Edwardian Ladies and Imperial Power

Women, Power and Politics
Series Editors: June Hannam and Pauline Stafford

Books in this series explore women's exercise of power in Britain and Europe from the ancient world onwards. In the expanding area of women's history this is an increasingly important theme, and one which provides a place for women's history and its insights within the traditional concerns of mainstream history. In view of the wide date range, 'power' is broadly conceived, involving, for instance, the religious and familial as well as the political.

Other published titles in the series:

Women and the Politics of Schooling in Victorian and Edwardian England
Jane Martin

Queens, Concubines and Dowagers: The King's Wife in the Early Middle Ages
Pauline Stafford

Edwardian Ladies and Imperial Power

JULIA BUSH

Leicester University Press

Leicester University Press
A Cassell imprint

Wellington House, 125 Strand, London WC2R 0BB
370 Lexington Avenue, New York, NY 10017–6550

First published 2000

British Library Cataloguing-in-Publication Data
A catalogue record for this book is available from the British Library.

ISBN 0-7185-0061-X

Library of Congress Cataloging-in-Publication Data
Bush, Julia.
    Edwardian ladies and imperial power / Julia Bush.
      p. cm.—(Women, power and politics)
    Includes bibliographical references and index.
    ISBN 0-7185-0061-X (hardcover)
    1. Great Britain—Colonies—Politics and government. 2. Women in politics—
Great Britain—History—20th century. 3. Imperialism—Social aspects—Great Britain—
History—20th century.   4. Power (Social sciences)—Great Britain—History—20th century.
5. Great Britain—Politics and government—1901–1910.   I. Title. II. Series.
   DA16.B87   1999
   325'.32'0820941—dc21   99–12380
                                                            CIP

Designed and typeset by Ben Cracknell Studios

Printed and bound in Great Britain by Cromwell Press Limited, Trowbridge, Wiltshire

Contents

List of Plates

Acknowledgements

My first debt of gratitude is to the four organizations whose histories are linked together in this book: the female emigration societies (united into the Society for the Oversea Settlement of British Women in 1920), the Girls' Friendly Society, the Victoria League, and the Primrose League. David Doughan of the Fawcett Library first led me in the direction of the emigration societies eight years ago, and the current project began from this basis. I was fascinated to discover that both the Girls' Friendly Society and the Victoria League are still working from their London headquarters and are still in possession of their own records. I would like to thank both organizations for permitting me to study in their archives and finding time to offer me assistance amidst their own busy commitments. Though the historical continuities are impressive, it is appropriate to emphasize here the extent to which both societies have re-created themselves in order to continue to provide service in a late-twentieth-century, post-colonial world. The Victoria League for Commonwealth Friendship nowadays lives up to its inclusive title by welcoming visiting members and others and also running a student hostel which accommodates young students from every part of the Commonwealth. I owe particular thanks to its Chairman, Colin Webber, to its General Secretary, John Allen (and his predecessor, Anna Keller), and to Barbara Johnson, who kindly read my full manuscript before publication. Unfortunately I have not been successful in tracing any organizational descendants of the Primrose League. I would like to thank the Bodleian Library for permission to work on its records.

My study of organized female imperialism has been greatly enriched by the opportunity to conduct research into the lives of individual women leaders. I wish to thank the following libraries and record offices for access to records, and to thank their staff for advice and guidance in my research: Bodleian Library, Oxford (Milner and Selborne papers); Churchill College, Cambridge (Chandos papers); British Library of Political and Economic Science, London School of Economics (Markham papers); Birmingham University Library (Chamberlain papers); Rhodes House Library, Oxford (Rhodes papers); Northamptonshire Record Office (Knightley papers); Hampshire Record Office (Selborne and Ridding papers); Centre for Kentish Studies (Talbot papers). I owe an additional debt to the descendants of the Edwardian 'leading ladies' and their associates who have kindly granted me permission to quote from private papers and autobiographies and to reproduce photographs: the Earl of Selborne (Maud and William Selborne); Viscount Chandos (Edith and Alfred Lyttelton); the Earl of Jersey (Margaret Jersey); Lady Violet Powell (biography of Margaret Jersey); Lady Mary

Clive (photograph of Lady Jersey and Lady Northcote); the Marquess of Salisbury (family photograph and Gwendolen Cecil's correspondence); Lord Tweedsmuir (Susan Grosvenor); Lord Midleton (William St John Brodrick's correspondence); Mr Charles Talbot (Meriel Talbot); Mrs Halcyon Palmer (Violet Markham). Professor Nuttall, the Fellow Librarian of New College, Oxford, granted permission to quote from the Milner papers. Quotations from the archives of the Royal Commonwealth Society are by permission of the Syndics of Cambridge University Library. Quotations from Joseph Chamberlain's correspondence are by permission of Birmingham University Library. In a more general sense, I am deeply grateful for the resources of the Fawcett Library, London Guildhall University and of the British Library and British Newspaper Library, without which this book could not have been written. Last but not least, I would like to thank the library staff of my home institution, University College Northampton.

Apart from the four organizations which provide the primary focus of the book, other associations have provided an important supplementary record of the Empire-related work of Edwardian women. I am particularly grateful for access to the records of the National League for Opposing Women's Suffrage at the Bodleian Library, and to the records of the National Union of Women Workers at the Fawcett Library and the British Library of Economic and Political Science. Like the Girls' Friendly Society and the Victoria League, the League of the Empire and the Mothers' Union have bequeathed modern descendant organizations whose traditions of service encompass visiting historians. I enjoyed the experience and benefited from the archives of the League for the Exchange of Commonwealth Teachers and the Mothers' Union, and was again impressed by the ability of formerly imperialist organizations to transform their political outlook while retaining respect and affection for their forebears.

Many historians have provided me with inspiration and intellectual stimulus. Their works are acknowledged in the Notes and Bibliography, but here I would like to offer particular thanks to those to whom I owe the most. Sheila Fletcher has provided inspiring friendship over a longer period than the composition of this book. Her Victorian girls have accompanied my Edwardian ladies over many years, and all along the way I have enjoyably benefited from her deep understanding of the world of the Lytteltons, Talbots and Gladstones. Catherine Hall provided helpful advice at an early stage in the book's development. During the final stages, the following friends and colleagues kindly read and commented upon sections of my manuscript: Sheila Fletcher, Sally Sokoloff, Peter King, Joyce Goodman, Catherine Pickles, Clare Midgley, Deborah Gaitskell, Karen Hunt, Jane Martin and Alison Oram. June Hannam, as Editor of the series, has provided help and encouragement throughout the process of research and writing. I am enormously grateful for the time and skills of these advisers. In addition, Angela John, Deborah Gaitskell, Joyce Goodman, Judith Rowbotham and Sheila Fletcher have been kind enough to supply me with copies of evidence from sources which I would not have otherwise uncovered. My thanks must be extended to include all those who have discussed ideas and sources with me at conferences and seminars over the past decade. I am also grateful to the Rector and the former Dean of Arts and Social Sciences at University College Northampton for granting me a sabbatical term in 1996 which finally made possible the production of a book. Further vital ingredients have been the meticulous secretarial support of Joy Knight, Emma Austin, Penny Hubbard and Charlotte Knight, and the photographic skills of Paul Bingham.

My mother, sister and husband have all offered encouragement and endured many years of the family inconveniences and obsessional conversations which accompany historical research. My final acknowledgements are to them, and to the fortitude of my children, Tom and Ruth. They have lived with this project more continuously than anyone else, so to them it is lovingly dedicated.

Abbreviated Titles of Organizations

BEL	British Empire League
BWEA	British Women's Emigration Association
CIL	Colonial Intelligence League
FMES	Female Middle Class Emigration Society
GFS	Girls' Friendly Society
GLW	Guild of Loyal Women
IODE	Imperial Order of Daughters of the Empire
NCW	National Council of Women
NLOWS	National League for Opposing Women's Suffrage
NUWSS	National Union of Women's Suffrage Societies
NUWW	National Union of Women Workers
PL	Primrose League
RCI	Royal Colonial Institute
SACS	South African Colonisation Society
SAX	South African Expansion Committee
SOSBW	Society for the Oversea Settlement of British Women
VL	Victoria League

To Tom and Ruth

1 British Ladies and the Empire

At the start of the twentieth century the British Empire was not short of admirers, and self-admirers. Patriots basked in the glow of imperial success, fanned by the expansionist policies and jubilee celebrations of the 1880s and 1890s, and tried, tested and ultimately crowned by victory in the South African war of 1899–1902. The coronation of Edward VII followed on the heels of victory. This event was marked in hundreds of schools by souvenir presentations of an illustrated history titled *King Edward's Realm . . . Story of the Making of the Empire*. The opening page reminded readers of both sexes that 'As Englishmen we have been born to a great inheritance, which we hold in common with our kinsmen in all parts of the Empire.' The book held in store 'a pleasant course of reading for young and old who desire to know something of the men who have made the Empire'. The reader was promised narrative continuity 'to help in sustaining his intelligent interest from page to page throughout the book'. It was perhaps needless to add, 'An endeavour has been made to foster that imperial spirit which takes a true pride in what our forefathers have achieved, which resolves to hold what they have won.'[1]

This unselfconsciously masculinist and Anglocentric text distilled the essence of much Edwardian imperialist propaganda. The scholarly writings of Dilke and Seeley and the political speeches of Chamberlain, Rhodes and Milner were successfully filtering through the press and the schoolroom to shape the world view of millions. Intrinsic to the imperial outlook was a self-definition of the British (often, inter-changeably, 'Englishmen') as a peculiarly gifted race with an insatiable need to exert their colonizing genius for the benefit of less fortunate others. When Joseph Chamberlain addressed the Royal Colonial Institute on 'The True Conception of Empire' in March 1897, he justified imperial rule in terms of happiness, peace and prosperity: 'In carrying out this work of civilisation we are fulfilling what I believe to be our national mission, and we are finding scope for the exercise of those faculties and qualities which have made of us a great governing race.'[2] For Alfred Milner, writing in 1913, imperialism was 'a question of preserving the unity of a great race, of enabling it, by maintaining that unity, to develop freely on its own lines, and to continue to fulfil its distinctive mission in the world'. As for those subjects of Empire beyond the pale of the anglicized white-settler Dominions, it was evident that 'they do not possess the gift of maintaining peace and order for themselves. Without our control their political condition would be one of chaos, as it was for centuries before that control was established.' Duty and responsibility, interest and honour all impelled the British to sustain their imperial burden, 'less perhaps for the material benefits which it brings us, than for its effect upon the national character – for it has helped to develop some of the best and most distinctive qualities of the race'.[3]

This spiritual creed of Empire was as attractive to many British women as it was to their male counterparts. It was an improving, self-reinforcing faith, designed to assert national vigour in an increasingly competitive world, but ultimately dependent upon the personal qualities of individuals. The female supporters of Empire were accustomed to a version of imperial history which virtually excluded their half of the British race. In between Queen Elizabeth and Queen Victoria, the coronation textbook recounted the exploits of Drake and Raleigh, Wolfe and Clive, Cook and Nelson. Even with an Empress of India on the throne, the nineteenth-century triumphs of Empire were portrayed exclusively as the work of male explorers, soldiers, traders and administrators. A concluding chapter dwelt with 'a thrill of pride' on the recent South African victory, which 'has given full proof that the spirit of their fathers is still active as ever, that the future of our race is as hard and well-knit as in days of yore'.[4] Nevertheless, this standard rhetoric offered women more than mere vicarious identification with male heroes. From amidst the catalogue of 'daring exploits' there emerged a symbolic Empire which depended heavily upon feminized imagery. Britannia ruled the waves, thus 'enabling the motherland to keep in constant touch with her daughter states in other lands'. The Empire was 'a whole family of English-speaking peoples'.[5] Milner wrote of 'the Mother Country' linked indissolubly to its Dominions by 'the bond of common blood';[6] and Chamberlain spoke with fervour of a 'vigorous and fruitful' mother, of 'troops of stalwart sons', and of colonial 'sister nations whose love and affection we eagerly desire'.[7]

The language of Empire was moulded first and foremost by its male exponents. But their choice of familial, and especially maternal, metaphor offered important meanings to women who wished to share in the self-congratulatory adventure. In the early twentieth century many leading imperialists turned their attention from the excitements of conquest to the longer-term issues of building a sustainable, civilizing Empire dependent upon female as well as male virtues. Reflection upon imperial values and prospects was the staple fare of the growing number of male-led imperial propaganda societies which developed in Edwardian Britain. The staid and gentlemanly Royal Colonial Institute (1869) was joined by the more vigorous and numerous campaigners of the British Empire League (1894), the Navy League (1897), the League of the Empire (1901), the National Service League (1902), the Tariff Reform League (1903) and the Overseas Club (1910). Some of these organizations admitted women, or established separate women's auxiliary groups. This was, after all, an era in which female citizenship as well as imperial citizenship was under hot debate. Whether or not male imperialists supported votes for women, few could ignore the increasing prominence of women's voluntary work, the improvements in female education, the gradual widening of women's career opportunities, and the consequent expansion of their political interests. Thus, in 1910, the Royal Colonial Institute invented a category of Lady Associates, allowing limited privileges in return for lower subscriptions while retaining its exclusively male Fellows as the main membership.[8] However, the often grudging and sometimes condescending admission of women to male-led imperialist conclaves proved insufficient for would-be female imperialists, who aspired to a contribution which reached beyond mere symbolic presence in imperialist discourse. The expansion of organized male imperialism was accompanied by a smaller-scale and much less well-known history of organized women's imperialism.

The formation of women's imperialist associations was not designed deliberately to challenge existing gender divisions, whether in Britain or in the Empire. To a large extent, it signified their willing acceptance. Women's contribution to Empire-building was believed to be innately different from that of men, and its value lay in those differences. The imperialist ladies of the Girls' Friendly Society (1874), the Primrose League (1883), the British Women's Emigration Association (1884) and the Victoria League (1901) were enthusiastic advocates of womanly imperial work which would complement and build upon male achievements. They adopted the emergent vision of a nurturing, familial Empire and gave it new substance by linking it to a range of practical imperialist work. Propaganda and behind-the-scenes political lobbying were important, but even more central to the female imperialist agenda were the tasks of guiding emigration, offering moral protection to women settlers, supporting church-building and missionary work abroad, and providing juvenile imperialist education and hospitality for colonial visitors at home. When the organized female imperialists acted assertively, it was so as to ensure that the special needs and contributions of women were not overlooked, and that the imperial project did not suffer from this oversight. Most of the upper-class and upper-middle-class women who predominated within organized female imperialism held very conventional views on gender difference. A small minority were self-proclaimed feminists, and a larger group (approximately half of the leadership) were supporters of votes for women. Interestingly, their divergent views on women's political status in Britain did not seriously disrupt their collective efforts to publicize and promote women's contribution to the British Empire. On this basis it seems reasonable to include the female imperialist associations within the ambit of a generously defined British women's movement.

The masculine imperial project was very evidently one of admiring self-definition. A study of organized female imperialism must also aim to explore subjective dimensions. The history of the ladies' associations is one of imagination and ambition as well as of visible activity. Why did a socially prestigious group of leaders decide to devote their time, energy and money to independent campaigning on behalf of the British Empire? How far were their campaigns merely an extension of earlier social activism? In what ways did they draw upon older traditions of upper-class female politics? The choice of certain gendered patriotic identities, and the neglect of others taken up by the male imperialist leagues, reveals more about the women imperialists themselves than it does about the needs of the British Empire. Evidence on the origins of female imperialist commitment is largely fragmentary and indirect. Women imperialists did not often compose coherent confessions of faith in the style of Milner or Chamberlain. Instead, they gratefully invited these gentlemen onto their platforms to make the grand, abstract speeches required on important occasions. Their extensive journalism, like their formal organizational records, focused mainly upon the practical work of the associations rather than upon their contribution to imperialist ideology. To some extent the lack of a coherent record of female imperialist thought reflects the reality of jumbled and inconsistent thinking, heavily indebted to ideas of male patrons. However, the associations and their leaders gradually found their own ways of expressing their views. Their outlook and motives, in all their variety and inconsistency, are pieced together throughout this book. The intention has been to investigate organized female imperialism on a broad front, linking motive to action and action to ideology. The choices which these women made, and their public and private justifications of their work, form an interesting addition to our understanding of Edwardian gender relations. Most of the leading ladies were, at least sometimes, reflective upon female roles. Their reflections related to individual lives and experiences, as well as to women's collective contribution towards an imperial future.

The printed publications and private official records of the ladies' associations are a rich, and historically rather neglected, source of evidence. But neither the motivation nor the general thinking behind organized female imperialism can be understood from these sources alone. In recent years feminist historians have opened up new perspectives on the relationship between women's personal lives and their engagement in the collective work of the Victorian and Edwardian women's movement.[9] It has become evident that women's organizations require detailed, intimate study upon their own terms, rather than simply measurement against male norms. Individual or grouped life histories are an essential basis for such studies, for it is by learning to travel more readily back and forth through (auto)biographical, social and political history that we can explore the nature of their interdependence. Fortunately, the upper-class leaders of female imperialism left an abundance of personal records. The opening chapters of this book draw heavily upon them in order to explain the social and political setting from which the imperialist associations emerged. In later chapters, the experiences and views of the same leading individuals are threaded through a history of key aspects of the associations' work.

Invaluable though autobiographies, journals and letters have proved, such documents have required careful reading. The illusion of direct access to personal experience remains no more than that. Upper-class Edwardian ladies had conscious and unconscious reasons for self-concealment as they penned their memoirs, usually in the interwar years. Many manuscript journals were similarly composed with a wider audience in view. *The Journals of Lady Knightley of Fawsley, 1856–1884* were published within two years of her death in 1913, though with the more recent decades discreetly omitted. The editor, her friend and fellow-imperialist Julia Cartwright, recorded Louisa Knightley's failed attempt to complete an autobiography a few years earlier, and her propensity for studying other published letters and diaries, 'with the object of improving her own Journal, and making it more interesting'.[10] When Edith Lyttelton accompanied her husband on government business to South Africa in 1900, she relayed a self-edited diary of her many conversations with Alfred Milner back to England, expressly for circulation among family and friends.[11]

Lady Frances Balfour, on the other hand, histrionically burned her letters at a Scottish lochside before publishing her carefully composed two-volume autobiography in 1930.[12] Even the most private of letters bear the inevitable signs of an intended readership. This becomes apparent from Edith Lyttelton's limited, self-deprecatory accounts of a busy public life in her loving epistles to an anxiously protective (and personally demanding) husband.[13] It is equally apparent in the Countess of Selborne's detailed and unashamedly political accounts of events leading to the South African Union of 1910, observed from the uniquely well-informed perspective of a Governor-General's wife and confidante.[14] Letters to her wider acquaintance were suitably guarded (and sometimes instrumental); those to different members of her family each recorded a different emphasis, only a wholly trusted adult daughter receiving the merest hint of criticism of the Governor-General's decisions and their impact upon Maud Selborne's own comfort and peace of mind.

Many of the most influential women imperialists were members of an imperial as well as a British elite. A study of organizational methods, in Chapter 4, demonstrates the extent to which female imperialism was dominated by a relatively small and close-knit leadership group. The ladies' associations were intensely hierarchical, both in outlook and in practice. Queen Victoria, even after her death in 1901, was the ultimate female imperialist icon; but the leading ladies were themselves prepared to be iconized and to use their social status and high-level political connections to advance their cause. A disproportionate emphasis upon the views and activities of a minority of well-documented leaders is thus less hard to justify in the context of organized female imperialism than it would be in the history of most other women's organizations, whether in this period or any other. The leadership of the female imperialist associations was defined by an inseparable combination of social class and gender, and the frequent use of the term 'ladies' in this book is intended to emphasize this point. In some senses class distinctions in the upper echelons of society were becoming blurred during the late Victorian and Edwardian decades. The perceptibly threatened status of the nobility is discussed in Chapter 2. However, there can be little doubt that titled lineage, social status and political power remained closely intertwined up to 1914. This was as true of the extra-parliamentary female imperialist associations as it was of the male governing elite with whom they were so closely connected. The Victoria League, founded in 1901, was in many ways the most archetypal of the Edwardian associations, drawing its leaders and its methods from all the pre-existing female imperialist groups and motivated into action at a climactic moment of Empire history. Nearly half of its ruling council, in the first year of its existence, bore titles which denoted their membership of the peerage and baronetcy. If we follow other recent historians in adopting a broad definition of aristocracy which includes the untitled landed gentry, many of whom were related directly or indirectly to the title-holders, then it becomes still more apparent that the female imperialist associations were dominated by an aristocratic leadership.[15] Such women put themselves forward as leaders, and were also deliberately sought out by less well-favoured organizations as a source of borrowed prestige as well as other assumed leadership qualities.

Privileged and influential British women often took up female imperialist work on the basis of a selective knowledge of Empire which had reinforced their patriotic and racial prejudices rather than promoting critical thought. It is difficult to glimpse the true complexity and diversity of the Edwardian Empire through the private or public records of the ladies' associations. Recent writing on European women's imperial roles has tended to emphasize their variety, as well as their significance for both imperial and domestic history;[16] but organized female imperialism attracted a relatively narrow stratum of the imperial ruling class. The 'Governor's Lady' and her close associates were especially prominent within the upper circles of the Victoria League. Inevitably, all the societies contained women whose experience of and commitment to imperial rule were confined to those colonies where 'Greater Britain' was already flourishing. They construed the Empire's future as bound up with the future of British settlement, and therefore devoted their efforts to Canada, Australia, New Zealand and (more problematically) South Africa.

By 1914 nearly one-third of the Empire's white population was living in these countries, all of which had become self-governing. It might have been a shock to many imperialist ladies to learn that, according to modern estimates, the Empire contained approximately six times more black and Asian people than white, of whom four-fifths lived in India.[17] However, these statistics would not have shaken their conviction that the strength and moral worth of the Empire lay emphatically with its 'British' minority. Racial pride stood at the heart of imperialism. Its gendered meanings for female imperialists, including interconnections with racial fear, will be considered further in Chapter 7. India inspired both pride and fear. Its importance and its imperial responsibilities were acknowledged to be immense, but were for the most part beyond the scope of the kinds of work which the female imperialist associations believed they did best. Other British women, including many leading feminists, became closely involved in 'protecting' Indian womanhood;[18] but the Victoria League made a self-defining choice to turn its back on India. Only the Girls' Friendly Society, of the organizations studied in this book, maintained a presence there on a scale which matched the very small proportion of British to Indian population. This society's minor (and controversial) transgressions of racial boundaries in India never seriously challenged the female imperialists' dominant aim to strengthen the Empire through its racially bonded 'white settler' colonies.

The women's imperialist associations adopted a blinkered view of the Empire which assimilated their social background, personal experiences and political ambitions. They joined with male imperialists in claiming a mystical unity for an Empire which was becoming ever larger and more heterogeneous. How was this unified and unifying miracle to be sustained? As usual, answers could be found in *King Edward's Realm*, the final chapter of which attributed 'Unity of the Empire' to 'Growth of Freedom', 'Imperial Spirit of our Race' and 'The Sovereign in Relation to the Empire'. Most female imperialists would have applauded such solutions. But among the uncomfortable realities which they ignored was the fact that the 'Growth of Freedom' in white settler colonies (where it alone applied) was already fostering colonial nationalisms that were resistant to British schemes for closer imperial federation. This detail was easily overlooked by women who were remarkably insensitive to the Anglocentrism of their own organizations. As relations with patriotic overseas organizations became more and more essential to the expanding work of the British associations, even the most loyal of Canadians, Australians, New Zealanders and South Africans were sometimes irritated by British women's assumptions of superiority. Colonial alliances were held together as much by a genuine appreciation of mutual practical benefit as by a shared faith in the United British Empire. The pleasures and pitfalls of these sisterly relations are investigated in Chapter 6.

Unity could, of course, become a problem closer to home. Each of the female imperialist associations was Anglocentric in its own way. All had some branches in parts of Britain beyond England, but the histories of Scottish, Welsh and Irish imperialism find a limited place in this book. The cultivation of consciously separate nations within the British Isles was very far from the agenda of British imperialism. Lord Milner proudly described himself as 'a British (indeed primarily an English) Nationalist'.[19] In his writings he acknowledged Britain's 'various stocks, and in spite of constant intermixture, strongly marked differences of type', but only to conclude that 'face to face with alien peoples, or with the unpeopled wilderness, they have realised their essential unity'.[20] His views were closely attuned to the outlook of a centralized, London-based female imperialism. The issue of Irish Home Rule, believed by Milner and many other imperialists to threaten the Empire, was deliberately shelved by the female imperialist associations. A number of their leading ladies were of Scottish origin, but most spent the annual social and parliamentary Season in London. A brief conflict flared in 1902, when Scottish members of the British Women's Emigration Association attempted to impose their own views about the moral suitability of certain candidates for emigration. 'Scotch' behaviour was criticized, and the epithet as well as the criticism resented. Fences were mended by a compromise which allowed slightly more organizational autonomy north of the border.[21] In 1907 the Victoria League's Edinburgh leaders began to gather together a Scottish federation of branches, such as the Girls' Friendly Society had long possessed. The Scottish GFS, unlike its small-scale Irish equivalent, was granted a special dispensation by the 'Parent Society' to organize along its own interdenominational lines.[22] But on the whole the female imperialist associations accepted the inevitability and desirability of direct rule from the imperial capital. This attitude reflected both their political views and their social standing, which in turn integrated their imperial work smoothly into the life of London High Society.

A more serious challenge to the unity of organized female imperialism might have arisen from the competing agendas of different societies, both male and female. Periodic concern was expressed about the problems of 'overlap'. Male propaganda societies made numerous attempts to persuade the Victoria League into closer collaboration, with the aim of future amalgamation. The Royal Colonial Institute tried more successfully to draw together the emigration societies in 1910. However, such approaches were often counter-productive, reinforcing the leading ladies' determination to assert their gendered independence. The prolonged amalgamation negotiations between the Victoria League and the League of the Empire were to become a source of bitter strife; two separate societies continue to pursue their separate paths nearly a hundred years later.[23] Failure to collaborate had many causes, some financial, some social, and some personal rather than political. The failures, whatever their cause, provide a marked contrast to the successful co-operation and friendly relations among the women's associations themselves.

The characteristic of successful co-operation further strengthens the case for regarding these associations as a significant grouping in their own right, and as a suitable subject for interconnected study. A number of explanations suggest themselves. In the first place it is apparent that the women imperialists were drawn together during the Edwardian years by a common core of beliefs and values. As has been demonstrated above, their outlook owed much to the broader currents of contemporary imperialist thought. However, the leading ladies fashioned their associations in their own image, and it was an image that they were prepared collectively to defend. Many of the women's societies were older than their male equivalents. The Girls' Friendly Society, the Primrose League and the British Women's Emigration Association moved gradually over two decades from their own varied and distinctive origins into the mainstream of an identifiably female imperialism which became embodied, from its foundation, in the

Victoria League. Between the death of Queen Victoria and the First World War, the major women's imperialist organizations were more closely intertwined than at any time before or since. Hence the relatively narrow chronological focus of this book, despite its acknowledgement of Victorian antecedents and of wartime and post-war successors to the Edwardian lady imperialists. The Edwardian agenda of organized female imperialism encompassed shared attitudes towards gender, race and social class. These fundamental ingredients of personal and political outlook synthesized into a common imperial ideal, a profound faith in its worldwide importance and a joint determination to contribute towards its fulfilment.

A second explanation of close and mutually supportive relations among female imperialist organizations lies in their successful adaptation of existing social networks. The aristocratic leadership of the associations dictated the extent to which they developed within an established annual cycle of upper-class work and entertainment, centred upon the traditional calendar of royalty and parliament. Though social boundaries were becoming steadily more permeable, the essentials of a High Society lifestyle survived surprisingly well into the first decade of the twentieth century, for the straightforward reason that they continued to serve the social and political needs of powerful vested interests. Society conditioned not merely the ladies' hierarchical social outlook, but also their chosen styles of imperialist activism. No hard and fast distinctions were possible between social and political activity when so much of the conduct of female imperialist affairs took place through informal encounters. The private and semi-private encounters between politically knowledgeable men and women form an important hidden chapter in the history of women's influence upon governments before they were permitted to vote.[24] Such channels of influence were fully exploited by Edwardian imperialist ladies. Still more vital to their associations were the many opportunities within an aristocratic lifestyle for wealthy and well-connected women to meet alone. Social ritual, as much as individual preference, dictated the methods of female imperialist politics. By the early twentieth century the gendered social rituals of the aristocracy intersected at many points with those of the upper-middle classes. This particular intersection has received less historical attention than it deserves, but is effectively demonstrated in studies by Barbara Caine, Pat Jalland and Mary Peterson.[25] Peterson concludes that 'the distinction between gentlefolk and the rest of Victorian Society is the largest rift in the Victorian social structure'.[26] During the late Victorian and Edwardian period an extensive network of women's social action developed, led primarily by those with the economic and social attributes of 'gentlefolk'. This alternative, and usefully complementary, arena of female contacts and joint endeavour served as an important extension to many aristocratic imperialists' social worlds. Female imperialism developed its own forms of social action on behalf of the Empire. However, its leaders drew upon both the organizational methods and the practical support of groups of women from a wider social background who shared similar gendered priorities around such issues as employment for 'respectable' women, moral reform and the protection of female travellers. An enormous number of women belonged to each other's organizations. This significant point is illustrated by the chart of female imperialist networks in Appendix 2. Among the leading imperialists were to be found several distinct subgroups of female reformers, including a substantial network of supporters of female suffrage.

Networking, and the shared attitudes which developed from it, will be explored throughout this book, but it is also important to convey an introductory sense of the distinctiveness of each of the main female imperialist associations. A fourth and final explanation of their ability to work together lies in the fact that much of their work was, in fact, amicably separate. Through a combination of historical evolution and deliberate planning, the women successfully avoided duplicating their practical imperialist activities, while usefully reinforcing each other when appropriate. Demarcation disputes were rare and were usually swiftly resolved. The Victoria League was easily persuaded to pass on emigration enquiries to the British Women's Emigration Association. The BWEA, in turn, happily drew upon the overseas hostel facilities of the Girls' Friendly Society. For many years these two societies shared a single redoubtable leading emigrator in the figure of the Honourable Mrs Ellen Joyce. Within the latter society she publicized emigration opportunities for young women. Within the former, she headed a specialized apparatus of financial support and practical advice for those who were already committed to emigration. Louisa Knightley was equally devoted to both societies, as well as belonging to the inner circles of the Primrose League and the Victoria League for good measure. Yet the complementarity of her various causes did not prevent her from drawing distinctions and establishing priorities. During the Edwardian years she too decided to put emigration to the 'Greater Britain' of the Dominions at the top of her political agenda.

At first acquaintance, the contrasts between the female imperialist organizations are perhaps more striking than their connections. The Girls' Friendly Society stood apart as much the largest and the oldest all-female organization. Closely linked to the Anglican Church, it claimed a quarter of a million members on the eve of the First World War. The vast majority of these members were young working-class women who were being trained by their social betters in the ways of Christianity, diligence and social purity as well as in the faith of female imperialism. The Empire may well have seemed distant from their lives. However, it gradually became a central aspect of the ideology conveyed by the Society's upper ranks. During the 1900s the Girls' Friendly Society was led by ladies who increasingly believed that their mission was to inspire members with a unified feminine, Christian and imperial vision. This was being fulfilled through a range of 'practical' Empire work, through education and through the building of colonial branches which were linked indissolubly to the Mother Country.

The Primrose League was another mass organization with a large working-class membership, estimated at 800,000 in 1914. From the outset it admitted both men and women as members and half of its membership was probably female in many areas. The League's characterization as a female imperialist organization is justified less by this estimate than by the fact that its leadership structure had opened up important, and partly separate, opportunities for upper-class women's political activism. In the 1900s the Ladies' Grand Council brought together more than 1500 guinea-paying subscribers, most of whom were also locally active as Primrose League organizers, or 'Dames'. Their executive committee was closely interlinked with the imperialist hierarchies of the Girls' Friendly Society and the British Women's Emigration Association. The general aim of the Primrose League remained the provision of a socially consolidating route into Conservative party politics, but by the turn of the century imperialist ideals had become an essential lubricant to this process. Upper-class ladies pressed the imperial cause at both local and national level. When the assertiveness of the Ladies' Grand Council received rebuffs from male leaders, a substantial number of Primrose Dames moved across to the Victoria League, where they had improved opportunities to set their own agenda.

Both the British Women's Emigration Association and the Victoria League were very much smaller organizations. They admitted a minority of male sympathizers, patrons and imperial 'experts' but maintained a strong female leadership which exerted its authority untramelled by male controls or the needs of a mass membership. By 1914 the Victoria League had around 6000 paying supporters, and the Emigration Association (with its sister organizations, the South African Colonisation Society and the Colonial Intelligence League) probably around 1000. Each society based its influence primarily upon the political connections and organizing abilities of an elite group of leaders rather than upon membership numbers. The British Women's Emigration Association was a direct descendant of earlier all-female societies which specialized in the selection, preparation and support of women emigrants. By 1909, the year of its twenty-fifth anniversary celebrations, its President was claiming that 'from its first inception' the Association had believed that 'the requirements of the Empire must come before the needs of the individual'.[27] This had become steadily more true over the years, as the Association moved beyond its original clerical and middle-class feminist origins and into the orbit of a socially elite female imperialism. The Victoria League represented the apex of female imperialism's social prestige, not only drawing together leading ladies from the executives of all the older associations but also linking them to a new patriotic intake from the highest levels of the British ruling class. Peeresses and wives of cabinet ministers and colonial governors were invaluable to the Victoria League's early strategy of exerting influence through powerful men. They continued to have their advantages as the League's work gradually settled into the 'practical' female imperialism of maintaining war graves, educating children and adults, and fostering closer Empire links through sponsorship, correspondence and large-scale hospitality.

With the exception of the Victoria League, each of the main female imperialist organizations has acquired the honour of a published history researched by a meticulous scholar.[28] Brian Harrison's study of the Girls' Friendly Society (1973), James Hammerton's of the British Women's Emigration Association (1979) and Martin Pugh's of the Primrose League (1985) have greatly benefited the present book. This book does not aim to subvert the conclusions of the earlier histories, but rather to supplement their separate, unitary narratives by exploring the themes which bound the main female imperialist organizations together during the Edwardian years. New juxtapositions inevitably shed fresh light upon each organization's work and create different emphases. A paradigm of female imperialist ideas, methods and achievements can be established, but it is one which must take careful account of contrasts as well as convergence. Female imperialism had a definable and sometimes influential collective existence, yet it continued to display multiple identities. This reflected not only the varied work of discrete associations, but also the complex lives of the main protagonists. The depth and direction of female imperialist commitment fluctuated, as these ladies threaded their way through the competing demands of family relationships, social duties and the alternative loyalties of party politics or other forms of 'women's work'. It is as important to avoid imposing an exaggerated retrospective unity upon the imperialist associations as it is to develop fresh insights into their many connections and shared ideas.

A further warning against the erection of rigid new boundaries and signposts is provided by a glance at some potential entrants to this study. Why have certain organizations been included and others excluded? The case for including the Primrose League has been made around its historic legacy to the Victoria League and the extensive, ongoing cross-membership between its Ladies' Grand Council and the other three main associations. The case against including the many other male-led organizations with substantial female memberships rests upon the inability of these women to assert a continuous and decisive influence over leadership policies. Though intersections of leadership sometimes existed, they were less extensive than in the case of the Primrose League. The Girl Guides and the Mothers' Union have also been excluded, despite their strong feminine and imperialist credentials, partly because their leaders were not fully integrated into the same exclusive social set as those of the other female-led associations. Even in 1900, the year of Colonel Baden-Powell's South African triumph, future Victoria League ladies corresponded disparagingly about his female relatives: 'the Baden-Powell family are pretty good at advertising themselves, I should say';[29] 'I am afraid that if not with him, with his family, Mafeking will involve some social sacrifices on our part!'[30] The Mothers' Union, like the Girl Guides, eventually developed an enormous range of colonial activities. Its clerical origins, in the drawing-rooms of Winchester's Cathedral close, were intriguingly close in time and place to those of the Girls' Friendly Society and the British Women's Emigration Association. However, an Overseas Committee of the Mothers' Union did not emerge until 1911, nearly thirty years after both of these other societies had turned their hand to imperial work. Mothers' Union foundress Mary Sumner would never have echoed Ellen Joyce's presidential boast of an 'Empire first' policy; nor was she to make the all-important social transition which resulted from Mrs Joyce's decision to hold joint office in the Girls' Friendly Society and the Emigration Association. It is possible to demonstrate that a majority of late Victorian and Edwardian women's associations had some form of ideological and organizational commitment to the Empire. Those which are studied alongside each other here were yoked together by particularly strong and influential bonds of common leadership. This did not cut them off from wider women's networks or from other, less feminized imperial causes, but it did develop certain defining qualities within their work in greater measure than within the work of adjacent organizations.

The primary purpose of this book has not been to isolate a distinctive and neatly bounded female imperialism. The imperialism of the Edwardian women's associations was a site of formative encounters and of untidy ideological loose ends. The value of a study of previously unexplored political conjunctions lies in the critical thinking which it provokes around more established explanatory categories as much as in the intrinsic interest of its subject matter. The book aims to contribute towards the ongoing process of restoring imperialism to the mainstream of British women's history and to the recuperation of a women's history of Empire which can be set alongside (and within) the many all-male successors to *King Edward's Realm*. The current state of historiography concerning women and Empire has been admirably summarized in the opening pages of Clare Midgley's recent *Gender and Imperialism* (1998). The present book continues the task of challenging masculinist 'Imperial History' as 'a key form of colonial discourse'.[31] It has become (evidently) important to understand the multiple dimensions of reciprocal relations between Empire, imagined ideals of Empire, and their adherents in each and every British social class. Detailed studies in relatively under-researched corners of this ideological territory, like the present one, can make their own contribution towards the wider theoretical re-mapping which both 'colonized' and 'colonizers' so fundamentally require. The post-colonial historical project is now thoroughly under way in many parts of the world. Further years of careful research are needed in order to bring it towards more complex and well-substantiated conclusions.

Another significant general aim of this study is to contribute to current discussion about relations between the Victorian and Edwardian women's movement, feminism and the suffrage campaign. The final chapter highlights the seeming paradox of strong female imperialist involvement in campaigns both for and against votes for women. How could suffragists and anti-suffragists continue to work together in the imperial cause? If suffrage was the touchstone of the Edwardian women's movement, must female imperialism stand excluded from its ranks? The answer to the first of these questions reveals the false polarities implied by the second. Continued joint work was perfectly possible when women shared a sense of common values and priorities which transcended the suffrage debate. The imperial cause was a true priority; so, too, was the establishment of the sound gender relations needed to underpin the Empire's moral and political future. Worthy and enduring imperial power depended upon a due respect for both sexes and for their different roles. It also depended upon a defence of social class boundaries, closely identified with the civilizing values which characterized some members of the British race rather more than others. The leaders of female imperialism were virtually unanimous in condemning unwomanly suffragette militancy and in opposing extension of a selective, socially hierarchical suffrage to include all adult women. They were also in profound agreement upon the need for imperial rule to draw upon women's talents and to defend their special interests. With or without the vote, women were vital to the Empire's future. As the Conservative suffragist Maud Selborne put it to an anti-suffrage fellow-member of the Victoria League executive, 'Some suffragists appear to think the vote is the end, whereas the right view seems to me that it is only a means – one of many – to obtain what we want.'[32]

The female imperialist societies provided a ladylike alternative means for women to contribute their gendered expertise towards an imperial future. By so doing, they could assert and develop their own organizational competence, as well as the wider significance of women's work. Even wealthy, titled ladies valued such personal reinforcement, and often built upon it to ease their transition from Victorian traditions of personal social service and private political influence towards a twentieth-century participation in public affairs. The parallels with the ambitions and personal growth experienced elsewhere in the Edwardian women's movement are inescapable. Whether or not the upper-class ladies of the female imperialist associations deserve a 'feminist' label seems largely irrelevant. If older historical definitions of the British women's movement have difficulty in encompassing them, then it is time to reconsider definitions rather than to exclude these women from the company of the publicly active and gender-conscious women among whom they surely belong.

The anti-suffragist and anti-feminist Ellen Joyce spoke for many lady imperialists when she addressed the Girls' Friendly Society Imperial Conference in July 1912 with a ringing call to place female imperialism (and women with it) to the fore:

> There is no bigger attitude or higher aspiration than to be one of the Daughters of a Christian Empire. The GFS has done the very best Imperial work that has been done, in sending women who have been under the highest influences from cultured, refined, religious women. to become the mothers of a race, not dwarfed by poverty; or cramped by pressure as in the Nest and Nursery of the Mother-Land; but free, contented, God-fearing women in the Great Garden of the British Empire. Let us enthuse ourselves and then enthuse others with the idea that the Empire and not the island is women's sphere . . . Empire building ought not to be left to accident. It is the finest, most interesting, the most satisfactory bit of work an Englishwoman can lay her hands to do.[33]

Ellen Joyce's speech brought together the varied and often implicitly contradictory aspirations of the female imperialist associations. In the Edwardian period the ambitious Empire-building of Rhodes, Chamberlain and Milner was tempered by the expensive losses of the South African War, yet fuelled by visions of a regenerative 'Great Garden' in which Britons might still flourish and outreach their less worthy competitors. The opportunities of Empire could be portrayed as doubly enticing for women of all classes whose lives seemed increasingly cramped by pressures and consciousness of gendered restrictions. The privileged leaders of organized female imperialism believed themselves to be working altruistically on behalf of Nation and Empire, and on behalf of their less privileged sisters both in Britain and the Dominions. However, regardless of formally adopted positions on feminism and the vote, they exhorted each other to imperial effort through language and activities which exuded their pride in women's power. The relationship between organized imperialism and the assertion of female power and female abilities was far from straightforward, but it undoubtedly existed, and its varied manifestations form the substance of this book's conclusions. Edwardian upper-class lady imperialists made their historically specific contribution to the construction of gendered national identity. The imperial project opened up enticing prospects for their direct and indirect participation in processes of social and political renewal both in Britain and overseas. By seizing their own organizational opportunity, as well as promoting suitable opportunities for humbler British women, the leading ladies of female imperialism sought to impose their gendered, class-bound values upon the national and imperial scene. In retrospect, they clearly failed to feminize the face of the Empire. They did little or nothing to alleviate the negative impact of imperial rule upon millions of colonized women, nor did they succeed in attracting the majority of British women to their cause. Yet their efforts did contribute in more limited ways to the revaluing of women's roles which was to prove a defining trait of the century ahead.

Notes

1. Rev. C.S. Dawe, *King Edward's Realm . . . Story of the Making of the Empire* (London: The Educational Supply Association, 1902), Preface.
2. J. Chamberlain, *Foreign and Colonial Speeches* (London: Routledge, 1897), p. 244.
3. A. Milner, *The Nation and the Empire* (London: Constable, 1913), pp. xxxii, xxxiii.
4. Dawe, p. 218.
5. *Ibid.*, pp. 8, 9.
6. Milner, p. xxxv.
7. Chamberlain, p. 248.
8. See the *Royal Colonial Institute Year Book*, 1912. The British Empire League, the Navy League and the Tariff Reform League also admitted women on special terms. Navy League women paid half the male membership subscription (*Navy League Year Book*, 1907–08). The British Empire League had some separate female branches, but though their educative work was valued there was little doubt where political authority lay. D. Porter (1976) described the Women's Association as 'content to remain a subsidiary partner of the Tariff Reform League' (PhD thesis, University of Manchester, p. 244), and dependent upon the League for finance and approval of its management and policies.
9. See e.g. B. Caine, *Victorian Feminists* (Oxford: Oxford University Press, 1992); M. J. Corbett, *Representing Femininity: Middle Class Subjectivity in Victorian and Edwardian Women's Autobiographies* (Oxford: Oxford University Press, 1992); C. Dyhouse, *Feminism and the Family in England 1880–1939* (Oxford: Blackwell, 1989); J. Lewis, *Women and Social Action in Victorian and Edwardian England* (Aldershot: Edward Elgar, 1991); S. Pederson and P. Mandler (eds), *After the Victorians: Private Conscience and Public Duty in Modern Britain* (London: Routledge, 1994); M.J. Peterson, *Family, Love and Work in the Lives of Victorian Gentlewomen* (Bloomington: Indiana University Press, 1989).
10. J. Cartwright (ed.), *The Journals of Lady Knightley of Fawsley, 1856–1884* (London: John Murray, 1915), p. xv.
11. Edith Lyttelton's diary, 1900. Chandos I, 6/3. Churchill College, Cambridge.
12. F. Balfour, *Ne Obliviscaris: Dinna Forget* (London: Hodder & Stoughton, 1930), p. xii.
13. Edith Lyttelton's letters to Alfred Lyttelton. Chandos I, 5/3.
14. Maud Selborne's South African correspondence. 9M68. Hampshire Record Office.
15. See D. Cannadine, *The Decline and Fall of the British Aristocracy* (London: Macmillan, 1996 edn), pp. 8–25; and M. Bush, *The English Aristocracy* (Manchester: Manchester University Press, 1984), pp. 1–10, for discussion of the definition of aristocracy. Cannadine and Bush include the landed gentry alongside the peerage and baronetcy as members of a wealth and status elite which helped to bind together the various British nationalities, and (at least until the 1880s) claimed a virtually unchallenged 'right to rule'.
16. See especially N. Chaudhuri *et al.* (eds), *Western Women and Imperialism* (Bloomington: Indiana University Press, 1992); C. Hall, *White, Male and Middle Class: Explorations in Feminism and History* (Cambridge: Polity Press, 1992); M. Strobel, *European Women and the Second British Empire* (Bloomington: Indiana University Press, 1991); V. Ware, *Beyond the Pale: White Women, Racism and History* (London: Verso, 1992).
17. Estimates from L. James, *The Rise and Fall of the British Empire* (London: Abacus, 1994), p. 353.
18. See A. Burton, *Burdens of History: British Feminists, Indian Women and Imperial Culture, 1865–1915* (Chapel Hill: University of North Carolina Press, 1994).
19. A. Milner, 'Credo', published posthumously in *The Times*, 27 July 1925.
20. Milner, 1913, pp. xxxv, xxxvi.

21. South African Expansion Committee Minutes, 4 November and 6 December 1901. FL2B,1/2. Fawcett Library.

22. M. Heath-Stubbs, *Friendship's Highway* (London: GFS, 1926), p. 166.

23. The late-twentieth-century descendants of the two Edwardian societies are the Victoria League for Commonwealth Friendship and the League for the Exchange of Commonwealth Teachers.

24. See L. Davidoff, *The Best Circles: Society Etiquette and the Season* (London: Croom Helm, 1973); P. Jalland, *Women, Marriage and Politics 1860–1914* (Oxford: Oxford University Press, 1988); K.D. Reynolds, 'Aristocratic Women and Political Society in Early and Mid-Victorian Britain', DPhil thesis (University of Oxford, 1995); E.S. Shkolnik, *Leading Ladies: A Study of Eight Late Victorian and Edwardian Political Wives* (New York: Garland, 1987).

25. B. Caine, *Destined to Be Wives: The Sisters of Beatrice Webb* (Oxford: Clarendon Press, 1986); P. Jalland, *Women, Marriage and Politics, 1860–1914* (Oxford: Oxford University Press, 1988); M. Peterson, *Family, Love and Work in the Lives of Victorian Gentlewomen* (Bloomington: Indiana University Press, 1989).

26. Peterson, p. x.

27. Ellen Joyce in *The Imperial Colonist.* 7/94. October 1909.

28. J. Hammerton, *Emigrant Gentlewomen: Genteel Poverty and Female Emigration, 1830–1914* (London: Croom Helm, 1979); B. Harrison, 'For Church, Queen and Family: The Girls' Friendly Society 1874–1920', *Past and Present*, 1973, **61**: 107–38; M. Pugh, *The Tories and the People. 1880–1935* (Oxford: Blackwell, 1985).

29. Louise Dawkins to Violet Cecil, 1 June 1900. VM 38, 259/7. Bodleian Library.

30. Gwendolen Cecil to Violet Cecil, 1 June 1900. VM 26, 101/29.

31. C. Midgley (ed.), *Gender and Imperialism* (Manchester: Manchester University Press, 1998), p. 5.

32. Maud Selborne to Violet Markham, 11 July 1913. VMar 26/30. BLPES.

33. E. Joyce, 'Thirty Years of Girls' Friendly Society Work' (London: GFS, 1912).

2 Society Lifestyles

The British Empire was a subject of interest, and even a source of pride and enthusiasm, for a great many Edwardian women. However, the female imperialist associations depended for inspiration upon a socially exclusive minority. This was true of the Girls' Friendly Society and the Primrose League with their broad memberships and elite leadership, as well as of the small, select emigration societies and the Victoria League, whose leaders' shared social privilege defined most aspects of female imperialism. Working on behalf of the Empire was a social as well as a patriotic duty, and as such was a recasting and an elaboration of existing duties and pleasures. Success depended upon the gendered upper-class skills which Society fostered. This chapter outlines the economic, social and political context of Edwardian High Society and introduces some of the attributes which female imperialism derived from it.

The decades during which organized female imperialism developed, from the mid-1880s to its heyday between 1900 and 1914, coincided with aristocratic decline. The imperialist mood of the 1900s was much less self-confident than it superficially appeared. At the heart of often vaguely expressed uncertainties lay a gradual move away from the absolute, unchallenged supremacy of landed wealth within upper-class society, and a corresponding reduction in the power of landed aristocrats and gentry to define the attitudes and behaviours of Society and government.[1] Wealth, social status and political influence had intertwined for centuries in the fortunes of patrician families. From the 1880s onwards, economic threats contributed to a fundamental undermining of social and political authority. The agricultural depression of the late nineteenth century varied considerably in regional impact, but in the worst-affected arable areas it caused catastrophic falls in estate incomes, sustained over decades rather than years. At the same time, the landed classes faced the arrival of the new rich in unprecedented numbers and as happy possessors of wealth from alternative sources in finance, business and industry. The landed classes did not give up their place lightly. There was a time lag before 'inherited habits of patrician behaviour' surrendered to economic realities.[2] There was also a period of economic adaptation and retrenchment, for example, through diversification of income sources and consolidation of estates around English family seats after Irish and Welsh land sales. To some extent, the British aristocracy had been adapting to new money throughout the nineteenth century. The difference after the 1880s is in the speed and scale of that adaptation and in the visibility of its social and political consequences.

One clear indication of combined economic and social change was the very substantial increase in the number of peerages that were granted for industrial and commercial achievements between 1885 and 1914. Plutocratic marriages, and even an Edwardian wave of noble alliances to actresses, further extended the bounds of Society. Reigning monarchs proved willing to legitimate social changes which they could not prevent by granting personal acknowledgement to ever-increasing numbers of new entrants at royal levees and drawing-rooms.[3] Davidoff estimates that by the end of the century up to 4000 families were active in London Society.[4] This strains the widely accepted contemporary convention of 'the Upper Ten Thousand', which is still more stretched by the figure of 30,000 families listed in the 1900 Court Guide as potentially eligible. A calculation in terms of families remained appropriate. Heredity was the cornerstone of Society, even at the end of the Edwardian period, and performance upon its public stage was very definitely a family enterprise.

Women's roles in this enterprise were distinctive from, though complementary to, those of male relatives and ultimately determined by personal attributes and abilities as well as by social necessities. At the most general level, women were both stage managers and leading players. Society operated by a process of exclusion as well as inclusion, and Society ladies assumed (after royalty) the main responsibility for determining who was in and who was out, and what was or was not acceptable behaviour. In the midst of the transformation which presaged its decline, Society clung to established customs and an established annual calendar: the London Season in summer, contrasting with country house living in autumn and winter; a spring and summer of entertainments linked to court presentations and the business of parliament, followed by a quieter rural spell with estate management and outdoor sports to the fore. But, as Davidoff and others have shown, these traditions were constantly reinvented throughout the nineteenth century. Society grew in complexity as well as in size, and the multiplication of its activities and ever-growing elaboration of its etiquette from the mid-nineteenth century onwards must be read as a defensive mechanism as well as an index of increasing wealth. Access rituals extended all the way from the Queen's formal approval of white-robed, ostrich-feathered debutantes to the compilation of dinner party guest lists and the leaving and receiving of visiting cards. Social performance extended from the choice of a London address to that of ballgowns, flowers and menus and of the front-of-house servants' liveries. Full social acceptance of newcomers, and the maintenance of status for the established upper classes, depended upon ostentatious conformity as well as upon securing suitable matrimonial alliances. The organization of elite social life provided a full-time career for many aristocratic ladies. A fair proportion of the family's fortunes depended upon their success, or so they believed and encouraged others to believe.

The relationship of Society life to the male politics of party and government was a long-established one. In origin, the timing and entertainments of the Season were tied to the parliamentary calendar. The aristocracy and gentry converged upon London when Parliament met and retired to the countryside when it dissolved. During the parliamentary session the female relatives of politicians not only found marriage partners and enjoyed themselves, but also cultivated a congenial social setting for the transaction of informal political business. A minority of the wealthy and ambitious became famous as political hostesses in the early and mid-nineteenth century. The Countess of Jersey, the Marchioness of Londonderry and the Duchess of Buccleuch held sway for the Tories, while Lady Waldegrave, Lady Spencer and Lady Cowper entertained the Liberals. The absence of highly structured political parties, whether in parliament or in the constituencies, provided a helpful context for such activities. There was much meeting and political brokering across party lines at assemblages such as Lady Palmerston's parties, while other London houses became trusted venues for small-scale, informal meetings of close political associates. Kim Reynolds warns against casting such hostesses as protofeminists;[5] but the compatibility of male and female political ambitions, pursued through differently gendered means, did not make women's role less visible or less important. Precedents were being set for late Victorian and Edwardian hostesses who performed some of the same roles while necessarily adapting to the changing nature of Society and politics.

By the turn of the century the increased size and more varied nature of Society and organizational changes within British politics were reshaping the relationship between London's political and social worlds. Contemporary observers noted that fragmentation had accompanied expansion. Society no longer formed a single, cohesive group whose members all knew each other personally. Meanwhile, politicians developed alternative venues for doing business, whether in the Houses of Parliament, in the proliferating private gentlemen's clubs, or at the offices of the main political parties. An expanding franchise swiftly made its mark upon the latter. The Reform Acts of 1867 and 1884, coupled with boundary redefinitions, anti-corruption legislation and local government reforms, looked set to transform the political establishment in the not-too-distant future. Though this was less than clear to many contemporaries, and at Cabinet level aristocratic privilege continued virtually untouched into the twentieth century, party professionals went busily to work from the 1870s onwards to set up the means of winning and exercising political power in a more democratic society. Late-nineteenth-century reforms in the Civil Service, the armed services and the judiciary further underlined the approach of a meritocracy. Would birth, landed wealth and 'merit' continue to converge around the upper-class scions of a judiciously expanded Society? On balance, the historians have concluded that by 1914 the writing was already on the wall.[6]

Yet there also remains evidence to suggest that unelected lady politicians were far from ready to bow out. New fissures in party politics opened up fresh opportunities for enterprising and determined hostesses. Liberal Unionists gathered at Devonshire House after the Home Rule split of 1886; Tory ministers found congenial company at Lansdowne House; and Grosvenor House was the chief base for the 'die-hard' opposition to the 1909 Budget and House of Lords reform. Female imperialism met with a friendly reception at each of the same grand houses, using them in turn as prestigious meeting places and lobbying their owners for various forms of support. Leading imperialist ladies provided a range of other fine social settings as an integral part of their political work. Either as political wives (in Pat Jalland's phrase),[7] or as the more fully committed political hostesses of earlier tradition, they brought existing experience of the intermingling of politics and social life to the work of the ladies' imperialist associations. The linkage of class and gender privileges to the Empire's cause reinforced older forms of female political intervention and influence at a time when these were coming under threat.

General conclusions about upper-class women's role in a changing society (and Society) can be tested against the life histories of prominent individuals. The twentieth-century proliferation of aristocratic memoirs is in itself evidence of the importance which these ladies attached to the customs and rituals of Society. In the cold draughts of a post-war world, there was an inevitable tendency towards nostalgia. Even Violet Markham, a businesslike Liberal who found her way into the female imperialist leadership through money and intellectual merit rather than ancient lineage, lived to lament 'the practical disappearance of a whole strata of society which was a precious element in the national life'. Not only the rich and titled, but the 'comfortably off' (on that ill-defined boundary between upper- and upper-middle-class) lived in ease and thereby defended 'the finer values'.[8] This faith in social hierarchy as an integral feature of national and imperial greatness was still more fervently expressed by many other autobiographers writing in the interwar years: no fewer than thirteen of the leading lady imperialists helpfully set pen to paper during this period.[9] Their memoirs tend to bear out recent research into female autobiography which shows the propensity of Victorian and Edwardian women for veiling female self-assertion and individual success behind accounts of the achievements of male others, or of the particular social groupings to which these women belonged.[10] Such stratagems were consciously adopted by some authors as a means of avoiding either indiscretion or undue feminine self-aggrandizement. The resulting record frustrates those historians in search of consecutive narratives of personal achievement (including organizational and political achievements), but nevertheless vividly conveys a sense of the upper-class social values which underlay female imperialism. Autobiographers were proud to record details of an era in national and imperial history, rather than simply an individual life story. This did not diminish their own importance, but rather set it accurately in context.

Society set-piece descriptions loom large in Edwardian ladies' autobiographies. So, too, do encounters with Great Men and Royalty. These relationships were significant within the development of female imperialism, and will be considered further in Chapters 3 and 4. This chapter focuses instead upon the contribution of memoirs and other personal records to our understanding of the leading imperialist ladies' educational background, their entry into Society and their experience of the rewards and deficits of upper-class married status. These aspects of personal life were fundamental in shaping the ideals and organizational methods of female imperialism. Idiosyncrasies and varied viewpoints inevitably emerge from the ladies' memoirs, diaries and letters. These provide salutary warnings against an exaggerated portrayal of unity. On the other hand, there is also compelling evidence of a bedrock of social and political assumptions which made possible the construction of alliances across the conventional divide of party and the potentially still wider divide of the suffrage issue. The leaders of female imperialism achieved purposeful agreement on imperial activism because they had so much else in common, including shared social values and a confident sense of gendered authority.

During the Edwardian period most of the leading lady imperialists were married women in their thirties, forties and fifties. They had received the kinds of education and upbringing available to girls of the upper classes in the mid-Victorian decades. Retrospective assessments of this education vary, but frequently emphasize its inadequacy for women who went on to lives of public work. As an education for Society, and for politics conducted largely through social channels, of course it had its strengths.

Very few imperialist ladies went to school. They therefore missed out on the growing public school ethos of manliness, militarism, Christianity and patriotism which so powerfully shaped the imperialist views of young men, except to the extent that it could be 'borrowed' from brothers or the (sometimes discouraged) literature of Newbolt, Kipling and Henty. By the 1880s the same spirit had entered the press. Violet Markham recalled,

> My first dim recollection of the great world outside the warm and sheltered circle of childhood is sitting on my Father's knee at the age of seven and looking at a picture of the defence of Rork's Drift in the *Illustrated London News*. The soldiers behind the sand-bags, the black figures with their spears in the foreground, made a picture rather alarming for a little girl.

The 'tragic death of General Gordon' was soon a second indelible memory.[11] But even the later appearance of a sub-imperialist fiction for girls in the 1880s and 1890s failed to place such images at the forefront of young ladies' education. 'Feminine abnegation in the face of imperial duty' or 'imperial philanthropy' were more likely to be central themes than military heroism, and adventurous heroines were rare before the 1900s.[12] Instead of studying world leadership, upper-class girls learned a haphazard variety of practical, social and intellectual skills laced with religious and moral conformity.

It was the lack of systematic thoroughness, and of established expectations of high standards, which many women lamented in adulthood. The same criticism was made of girls' schools (by the minority who attended them) as of the far more common governess education. Mary Ward, granddaughter of the famous headmaster Arnold of Rugby and herself a well-known novelist, claimed that her decade of miserable boarding school education was

> particularly wasted. I learnt nothing thoroughly or accurately . . . nor was it ever possible for me – who married at twenty – to get that firm hold on the structure and literary history of any language, ancient or modern, which my brother William, only fifteen months my junior, got from his six years at Rugby and his training there in Latin and Greek.[13]

Girls from moneyed rather than intellectual upper-middle-class backgrounds often combined a mainly private education with short periods at school. Elizabeth Haldane, as an only girl with four brothers, also drew envious contrasts. Her brothers 'pursued the ordinary well-trod paths of school and university' while her own education became 'extraordinarily scrappy'.[14] Violet Markham moved on from 'various governesses' to eighteen months at a genteel boarding-school on Ham Common. Between thirty and forty girls received

> a liberal, if in some respects limited, education . . . Here and there a girl sat for the Cambridge Higher Local Examination, but this was quite exceptional and the exception did not include myself. I have often wondered why it was never suggested that I should present myself for this exercise which would have pruned and lopped my rather untidy mind.

Elocution classes were unexpectedly helpful to Violet's later public-speaking career, but the limitations included 'no science, no economics, no social history'; and when, in the interwar years, she found herself serving upon a range of government committees, lack of mathematics proved 'a sad and lifelong stumbling block'.[15]

Governesses were remembered in later life with a mixture of affection and contempt. At the lower end of the market, Violet Cecil (whose parents separated when she was five) recalled 'a succession of governesses' who taught her in hired rooms near her mother's 'very small house'; while, presumably at her father's expense, one brother 'left Rugby for Sandhurst and his regiment in India', and the other 'left Harrow for Cambridge and went on a journey round the world'.[16] Far more memorable than the governesses were her encounters with her unconventional mother's artistic and literary friends, including Wilde, Whistler, Sickert and Burne-Jones. At the upper end of the governess range, the Leigh family's Miss Custarde was an almost mythic combination of extreme accomplishment and extreme moral rectitude. She successfully introduced Margaret Leigh (the eldest of seven) to the higher realms of art and literature, but failed to instil her own talents for music and needlework. Known by her family as 'the Head Girl', Margaret was not the most compliant of pupils and resisted moral bludgeoning.[17] Susan Grosvenor's governess was another moral tyrant, but a less talented one. She was remembered as having 'absolutely no teaching ability at all'. Fortunately, the Grosvenors' wealth softened this verdict by financing

> good classes when I was in London . . . I learnt drawing and studied languages and French, German and Italian literature; but it was all unrelated and uncoordinated . . . I still mourn the fact that I was never taught to concentrate or to have exactness of mind when I was a child, and that I was never told of their vital importance in later life.[18]

Daisy Warwick wrote with contrasting warmth of 'a joyful pursuit of knowledge and explorations into the realms of taste and feeling, under the guidance of a much-loved Miss Blake'. Two governesses and a tutor ministered to seven children in the grand setting of Easton to which Daisy (most unusually) had inherited her own right at the age of five. But grandeur did not absolve the daughters from moral training, and Miss Blake was 'inexorable as any *grand dame* of old on matters of etiquette and manners'. More enjoyable were studies of history, literature, music and art upon a lavish scale, including access to literature in three languages, to Patti at the Albert Hall, to the Royal Academy, National Gallery and 'catalogues of the Louvre pictures and of the Florentine galleries'. Though 'geography had not yet entered the scientific stage', there were opportunities to share 'national excitement in the distant exploits of Livingstone, and, later on, Stanley'. As for science itself, this was merely

> a timid nibbling at botany, geology and so forth . . . early science lessons meant lying on my back on the grass on summer evenings while Miss Blake taught me the names of various stars and constellations, or lying flat on the top of a narrow wall gazing upwards to become conscious of the earth's movement.[19]

Like other leading ladies, Daisy Warwick later turned a brave face on the incompleteness of her education. She developed a 'passion for books' and learned to educate herself. Elizabeth Haldane also believed that intelligent girls could find their own way, like 'chickens pecking around till they did so! One emerged terribly ignorant in some directions, but really interested in others.'[20] Religion was a serious curb on adult and children's behaviour in her Edinburgh household, dominated by a Calvinist father.

However, at the wealthy and aristocratic end of the social elite, youthful freedom left happy memories despite the strictness of governesses and the regularity of family prayers. The future Countess of Warwick rode a stable-full of unsuitably fierce horses; the girls of the Lyttelton and Talbot families joined their brothers at cricket as well as on horseback;[21] and the notoriously untamed Tennant sisters (one of them later to become Margot Asquith) took free choice to extremes:

> We were wild children and, left to ourselves, had the time of our lives. I rode my pony up the front stairs and tried to teach my father's high stepping barouche-horses to jump – crashing their knees into the hurdles in the field – and climbed our dangerous roof, sitting on the sweep's ladder by moonlight in my night-gown.[22]

It is clear that the wider dimensions of a privileged upbringing could compensate for some of the deficiencies in girls' education. Though imperialist ladies considered themselves to be incompletely educated, they were well-read and often accomplished at more than a purely superficial level. Not only Mary Ward but also Margaret Jersey, Frances Balfour, Edith Lyttelton and Violet Markham became successful published authors. Violet Cecil in later life succeeded her brother as editor of the *National Review*, and in her youth made repeated efforts to develop her artistic talents. As leaders both in Society and within female imperialism, these were exceptional women who had unusual ability and strength of character. Their consciousness of an educational deficit was undoubtedly replicated among less exceptional women of the same social class and must be considered a significant factor within the female imperialist associations.

As childhood gave way to adulthood, formal education came to an end but the social education of young ladies intensified. Social and intellectual training were by no means opposite poles. Success in Society demanded more than mere physical beauty and nice manners, and active female imperialists were frequently among those who sought and achieved social brilliance rather than mere acceptability and correctness. The final stages of a young lady's preparation to enter Society united both mental and physical grooming, often in a Parisian setting. Violet Maxse's father, bolstered by an inheritance, provided two successive winters in the Boulevard St Germain, where Violet worked at her art, her French and her violin, attended innumerable plays and posted home copious descriptions and sketches of the latest fashions. Dinner party guests included Georges Clemenceau, an old family friend, the artists Edgar Degas and Mary Cassatt, and Joseph Chamberlain with 'his charming young American bride' (later a somewhat retiring female imperialist herself).[23] Even Elizabeth Haldane, whose Scottish upbringing had been the opposite of bohemian, was judged in need of a winter in Paris with her mother and a maid. Margaret Leigh wintered in the South of France with her parents and toured Italy, the Netherlands and a romantically remembered southern Ireland during her teenage years. This proved to be the beginning of a lifelong enjoyment of travel, as well as the completion of an education. Like many other lady imperialists, she began a habit of systematically recording her journeys for the education of others.

Margaret Leigh's triumphant progress through her first London Season was to be a textbook example of successfully completed rites of passage. Like every other entrant, she donned her white gown, veil, flowers and ostrich feathers and overcame the perils of curtseying and retreating backwards from royalty while wearing the court-regulated three-yard train. Parties and balls followed, during which strict chaperonage ensured limited contact with highly suitable young men. Dancing was supplemented (or, in Lord Jersey's case substituted) by 'little walks', since seated conversation between opposite sexes was considered bad form at balls. 'At one of the last balls of the season, Lord Jersey realised that Miss Leigh would be leaving London, and that the little walks would cease. He presented himself to Lord Leigh as a suitor, and on July 18th 1872 the engagement was settled.'[24] Margaret later told her grandchildren that she had met her husband only twelve times, and under extremely restrictive circumstances, before accepting his proposal. She had done what was expected of her. Suitable marriages were the key to successful perpetuation of the hereditary landed aristocracy and thence to upper-class domination of national life.

Even less conventional women than Margaret Jersey often married little-known men in haste, or married with an evident eye upon social suitability rather than romantic bliss. Margot Tennant's calculating betrothal to Henry Asquith, widowed father of three and foreseeably a future premier, was the subject of disapproval and warnings in 1894. In this case, political ambition and financial considerations dominated the equation rather than titles or landed status. Louisa Bowater's wedding, as a youthful and impecunious bride, to Sir Rainald Knightley, twenty years her senior, was almost equally calculated, though it soon matured into a love-match. Daisy Maynard became a highly suitable Countess of Warwick before setting out on her 1890s career as a member of the Marlborough House 'fast' set and mistress of the Prince of Wales. Violet Maxse, like Margaret Leigh, was swept away amidst the excitements of the Season. In her case it was the Dublin Season of 1894, where there were amusing imperial overtones in the faithful replication of London social ceremonies at the court of the Viceroy, Lord Houghton. 'It's all like playing at houses as one used to when one was little,' commented Violet to her mother. But although she found it difficult to take her second 'royal' presentation as seriously as her first, she enjoyed a second debutante outfit ('Everyone told me that it was the prettiest dress in the room'), and was soon at full stretch in a 'giddy whirl' of entertainments. 'This week we go out every night – tonight to the play. It is Lord E. Cecil's party, he is commonly called "Nigs" by his family and Ned by his regiment. Tomorrow a dance, Wednesday a concert, Thursday a "State Ball", the first that has been given since the Duke of Marlborough's time, Friday and Saturday dinner parties. Isn't it a life?'[25] Within a fortnight Violet and Lord Edward Cecil were engaged.

It was customary for an engaged girl, and even more so for a married lady, to become gradually incorporated into the family and social circles of her fiancé/husband. Even when women were socially acceptable to their new husbands' families, they often needed to make significant adjustments to lifestyle and attitudes in order to 'fit in'. Violet Maxse was a case in point. Edward Cecil remained on military duty in Dublin while Violet endured an alarming post-engagement lunch with the Cecil family in London. A more pleasurable first visit to Hatfield, the ancestral home, followed soon after. Meanwhile Violet was receiving half-joking warning letters from her acquaintances in different 'sets': 'Mr Burne-Jones said the Cecils carried their wives off to an inaccessible fastness and there chewed their bones. Mr Asquith said gloomily that our spheres would no longer cut across each other.'[26] The potential conflicts revolved around deeper issues than merely party politics. Friendships, and even marriages, across party lines were by no means uncommon in the late Victorian and Edwardian period. Violet Maxse's Liberal Unionist background was acceptable enough at Hatfield (where she moved rapidly into Tory patriot mode). Maud Cecil (Lord Edward's eldest sister) maintained her Conservatism when she married into the Whig Selborne family and eventually had the satisfaction of being joined by her husband after his passage through Unionism. Frances Campbell was also descended from the Whig aristocracy as daughter of the Duke of Argyll, but found her marriage partner in Eustace Balfour, nephew of Lord Salisbury and brother of Conservative premier Arthur Balfour. After a particularly unhappy marriage, she left a frank account of her own first impressions of the Balfour household. The Balfours

> were all conspicuously talented, but in directions with which I was totally unfamiliar. An austere reserve kept them silent on subjects in which we were vociferous. Their logical faculties bordered on the dry as dust; their emotions were held in strict control; their natural bent was to try all things, and to prove for themselves all things. Any display of excited or unreasonable feeling was foreign to their nature.[27]

In time, Frances became close to many members of her new family, including in particular Arthur Balfour and her sister-in-law (and fellow imperialist) Betty Balfour. However, she retained a proud consciousness of her former unmarried identity and, like Violet Cecil, was reluctant to pay the full price of surrendering it. 'Difficulties of Getting Married' was her page-heading for the foregoing section of her autobiography.

Most upper-class women found the difficulties of marriage more than compensated for by its advantages. Weddings fulfilled a strong social expectation, linked to the equally strong expectation of motherhood. Whether or not the matrimonial path ran smoothly, a married woman achieved improved status and access to a range of authoritative new roles. For those who chose to participate, the pleasures and duties of the London Season continued unabated. Debutantes were the pawns in a game largely controlled by matrons. Nor did the interplay of sexual liaisons necessarily end in marriage. There were many discreet 'affaires' from royalty downwards, and some at least of the imperialist ladies chose to exercise their powers in this direction. Upper-class friendship networks were an essential base for the work of the female imperialist associations. Men developed their own single-sex networks through politics, business, clubs and the sporting fraternities of shooting and golf. But mixed-sex and female socializing relied heavily upon the efforts of married women with homes of their own and opportunities to entertain. Friendship and the exercise of 'influence' were often so closely intertwined that they became indistinguishable. Married women shared in this form of political power, and not only on behalf of their husbands' careers. It was in the nature of 'influence' to demand discretion, but there are plenty of recorded instances of requests made and granted, and cabinet ministers' ears successfully bent on matters of concern. Daisy Warwick made inflated claims for her personal 'influence', alleging to have single-handedly set up the early discussions with colonial premiers which resulted in 'the birth of Mr Chamberlain's Empire movement'.[28] More convincing are Violet Cecil's account of lobbying Lord Salisbury on the subject of military hospitals in South Africa after her return from that country in 1900[29] and Mary Jeune's description of another dinner party at Hatfield when it was her 'happy fate' to sit next to the premier.[30] Margot Asquith's account of debating political ideas and personalities during a youthful drive alongside William Gladstone shows similar respect for a senior statesman who was prepared to take women seriously.[31]

More equal companionship was to be found among contemporaries enjoying mixed-sex company in one or another of London's social 'sets'. The best-known (and most self-publicizing) of these was the Souls, formed in the 1880s around Arthur Balfour, George Curzon and the Tennant sisters. The 'set' was a friendship group of married couples, together with a minority of bright young single women and confirmed bachelors such as Balfour himself. They united loosely around shared social enjoyments laced with intelligent wit. Formal politics were a subordinate aspect of their discussions, and the cross-party friendships that were forged so agreeably in the last decades of the century provided useful ballast for the equally 'non-political' female imperialism of the Edwardian years. In July 1889 George Curzon hosted a famous Souls' dinner party at a London club.[32] The records of the Victoria League fifteen years later show how long-standing such social ties could become. Seven of Curzon's lady guests were among the League's Council members; the family names of several others appear in the membership lists; and the Victoria League was profiting from the male Souls' achievement of high office. Balfour (then Asquith) became Prime Minister; Curzon was Viceroy of India; Brodrick served in the Foreign Office and then as Secretary of State for War; Lyttelton was Colonial Secretary and married a fellow-Soul who became one of the Victoria League's leading organizers.

By the end of the nineteenth century Society entertainments were more varied and numerous than ever before. No single hostess could hope to achieve the mid-century predominance of Lady Jersey and Lady Palmerston. However, adaptations were possible in this sphere of social life, as in others, and from 1880 to 1914 there were still a number of married women who regarded themselves as 'specialists' in large-scale political entertainment. Recalling the 1880s and 1890s, the Countess of Warwick carefully distinguished 'political' from 'social' hostesses. Among the former, Lady Londonderry and Lady Lansdowne led the way for the Conservatives and Unionists, and Lady Spencer and Lady Tweedmouth for the Liberals.

> In spite of invitations being restricted to friends and acquaintances, five hundred was no large figure for a political reception, which would start at nine o'clock and be over at midnight. Supper would be an affair of the buffet, but would be of irreproachable quality. There were no sterner critics of champagne, *foie gras*, quail, and the rest of the familiar luxuries, than the people who attended receptions.

A minimum of £500 was budgeted for refreshments and floral decorations. Equally lavish hospitality was provided at official government receptions, where again the hostess's role was central. Lady Salisbury's Foreign Office receptions were 'dazzling both to the eye and to the mind', crowded not only with politicians and senior civil servants, but also graced by the presence of British and foreign royalty and 'foreign attachés in uniforms of infinite splendour'.[33]

On a slightly smaller scale, Mary Jeune and Margaret Jersey kept up more personal traditions of political entertaining, mingling diverse politicians with their literary friends. Ladies' knowledge of politics and their ability to exert 'influence' benefited enormously from such occasions. As the ambitious wife of a titled lawyer rather than a politician, Mary Jeune's enthusiasm for such gatherings was very much her own. Her autobiography records with precision the impact of an ever-widening Society upon her style of entertaining. It eventually became 'more convenient to receive on a larger scale and less often . . . I think I may fairly say my parties were popular. They were very mixed, and sometimes very crowded.' Mary Jeune's boastful account of famous and satisfied guests concluded with an emphasis upon the demanding nature of her own role.

> The position of the hostess is not a bed of roses, and besides the initial difficulty in London of first of all finding a suitable day, and then selecting her guests so that they may be both agreeable and sympathetic to each other, she has to reckon with the endless accidents which very often destroy what promised to be the realisation of her ideal. Everyone knows the perpetual defeats and disappointments which a hostess encounters in London, where the competition is so keen.[34]

Margaret Jersey was among Mary Jeune's competitors, and apparently fell out with her at one stage over having successfully filched Joseph Chamberlain into her orbit of influence and entertainment. Perhaps Chamberlain did find Osterley House and its hostess more enjoyable than the Jeune establishment. Certainly by the mid-1890s the younger woman was vigorously taking the initiative in cross-party entertaining with a combined imperialist and literary flavour. In its pleasant surburban park, Osterley was ideally situated as a weekend retreat during the Season. Away from the crush of London receptions, the formality of dinner parties and the pressures of parliament, politicians and their female friends and relatives gathered to relax and talk. Violet Markham remembered the pleasures and exertions of an Osterley weekend, to which her Victoria League work drew her despite her Liberal politics. A Saturday afternoon garden-party was followed by a more intimate evening for two dozen house guests. After Sunday morning church,

> a whole new set of guests would appear first for lunch, then for tea, then again for dinner. Sometimes these contingents overlapped each other. On Sundays we dined off the famous Osterley gold plate, the only times in my life I have had that experience. On Monday morning I would crawl back to London worn out with so much conversation, all of it worthwhile, for Lady Jersey's guests were not social butterflies but included outstanding figures in politics, literature, and the arts.[35]

Violet's background, as the daughter of a wealthy Midlands mineowner, was not one that would have opened Osterley's doors a generation earlier. Yet this potentially critical upper-middle-class visitor evidently felt that aristocratic traditions of combined political and social entertainment were being usefully prolonged.

Neither Lord Jersey nor Sir Francis Jeune pursued outstanding political careers, despite some involvement in government. But the wives of more prominent politicians, while not necessarily aspiring 'political hostesses', found themselves increasingly drawn into active roles related to their husbands' careers. Their consequent knowledge of politics and acquisition of political skills stood them in good stead as active female imperialists. Jennie Churchill noted in her autobiography how her own political involvement grew alongside her husband's during the 1880s. The 'ultra-political' ladies in regular attendance at the House of Commons included Mrs Gladstone, Miss Balfour (Arthur's sister, and later Secretary of the Victoria League) and Mrs Chamberlain. By the date of her book (1908), a good deal had changed.

The present generation are full of the desire of being, or appearing to be, serious. To be beautiful and rich is not sufficient; the real social leaders of today are not content with these accidents of birth and fortune. They aspire to political influence, or to be thought literary and artistic; and society follows the lead.[36]

To this rather jaundiced explanation of increased attendance might, of course, be added recent changes in the world of politics. Wives attended not only to gossip and 'be seen', but also to equip themselves to provide necessary support in the social world of politics and the rough-and-tumble of democratizing constituency work. Jennie Churchill proved herself to be supremely able in all these spheres at an early date; it was her tragedy that her erratic husband bowed petulantly out of the Cabinet just as her own political talents began to flower. Her legacy as a founder of the Primrose League was taken up by others in the next generation.

Not all political wives were enthusiastic, but Jennie Churchill was far from alone in enjoying the surge of power and confidence which came from participation in election campaigns. Louisa Knightley's elderly husband was notably ill-equipped for an advancing democratic age. He had taken over his father's Conservative seat of South Northamptonshire in 1852 and, as a descendant of the Knightleys of Fawsley who had been in residence since the fifteenth century, felt entitled to expect political continuity on his local patch. The Franchise and Redistribution Acts of 1884 and 1885 put this in jeopardy by granting votes to agricultural labourers and redrawing his constituency boundaries to include towns with a strong Liberal and Radical influence. In the 1885 election Sir Rainald faced a political opponent for the first time in seventeen years and the necessity for an organized campaign. Louisa Knightley came to his rescue.[37] With spectacular efficiency, she drew upon information from the Central Conservative Office as well as local knowledge to set up local committees (including Ladies' Committees) and plan meetings and canvassing. A month before election day she wrote in her diary, 'I am proud to think that I shall soon, I hope, have arranged for the canvassing of every village in the division.'[38] Her personal role had been so conspicuous that it drew down political abuse upon her head, allowing Sir Rainald to leap chivalrously to her defence and thereby increase their popularity as a married couple. In fact Louisa was a firm believer in organization as opposed to mere personal charisma, male or female. The success of the campaign owed much to her foresight in mobilizing other people to work for her husband's cause, including the members of a Daventry (Knightley) Habitation of the Primrose League. Her own elevation as a Primrose League Dame is briskly recorded: 'It sounds all rubbish, but the objects "the maintenance of Religion, of the Estates of the Realm, of the ascendancy of the British Empire", are excellent, and I can quite believe that the paraphernalia helps to keep Conservatives together; means, in short, an army of unpaid canvassers.'[39]

Maud Selborne was similarly able to use the combination of a historic family name and excellent organizing skills to support her brothers, and eventually her son, in Edwardian election campaigns. As the wife of a peer she could have opted out of such work, but there is every sign that she enjoyed it.[40] Edith Lyttelton, on the other hand, undertook election work out of duty rather than enthusiasm. In 1903 Alfred Lyttelton stood for a by-election on accepting office as Colonial Secretary, and promptly succumbed to an attack of jaundice. 'With many misgivings' Edith stepped in to address his meetings, knowing that she lacked the advantages of locally respected status and knowledge and that the national issue of tariff reform would give impetus to their Liberal opponent. 'I never did more than give as clearly as I could some short message from him, but I was well backed by the Press and a great deal of sympathy for him was aroused in this way.'[41] The result was a narrow Unionist victory. Other passages in Edith's biography of her husband give an interesting insight into the less conspicuous functions of political wives and also into this particular marriage relationship. Alfred was heavily reliant upon her encouragement and advice. Throughout his life he struggled against 'an inner sense of failure and mistrust of his own powers'.[42] The decision that he should suspend a lucrative legal career to enter politics in 1894 was taken jointly, after Edith had been privately lobbied by third parties to secure this result. A family home was purchased in Great College Street, in the shadow of the Houses of Parliament, and Edith took up political entertaining on her husband's behalf. Guests included imperialist politicians and wives who supported female imperialism from both main political parties; and Alfred's parliamentary interests within Britain centred upon issues which also interested his wife. She studied political affairs closely, reading parliamentary papers as well as attending debates, and undoubtedly enjoyed the development of a partnership of ideas. Alfred was strongly influenced by her views. Like Rainald Knightley, he grudgingly came round to support women's suffrage, while at the same time constantly urging his wife to avoid overstraining herself by independent organizational and political work. Efforts on a husband's behalf were more acceptable.

The social and political roles of married upper-class ladies naturally extended from the busy London Season into the quieter lifestyles of country house existence during the autumn and winter. As we have seen, class boundaries with the upper-middle-class were becoming blurred by the turn of the century, and it would be inaccurate to pin a stereotyped image of the 'lady of the manor' upon all the leading female imperialists. Many did not have a palatial country seat to retire to, but the annual rhythm of social life was shaped by those who did. Hospitality had become far more catholic, and wealth and talent were often acceptable entry tickets, so that during the pre-war decade there were probably larger numbers of people than ever before attempting to share the pleasures of an aristocratic lifestyle. At the same time that lifestyle, in the country as well as in the capital, was being perceptibly undermined and transformed. Old-style country house entertaining, which had earlier taken up several months of the year, lingered on particularly in the parts of Britain more distant from London. The Warwicks had a home in Scotland as well as a castle in England, and Rhodes, Chamberlain and the Prince of Wales were among those who enjoyed their splendid hospitality. The Balfours spent much time at Whittinghame, thirty miles outside Edinburgh. Frances Balfour and Mary Jeune enjoyed revisiting their Highland parental homes, and the Haldanes also entertained extensively, though on a smaller scale, in their family house at Cloan. When Alfred and Edith Lyttelton decided to purchase a country retreat (to avoid endless perambulation around other people's houses, which Edith had grown to dislike), they decided upon a newly built house on the Muirfield golf-links at Gullane. This was conveniently close to Whittinghame, and contingents of guests travelled there with such regularity that Edith 'found life there even more exhausting than in London' and eventually sold up in favour of the rural peace of Sussex. The Edwardian popularity of golf and shooting was a sign of the changing times. These were less definitively the country sports of the landed aristocracy than were traditional fox-hunting and deer-stalking. Daisy Warwick wrote feelingly in her autobiography about the extreme boredom of ladies at Victorian country house parties that were dedicated exclusively to male sport. In Frances Balfour's memories of country life at Whittinghame she tells of a significant encounter between the old and the new. When Joseph Chamberlain came to stay he 'quite simply expressed his astonishment' at the extent of Arthur Balfour's estate. It also transpired that Chamberlain 'played no games', which may be one of a number of reasons for his popularity among the female imperialists.[43] In general, sport was one of the fault lines between male and female lifestyles. Violet Cecil first met (and learned to admire) Margot Asquith on the hunting field. This was an unusual exception, and when hunting extended to the imperial context of Big Game it still more emphatically signified the Empire as a man's world.[44]

Country lifestyles were not necessarily idle for ladies, however. Even being a guest could be demanding when mountains of baggage needed to be transported, servants organized and clothes changed four times a day. When a lady was staying on her own estate her organizational roles multiplied. For many women of the landed gentry, as opposed to the wealthiest aristocracy, country living was almost a full-time career, interrupted only by short interludes of town visiting and (if possible) a trip to London during the Season. Louisa Knightley relished life on her medium-sized country estate, though she enjoyed London Society life as well. As the young bride of a traditionalist husband, she devoted herself to tasks of household and neighbourhood management. The editor of her published journal, friend and Northamptonshire neighbour Julia Cartwright, described these early years: 'Whether her neighbours were dull or interesting, clever or stupid, Lady Knightley was determined to have a share in their joys and sorrows, and if possible make Fawsley a centre for rich and poor alike.'[45] At first her entertaining focused upon landed neighbours (such as the Cartwrights) and particularly the ladies of these families. Philanthropy gradually extended beyond the established custom of Christmas hand-outs of warm clothing, bedding and beef. Like other great ladies, Louisa Knightley treasured her detailed knowledge of the poor and believed that her personal contact with them was a moral as well as a practical support.[46] However, she was also influenced by the rising tide of middle-class philanthropy in towns and cities, and judged it useful to distinguish the deserving and to promote collective self-help. Towards the end of the century she made every effort to mesh her private charity into the emerging activity of elected local government, seeing no incongruity in presiding over her local parish council and moving on from patronage and management of village schools to a co-opted place on the first County Education Committee. Her work in parliamentary election campaigns fitted comfortably within this general frame. So, too, did her dedicated efforts for the Girls' Friendly Society which began at local level and ended up on an imperial plane. Her patriotic sense of duty was deeply imbued with a class-based view of her gender role. Alongside (and within) this stood her deep-seated faith in Anglican Christianity.

A combination of old-fashioned charity and more systematic forms of help for the poor was an inescapable feature of country life for upper-class Victorian ladies, though of course not all pursued these duties with equal energy. Daisy Warwick wrote, 'I was compelled more or less to play Lady Bountiful at Easton. I got to understand the miseries that life brings to the poor, and I wished to mitigate some of those hardships.'[47]

Violet Cecil, who seems to have had little personal interest in such activities, remembered semi-humorously her mother-in-law's assistance to the sick cottagers. It consisted (in the legend, at least) of mixing together the Cecil family's left-over medicines with an equal quantity of best port wine, and was extremely popular.[48] Margaret Jersey adopted the businesslike style of Louisa Knightley, though with less religious fervour. In later life she joked that 'She Gave Away Prizes' would make her a suitable epitaph, since 'she doubted if there was a child in Middlesex who had not received a prize from her hands'.[49] Bountifulness, in all its varied forms, certainly persisted into the Edwardian years. Its changing emphases are illustrated by the lady imperialists' increasing involvement in urban social work as well as country charity. Susan Grosvenor risked her mother's disapproval by opting for voluntary work at the Charity Organization Society's Baker Street offices, then at Mary Ward's Passmore Edwards settlement in Bloomsbury.[50] Violet Markham used her 1901 inheritance to establish a settlement in Chesterfield, near the family home where she had already 'found intolerable the life of a young lady of leisure', and volunteered as a School Board manager.[51] Edith Lyttelton was involved in the London campaign against sweated labour. Elizabeth Haldane developed a serious level of commitment and expertise in a whole range of areas, including child welfare, the Poor Law and the development of the nursing profession. Constance Battersea and the Countess of Aberdeen were equally versatile. The connections between these burgeoning philanthropic activities and the development of women's organizations and women's politics were complex and will be considered further in later chapters. At this stage it is worth noting the near-universality of philanthropic experience among the women who joined together to work for female imperialism.

In country settings, philanthropy was regarded by men and women alike as a female contribution to estate management. Ladies were required to exercise a range of managerial skills, and an ability to organize authoritatively was a far clearer badge of a Victorian lady's upper-class status than the decorative idleness so often attributed to her. The existence of patrician comforts depended entirely upon the labour of servants, whose appointment and supervision was very much the mistress's province. In the largest homes supervision might be delegated to a few senior servants, but most ladies prided themselves on taking personal responsibility for domestic arrangements. The autobiographies have rather little to say on this subject, perhaps considered too humdrum for inclusion, but frequently note the post-war absence of servants as a key transformation of modern life. Only Violet Markham, whose family home was on a relatively modest scale, gives the subject the importance it deserves. Her chapter on 'Domestic Economy' records the precision with which her mother kept house, leaving intact the accounting systems and management practices which Violet herself inherited in 1912.[52] Not for nothing was it expected that the young daughter of such a family would bring useful skills into the work of Chesterfield's schools.

Beyond managing entertainment, charities and servants, and their associated finances, how far did women act as partners in the government of town houses and country estates? Reynolds, Jalland and others show that full-scale economic management remained by and large the province of men. Upper-class ladies were not usually financially helpless, however. The upper-class practice of defending female wealth through entail and marriage settlements ensured that there was one law for the rich and another for the poor in the matter of married women's property.[53] The marriage settlements of Mary Curzon, Maud Selborne and Violet Cecil demonstrate that none of these wives depended entirely upon husbandly hand-outs. A wife's economic status, like her social status, nevertheless remained closely tied to her husband's. He would expect to influence her financial affairs without requiring legal sanction. She would not usually expect much consultation on major economic decisions, and none at all on minor ones in areas beyond the sphere of domestic management. There were some exceptions to this rule, including of course those women who were thrown back on to independent financial responsibility by widowhood, or who were unmarried and living with no close male relatives; but here too there were often male experts to step into the breach. Louisa Knightley's diary of the 1900s contains some sad passages on meetings with her steward and her solicitor, as agricultural depression and mounting estate debts caught up with Fawsley. Her predominant mood regarding estate management seems (most unusually for her) to have been one of resigned helplessness. Violet Cecil's financial correspondence with her estranged husband in Egypt, during the same period, suggests a more proactive response to financial difficulties. But she continued to accept his decisions in this area, if in no other, as final.

Most of the female roles described above were closely linked to marriage. It is evident why upper-class women were keen to attain this respected status. However, unmarried aristocratic women were unlikely to find starvation staring them in the face, and many led busy lives which might include service to the female imperialist cause. For some unmarried ladies, care of a brother or other relatives brought responsibilities similar to those of upper-class wives. Elizabeth Haldane seems to have harmoniously combined support for her brother Richard (a keener imperialist than she was) with a life of independent achievement in social work and literature. Alice Balfour's less successful career centred around her position as surrogate wife to her brother Arthur Balfour. In this capacity she invited the Victoria League to its inaugural meeting at 10 Downing Street. She also held high office in the Primrose League, but proved incapable of developing her independence further, despite wide interests in art, music and philanthropy as well as politics. Keeping house and acting as hostess for Arthur was time-consuming yet unrewarding, for she could never attain the assured rank of 'wife and mother' and was threatened by the more dynamic presence of her sister-in-law, Frances Balfour.[54] Maud Selborne's sister, Gwendolen Cecil, took over after her mother's death as confidante and domestic manager for Lord Salisbury and (later) the rest of the resident Hatfield family. She apparently had few regrets about her lack of a marriage partner. Like Violet Markham, who remained single until she reached the advanced age of 43 in 1915, she seems to have relished the opportunity to develop her own work and interests.[55] Violet struggled with the concept of matrimony. On the one hand she was strongly attracted towards it because of her conservative views on women's natural sphere. She cared dutifully for her ageing mother through the Edwardian years, as well as providing her brother Arthur with 'wifely' political support. On the other hand she had unusual opportunities for striking out alone, as an economically independent single woman of strong intellectual ability. Her late marriage to a man who encouraged her to follow her own interests was the best available compromise.

Several of the leading female imperialists were married women who were either emotionally distant from their husbands or widowed. Louisa Knightley and Laura

Ridding both became noticeably more active in public affairs after their husbands died. To varying extents, Margaret Jersey, Violet Cecil and Frances Balfour all found themselves with incompatible partners and acted independently in their public work. Together with Alice Balfour, Violet Markham, Gwendolen Cecil and Meriel Talbot (another satisfied spinster), these relatively free-standing women were a very important source of energy and commitment for the imperialist cause. However, the status of wife and (preferably) mother retained great importance for that cause. Insofar as female imperialism had an ideology of its own, it centred on the value of British women's family roles for the Empire as a whole. Organization and propaganda were validated by the leadership of women who performed those roles at the most prestigious levels of British society.

At a more practical level, the role of a wife (even a surrogate wife) opened up a wide range of social contacts and responsibilities. Whether in the world of country house life or of London politics and Society, married status implied a demanding array of duties and bestowed authority during their performance. Motherhood was, as we shall see, an overarching symbol within female imperialism. However, its practical impact upon the lifestyles of lady imperialists was less significant than that of wifehood. Patterns of mothering varied among the women in this study, but there was universal dependence upon nurses and governesses for daily childcare, and near-universal willingness among married ladies to put the interests of husbands above those of children. As Chapter 3 reveals, both Violet Cecil and Edith Lyttelton left their small children behind in order to accompany their husbands to South Africa. When Alfred Lyttelton begged his wife to work less hard for female imperialism, it was on the basis of his needs and her health rather than those of their children. Even childless women, such as Louisa Knightley, felt empowered by their class and gender status to advise poorer mothers at home and overseas on how to improve their family care for the sake of an imperial future. It was possible to claim the mantle of superior motherhood without much direct experience.

Lady imperialists were not the first political organizers to practise only partly what they preached. Not all were model wives and mothers, and a minority took advantage of being neither. What they shared, and deployed within the female imperialist movement, were the learnt attitudes and the perceived status associated with integrated class and gender roles. Their upper-class female lifestyles made possible their imperialist politics, both in conceptual and in practical terms.

Notes

1. See in particular D. Cannadine, *The Decline and Fall of the British Aristocracy* (London: Macmillan, 1996 edn). This monumental study begins in the 'Troubled Decade' of the 1880s, and adds very substantially to earlier works such as F. M.L. Thompson, *English Landed Society in the Nineteenth Century* (London: Routledge & Kegan Paul, 1963); M. Bush, *The English Aristocracy* (Manchester: Manchester University Press, 1984); W.D. Rubinstein, *Elites and the Wealthy in Modern British History* (Sussex: Harvester, 1987); and J. Beckett, *The Aristocracy in England 1660–1914* (Oxford: Blackwell, 1989).
2. Cannadine, p. 137.
3. See N. Ellenberger, 'The Transformation of "Society" at the End of Victoria's Reign: Evidence from the Court Presentation Records', *Albion*, 1990, 22 (4): 633–53. Ellenberger found that court presentation was being successfully used on a large scale to legitimate new arrivals

into Society by the end of the nineteenth century. Holders of hereditary titles increased by 11 per cent between 1850 and 1900; but numbers received at court increased much more steeply, approximately trebling between 1840 and 1900.

4. Davidoff (1973) discusses the growth of London Society and its implications in *The Best Circles*, Chapter 4. She quotes Beatrice Webb's description of Society in the 1880s as 'a shifting mass of miscellaneous and uncertain membership, it was essentially a body that could be defined, not by its circumference, which could not be traced, but by its centre or centres' (p. 63).

5. See K. Reynolds, 'Politics without Feminism: The Victorian Political Hostess', Chapter 4, in C. Campbell Orr, *Wollstonecraft's Daughters: Womanhood in England and France, 1780–1920* (Manchester: Manchester University Press, 1996).

6. See Thompson, p. 326; Cannadine, p. 351.

7. P. Jalland, *Women, Marriage and Politics 1860–1914* (Oxford: Oxford University Press, 1988). Jalland analyses the roles and attitudes of politicians' wives, deliberately focusing upon 'aspects of women's personal lives, which have been seriously neglected, rather than on women's public involvement' (p. 5).

8. V. Markham, *Return Passage* (London: Oxford University Press, 1953), p. 136.

9. The Countess of Aberdeen, Margot Asquith, Frances Balfour, Constance Battersea, Millicent Fawcett, Elizabeth Haldane, Margaret Jersey, Louisa Knightley (edited journals), the Marchioness of Londonderry, Edith Lyttelton, Mary Ward, the Countess of Warwick. Pre-war autobiographers included Jennie Churchill, Mary Jeune and Dorothy Nevill; post-Second World War volumes of reminiscence came from Violet Markham, Violet Milner (formerly Cecil) and Susan Tweedsmuir (formerly Buchan, née Grosvenor). These women are usually referred to in the text by the surname which they most frequently used during their active involvement in organized female imperialism. Maiden names are necessary at some points in this chapter. Brief biographical details of leading ladies are provided in Appendix 3.

10. See M. Corbett, *Representing Femininity: Middle Class Subjectivity in Victorian and Edwardian Women's Autobiographies* (Oxford: Oxford University Press, 1992); J. Barbre *et al.* (eds), *Interpreting Women's Lives: Feminist Theory and Personal Narratives* (Bloomington: Indiana University Press, 1989); S. Benstock (ed.), *The Private Self: Theory and Practice of Women's Autobiographical Writings* (London: Routledge, 1988); J. Swindells (ed.), *The Uses of Autobiography* (London: Taylor & Francis, 1995).

11. Markham, p. 15.

12. See J. Rowbotham, *Good Girls Make Good Wives* (Oxford: Blackwell, 1989), pp. 188 and 215. Bessie Marchant produced a steady supply of more adventurous colonial heroines in the Edwardian period; for example, Canadian Nell in *Daughters of the Dominion* (1909) and South African Molly in *Molly of One Tree Bend: A Story of a Girl's Heroism on the Veldt* (1910). Both girls ultimately sank gratefully into a hero's protective embrace.

13. M. Ward, *A Writer's Recollections* (London: Collins, 1918), p. 129.

14. E. Haldane, *From One Century to Another* (London: Alexander Maclehose & Co, 1937), p. 60.

15. Markham, pp. 40–3.

16. V. Milner, *My Picture Gallery 1886–1901* (London: John Murray, 1951), p. 4.

17. V. Powell, *Margaret Countess of Jersey* (London: Heinemann, 1978), p. 16.

18. S. Tweedsmuir, *The Lilac and the Rose* (London: Gerald Duckworth, 1952), p. 92.

19. F. Greville, Countess of Warwick, *Life's Ebb and Flow* (Plymouth: Mayflower Press, 1929), pp. 19, 23, 25.

20. E. Haldane, *From One Century to Another*, p. 60.

21. See S. Fletcher, *Victorian Girls: Lord Lyttelton's Daughters* (London: The Hambledon Press, 1997). The daughter of the eldest of these daughters became, in turn, a proficient cricketer

as well as the administrative mainstay of the Edwardian Victoria League. I am indebted to Sheila Fletcher for this information, drawn from unpublished family papers.

22. M. Asquith, *The Autobiography of Margot Asquith* (London: Weidenfeld & Nicolson, 1920/1922; 1995 edn), p. 16.
23. Milner, p. 18.
24. Powell, p. 29.
25. Milner, pp. 51–5.
26. *Ibid.*, p. 58.
27. F. Balfour, *Ne Obliviscaris: Dinna Forget* (London: Hodder & Stoughton, 1930), p. 173.
28. Greville, p. 143.
29. Milner, pp. 224–5.
30. M. Jeune, Lady St Helier, *Memoirs of Fifty Years* (London: Edward Arnold, 1909), p. 266.
31. Asquith, pp. 100–1.
32. *Ibid.*, pp. 119–25. Margot Asquith reproduces Curzon's welcoming poem, which lauded each of his guests individually.
33. Greville, pp. 49–52.
34. Jeune, p. 188.
35. Markham, p. 238.
36. J. Churchill, *The Reminiscences of Lady Randolph Churchill* (London: Edward Arnold, 1908), pp. 87–8.
37. See P. Gordon, 'Lady Knightley and the South Northamptonshire Election of 1885', *Northamptonshire Past and Present*, 1982, 6 (5): 265–73.
38. Louisa Knightley's journal, 23 October 1885. Northamptonshire Record Office.
39. *Ibid.*, 12 May 1885.
40. See e.g. her comments on the January 1910 election campaign: 'with a son and a son-in-law, and two brothers standing, it is too thrilling', she wrote to her daughter, Lady Howick, on 19 December 1909 (9 M 68, 193. Hampshire Record Office). In the December 1910 campaign she was active in her brother Robert Cecil's cause: 'I am quite sure this seat could have been won if a decent organisation had been started here three months ago', she wrote to her husband, William Selborne, on 7 December 1910 (MS Selborne adds. 3, 119. Bodleian Library).
41. E. Lyttelton, *Alfred Lyttelton* (London: Longmans, Green & Co, 1917), p. 288.
42. *Ibid.*, p. 79.
43. Balfour, p. 357.
44. See J. MacKenzie, *The Empire of Nature: Hunting, Conservation and British Imperialism* (Manchester: Manchester University Press, 1988). Lord Curzon and Lord Selborne were enthusiastic big game hunters and made the most of opportunities offered by occupation of the British government's highest posts in India and South Africa respectively. Hunting exploits were retailed to their female correspondents, including an unimpressed Maud Selborne (who did her best to exclude animal trophies from the Hampshire family home). Alfred Lyttelton, former Colonial Secretary, regarded an East African hunting trip in 1912 as one of the highlights of his career. 'Alfred gets a lion' is recorded in loving detail by his wife: 'he knew it was not very likely that he would have a chance, but he could not help desiring it intensely' (Lyttelton, p. 390).
45. J. Cartwright (ed.), *The Journals of Lady Knightley of Fawsley (1856–1884)* (London: John Murray, 1915), p. 183.
46. See J. Gerard, 'Lady Bountiful: Women of the Landed Classes and Rural Philanthropy', *Victorian Studies*, 1987, 30 (2): 183–209.
47. Greville, p. 72.
48. Milner, p. 84.
49. Powell, p. 53.

50. Tweedsmuir, pp. 88–90.
51. Markham, p. 63.
52. Markham, Chapter 4. Appendices include a chart of servants' wages, 'Staff rules at Tapton House' and 'Menus and criticisms of dinners and parties from my mother's notebook', pp. 244–9.
53. See Jalland, pp. 58–72, and autobiographical evidence of lady imperialists.
54. *Ibid.*, pp. 268–72.
55. See K. Rose, *The Later Cecils* (London: Weidenfeld & Nicolson, 1975), Chapter 10; and Jalland, pp. 281–2; see also Gwendolen Cecil's correspondence with Violet Cecil and Maud Selborne, in the Milner and Selborne MS collections at the Bodleian Library.

3 The Imperial Turn

Despite significant changes in Society, Edwardian imperialism carried forward many older traditions of upper-class feminine influence. Political wives and hostesses were as busy as ever, though the days of the exclusive, power-brokering salon were largely over. The Season and country house parties continued to provide social and intellectual meeting grounds for wealthy men and women. Meanwhile, a growing number of ladies extended their organizing abilities by contributing to organized female philanthropy in all its late Victorian abundance. Through so doing they learned to work alongside, as well as on behalf of, women who did not share their own social status. For some women, a sense of imperial mission merely projected existing philanthropic activity on to a worldwide stage. For others, an interest in the ideal of imperialism might develop from evolving press coverage and parliamentary debate, from the Liberals' split over Irish Home Rule, from the Tories' efforts to incorporate Empire into popular politics, or from Queen Victoria's royal example. The tone of female imperialist propaganda was usually conformist, and its chosen activities drew upon organizational continuities and acceptable female roles. Nevertheless, the appearance of women's associations which put imperial politics to the fore did imply new thinking. At the least, it indicated that women expected their partnership in the imperial enterprise to be taken seriously. In its more assertive forms, female imperialism also implied that women's creative and practical contributions to the Empire had been greatly underestimated and that this was detrimental to the Empire's future.

How did Edwardian ladies acquire such views, and why did they decide to act upon them? Learning to 'Think Imperially' (as a contemporary exhortation put it) was a different experience for different women and did not happen to everyone. The imperial aspects of upper-class lifestyles are an inescapable departure point. Perhaps the most powerful influence of all was the active engagement of family members in Empire-building, whether in political, economic, military or administrative spheres. Few, if any, aristocratic families stood entirely apart from the process. If the government of Britain remained disproportionately aristocratic, this was still more true of an imperial rule which offered promotion opportunities within the peerage and fast-track ennoblement for untitled entrants. From 1877 India required suitably noble Viceroys to represent its Empress. As Canada united in 1867, Australia moved towards Federation in 1900, and New Zealand gained Dominion status in 1907, the openings for High Commissioners and Governors continued to expand. Every top-rank post demanded a host of proconsular attendants and administrators, so that the circle of aristocratic opportunity widened to include younger sons and distant cousins. High salaries enabled some upper-class families to maintain lifestyles they could no longer afford in Britain, and despite the relative lack of political power exercised even by senior imperial post-holders, few turned down such opportunities when they arose.[1] The Armed Services were another enclave in which patrician families sustained a leadership role that carried them to the forefront of imperial conquests and the defence of imperial power. Landed and military status were historically linked and even by the end of the nineteenth century, when middle-class entrance to public schools and competitive examinations for officer status were beginning to erode aristocratic influence, upper-class officers were an elite within the commanding elite. The attractions of officership for an increasingly wide range of men included its association with high social rank, as well as with Empire. Similar attitudes influenced entrance to the higher levels of the clergy in the late Victorian and Edwardian period. Titled connections both predisposed young men to enter the clergy and assisted their path to promotion, as the Anglican Church followed the flag and replicated its formal hierarchies in distant parts of the world.[2]

A very high proportion of active female imperialists had relatives who served the Empire at senior levels in government, the Armed Services or the Church. For some, these personal links opened up the possibility (or necessity) of imperial travel and even many years of residence in the Empire. When such women returned to London Society they were welcomed into female imperialist associations as valued 'experts', whether or not they had in fact taken an interest in local affairs during their time abroad. The Victoria League made a particular point of head-hunting titled expatriates, deemed invaluable for its educational and colonial hospitality programmes. Few government or military postings involved a lifetime's overseas service. Even when husbands (sometimes fathers or brothers) were in long-term appointments, female relatives seem rather frequently to have broken their exile by visits to Britain and often came for longer periods to accompany children or to attend sick or elderly relatives. The female imperialist associations drew upon personal links at many different levels. On the one hand the status of the wives of Governors or resident military commanders or bishops made them eminently suitable as patrons and (hopefully) activists within the colonial associations affiliated to British female imperialism. On the other hand even former residents who had no intention of returning to imperial outposts were assumed to be knowledgeable, and to retain some influence abroad. They were also assumed to be committed to the types of women's work which the imperialist associations favoured. For female imperialism signified a commitment to Empire-building over and above a philanthropic commitment to assisting individual women. Who could be more suited to this task than ladies who had already shared in the imperial responsibilities of male Empire-builders?

Margaret Jersey, Violet Cecil and Maud Selborne were all strongly influenced towards imperial work through their experience as resident wives abroad. Margaret Jersey delighted in foreign travel, seizing every opportunity during her early married years to escape to the Mediterranean, or to tour Europe with her close friend Mary Galloway. According to her biographer, she was 'at once charmed with the idea of India' when invited to visit a friend who had become Governor of Madras in 1888.[3] Her carefully diarized travels led to a published article in *The Nineteenth Century* which evidenced both her pleasure and her serious interest in studying the outcomes of imperial rule. Queen Victoria received a copy and invited the Jerseys to dine and sleep at Windsor on the strength of it. An offer of the Governorship of Bombay followed soon after, but Lord Jersey declined on health grounds. The next year found Margaret touring Egypt, in the company of Mary Galloway and with the assistance of Colonel (later Lord) Kitchener. In 1890 her husband was prevailed upon to accept the more congenial Governorship of New South Wales, and the family set sail for a three-year stay in one of the leading 'white settler colonies'. Margaret's cousin went as one of Jersey's aides-de-camp; her brother Rupert Leigh was another, and was therefore conveniently available to chaperone Margaret on social visits to the Governor-General of New Zealand and to Samoa, where she was hosted by the British Land Commissioner, brother of the novelist Rider Haggard and an old acquaintance of Osterley days.

A few years later Violet Cecil began her imperial travels by following her husband's posting with the Grenadier Guards to Gibraltar. Her autobiography dramatically records:

> In the autumn of 1897 an event occurred which changed the current of my life by sending me abroad into places where England – the England that won the Empire – was at work . . . Sir Alfred Lyall, whose very distinguished career had been spent in India, said, as he saw me off at the station: 'You will never come back', and in the sense that he meant it, I never have. For once you have seen Englishmen at work at their self-appointed great task, the dear Island itself seems cramped.[4]

Hindsight apart, there is no doubt that different vistas soon opened up before Violet's eyes. Within weeks she began bombarding an intimate correspondent at the War Office with her views on imperial defence.[5] A visit from her father (himself a retired admiral) made possible a quick trip to Morocco, which she found 'quite without what we call civilisation' apart from a dinner party with the resident British Minister.[6] A few months later Lord Edward was summoned into Kitchener's service in Egypt. Violet packed off her infant son to her in-laws at Hatfield in order to spend a couple of months in Cairo and travelling up the Nile to Aswan. Her companions were Sir Clinton and Lady Dawkins, who were soon to be despatched to Lord Curzon's viceregal court and thereafter joined her in the Victoria League.

Maud Selborne's career as wife of the last South African High Commissioner before the 1910 Act of Union was to last five years, with a number of interludes in Britain. A less romantic (and xenophobic) imperialist than Violet Cecil, she made a very deliberate transition into imperial work as a result of her husband's career move. This required a suppression of earlier prejudices, for when a move to South Africa was first mooted in 1900, Maud had taken the initiative in scotching the idea. Lord Salisbury was prompted by his daughter into giving prime ministerial advice to his son-in-law which reflected his own relative coolness on the subject of Empire.[7] Selborne was in any case reluctant to give up his family life, his estates management and his local militia, together with the chance of promotion within a newly elected Conservative ministry, according to St John Brodrick, who wrote to tell Violet Cecil all about it.[8] By 1905 both Maud and her husband felt the stature of the job on offer had increased sufficiently to make it more attractive. The South African War had been won, Milner had departed, and Selborne was appointed to step directly into his shoes as Britain's foremost representative in an era of social, economic and political reconstruction leading towards establishment of a new Dominion. As an unusually strong political partnership, the Selbornes relished their role as Empire-builders, and it was inevitable that Maud would move from a passive to an actively pro-imperialist stance.

Examples of ladies whose family ties became imperial ties could be endlessly multiplied. The unmarried daughters of Sir Bartle Frere, an earlier South African High Commissioner and Governor whose belligerent policies against the Zulus had disastrously backfired, were leading figures in the British Women's Emigration Association and the Victoria League. Lady Loch, wife of a South African Governor in the 1890s, became a combative member of the emigration association's South African Expansion Committee. Laura Ridding, Selborne's sister, visited South Africa in 1908 and returned to take up imperial emigration alongside her existing work for the Girls' Friendly Society, the Mothers' Union and the National Union of Women Workers. Gwendolen Cecil, Edward Cecil's sister and Selborne's sister-in-law, expanded her imperial work in the 1900s beyond the Primrose League to include an influential role within the South African Colonisation Society and the Victoria League. Dora Gore Browne, favourite poet of the emigration associations, was led into imperial propaganda through her sisterly visits to the Rector of Pretoria, as well as through her lifelong association with the Winchester circle of religious imperialist ladies.

The Lyttelton and Talbot ladies were nearly as ubiquitous in the circles of female imperialism as those of the Cecil and Balfour families. Lyttelton links to the Antipodes went back to the early nineteenth century (when they helped to colonize New Zealand). Sir Neville Lyttelton's late-nineteenth-century military career took in an unusually large number of imperialist hot spots, including Afghanistan, Egypt, Ireland and the South African War, from which he emerged as Commander-in-Chief.[9] It is not surprising to find his wife Katherine presiding over the South African Colonisation Society's Transvaal organization, then moving on to its London executive after her return to Britain. Sir Neville's brother, Alfred Lyttelton, was Colonial Secretary from 1903 to 1905. His wife Edith took a major share in Victoria League work, to which she also recruited the wives of two other influential family members. Kathleen Lyttelton's husband Arthur was Bishop of Southampton, and Lavinia Talbot (née Lyttelton) had an even more useful husband who, as Headmaster of Eton, was promptly signed up as a Victoria League vice-president. The Talbots intermarried several times over with the Lytteltons. Meriel Talbot, full-time Secretary of the Victoria League from 1901 to 1916, and later secretary to the government-sponsored successor to the BWEA and editor of *The Imperial Colonist*, was the invaluable outcome of another such union. Lady Talbot, wife of Sir Reginald Talbot (an Australian Governor and retired general), was an executive committee member of the leading emigration societies. She was also a Victoria League Council member and by 1909 had been joined there by a group of her female relatives. Bishop Edward Talbot, singled out by Cannadine as a 'self-consciously grand' patrician prelate,[10] was Meriel Talbot's uncle and another influential friend of Empire and of female imperialism.

How much did family links to the Empire really give these women (and men) in common? Clearly not an indefinite amount, given the diversity of male imperial careers and the diversity of the Empire itself, not to mention the variety of convictions and abilities which different women brought to their imperial work. These multiple connections and interconnections are nevertheless a highly important feature of the ladies' associations. Most female imperialists believed that they knew the Empire and that their task was to bring home its future potential to their fellow-Britons. Their belief was frequently based upon personal and family experience. High-status imperial postings, or close contact with family members who held them, fostered a sense of shared duty and a confidence in the power of upper-class women to contribute towards its fulfilment from their existing fund of talents and experience.

Even for women who did not travel the world, a London drawing-room or dinner party encounter with a charismatic imperialist politician, governor or general might produce an imperial turn and the illusion of personal connection. Joseph Chamberlain was a considerable social success, but no imperialist came near to equalling Cecil Rhodes' triumphs during his infrequent but never-forgotten appearances in Britain. 'Men and women trembled before him,' recalled Margot Asquith, whose own view of Rhodes was a jaundiced one linked to her husband's refusal to serve on the official inquiry into the infamous Jameson Raid. She denied any wish to meet the great man herself, but at a Downing Street party in 1899 observed 'the circle of fashionable ladies crouching at Cecil Rhodes' feet. He sat like a great bronze gong among them: and I had not the spirit to disturb their worship.'[11] Jennie Churchill was another potential sceptic with a keen sense of humour, but her autobiography lovingly reproduced two notes in Rhodes' blunt, unflattering style with the comment: 'A man of big ideas, he knew what he wanted, and made for his goal.'[12] She successfully appealed for his support to help launch her wartime scheme to fund a hospital ship for South Africa. Mary Jeune met Rhodes for dinner and took him to the theatre with her friends. The conversation turned to gardening, and afterwards Mary ordered 'a large variety of carnations' for despatch to his Cape Town gardener, despite the fact that 'he impressed me as a man to whom the small things of life were of but trifling interest; he had one great aim and one great ambition in his life, and in pursuit of that he forgot everything else'.[13]

The most dramatic conversion to imperialism under Rhodes' influence was undoubtedly that of Daisy, Countess of Warwick. Introduced by the famous editor W. T. Stead, she immediately decided that 'Cecil Rhodes was that strange, unmistakable thing, a man of genius. His big ideas lifted him right out of the common, well-worn paths . . . I reciprocated his friendship with all my heart.'[14] This is borne out by a remarkable letter which survives among Rhodes' own papers. Dated September 1898, and scrawled across multiple sheets of luxuriously embossed Warwick Castle notepaper, it passionately proclaimed her desire (and ability) to become 'one more worker for the Cause'. She confessed '*still* the personal hero worship is not quite merged in enthusiasm for the Cause' and regretted the impossibility of private talk in London ('the Butterflies surround you when you come there !!!'), concluding, 'Do not dream of answering this. I know that you never write letters and this letter requires no reply.'[15] Six months before his premature death in March 1902 they sat together on the Scottish moors, 'he telling me of all his wonderful ideas . . . he was sure God would not let him die before he had done his work, and this work he conceived to be, to bring about the Union of South Africa'.[16] In practice, of course, the Countess found it less easy than she had hoped to deliver up the English public in support of Rhodes' schemes. Though much admired in her youth, by the 1900s she was regarded by most patriotic ladies as both eccentric and dangerously socialistic. Her practical work for the Empire was to be largely confined to isolated efforts to train female emigrants in rural skills, divorced from female imperialist sponsorship of similar schemes elsewhere.[17]

The limited nature of the Countess of Warwick's imperial achievements highlights the value of collective organization, even for the richest and most nobly born supporters of Empire. The Victoria League made a fresh start in 1901, but benefited hugely from existing networks of potential supporters. Most members of its executive committee were already active in one or more of the emigration associations, the Primrose League or the Girls' Friendly Society. The appearance of this new and more single-minded league in 1901 prompts examination of the late-nineteenth-century evolution of the earlier associations. In what ways was their work already converging around imperialism by 1900? The evidence suggests that the Victoria League was built upon solid foundations. However, the distinctive background and methods of each of the older societies left its mark upon Edwardian female imperialism, ensuring that it remained multiple and diverse even during its years of greatest unity. Separate identities were the product of separate histories and a source of strength so long as the interlocked leaderships of the major associations remained committed to constructive co-operation.

The oldest association was the Girls' Friendly Society, formed in Winchester in 1875 as 'a fellowship of young girls whose bond of union is purity and prayer'.[18] The founding members were wives of senior clergy and members of the local gentry who shared a common view on upper- and middle-class women's responsibility for protecting working-class girls. Social hierarchy was thus built into the GFS from the start. Only Anglican ladies could become guardian associates, since only they were qualified to provide the necessary religious and secular guidance. The influences of Christianity, philanthropy and of current social purity campaigning were everywhere to be seen in the early years; the influence of Empire almost nowhere. Among the first associates of the GFS was Louisa Knightley, busily settling into her Lady Bountiful role on her Northamptonshire estate. 'I do really think it is the thing which I have so long wanted' she wrote excitedly in her diary, after hearing about the Society from a neighbour, Lady Dryden. On Easter Day she enlisted 'four of my own maids as members of the GFS'. Within two years she was attending London meetings of branch secretaries, and edging her way into the leadership. A GFS picnic festival at Fawsley in June 1878 was attended by eighteen ladies and gentlemen and more than sixty members, and Louisa exulted in the 'real pleasure in sharing the delights of this beautiful place with those who have so few pleasures'.[19]

Margot Asquith described her sister Laura's recruitment of local mill-girls in similarly uncomplicated terms.[20] However, another early member of the GFS was Winchester resident Ellen Joyce, a clergyman's wife who (during an early widowhood) went on to become the Society's leading imperial spokeswoman, and president of the British Women's Emigration Association. At the GFS Imperial Conference in 1912 she stated emphatically: 'It has been my great honour and happiness to have been associated in the Imperial movement with the Imperial Workers of the GFS from the year 1882. Our Foundress, Mrs Townsend, is one of the earliest Imperialists.'[21] From the 1880s, if not from the 1870s, the GFS did indeed take on a decidedly imperialist hue. Mrs Joyce set up its Emigration Department in 1883, along lines which presaged the wider emigration work she entered a year later. Emigrants were to receive the full cloak of GFS's moral protection, from the point of preparation and departure to the point of arrival and installation in their new colonial homes. This necessitated close contact with women in those 'white settler colonies' deemed fit to receive the Society's members. Emigration work and the expansion of GFS overseas branches proceeded hand in hand, and the Society's motto 'Bear ye one another's burdens' began to take on new meanings. But a sisterhood of true equals was no more part of its imperial than of its domestic outlook. The signature of formal treaties between the English society and its overseas offshoots from 1882 onwards was expressly designed to deter strong-minded colonials who might presume 'to appropriate the *name* without adopting the *principles* of the Society'.[22] In theory at least, these principles were immutable and within a couple of years colonial treaties were meekly signed by the central GFS committees in New Zealand, the Australian states and most Canadian provinces.

Personal morality remained central to the GFS's view of Empire. But the colonial treaties encouraged the GFS to gradually change the emphasis of its work and to focus more explicitly on the future of the Empire itself rather than only on the opportunities and challenges which it provided for individual members. A growing engagement in imperial missionary work reinforced this tendency. During the 1890s the society's journals recorded (and encouraged) members' efforts to save their pennies towards support for 'Our Missionary' in India and Japan. Collective altruism aligned itself with the imperialist virtues of religious and racial superiority. The Anglican Church itself was becoming increasingly conscious of its worldwide responsibilities and the periodic Pan-Anglican Synods in London were linked to parallel meetings in the colonies. In 1896 the GFS Central Council institutionalized such meetings by establishing a colonial committee, chaired by Mrs Townsend and including colonial delegates alongside British GFS leaders. The new committee's aim was 'to bring the leaders of the Society in the mother country and those in distant lands more into touch with one another'; one of its earliest decisions was to introduce an annual 'Day of Intercession for the GFS throughout the Empire'. The new committee also brought the GFS closer to the British Women's Emigration Society, and promoted the spirit of imperial unity within both associations. Miss Lily Frere moved across from the BWEA 'as representative for South Africa' and both the Hon. Mrs Victoria Grosvenor (already active in the BWEA) and Lady Louisa Knightley (soon to lead the South African Colonisation Society) became GFS vice-presidents.[23]

The BWEA itself had clearly broadened and strengthened its commitment to Empire by 1900. Unlike the GFS it never aspired to a mass membership, nor (until 1902) sought to influence a wider public through a published journal. The first female emigration society was formed in 1862, in close association with the feminist Society for Promoting the Employment of Women, and unquestionably prioritized the needs of distressed gentlewomen over those of the Empire. Important continuities of personnel, ideas and finance linked this society to two new ones founded in the early 1880s and eventually to the amalgamated group entitled the United British Women's Emigration Association in 1888. The BWEA remained deeply concerned by the poor employment prospects for women in Britain and particularly by middle-class female poverty. Its emphasis in the 1880s was philanthropic rather than feminist, but it was a philanthropy charged with a strong gender consciousness. The Association's commitment was to emigration by women and for women, since their organizing talents and their needs as emigrants differed from those of men. The ease with which

Ellen Joyce (and later Louisa Knightley) moved back and forth between the GFS and emigration work is not surprising, given the emphasis within both movements on women's need for moral protection. Vigorous efforts were made in the 1880s to dispel rumours that the BWEA's concealed and unrespectable aim was the export of marriageable young women for Empire service. Refutations of this imperialist slur read rather curiously alongside the Association's later boasts of Empire-building success. However, from the perspective of Mrs Joyce, the inconsistency was not a major one. She saw the needs of individuals and of colonies as neatly dovetailed under her own indispensable leadership. Her intention by the 1890s was both to help deserving women and to serve the Empire. Her enthusiasm for the latter had been strengthened by her tours of Canada in 1884 and 1890, and her visit to Cape Colony in 1893. By 1900 the BWEA's leading committees, like those of the GFS, reflected the gathering momentum of an imperial turn. Clerical wives were outnumbered by returned colonial residents. The sudden acceleration in BWEA work at the end of the South African War was to confirm the Emigration Association's status as a significant contributor to female imperialism.

The Primrose League stands apart from the GFS and BWEA as an organization founded in 1885 with an explicitly political mission and an all-but-explicit allegiance to the Conservative Party. In 1900 it contained a larger number of upper-class women than any other association. Among the leading Edwardian female imperialists, these included long-time members Margaret Jersey (who presided over the Primrose League Ladies' Grand Council before moving on to the Victoria League), Louisa Knightley, Lily and Georgina Frere, Gwendolen Cecil, Jennie Churchill, Alice and Betty Balfour, Susan Malmesbury and Meresia Nevill. The League was not only a source of recruits to other, female-led associations, but must also be seen as a training ground in its own right for both political organization and imperialist propaganda. The founding principles of the Primrose League included a commitment to 'the maintenance of Religion, of the Estates of the Realm, of the ascendancy of the British Empire'.[24] These ideals were seen not merely as compatible, but as closely related and indeed inter-dependent. The entertainment value of Empire was increasingly exploited in the League's programme of popular activities in the 1880s and 1890s. Lantern lectures, songs, recitations and dramatic sketches, and tableaux vied for a place in village halls as imperial successes were celebrated and curiosity and hero-worship satisfied. However, the serious intent of such propaganda should also be acknowledged. Imperialist ladies were often cynical about the pseudo-antique ranks and rituals of the league and pragmatic about its election-winning potential, but this did not prevent them from valuing their organization's creed when it touched upon their own concerns in religion, government and Empire. Most female imperialists hoped that the Primrose League would strengthen social solidarity and national greatness by opening up colonial opportunities for all classes. Its work encouraged both British politicians and the British public to lift their aspirations above the humdrum level of day-to-day party politics.

It may be concluded that the Girls' Friendly Society, the British Women's Emigration Association and the Primrose League were already tilling fertile imperialist soil at the end of the nineteenth century and that they did so largely through the efforts of a committed upper-class female leadership. The South African War of 1899 to 1902 was nevertheless a transformative event for organized female imperialism. It represented a major shock and discontinuity for the governing classes and large sections of the British public. This was underlined by Queen Victoria's death during the last year of the war and by the near-fatal illness of her successor on the eve of his coronation. National confidence was first severely dented then ultimately reinforced in ways which favoured a more proactive development of the Empire. South Africa emerged as a future new Dominion, thanks not only to the 'heroism' of British troops but also to the support of volunteer contingents from Canada, New Zealand and newly federated Australia. Imperial ceremonies multiplied around the departure and arrival home of troops, the granting of medals, the royal funeral and the ultimately splendid coronation of Victoria's son. Critics of the war (of whom there were plenty) required energetic rebuttal; its victims required women's care and its victors their support and applause.

Though certain activities (such as emigration to South Africa) came temporarily to a halt, a thousand new avenues opened up for female imperialists to demonstrate their wartime patriotism through word and deed. Some moved into action as freelance individuals, while others turned to existing societies and (eventually) the Victoria League. War funds multiplied confusingly as ladies competed to supply comforts to their favourite regiments. Violet Cecil's London correspondents had to explain to her that, though she was close to the scene of the action in Cape Town, her appeals on behalf of refugees, soldiers and hospitals could not monopolize the society's generosity. Gwendolen Cecil reported encouragingly at first:

> I wrote to the papers at once and am now struggling in a sea of sponges, towels and soap combined with cheques. I hope to get it all off next week – about 2000 cakes of soap, and 100 each or more of the remaining articles. I hope you'll know what to do with them when they arrive.[25]

A fortnight later, 'It simply rains soap upon me and my father is beginning to complain of the smell as of many grocers which pervades the front hall.' By March, compassion fatigue was setting in, however: 'The pillow-pyjama fund is progressing – but not quite so quickly as last time and I doubt if I can do the trick a third time.'[26] Soon after, St John Brodrick wrote: 'I see you want more things for men at the front and shall energise for you – but if you don't get response it's because there are *so* many funds – for instance – Lady White got £4000 comforts for Ladysmith; Lady Roberts for Colonial Horse; each Cavalry regiment has a collector.'[27]

Many lady patriots were keen to join Violet Cecil and other ringside spectators at the battle front. Some sailed for South Africa to visit husbands or brothers, and some expressed an ill-focused ambition to nurse the troops, but for many it was simply (as Violet Cecil described it) a case of wanting 'to be "in" on all the excitement'.[28] By April 1900 this influx had become so noticeable that it attracted a royal reprimand, conveyed by Chamberlain to Sir Alfred Milner. Milner responded with a published rebuke to female war tourists which was stern enough to alarm even Violet Cecil. Fortunately Gwendolen Cecil could reassure Violet, after a visit to Windsor, that she 'had not been included in the Queen's disapproval'.[29] Jennie Churchill's hospital ship, in which she eventually set sail for South Africa in December 1899, also received Victoria's blessing, together with the royal gift of a Union Jack. It was funded through the efforts of a committee of American women resident in London, and in the teeth of widespread

American disapproval of the war. Members of the committee included several who later joined the Victoria League.

The Victoria League itself was very clearly a direct outcome of the South African War. Founded in 1901, its leadership and initial membership was almost exclusively from Society's top drawer, and its aim was unambiguously to promote imperialism. As we have seen, many entrants had gained previous experience of working for Empire through other organizations, but the Victoria League made its distinctive contribution by crystallizing the emotional aftermath of the war into an effective and perhaps unusually single-minded association. As with earlier societies, its origins can be traced back to a collective decision by a small group of ladies. Violet Cecil and Edith Lyttelton were the key individuals involved, to be joined shortly after by Violet Markham who became probably the most able member of the Victoria League executive. Coincidentally, these three women's paths had converged in Cape Town between 1899 and 1900. The impact made on them by their visits is worth recording in some detail. Their experiences helped to set the future course of the League which, in turn, influenced the agendas of the older societies. At the same time, their personal histories further illustrate the interdependence between upper-class women's social and political worlds.

Violet Markham was the first Cape Town arrival. Her visit lasted from June to October 1899, when she set sail for home a week before war broke out. She could not be accused of being a war tourist, but was no normal tourist either since she devoted her visit to extensive enquiries into the social and political situation which later furnished her with much of the material for two books defending Milner's policies in particular, and the concept of a British South Africa in general. Her family had despatched her to South Africa for health reasons (she was diagnosed, like so many other gifted Victorian women, as suffering from neurasthenia); but her self-appointed task as a leading apostle of Milnerism was rapidly decided upon when she met the High Commissioner face to face in the gardens of the Mount Nelson Hotel:

> He was perfectly charming to me . . . It was quite impossible to realise he was a celebrity, so simple and kind he was in manner as I chatted away at my ease. He seemed harassed and his mind was clearly running all the time on South African affairs; however I did my best to keep him off that topic of conversation. I don't know when I have been more attracted to anyone . . . Tonight I talked to the man, in the future I shall only converse with the Governor which is rather a different thing.[30]

Miss Markham's personal liking for Milner fuelled an existing strong admiration for his administrative talents. As she recalled in her autobiography, an earlier visit to Egypt had prompted her to read Milner's analysis of British imperial rule. *England in Egypt* illustrated for her 'the decisive influence of certain books on one's whole way of thinking . . . It shook me away from my liberal moorings and made me for a long time a convinced Imperialist.'[31] Milner was by no means unaware of the powers of literature himself and was soon giving Violet generous assistance with her forthcoming propaganda work by providing introductions to politicians, industrialists, educators and administrators, together with numerous opportunities to share his Government House dining-table. Within a fortnight she had developed decided opinions on 'the dolt-headed Boers': 'I feel sure they won't fight but I feel equally sure it will require a display of military strength before they give way . . . Unless the Government back up

Sir Alfred at this crisis we may as well haul down the English flag in South Africa.'[32] She had also dispelled her initial puzzlement over entrenched 'race hatred' between Dutch and British, but still more importantly between blacks and whites. Her views on the latter divide went beyond Milner's own, and were soon to become common currency within the Victoria League.

On the eve of her departure, Violet described to her mother a flattering late-night chat with Violet Cecil:

> She had been dining with the Governor and she said, Sir Alfred has been talking a great deal about you tonight and with much enthusiasm. He says though they can ill afford to lose one nice person in a place like this he is very glad for the sake of the cause you are going home because it's so necessary at present to stir up public opinion in England and he thinks you can be of great use in that way knowing the facts as you do! I must say I felt very pleased with this word of approval from the Chief and it sends me home with double energy for the fray in England.[33]

Within days of stepping ashore she was addressing pro-war meetings, defending Milner in the press and working up to ten hours a day on the first of her South Africa books. More compliments and encouragement from the Chief followed its publication, and confirmed Violet's commitment to longer-term work for Empire.

Edith Lyttelton's visit to South Africa was the result of her husband's appointment to head a government enquiry into Transvaal monopolies. Chamberlain expected the outcomes to assist post-war economic and political reconstruction, but the war dragged inconveniently on, leaving the Lytteltons stranded for a month in Cape Town in the autumn of 1900 before they could move up-country to begin the real task. Like Violet Markham before her, Edith soon took a strong personal liking to Milner. This may well have been reciprocated, since she was an attractive and famously quick-witted socialite, with the added advantage (from his point of view) of close friendship with Balfour and Asquith dating back to her youthful membership of the Souls. On her first day in Cape Town she delightedly discovered that 'he talks with absolute unreserve about the whole situation past and present'. Two days later she noted in her diary: 'The adoration of everyone about him for the Governor is very remarkable. His quick sympathy often makes people fancy him weak, but it is really one of the sources of his strength.' Soon after, Edith and the Governor enjoyed

> a most delightful and intimate talk. He told me all about the different characters of the people on his staff, and talked a great deal about himself and his own ambitions and desires, perhaps rather too private to put down here. But it was interspersed – as indeed his talk was all day long – with every kind of interesting discussion about the future of this country.

The next day 'a clandestine appointment' was achieved. Milner successfully 'dodged the ADCs' and walked with her on Table Mountain, discussing the deficiencies of Cape Colony's parliamentary government, the probability of Boer farmers going downhill if they failed to opt for anglicization and the long-term economic prospects for South Africa. Other private walks followed, and even a secret picnic planned jointly with Violet Cecil:

> We managed to avoid the guards and the Staff, and off we drove up the Kloof Road. I had sent Lawrence on in front with the tea packed into my bonnet box. It was great fun, Sir

Alfred being like a boy out of school – right away from Government House and its journalists and incessant interviews.[34]

The informality of such contact did not diminish its political impact. At the end of September Edith wrote to her sister-in-law, Kathleen Lyttelton: 'I see a great deal of Alfred Milner and am immensely impressed by certain things in him. His ideas on the future are thrillingly interesting, so big and full of vision.' It was an imperial vision which begged to be shared. Her diary was pressed into service as a record for the Chief's daily utterances and she rapidly organized its circulation among her family and friends even before her own return to England ('I thought when I left England it was going to be a squirrely one instead of a political . . . Mummy takes out any of the pages which on the whole I think perhaps it is better not to circulate').[35] In October 1900 a 'patriotic address' from Mrs Alfred Lyttelton was read to the National Union of Women Workers' Brighton Conference, where Louisa Knightley listened with intense admiration.[36] During the latter part of her South African stay Edith travelled to the Transvaal with her husband and further extended her repertoire of imperialist propaganda by attending her husband's Commission, where the economic crimes of greedy capitalists (supported by the Boers) were described in detail. She also heard firsthand accounts of the fighting during a visit by Neville Lyttelton, who to her delight brought her brother Christopher with him as his aide-de-camp. Most touching of all was an encounter with Lord Roberts, whose own son had recently died on the battlefield. Before leaving for home Edith attended the military review which marked Britain's formal annexation of the Transvaal. The Lytteltons' journey to Durban for the voyage home took in the sites of famous battles and sieges. Edith gladly accepted a gift of souvenir Boer bullets from Colenso ('though one naturally likes the relics best which one picks up oneself').[37] By the end of the year she was back in London, fulfilling her duty to Milner, Roberts, Rhodes and Baden-Powell by planning the launch of the Victoria League.

Violet Cecil had a longer and more complex relationship with Milner than either Violet Markham or Edith Lyttelton. Her autobiography primly records that, before her arrival with Lord Edward in South Africa, 'I had known Sir Alfred Milner very well for years.'[38] They had in fact exchanged love letters through much of the 1890s, both before and after her marriage. Intimacy was rapidly re-established when Lord Edward conveniently disappeared to join the siege of Mafeking and Violet established her sway over the Cape Town social scene. At Cecil Rhodes' insistence, she became a permanent house guest at Groote Schuur. Violet Markham acidly noted both her 'wonderful fascination and cleverness' and the fact that she 'has always a train of men about her'.[39] To her social brilliance she added a much-publicized record of war service, devoting some part of every day to receiving refugees at the railway station and improving the organization of local hospitals. Entertaining a ceaseless flow of visitors was another act of duty to relieve Government House, but it also provided a matchless source of news from the war zone and the outside world. Private walks and talks with Milner were sustained, even at the height of the war crisis. Multiple sources confirm that he developed a strong dependence upon her company – whether or not this led to a sexual liaison. Once the first few anxious months were over, Violet showed every sign of enjoying her position. Among its attractions was the fact that her own news and influence became much in demand. St John Brodrick (by now Under-Secretary at the

Foreign Office) was still among her most assiduous correspondents. His weekly letters contained flattering confidences, and opinions clearly intended to be conveyed to Milner ('Tell this not beyond Milner . . .').[40] In return, she bombarded him (and hoped, by extension, to bombard the government) with Milnerite pleas and viewpoints. Gradually, as Violet's letters became less affectionate, Brodrick's replies began to display a touch of irony. He became impatient of her insistent demands for specific decisions, and for 'jobs for all your friends'.[41] In April 1900 he shrewdly summarized Violet Cecil's war, in words which presaged her Victoria League career:

> I am now a total disbeliever in the deserted, sorrowing grass-widow – dragging along a dreary existence with longing for child and friends at home. Every returning friend brings me fresh evidence of a bustling, buoyant and beloved figure, dominating Cape Town society, pervading South African politics, bullying doctors, harassing Gatliffs, and routing any chance adventurers or adventuresses embarking on the same track . . . I have so often written as if you were sorrowing that I now record my deliberate conviction that, with intervals of depression, you are having the loftiest and most antique time of your life; that you have not the least desire to come home.[42]

On this last point, at least, there was agreement. 'It was a pang to leave South Africa' wrote Violet in her autobiography. 'Such a crowded fourteen months of my life had been lived in that beautiful country.'[43] She did not add that she hated leaving Milner and that her marriage was reaching the stage of irretrievable breakdown, though by now she was expecting a post-Mafeking baby. Consolation was to be found in furthering the cause at home. Within a few months the Victoria League was formed, its birth narrowly preceding that of Violet's daughter. Within days of the latter event Milner arrived in Britain for a triumphal visit, intended partly to prove that he had the government's full backing. Amidst engagements which included a Cabinet welcome at Waterloo, bestowal of a peerage and a grand City dinner, he found time to spend at Violet Cecil's bedside.

It would be misleading, if somewhat plausible, to judge the League solely as Milner's offspring. The South African War was the catalyst rather than any single person. According to Violet Cecil's account, the direct inspiration to organize came from the third generation South African loyalist Dorothea Fairbridge rather than from Milner himself. She had already set up a Guild of Loyal Women in Cape Province, and met with each of the visiting English ladies to discuss it. The Guild's representatives were in England when the first Victoria League meeting was held, and in fact succeeded in embarrassing Violet Cecil on that occasion by their over-enthusiasm and lack of social polish. The first meeting was a very grand affair. Held at 10 Downing Street at Alice Balfour's invitation, it was organized jointly by Edith Lyttelton and Violet Cecil and attended by the great ladies of both main political parties, dressed in deep mourning. With Lady Jersey in the chair, they resolved to form an association of 'women of the British Isles who are in sympathy with Imperial objects and desire a close union between the different parts of the Empire'. The title 'Victoria League' was chosen 'in memory of our late Gracious Queen, and with the desire to continue the great work of closer union . . . for which she did so much'.[44] Those present included many with South African connections, among them Georgina and Lily Frere, Mrs Lyttelton Gell and Mrs Fawcett, returned from leading a government-sponsored enquiry into conditions in the concentration camps. Violet Cecil's contingent included Lady Hilda Brodrick, as well as her sisters-in-law Gwendolen Cecil and Mrs Leo Maxse, wife of the editor of *The National Review*. From the upper social ranks of the Conservative Party came Lady Jersey and the Duchess of Marlborough (sister-in-law to Jennie Churchill), counterbalanced by the Liberals Lady Tweedmouth and the Countess of Carrington. Rank and influence were to be very important within this association from the outset. Before the meeting Violet Cecil compared herself humorously to 'a terrier trying to catch several ducks in a pond' as she rounded up ladies of distinction;[45] and Margaret Jersey made a point of reading aloud 'the list of ladies who had already joined the General Committee' as she introduced 'the aims and advantages of the proposed Association'.[46] In the words of Lady Jersey's autobiography, the Victoria League's first executive 'was composed of the wives and sisters of Cabinet Ministers, of wives of leaders of the Opposition, and other representative ladies'.[47]

At its inaugural meeting, the League pledged itself 'to become a centre for receiving and distributing information regarding the different British dominions, especially information of importance to women'. It also resolved to promote 'any practical work desired by the Colonies and tending to the good of the Empire as a whole'.[48] This opened the way for a flood of Victoria League initiatives linked to South Africa. Funds were set up to aid British refugees and Dutch women and children in the camps, and, most poignantly, to support the work of the Guild of Loyal Women in locating and tending British graves. More than £8000 was eventually subscribed for the latter purpose. The impact of the war upon the League therefore continued into peacetime. Milner remained ultimate arbiter on its South African work for as long as he stayed in power. This is evidenced by early executive committee minute books, which record frequent appeals for his advice or authorization. No doubt there were many behind-the-scenes contacts too. Milner continued to correspond privately with the League's leading ladies and was soon to prove his worth as one of the most influential trustees managing Rhodes' posthumous fund for imperial education. He was undoubtedly a powerful and useful patron, but it would be wrong to overlook the fact that the Victoria League had benefits to offer Milner in return. Not only did it pursue public work on behalf of a shared imperialist cause, but also the social and political composition of its leadership offered him prospects of strengthening his own influence upon the government and the British ruling class. This was a significant consideration as the war receded; the Chinese labour controversy dogged his final year in office, and in 1905 he found himself back in Britain and threatened with the political wilderness.

The Victoria League was not the only female imperialist organization which success-fully seized upon opportunities offered by the South African War. The war produced a climax of Primrose League activity as its members distributed over 100,000 patriotic leaflets in the first month, rallied around the flag at innumerable meetings, and made an important contribution to the Tory success in the 'Khaki' election of 1900. In the aftermath of this election there were the usual fulsome tributes to lady canvassers, but a familiar difficulty persists in identifying more precisely the extent of Primrose League women's wartime activities. The Ladies' Grand Council certainly worked hard in support of the mass patriotic rally of the Primrose League at the Albert Hall in May 1901. The meeting passed a resolution recognizing 'with the highest satisfaction the Growth of Imperial Sentiment, as exemplified by the assertion of British Supremacy in South Africa, the Federation of Australia, and the unanimous support afforded to the Mother Country by the Colonies and allied portions of the Empire'. Arthur and Alice Balfour were welcomed into the hall by 'round after round of cheering', and to the strains of 'Rule Britannia'. The Duchess of Marlborough presented Champion banners to the habitations of Sleaford, Enfield, Southport and Bayswater, but made no speech.[49] For the Ladies' Grand Council, however, such events were not always an unmixed pleasure. At the previous year's Albert Hall rally, part of the would-be audience had been turned away, despite the fact that 'all applications sent through the Ladies secretary had been sent downstairs at once, stamped and with LGC in blue on them'.[50] This was not the first time that the ladies had felt snubbed; as on previous occasions, they responded with a request for more efficient arrangements (and greater autonomy) in the future. By May 1901 the Victoria League had already made its entry upon the scene. Its progress was formally reported to the Ladies' Grand Council by Lady Jersey in the week of the Albert Hall meeting.[51]

The Girls' Friendly Society greeted the war more quietly, but with enthusiasm. Its members were encouraged to reflect upon (and act in) the spirit of true womanly patriotism. *Friendly Leaves*, the main GFS membership journal, published a poem in May 1900 entitled 'Daughters of the Empire': 'Do you not long to take your part?' it began, then proceeded to explain how women, too, could serve:

> The task that you are called to do
> Is quite as hard as War's brave deeds,
> True British pluck will pull you through –
> See to the wounded soldier's needs!
> Brave Daughters of the Empire, come,
> Give to your Queen, assist your Lord,
> From village, shire and city home,
> Give of your wealth with open hand!
> From North and South, from East and West,
> Joint Daughter-hearts from distant shores!
> Your Empire asks of you your best –
> Pour out your richest love and stores![52]

The popularity of these lines is signalled by the fact that the poem was reprinted for sale through 'all booksellers' (and at reduced rates to GFS members), profits to be sent to the Mansion House War Fund. The poem was also presented to Queen Victoria, who accepted it 'with much gratification'.[53] Its sentiments were echoed at innumerable local meetings and certainly helped to accentuate the turn towards imperial work which was already underway in the 1890s.

Louisa Knightley made a second important journalistic contribution in January 1901 with a leading article in *The Girls' Quarterly*, a journal read mostly by GFS Associates. Under the heading 'The Empire and the GFS', she began by observing:

> The idea of the Empire is one which in the last few years, and still more in the last few months, has so completely entered into all our minds – is, so to speak, so much 'in the air' – that the title of my paper will not excite the surprise it certainly would have done some years ago.

Invoking Edith Lyttelton's 'patriotic address' to the National Union of Women Workers, she underlined the relationship between Empire-building and Christian righteousness:

> If the British race is to further the Kingdom of God throughout the vast dominions over which our beloved Queen bears sway, it must be by having a high standard themselves, and living up to it. And who, but the women of that race, are to raise the standard?

She then recounted the 'beautiful story' of a wounded British soldier who was rescued by a Boer commander on the strength of a letter from his mother, discovered in his pocket, which counselled her son towards Christian chivalry. 'Men are more influenced by women than we at all realise', observed Lady Knightley, then concluded with reflections on the power of the GFS to 'raise the standard': 'Let us go forward, praying ever for His grace, that we may be enabled to bear our part, however small, in the ennobling and sanctifying of the great Empire in which His Providence has placed us.'[54]

The Girls' Friendly Society prided itself on successfully linking the highest idealism with the most useful forms of practical action. While members saved their pence for war funds, knitted for the troops and assuaged personal anxieties with a mixture of patriotism and prayer, the GFS Colonial Committee was planning post-war reconstruction. It was agreed that the formation of GFS branches and the expansion of the Anglican Church in South Africa were urgent priorities. Under the influence of Ellen Joyce and Louisa Knightley, the issue of female emigration also came strongly to the fore. In July 1901 a South African sectional committee was established, with Mrs Townsend herself in the chair and Louisa Knightley as vice-chair; other members included Lily Frere and Mrs Bairnsfather, Secretary of the GFS in Cape Town and an enthusiastic emigrator. By this time it was clear that there would be plenty of South African emigration work to go round and that the GFS could work in productive alliance with the recently formed South African Expansion Committee of the BWEA. Meanwhile, the GFS committees were free to consider other work. Ellen Joyce pressed the Society to set up yet another journal, this time dedicated to colonial work. The appointment of a full-time GFS organizing worker for South Africa was also under serious discussion. As the war ended, the sense of urgency grew. Ellen Joyce reported to the Colonial Committee in June 1902: 'The idea which is most deeply impressed on my mind as regards the whole work of the GFS in the Colonies, is the greatness of the opportunity and our absolute powerlessness to take advantage of it *with sufficient speed*.'[55] By the following year funds had been raised and Lilian Beckwith set off for South Africa to expand the GFS and strengthen its British links. Extensive journal coverage ensured that the Society's many thousands of associates and members felt fully involved in this and every other GFS imperial venture.

Louisa Knightley's diary reveals her view that the main female contribution to post-war reconstruction came from the South African Expansion Committee (under her own chairmanship), rather than from the GFS, the Primrose League or even the Victoria League. The South African War certainly caused a dramatic upheaval within the long-established Emigration Association. In general terms, it ended Ellen Joyce's monopoly over decision-making and methods. Old South Africa hands, led by Lady Loch and the Frere sisters, had tried and failed to take over the BWEA executive committee from within during 1900, but 1901 brought forward Lady Knightley as an invaluable new recruit whom even Ellen Joyce liked and trusted. Louisa's turn to emigration work had everything to do with the war in South Africa, though she did not actually visit the country until four years later. As a widow in relatively straitened circumstances, she did not mingle quite as regularly in London Society as other leading imperialist ladies, but her diary nevertheless suggests the influence of wartime socializing upon her political outlook. Guests at Fawsley included several with South African experience. Military heroes were soon to be encountered, both in Northamptonshire and London. In April 1901 'Captain Lowndes sat by me at dinner and told me a little about Kimberley'; in June she found herself dining with 'a family of heroes', all of whom had fought in Africa; other social engagements included the difficult task of comforting the bereaved.[56] The war was present in the sermons to which she so attentively listened. It was present in pictures at the Royal Academy, in the newspapers, in the business of government (which she sometimes followed from the Gallery) and in the military parades she enjoyed in London parks.

The all-important invitation to join in emigration work was issued by Ellen Joyce on 26 November 1900, soon after Edith Lyttelton's Brighton address had independently moved Louisa to record her strengthened sense of imperial mission. She was soon succeeding where Ellen Joyce had sometimes failed, by bringing together South African 'experts' with British women who already considered themselves expert in tried-and-tested emigration methods. Emigration was at a standstill during the war, but it was evident that government support for an anglicized post-war South Africa would reinforce and multiply the committee's work. Milner and Chamberlain had every intention of recruiting the female emigrators to their own cause. The South African Expansion Committee (renamed the Colonisation Society in 1902) was therefore pushing at an open door when it demanded cheap travel and government investment in South African reception facilities. Milner fitted a private meeting with the South African Expansion Committee into his crowded schedule in June 1901 and succeeded in weaving his usual personal spell over Louisa Knightley at a ladies' luncheon:

> I had the good fortune to sit next to Lord Milner, who is just a good-looking, gentleman-like looking man, but who impressed me greatly by his wonderful power of listening. He told me that one of his staff has great capacities for listening – that all sorts and conditions of people confide in him, so he (Lord Milner) got much information, but I suspect that he does a good deal in that line himself. After luncheon we all sat about in the Imperial Institute Museum in an informal way and he both asked and answered questions in a delightful way giving us much information and in a cautious manner promising some help in aided passages.[57]

A few months later he addressed a public letter of support to the committee, to be republished proudly on the front page of the first edition of *The Imperial Colonist* in January 1902.

Milner's support soon extended beyond mere words to the establishment of a Women's Immigration Department in the Transvaal, offering a £5 subsidy towards the passage costs of each female immigrant, hostel accommodation at Cape Town and free railway passes to the immigrant's place of destination. In a telegram to Chamberlain, again published triumphantly in *The Imperial Colonist*, Milner confirmed the emigration society's official recognition as the government's preferred selection and advisory agency.

Joseph Chamberlain offered free passages to women emigrants in returning empty troop-ships. Further substantial support came from mining magnates and financial interests in South Africa, and patriotic male and female writers in the British press. Briefly, the spotlight upon organized female emigration was intense. All the ladies' imperialist associations basked·in the glow of favourable publicity. Yet, from the point of view of the South African Colonisation Society, there was a price to be paid. Could the BWEA's established standards of selection and protection be upheld when Milner demanded a minimum of fifty new emigrants each fortnight? The South Africans wanted domestic servants, whereas the female emigrators still preferred to assist the genteel poor. Eventually these dilemmas were resolved by Milner's acceptance that a policy of quantity before quality could prove counter-productive, and by a slow-down in demand as the Transvaal's economic situation deteriorated. But this was not before the Colonisation Society had also made its own compromises, demonstrating beyond any doubt that its leaders now believed themselves to be acting first and foremost in the cause of Empire.

From 1904 onwards the predominance of South Africa in the affairs of female imperialism became less marked. The war receded into the past, the anglicization of South Africa gradually ran into difficulties, and the countervailing attractions of Australia, New Zealand and particularly Canada reasserted themselves. Committed imperialists reminded each other that they were working for the future of the Empire as a whole rather than for any single territory, a point reinforced by the build-up towards events such as the Colonial Premiers' Conference of 1907 and the Pan-Anglican Congress of 1908. Nevertheless, the South African War was of lasting importance for organized female imperialism, and probably the single most important reason why it made strong progress during the Edwardian years. The Victoria League and the South African Colonisation Society emerged directly from the war. Led by upper-class women with a high level of both ability and influence, these new bodies helped to focus the work of the larger, older, more amorphous societies upon the contribution which women could make to imperialism. The war greatly expanded the circle of ladies who were not merely interested in the Empire, but were prepared to organize and work for it.

Notes

1. See D. Cannadine, *The Decline and Fall of the British Aristocracy* (London: Macmillan, 1996 edn), pp. 588–602; and *Aspects of Aristocracy* (London: Penguin, 1995), pp. 109–29. In the former work Cannadine enjoyably lampoons the Empire's 'Great Ornamentals'; in the latter, his case study of the imperial career of Lord Strickland concludes that aristocracy and Empire 'declined and fell together' as the twentieth century unfolded.
2. See Cannadine, *Decline and Fall*, pp. 255–62.
3. V. Powell, *Margaret, Countess of Jersey* (London: Heinemann, 1978), p. 83.
4. V. Milner, *My Picture Gallery 1886–1901* (London: John Murray, 1951), p. 103.
5. Violet Milner correspondence with William St John Brodrick, November 1897–January 1898. On 21 November 1897 Brodrick replied flatteringly: 'I like your artillery idea for fortresses so much – would gladly get a talk with Lord Salisbury just now about it.' VM 35, 176/5. Bodleian Library.
6. Milner, p. 106.

7. Salisbury's views were relayed to Selborne by his wife in October 1900. MS Selborne 100. Bodleian Library.

8. St John Brodrick to Violet Cecil, 27 September 1900. VM 35, 176/99.

9. See N. Lyttelton, *Eighty Years: Soldiering, Politics, Games* (London: Hodder & Stoughton, 1927). Like many other male imperialist autobiographers, he makes no mention of his wife's work or of her contribution to his own career.

10. Cannadine, *Decline and Fall*, p. 258.

11. M. Asquith (ed.), *The Autobiography of Margot Asquith* (London: Weidenfeld & Nicolson, 1995), p. 227.

12. J. Churchill, *The Reminiscences of Lady Randolph Churchill* (London: Edward Arnold, 1908), p. 294.

13. M. Jeune, Lady St Helier, *Memoirs of Fifty Years* (London: Edward Arnold, 1909), p. 229.

14. F. Greville, Countess of Warwick, *Life's Ebb and Flow* (Plymouth: Mayflower Press, 1929), p. 134.

15. Countess of Warwick to Cecil Rhodes, 28 September 1898. Rhodes Papers. MSS Afr. S228. C28, 91–92. Rhodes House.

16. Greville, p. 135.

17. See details of the Lady Warwick Hostel, founded through her patronage in 1898 and linked to Reading College. The imperialist aims of this agricultural training scheme were linked into a wider vision of improved education and employment opportunities for women. The Countess sent details of the scheme directly to Cecil Rhodes. Rhodes Papers. MSS Afr. S228. C28, 139–142.

18. M. Heath-Stubbs, *Friendship's Highway* (London: GFS, 1926), p. 4.

19. Louisa Knightley's journal, 26 February and 16 April 1876, and 11 and 27 June 1876. Northamptonshire Record Office.

20. Asquith, pp. 22–3.

21. E. Joyce, 'Thirty Years of Girls' Friendly Society Work' (London: GFS, 1912).

22. A. Money, *History of the Girls' Friendly Society* (London: GFS, 1897), p. 149.

23. *Ibid.*, p. 153. See also Minute Book of GFS colonial committee 1896–1906, 15 November 1897, 14 November 1898 and 20 November 1899.

24. These words formed part of the formal pledge of allegiance undertaken by those joining the Primrose League and were quoted in Louisa Knightley's Journal on the date of her own initiation, 12 May 1885.

25. Gwendolen Cecil to Violet Cecil, 10 February 1900. VM 26, 101/17.

26. Gwendolen Cecil to Violet Cecil, 23 February 1900. VM 26, 101/18; and March 1900. VM 26, 101/20.

27. St John Brodrick to Violet Cecil, 22 March 1900. VM 35, 176/73.

28. Milner, p. 183.

29. *Ibid.*, p. 185.

30. Violet Markham's diary, 9 June 1899. Markham papers. VMar 17/5. British Library of Political and Economic Science.

31. V. Markham, *Return Passage* (Oxford: Oxford University Press, 1953), p. 48.

32. Violet Markham's diary, 21 June 1899. VMar 17/5.

33. Violet Markham to Rosa Markham, 26 September 1899. VMar 27/49.

34. Edith Lyttelton's diary, 28 and 30 August, and 1, 2 and 13 September 1900. Chandos I, 6/3. Chandos papers. Churchill College, Cambridge.

35. Edith Lyttelton to Kathleen Lyttelton, 26 September 1900. Chandos II, 3/14.

36. Louisa Knightley's journal, 23 October 1900.

37. Edith Lyttelton's diary, 1 November 1900, quoted in E. Lyttelton, *Alfred Lyttelton* (London: Longmans, Green and Co, 1917), p. 259.

38. Milner, p. 132.

39. Violet Markham to Rosa Markham, 26 September 1899. VMar 27/49.

40. St John Brodrick to Violet Cecil, 21 December 1899. VM 35, 176/59. On this occasion the 'secret' news was that both Germany and Russia had renewed their non-intervention assurances, despite British military setbacks. On 1 December 1899 Brodrick asked Violet Cecil to 'find out quietly who Milner would like' to administer the Transvaal after eventual British victory. VM 35, 176/55.

41. St John Brodrick to Violet Cecil, 18 May 1900. VM 35, 176/81.

42. St John Brodrick to Violet Cecil, 27 April 1900. VM 35, 176/78.

43. Milner, p. 215.

44. Victoria League Executive Committee Minutes 1901–1903. Minutes of a 'preliminary meeting' on 2 April 1901.

45. Milner, p. 237.

46. Victoria League 'preliminary meeting' Minutes, 2 April 1901.

47. M. Villiers, Countess of Jersey, *Fifty-one Years of Victorian Life* (London: John Murray, 1922), p. 380.

48. Victoria League 'preliminary meeting' minutes, 2 April 1901.

49. *Primrose League Gazette*, 1 June 1901.

50. Primrose League Ladies' Grand Council Executive Committee Minutes, 18 May 1900. Bodleian Library.

51. Primrose League Ladies' Grand Council Executive Committee Minutes, 3 May 1901, 18 May 1900.

52. *Friendly Leaves*, May 1900. GFS.

53. Details of the poem's distribution were also published in *Friendly Leaves*, May 1900.

54. *The Girls' Quarterly*, January 1901.

55. GFS Colonial Committee Minutes, 16 June 1902.

56. Louisa Knightley's journal, 14 April and 13 June 1901.

57. Louisa Knightley's journal, 19 June 1901.

4   Organized Ladies

The organizational practices of the ladies' associations have much to teach us about the politics of female imperialism. To the extent that these women did develop a coherent vision of their feminine contribution to Empire, it is more fully expressed through their chosen activities and methods of work than through the rhetoric of imperial propaganda. The discourse of published books, articles and speeches, even when supplemented by private diaries and correspondence, presents an incomplete picture of emergent views when studied apart from the record of the associations' day-to-day business. Minute books, annual reports, membership lists and balance sheets together reveal key characteristics of political outlook. Imperialist women adopted and adapted these conventional tools in ways which reflected their gendered social values as much as their imperial ambitions. In this chapter four aspects of organizational practice are analysed in some detail in order to explain more clearly where female imperialism came from, what it stood for and the directions in which it was evolving by 1914. The formalized relations among upper-class leaders, and between leading ladies and their followers, provide revealing evidence of their evolving attitudes towards the wider worlds of both Britain and its Empire. Success and failure in joint work with organized male imperialists served to underline the centrality of gender to political behaviour and imperial outlook. Finally, the idealized yet visibly active links between royalty and the female imperialist associations reinforced the gendered social hierarchy which so importantly underpinned their work.

Leaders, committees and paid workers

Leadership was highly important within the imperialist associations, but it was characteristically a collective process rather than a performance by outstanding individuals. Female imperialists were convinced of the importance of committees. In the world of male politics, formal routines were considered essential to the efficient conduct of business. The ladies' associations consciously tried to establish their credentials by replicating such formalities. Many upper-class women had experienced committee work in the course of their philanthropic activity, or (less frequently) in the contexts of local government or of specific activities elsewhere in the women's movement. They were confident of their ability to contribute to committees and even to lead them, though usually less so of their ability to make a speech or to frame a fully developed argument around the politics of female imperialism.

For these associations, as for so many others, it is the formal record which has survived most completely. Yet the leading ladies' private papers show how much of the work of committees in fact went on behind the scenes and between meetings, during informal gatherings at each other's houses or during the round of London entertainments in which so many participated. The pre-history of the Victoria League, described in Chapter 3, illustrates this point. It is further borne out by Louisa Knightley's diary during the period when she assumed leadership of the South Africa Colonisation Society. 'I feel it is so important to learn all the personal equations in this difficult and important business', she wrote in the early months of her chairmanship. Her social round included tea with Lady Malmesbury 'and talk about the big scheme of Women's Emigration to South Africa which her husband, Sir John Ardagh, is anxious to start', 'luncheon with Lady Brassey to talk South Africa', and lunch at Osterley 'and very pleasant it was. Much S.A. talk – as many of the Committee were there.' Even, as a necessary sacrifice, 'Had Mrs Joyce and Mrs Gell to talk South Africa . . . missed meeting on the better observance of Sunday among the upper classes.' Hospitality at Fawsley soon included a week-long visit from Mrs Joyce, 'brimming over with Emigration', as well as visits from Canadian and South African travellers who satisfied her thirst for 'personal' contact with the colonies too.[1] The correspondence of Edith Lyttelton and Violet Cecil equally brimmed with lunches, teas and drawing-room chats with fellow Victoria League committee members between 1901 and 1902, to an extent which makes it seem unlikely that any committee could function smoothly without its members sharing the same social circles.

Such activities supplemented committee meetings, but could not substitute for them. This was particularly true of the larger and more truly national organizations. As the biggest all-female association (and, at leadership level, probably the least aristocratic) the Girls' Friendly Society developed the most elaborate committee structure. From a founding meeting of five women there appeared a fully fledged Constitution within six years, linking the society to the diocesan organization of the Anglican Church. Elected councils with their own officers and subcommittees advised presidents at both diocesan and central level, while the central organization came also to rely increasingly heavily upon paid professional workers in each of four specialized departments. A central finance committee was headed by three male trustees: Lord Brabazon (Meath), later founder of the Empire Day movement; the Reverend Sir Talbot Baker; and Mr Townsend, 'husband of the Foundress'.[2] There were multiple messages within this chosen structure. First, the society underlined its links to the National Church by appealing to its male hierarchy for active co-operation. By 1882 twenty-five out of twenty-six dioceses across Britain were represented on the GFS Central Council. Second, though the Constitution delegated a certain amount of work, expense and responsibility, a strong central authority was maintained. The cult of 'the Foundress' was to be expanded into a wider glamorization of upper-class female leaders, whose portraits and life-stories frequently adorned the Society's journals. In addition, the creation of central departments staffed by salaried officials amounted to an assertion of headquarters control and a recognition that a large-scale national organization could not be run by well-born, high-minded amateurs alone. The first professional secretary was presented to Mrs Townsend as a surprise birthday gift from associates and members after her health broke down 'under the heavy strain of the work' in 1879.[3] The appointment of male financial 'experts' provides further insight into the Society's views on hierarchy. The GFS soon developed a strong financial base, due to its astonishingly successful expansion and its virtuously thrifty attitude towards collection of membership subscriptions. However, during the Edwardian years its financial management remained dominated by men, despite the fact that other committees were almost exclusively female. Despite some ambiguities around gendered ability and the desirability of collective, representative rule, it is apparent from the formal record of GFS business that effective leadership remained in the hands of a minority of leading ladies, assisted by full-time staff at the London headquarters.

The emigration societies, being much smaller organizations, never aspired to the type of complex organization which characterized the Girls' Friendly Society. The earliest female emigration societies were merely loose groupings of 'workers' for the cause who came together to set up a joint loan fund, but in other respects intended to continue with existing independent philanthropy. There was built-in resistance to a strong central committee and investment in a professionally staffed office. The Female Middle Class Emigration Society of 1862 initially took advantage of its close links with the organized feminism of the Langham Place circle,[4] but before long its solitary paid worker and small committee of patrons and workers were struggling to keep the work properly organized. Only four reports were published between 1862 and 1886. In the early 1880s a cluster of new societies appeared, including the United Women's Emigration Association (1884). This body framed the selective and protective set of 'regulations for workers' which were accepted as essential guidelines into the Edwardian period. However, its organizational structure remained deliberately fluid, pledging emigrators to 'work in harmony and concert', but at the same time strictly guarding their autonomy.[5] In 1885 two of the association's most effective leaders refashioned this unworkable structure in the interests of expansion and greater efficiency. Ellen Joyce and Adelaide Ross were both Anglican clergy wives, with experience of more effective organization in the GFS and male-led church emigration associations. They set up a council of 'influential' male and female patrons, alongside a working committee of women assisted by three chaplains, and appointed a full-time female secretary and the Reverend Talbot Baker (GFS Trustee) as Treasurer. Scottish emigrators, led by Frances Balfour's sister, Lady Victoria Campbell, agreed to organize from within a unified British association in 1888.

Nevertheless, the British Women's Emigration Association of the 1890s remained somewhat minimalist. Both Miss Lefroy and Mrs Joyce (as vice-president) worked from their homes until 1893.[6] Benevolent despotism continued to be Ellen Joyce's preferred form of management into the twentieth century and was reinforced by the BWEA's willingness to nominate her as its 'Organizing Referee', with a right of final decision on the suitability of individual emigrants. Her authoritarianism received a warning jolt from the secession of the South African Colonisation Society in 1902, achieved tactfully under Louisa Knightley's leadership but clearly designed to establish independent action. Still more significantly, the Colonial Intelligence League for Educated Women was established by female members of the Grosvenor family in 1910 with the intention of specializing in a field upon which the BWEA already prided itself. Both of these Edwardian organizations chose conventional committee structures and established central offices. The CIL in particular seemed determined to break the historic link between female voluntary work and amateurism, and successfully poached a leading Victoria League administrator to run its office.[7] Louisa Knightley had tended to side with Ellen Joyce in resisting the formation of this new and 'overlapping' association, but was soon forced to admire its energetic expansion and success in drawing professional educators into the work of assisted emigration.[8] The CIL had little time to prove itself before the outbreak of war halted its work. However, its revised methods clearly illustrate the evolution of female imperialist organization during the preceding decade. The Grosvenor ladies were impeccably aristocratic and drew as heavily as any other group of imperialist women upon their family and social connections when they set up CIL finances and committees. Yet they also took a positive view of the organizational lessons to be learned from a wider range of Edwardian women's social action. In this sense the CIL was both the last of the older, patrician-led female imperialist associations and the precursor of the broader patriotic women's organizations which emerged at the end of the First World War.

The Primrose League, as we have seen, had a well-funded London office in which the Ladies' Grand Council occupied space, but failed to exert a decisive influence. After 1900 some of the leading women of the Primrose League decided to channel their main efforts for imperialism into the female-run societies dedicated to this work, particularly the Victoria League. It is interesting to note that the Ladies' Grand Council's various attempts to assert itself during the previous two decades had found expression through debate about committee relationships and office arrangements rather than open discussion of political ideas or (still less) gender roles. The structure of the Primrose League reflected internal power relations, and these in turn reflected political outlook. In the late 1880s the Ladies' Grand Council had over a thousand members paying an annual subscription of a guinea and was conscious that almost half of the upper tier of membership in the country as a whole was female. They made successive approaches to the ruling Grand Council of the League, proposing reforms which would have affected the latter's authority over both the Ladies' Council and the local Habitations (branches), where women's presence was strong. Not surprisingly perhaps, all such requests were rejected. The Grand Council would not decrease the percentage of Tribute (funds) which it kept for its own purposes; it would not form Divisional Councils in each constituency with powers to issue their own Knights and Dames diplomas; and it emphatically would not tolerate the Ladies' Grand Council arrogating to itself the power to award the League's Special Clasp.[9] A joint consultative committee was set up in July 1887 to try to iron out future disagreements. The Ladies' Grand Council was less than impressed by the outcomes, which included the offer of a more influential role in organizing entertainments and the opportunity to study (but not discuss) the agendas of Grand Council meetings.[10] By the turn of the century most leading women seem to have accepted the inevitability of their subordination within the League's central organization, though within the Habitations they were continuing to prove their organizing powers.

The Victoria League had the advantage of making a fresh start, unencumbered by past organizational history. However, its leaders were influenced by the traditions of the various societies to which they already belonged, and governed by the League's financial limitations. Like the BWEA and SACS, the Victoria League had no real intention of recruiting a mass membership and was initially unconcerned about keeping up democratic appearances. The significance of a 'representative' executive committee related only to the balance of political party allegiances. Efforts to keep down office expenses exacted a familiar toll when Edith Lyttelton resigned as honorary secretary 'on account of ill-health and over-work'.[11] Meriel Talbot soon proved to be an ideal replacement as Edith's niece and a lady of aristocratic pedigree who was nevertheless ready and able to develop a career as a salaried administrator. By 1915 the League had achieved ten paid workers, alongside five honorary ladies responsible for various departments of its work. Like the emigration societies, the Victoria League relied heavily upon wealthy patrons, and eventually the Rhodes Trust. Like the Primrose League, it perceived the financial usefulness of a large council of guinea subscribers. Like the Girls' Friendly Society it also perceived the usefulness of the small subscriber, though the Victoria League was unable to instil equal diligence into its local collectors.[12]

Council meetings were annual, crowded and formal affairs, dominated by invited male speakers. Effective business remained in the hands of an executive committee which mysteriously received exactly the desired number of nominations each year.[13] Following the BWEA, the Victoria League emphasized the centralized nature of its work by establishing general subcommittees in areas such as education, literature, branches and hospitality. At least one executive committee member participated in each, an innovation which possibly owed something to Frances Balfour's erratic activities as secretary to the hospitality committee from 1902 to 1903. Her autobiography contains a flippant account of her mistakes in this role; and after she resigned the executive took the unusual step of formally deprecating her attitudes.[14] Thus an untidy shred of discordant reality creeps occasionally into the formal record, providing a salutary reminder of its incompleteness.

Followers and local organization

Varied central organization reflects the differing and evolving outlook of female imperialist associations on relations between leaders and followers, between their London headquarters and the rest of the country and ultimately the rest of the Empire. Imperialist organization in the colonies will be considered in Chapter 6, together with the related issue of the status of Scotland, Wales and Ireland within the British associations. The importance of an upper-class female leadership within these associations has already been established. The dominance of Society ladies is self-evident within the Victoria League and (to a slightly lesser extent) the emigration societies. It is also apparent in the imperialist aspects of GFS work, though this large organization permitted a limited devolution of responsibility in relation to its work overall. The Primrose League, as a mixed-sex organization led by men, could not encompass an equally evident reliance upon its outstanding women. However, it did share the other associations' deep respect for social rank, translated in practice into a corresponding reluctance to devolve power, let alone to establish truly democratic organization.

During the 1900s both the Girls' Friendly Society and the Victoria League appeared to bend somewhat with the democratic wind, though neither abandoned a leadership stance of matriarchal upper-class authority. The Foundress, Mrs Townsend, was to the fore in urging the GFS to move with the times, both by broadening the social base of its membership and by involving members in running their own affairs. She concluded the 1897 history of the Society with a bold statement, written more in anticipation than as a description of current reality:

> We are no longer an association of ladies working for girls chiefly of one class, but a band of women, of all ranks, ages and occupations, invited to share in the same work and to uphold the same principles, each according to her powers . . . Must we not set ourselves to rise to the measure of our own capacities, that in our methods, our machinery, our literature, our ideas, we may find means definitely to organize the working powers of our vast and varied Membership which is now able to carry the ideal of the Society into every sphere of life?[15]

Two years later the Society established a single Members' Department. There was also a renewed drive to bring 'leisured and educated girls of the upper and middle classes' into membership as a step towards what Mrs Townsend called 'the real ideal of the Society – that every *Member* should have been a *Candidate*, and every *Associate* should have been a *Member*'.[16] Brian Harrison's analysis of the social composition of GFS membership shows that, in practice, the ideal came nowhere near achievement.[17] The GFS remained stronger in the south than in the north, in the country rather than in the towns, and among servants rather than factory girls. Almost half of the Edwardian membership were servants, and in 1911 only 3257 of 194,617 members were 'leisured educated girls'. The proportion of associates to members was also declining, as varied leisure and work opportunities opened up for middle-class and upper-class women.

Perhaps more successful, however, was the attempt to give members an active role. Older members were encouraged to stay with their branches as helpers, even after marriage, and members' committees took over some of the humdrum aspects of local organization. The Society's numerous journals reflected these developments. A regular column appeared in *Friendly Work* entitled 'The Members' Committee Room', with the dual purpose of gathering in members' views on organization and handing out advice. The reports of branch activities indicate an ever-increasing choice of good deeds and entertainments for members. Included in the choice was work for the Empire, and here too members were encouraged to take some initiative. The work of 'Our Missionary' depended upon myriad local efforts, and schemes to link individual British branches with GFS branches overseas were promoted as 'distinctly members' work'.[18] The Society was building its own forms of popular imperialism. Like the Primrose League, it was also demonstrating that the active participation of members at local level could be comfortably assimilated and even used to strengthen a hierarchical organization based upon social deference. Dutiful GFS members helped their associates; they did not usurp their role as leaders and moral guardians. Neither did they aspire to influence the national leadership.

The Victoria League appeared to be a most unlikely candidate for 'democratization'. Yet by 1914 it had, almost unintentionally, acquired a string of local branches and had even made some adaptations in its central organization in order to broaden its appeal. Education and propaganda work were important to the Victoria League. However, its aristocratic origins sapped its will and ability to develop a systematic plan for educating the public into fuller appreciation of Empire. The first regional branches of the League emerged in a piecemeal fashion as individual enthusiasts left London for their suburban, seaside or country homes. The public lecture programme which began in 1902, with the aid of 'a beautiful magic lantern' donated by Lady Jersey,[19] does not seem to have been directly linked to branch-building. An organizing secretary was appointed, but the most effective initiatives remained at local level, with the result that branches were soon diverse as well as more numerous. Branch reports in the fourth Annual Report record drawing-room meetings in Hove, town hall lectures in Cheltenham and a range of activity centred on local schools in Harrow. Newlands Corner in Surrey had close links with a local rifle club and a strong line in amateur dramatics, while Harrow was soon pressing the League to enrol junior members. Five or six new branches were formed each year, but others fell away, and attempts to pull these efforts together by summoning branch representatives to the London office met with little success.[20]

This untidy situation concerned at least a few of the Victoria League's leaders. In 1904 Violet Markham became the first chair of a new branch committee and in 1911 she was the guiding force behind a more ambitious attempt to broaden the League's appeal. As an active Liberal with a strong interest in social questions, she was keen to demonstrate the relevance of Empire to the working classes, both by directing the Victoria League's attention to industrial, health and town-planning issues, and by setting up branches in the main industrial cities. An uncomfortable public meeting in Oxford finally spurred her into action. The Dean of Balliol presided and Miss Markham and Miss Talbot spoke, but, as she reported back to the executive,

> The audience gave the impression of hostility to the subject and of considerable indifference to the conditions prevailing in the Colonies. Miss Markham felt strongly that the meeting revealed the need for getting the educational work of the League into the industrial centres, and also that the League's central organisation requires alteration to secure a wider class representation.[21]

Interestingly, the executive decided to back her on both counts. A northern tour was planned, somewhat in the pattern of Meriel Talbot's recent colonial tours. Soon Miss Markham and Miss Talbot were braving the citizens of Sheffield and Newcastle, where they received a more friendly reception than in Oxford as the ground had been prepared by prior conversations with patriotic councillors and trade unionists. Salaried organizers were needed in northern outposts to undertake 'pioneer work' beyond the scope of upper-class volunteers.[22] This domestic mission was sustained until the outbreak of war, but lost important momentum when Violet Markham left for a period abroad after her mother's death in 1912. Changes were duly made to the League's constitution in 1912 so that, in theory at least, the power of decision no longer rested solely with a council of those who could afford an annual guinea subscription. In practice, there was very little real change in the League's priorities and methods. 'Democratization' was soon submerged by wartime activities which aristocratic ladies could undertake with greater confidence and conviction.

It may be concluded that, despite these diversions within GFS and Victoria League history, none of the female imperialist associations strayed far down the path to democracy. To have done so would have undermined the basis for their existence. In their different ways each of these associations was committed to the exercise of elite leadership and to keeping followers in their proper place. This was the case whether the followers were hundreds of thousands (as in the GFS and the Primrose League) or merely a few thousand (as with the Victoria League). The emigration societies upheld their own historic traditions by making virtually no effort to recruit a membership, though they valued subscribing sympathizers and friends who were prepared to help spread the word to prospective emigrants. The BWEA, the South African Colonisation Society and the Colonial Intelligence League were associations which consisted entirely of leaders, some of whom took on greater responsibility than others, but all of whom believed they had the necessary wealth, rank and education to understand the needs and imperial purposes of emigration better than the emigrants themselves.

The female imperialist associations remained satisfied with the fact that their organizations were London-based and London-focused. London was, after all, the heart of the Empire and the seat both of government and High Society. In terms of influence, these associations required a London base. Both the Victoria League and the emigration societies relied upon the financial patronage of the wealthy and sought to make an impact upon government policies related to Empire. The Primrose League was linked to the upper tier of the Conservative party, and of course to Parliament. The Girls' Friendly Society had originated elsewhere, but stood to benefit from the proximity of major Anglican events and institutions in the capital city. A London base for female imperialism thus seemed to be a foregone conclusion to its leading ladies. Any disadvantages were much less obvious. Provincial impatience with London's (and England's) assumed status as the hub of the world was rarely expressed, but is perhaps reflected in the relative difficulty of branch-building in more distant parts of Britain. It was to be more clearly reflected in the sometimes uneasy relationship between the Mother Country's imperialist associations and those of the Dominions.

Organizing with men

To a certain extent, all female imperialist work involved organizing with men. Gender rivalry was not absent from the ladies' associations, but only a minority of the activists were highly sensitized to it and it was normally kept well below the surface. The public face of female imperialism was one of friendly co-operation. Imperialist women were conscious of their ability to influence male power-holders and visualized themselves as partners in a common cause, donating their own particular talents and ensuring that female interests and contributions were not lost sight of. Work with men was sometimes seen as problematic in organizational terms, however. What role should men be permitted to play within the women's own organizations? Further, how far should the female imperialists go down the road of collaboration with male imperialist leagues and other associations?

Policy on male participation varied considerably. At one end of the spectrum the Primrose League had a majority of male members and was led by a male Grand Council. Its only qualification for even partial inclusion within a study of organized female imperialism is its importance as a training ground (and ongoing source of members), and the continuing existence of the Ladies' Grand Council as a focus for female leadership. At the other end of the spectrum, the Girls' Friendly Society stood squarely upon a platform of organization by women for women. This was as true of its imperial work as of any other branch of its activity, and was undermined only by its reliance upon male financial advisers and (of course) an all-male Anglican clergy.

The position was rather more complex within the emigration societies and the Victoria League. Organized female emigration, like the GFS, had strong clerical links, and its committees of the 1880s typically contained a sprinkling of clergy alongside philanthropic women who were sometimes themselves clerical wives. By the 1900s, and particularly under the influence of the South African War, the composition of the leadership had shifted to favour an important group of Society ladies with imperialist views, and often colonial or political connections. Larger-scale female emigration depended upon achieving male support, both in financial and political terms. The (almost) all-male line-up of speakers was particularly characteristic of emigration platforms, and Joseph Chamberlain, Alfred Lyttelton and Alfred Milner were successively 'captured' as speakers. In June 1904 the SACS Annual Meeting boasted the Duke of Marlborough (Under-Secretary for the Colonies) in the chair, with Sir Neville Lyttelton, Sir Henry McCallum (Governor of Natal) and Mr Evelyn Cecil MP as speakers. The vote of thanks was proposed by Major-General Sir John Ardagh. Louisa Knightley, as the solitary female speaker, confined her comments to brief support for the motion in praise of the Society's work. Apart from this, the women's role was confined to attendance upon HRH Princess Christian, a silent guest who 'arrived punctually at three o'clock, and was received by the Duke and Duchess of Marlborough, by the Vice-Presidents Susan, Countess of Malmesbury and Miss Balfour, and the other members of the Executive Committee'.[23]

The formal ritual of such an occasion does not, of course, reflect day-to-day working practices. Neither the BWEA, SACS nor the CIL formally excluded men from committees; on the other hand male members remained a small and apparently rather uninfluential minority. Their status seems to have been largely confined to that of visiting 'experts', and minute books indicate that male attendances were comparatively rare even when men were listed as committee members. The male presence threatened to become a significant issue when the Colonial Office demanded representation on the SACS executive in return for its sponsorship of organized emigration at the end of the South African War. However, in practice 'the Colonial Office men' (as Louisa Knightley referred to them) seem to have been sleeping members; Milner and Chamberlain never truly tested the Society's determination to run its own show along well-established, female-dominated lines.[24]

The Victoria League gave more thought to policy-making on male participation than the other associations. At its inaugural meeting the League defined itself as 'a Women's Association', but it rapidly became apparent to most executive committee members that the exclusion of men might be tactically unwise. On 21 May 1901,

> The question of admitting men within the scope of the League was discussed, Lady Jersey reporting on an interview with Lord Eustace Cecil who was considering the formation of an Association of the kind for men . . . The committee decided to omit from the Constitution any statement which debarred men from admission.

However, there were clearly some dissenters, for when the same issue was raised again at a meeting of eighty council members the following day a subcommittee was appointed to 'confer on the question'. In June 1901 'It was agreed that the EC for the League should confine itself at first to working with women only', and the idea of a single-sex imperial ladies' club began to gather support.[25]

Over the next few years the Victoria League found itself bombarded with invitations to join forces with (or be swallowed up by?) associations led wholly or predominantly by men. Its adherence to its founding intentions is evident in its determination to maintain an independent though co-operative existence. Once the League had carved out its own niche within organized imperialism, the decision to carry on the work through mixed-sex committees was eventually taken on grounds of expedience. During 1905 a small number of men appeared in the council membership and in 1907 they were invited on to the executive committee. In the sixth Annual Report the executive committee was listed as eight men and twenty-one women, and the vice-presidents (paying five guineas each for the privilege) included the headmasters of four leading public schools and the leaders of both main political parties. In the following year they were joined by the Lord Mayor, the Earl of Cromer, Viscount Milner, Rudyard Kipling and Sidney Webb. Meanwhile, the core business of the Victoria League remained very much as it had been, though presumably benefiting from the enhanced 'influence' and financial support which accompanied the male entrants. The League certainly concluded that mixed-sex membership was a success, for soon afterwards its secretary, Meriel Talbot, was chivvying colonial female imperialist associations in the same direction. Male influence on the League's committees was more visible than on those of the emigration societies, but very far from predominant. In the eyes of the male leagues, and probably those of the public, the Victoria League continued to be mainly concerned with aspects of 'women's work for Empire'.

Organizational records contain interesting evidence on the women's associations' external, as well as internal, partnerships with male sympathizers. The independence of the Girls' Friendly Society was unassailable, since it was an association with a distinctively feminine moral role. The Primrose League's potential female leadership had been successfully controlled by the 1900s, so the issue of external partnerships never assumed a gendered perspective. The female emigration societies and the Victoria League, on the other hand, devoted much time and energy to ducking and weaving among competitor organizations which were larger and better-funded than themselves. The Victoria League had laid itself open to external approaches by its founding pledge to 'invite the alliance of and offer help and cooperation to such bodies of a similar nature as already exist, or as shall hereafter be formed, in other parts of the Empire'.[26] Overseas links were probably more clearly envisaged at the inaugural meeting than links with similar British organizations. However, the League's most persistent suitors soon proved to be the London-based British Empire League, together with the Navy League, the Empire Day movement, the National Service League and the Royal Colonial Institute. The Victoria League and the mixed-sex League of the Empire also pursued a long and tortuous mutual courtship which will be discussed in Chapter 8. Some form of amalgamation between these two organizations really did seem plausible for several years. The same was probably never true of the Victoria League's relationship with the large male leagues, simply because the balance of power was too uneven. The leading ladies of the Victoria League drew the line firmly at collaboration, refusing closer ties which would have robbed female imperialism of its distinctive voice and diminished the profile of its work.

All the male leagues had some female adherents, though in every case they were a minority recruited on different terms and expected to engage in different work from male members. The evident usefulness of women supporters (especially those as well-connected as the Victoria League members) whetted the appetite of male leaders for co-operation and eventual formal alliance. First off the mark was the British Empire League, with its June 1901 approach to the Victoria League executive through Lady Brassey, wife of one of its founders and a friend of Louisa Knightley. Margaret Jersey not surprisingly stalled at her blunt suggestion 'that the Victoria League become the Women's Branch of the British Empire League';[27] but over the next two years she welcomed such collaborative opportunities as a joint fund-raising ball (in July 1902), and joint sponsorship of Empire Day events. During 1904 to 1905 the Victoria League ladies apparently reconsidered the possibility of an amalgamation, but only on their own terms. The British Empire League refused to countenance a Women's Branch which would be a self-managing and semi-independent entity, and during 1906 relations noticeably cooled.[28]

Contacts with the Navy League followed a similar trajectory, from warm expressions of support, through some useful practical co-operation, then ultimately to a firm Victoria League rejection of a relationship that was too close for comfort. There was no question of amalgamating with a body which had a much narrower brief and a less socially exclusive leadership than the Victoria League, but the Navy League was refused the League's support in February 1909 when it wanted to exert joint pressure on the government to achieve 'the more extended use of the National Flag over schools'.[29] Even Lord Meath met with a declaration of independence when he pressed a little too hard for the Victoria League's official support. In 1906 the executive refused to adopt his leaflets as League pamphlets ('Lady Jersey and Lady Carrington to prepare suggested alternatives').[30] The following year they also rejected his offer of 'Empire Movement' cards to be included with the League's own Empire Day communications to schools. Many Victoria League members were individual supporters of the male-led leagues and, especially in the case of the Navy League and National Service League, applauded their work. Violet Cecil and Rudyard Kipling jointly set up a local branch of the National Service League near their homes in Sussex.[31] However, the Victoria League executive continued to defend the need for cautious autonomy when it was consulted by its Ipswich branch about the advisability of joint activities with the National Service League in 1911.

There were only two exceptions to the Victoria League's rejection of formal alliances. On the eve of the First World War it judged the large and loosely defined Overseas Club to be a harmless (even useful) addition to its own efforts to promote intercolonial hospitality, and agreed to put its own overseas branches 'in touch' with Evelyn Wrench and his followers.[32] More significantly, between 1912 and 1913 the Royal Colonial Institute succeeded in drawing the Victoria League into a standing joint committee for information exchange and discussion of possible future 'practical co-operation'.[33] This prospect was certainly viewed with more enthusiasm by the Institute than the League. The first two half-yearly informational reports of both organizations (included in the joint committee's minutes) provide a useful overview of their similarities and differences.[34] The Royal Colonial Institute remained largely a gentleman's club, with its 6000 male fellows and its luxuriously appointed London headquarters. Formal dinners and lectures were the main scheduled events; aspirations to extend public lectures 'throughout the United Kingdom' and to spearhead 'co-ordination of existing

Societies engaged in Imperial work' had made only limited progress by 1914. Most Colonial Institute lectures took the form of papers from 'distinguished men', either on specific professional issues or on general aspects of 'Imperial Outlook'. In contrast, the Victoria League continued with its relatively underfunded and small-scale 'practical' work concerning hospitality and education, sponsoring few large set-piece events and investing increasing amounts of effort into work in the provinces and work with children.

The BWEA's separately developed links with the Royal Colonial Institute provide a further illustration of inter-organizational collaboration which achieved limited success, but ultimately highlighted differences in style and content between male- and female-led associations. In May 1910 the Colonial Institute took the initiative in calling together the largest and most broadly representative British emigration conference organized thus far. Its aims were to promote future co-operation, and particularly to consider means of 'diverting as far as possible the stream of emigration now going outside the British Empire'.[35] The female emigration societies were naturally prominent among the twenty-five organizations represented at the conference, and were strongly represented on the RCI's Joint Standing Committee on Emigration set up in its wake. Anxious to gain (or regain) the initiative, the female emigrators soon pushed their concerns over the protection of young women to the top of the new committee's agenda. An all-female subcommittee was appointed to look into allegations concerning the poor reception of female emigrants in some parts of Australia, to be convened by Miss Grimes of the Church Emigration Society and to include Lady Knightley, Lady Talbot and Miss Vivian from the BWEA and SACS. Trouble followed and is copiously documented in the meticulous records of the Royal Colonial Institute.[36] The ladies' subcommittee exceeded its brief by making direct (and tactless) approaches to Australian government representatives. Worse still, they usurped the name of the Colonial Institute to justify their intervention. The ladies found themselves embarrassingly caught in the middle as the Institute hastily mended fences with irate Agents-General, its secretary and chairman not scrupling to put their good relations with these gentlemen above any consideration of support for its subcommittee or the emigrants themselves. A humiliating climb-down was ordered, and achieved, before the women members of the standing committee were eventually allowed to make a limited contribution to a report from the Royal Colonial Institute to the Prime Minister, as chair of the 1911 Imperial Conference, on general issues concerning emigration to the Empire.

This episode perhaps illustrates more clearly than any other single recorded event the reasons why female imperialists were cautious about entering into close collaboration with male leagues. As relatively small but independent organizations, the emigration societies and the Victoria League developed their own voice and their own methods of doing business. As minor adjuncts of larger, better-funded, male-led organizations, they might hope to strengthen their channels of political influence, but at the cost of loss of control and probable de-prioritization of aspects of imperial work which they themselves believed to be of the highest importance.

Royal support

The style and achievements of the female imperialist associations owed a great deal to their consistently strong royal support. In this area, at least, they were often able to out-trump the male-led leagues and even the Colonial Institute itself, for the ladies' associations could plausibly claim to have inherited the mantle of Queen Victoria's own views on Empire. They could also demonstrate close personal connections between their leaders and female members of the royal family, and publicize the active participation of two of Victoria's daughters in their organizational work.

The Queen's death on 22 January 1901 stirred emotions already brought to a high pitch by the defeats and victories of the South African War. Autobiographical accounts of Victoria's departure describe a national unity of grief in which these authors deeply shared. 'People who remember those winter days need no description of their impact, and those who are too young to recall them can never realise what it meant to feel as if a whole Empire had become one great orphaned family', wrote Margaret Jersey.[37] Violet Markham recalled 'A rising tide of dismay and sorrow unprecedented in history . . . the mother of her people lay dying; was England dying with the Queen?'[38] On the day of the funeral Violet Milner stood on the balcony of a friend's house in Buckingham Gate, alongside Edith Lyttelton, Mary Ward, Louise Dawkins, Mary Elcho and other future Victoria League stalwarts. Her diary captured the solemn drama of the moment when 'the great crowd turned silently towards Her as She came by and our eyes followed Her round the curve into the park'.[39]

For the lady imperialists, Victoria's death confirmed profound faith in the mystical unity of domestic virtue and ruling authority, binding the Queen to her people and Britain to its worldwide Empire. Over subsequent months, the ladies' associations vied for ownership of the Queen's legacy. *The Primrose League Gazette* caught their mood in one of hundreds of poetic tributes:

> It was as a woman that we loved her most,
> The mother of the people of her realm.[40]

The Victoria League was founded as a memorial to the Queen. Although the British Women's Emigration Association's vote of condolence drew attention to her personal interest in its work, the Girls' Friendly Society was probably in the best position to bind Victoria's virtues and her memory into its British and imperial mission to women. As its patron, the Queen had so heartily approved of its work that she herself took on an associate's guardian role in relation to several young girls. Thus *Friendly Leaves* could, with some justice, claim 'She was our Patron, and she *is* our example.'

In a twelve-page illustrated, black-bordered tribute, Mrs Townsend described Victoria's family life, her imperial greatness, her links to the GFS and her gift of moral authority: 'We cannot all be queens, you will say, or govern Empires or guide the State or live surrounded by the splendour of a Court. Yet every woman is destined to be, in some fashion, the queen of a kingdom in the kingdom of home.'[41] The interconnectedness of home-building and Empire-building was to become one of the most powerful themes of Edwardian female imperialism. Historians have examined the inherent contradiction between Victoria's love of private domesticity, her hostility to feminism and her strong exertion of her own imperial rule.[42] It was a contradiction which could be resolved by equating, rather than contrasting, the ideals of home and Empire. Such an equation made sense to lady imperialists engaged in the work of emigrating future colonial mothers, or educating the youth of the Mother Country. They believed they were truly building the Empire in ways which only women knew.

Queen Victoria thus became immensely important as an icon and inspiration for female imperialism, but royal support for the cause also extended in organizational directions. A number of female members of the Royal Family took a direct personal interest in the ladies' associations both before and after the Queen's death. The value of such support is a reflection of the royals' status as the leaders of Society, as well as rulers of an Empire. There was a significant difference between formal patronage and active involvement, and the societies enjoyed the benefits of both. Undoubtedly this fact reinforced their upper-class leadership and the extensive aristocratic support for organized female imperialism.

Among the leading ladies, Margaret Jersey, Frances Balfour and Louisa Knightley all had strong royal connections which they used to benefit their associations. Margaret Jersey's childhood memories included a visit by the Queen to her family home. Her husband was a member of the Villiers family, whose varied royal connections went back to King James I, and he was both a godson of the Queen and a Lord-in-Waiting at her Court from 1875. This appointment, and Jersey's later governorship, gave Margaret opportunities for personal contact with the Queen, whom she had also impressed with her article about India in 1889. Frances Balfour, as sister of the Duke of Argyll, was sister-in-law to the Queen's fourth daughter, the Princess Louise. Louisa Knightley, though of less elevated noble status, had probably the closest royal links of all. Her father was Equerry to Prince Albert, and Groom-in-Waiting to Queen Victoria. By a curious coincidence, he died on the same day as Prince Albert himself while in the process of escorting one of the youngest royal children to Cannes. Twenty-year-old Louisa and her mother remained in the South of France with Prince Leopold, returning several weeks later to a grateful welcome from the bereaved Queen. Louisa formed a close personal friendship not only with Leopold (and later his wife) but also with his elder sister, the Princess Helena. As Princess Christian (wife of a Prince of Schleswig Holstein), she became an active female imperialist. The death of her eldest son in the South African War merely confirmed her devotion to securing the future of Britain's Empire. Queen Mary, too, became a friend of Louisa Knightley, and paid her a deathbed visit at Fawsley in September 1913.

This type of personal relationship with royalty was (in those days) treated with the utmost discretion in personal memoirs. It is therefore difficult to assess exactly how far the female imperialists pushed their cause within royal circles, but organizational records contain evidence which proves that they did do so. The Girls' Friendly Society secured Queen Victoria's patronage by a formal approach through one of its diocesan presidents in 1880. However, as soon as the South African Colonisation Society had established its separate existence in 1901, its executive suggested that Louisa Knightley should make a personal approach to Queen Alexandra to act as Patron and to Princess Christian to act as Vice-Patron and a voting member of the committee. A further royal *coup* was achieved in 1904, when Louisa Knightley chaired a private conference in Princess Christian's own home for discussion of emigration methods. The 'full and free discussion' on this occasion, dominated almost entirely by female speakers, presented a notable contrast to the customary formalities of public meetings.[43] In 1911 Princess Christian agreed to act as president of the Colonial Intelligence League, Louisa Knightley being among the vice-presidents. Over the next three years the 'Princess Christian Appeal' on behalf of the South African Colonisation Society attracted substantial donations both in Britain and South Africa.

Margaret Jersey also found her services in demand to act as a royal intermediary on behalf of the Victoria League. In 1908 she agreed to ask Princess Louise to preside over an appeal in support of the Canadian Tercentenary celebrations. Four years later there was a slight stir on the Victoria League executive when it was revealed that their arch-rivals, the League of the Empire, were trying to 'poach' Princess Louise as a patron for their forthcoming imperial education conference. As the Minutes decorously report: 'communication had passed between representatives of the Victoria League and HRH on the subject and . . . it was considered desirable that the Princess should be brought into closer touch with the work of the Victoria League.' This outflanking move was a notable success, for in October 1912 the Princess accepted a public link – '[she] did not usually give her patronage at the same time as Princess Christian, but wished to make an exception in the case of the Victoria League.' Something of a clean sweep had in fact been achieved, as the Princess of Wales had also been signed up as a patron.[44]

Royal support for organized female imperialism thus represented, and was known by Society to represent, far more than mere permission to use royal names to adorn notepaper and reports. The societies' work had attracted genuine royal interest and approval. This point was underlined to a wider public on every possible occasion. It not only reinforced the social elitism of the female imperialist leadership, but also contributed to the self-confidence of the movement as a whole. Queen Victoria had fulfilled her duty as Queen, Empress and Head of the Church by carrying out 'women's work for Empire' in its highest form and at the highest levels. Who more suitable to take up their share of her burden than her royal daughters, their aristocratic friends and other loyal women among her British subjects? All the projects of female imperialism shared a little of the aura of her royal, and feminine, authority.

Notes

1. See Louisa Knightley's journal, 4 June 1901, 13 February 1901, 29 June 1901, 1 July 1901 and 2 March 1901. Northamptonshire Record Office.
2. See M. Heath-Stubbs, *Friendship's Highway* (London: GFS, 1926), pp. 8–10. The author described the GFS Constitution as 'Like a good architectural design, to serve as a pattern and basis for all future developments' (p. 8).
3. *Ibid.*, p. 9.
4. A loan from Barbara Bodichon provided the basis for the original central loan fund, supplemented by an appeal through *The Times* from Maria Rye, a leading member of the Society for Promoting the Employment of Women. The Emigration Society shared the same London address as *The English Woman's Journal* and the National Association for the Promotion of Social Science.
5. United English Women's Emigration Association statement of aims, in its finance committee minutes 1885–1886. FL2A. Fawcett Library.
6. U. Monk, *New Horizons: A Hundred Years of Women's Migration* (London: HMSO, 1963), p. 15. The early history of assisted female emigration is usefully summarized in the Fawcett Library's catalogue of the Female Emigration Societies' papers.

7. Eleanor Percy-Taylor, who had made a name for herself as a Victoria League lecturer and proved herself as an administrator by standing in for Meriel Talbot as secretary during her World Tour of 1909 to 1911.

8. See Louisa Knightley's journal, 27 April 1910, 20 February 1911, 13 November 1911, 4 December 1911, 8 March 1912 and 3 May 1912. Lady Knightley eventually played a key role in mending fences between the CIL and the BWEA, by offering to become a CIL vice-president after a majority of the BWEA Council had agreed that Caroline Grosvenor 'should retire' from that body. As she commented with her usual wry humour, 'it was perhaps as well that Mrs Joyce was not there' at the decisive meeting on 3 May 1912.

9. See the Primrose League Ladies' Grand Council Executive Committee Minute Book, meetings of 18 January 1887, 11 February 1887 and 11 March 1887. PL10. Bodleian Library.

10. *Ibid.*, 11 November 1887.

11. Victoria League First Annual Report, 1901–02 (1902).

12. See Appendix 1.

13. Victoria League Executive Committee Minutes reveal the behind-the-scenes juggling which succeeded in averting divisive elections while at the same time preserving a balance of Liberal and Conservative leading ladies; for example, on 11 May 1906, when surplus Conservative candidates were tactfully weeded out on the basis of poor attendance during the previous year.

14. Victoria League Executive Committee Minutes, 19 July 1904.

15. A. Money, *History of the Girls' Friendly Society* (London: GFS 'L'Envoi', 1897).

16. Heath-Stubbs, p. 21.

17. See B. Harrison, 'For Church, Queen and Family: The Girls' Friendly Society 1874–1920', *Past and Present*, 1973, **61**: 120.

18. *Friendly Work*, July 1905.

19. Victoria League First Annual Report, 1901–02 (1902).

20. Victoria League Sixth Annual Report, 1907 (1908).

21. Victoria League Executive Committee Minutes, 21 January 1911.

22. Victoria League Eleventh Annual Report, 1912 (1913).

23. *The Imperial Colonist*, III/30. June 1904.

24. See correspondence from Alicia Cecil, on behalf of SAX/SACS, to the Johannesburg ladies' committee receiving its emigrants, between December 1902 and November 1903. South African Colonisation Society, 3/1–2. Fawcett Library. These letters vividly reflect the stresses of attempting simultaneously to satisfy the Colonial Office, Lord Milner, the SAX/SACS committee and the Johannesburg committee.

25. Victoria League Executive Committee Minutes, 21 May 1901, 7 June 1901 and 21 June 1901.

26. Victoria League Executive Committee Minutes, 'preliminary meeting' on 2 April 1901.

27. Victoria League Executive Committee Minutes, 21 June 1901.

28. See Victoria League Executive Committee Minutes, 3 May 1906, which record open conflict between the two Leagues over the establishment of competing branches in Manchester.

29. Victoria League Executive Committee Minutes, 12 February 1909.

30. Victoria League Executive Committee Minutes, 29 November 1906.

31. See correspondence between Violet Cecil and Rudyard Kipling during 1910. VM44. Bodleian Library.

32. Victoria League Executive Committee Minutes, 17 October 1910.

33. Victoria League Executive Committee Minutes, 20 February 1912.

34. Minutes of the Royal Colonial Institute's 'Joint Committee with the Victoria League and Other Bodies 1913–19'. Royal Commonwealth Society Archives. Cambridge University Library. The first pair of half-yearly reports covered the six-month period from January to June 1913.

35. See the Minutes of the Royal Colonial Institute's Empire Migration Committee, 1910–14. Royal Commonwealth Society Archives. The objectives of the conference were agreed at a meeting on 25 April 1910.

36. See the RCI Empire Migration Committee Minutes, 3 November 1910, 17 November 1910, 1 December 1910 and 12 January 1911; supplemented by the RCI Emigration Letter Book 1910–14, which contains agitated (and exculpatory) correspondence from the RCI Secretary to the offended Australian Agents-General. The papers of the RCI emigration committee also include an almost verbatim record of the first meeting of the ladies' subcommittee which investigated damaging rumours about neglect of female welfare by various Australian state governments. This record (including the committee members' expressions of outrage) unfortunately reached the hands of the Agents-General and substantiated their complaints to the higher authorities of the Royal Colonial Institute.

37. M. Villiers, *Fifty-one Years of Victorian Life* (London: John Murray, 1922), p. 380.

38. V. Markham, *Return Passage* (Oxford: Oxford University Press, 1953), p. 69.

39. Milner, p. 234.

40. *Primrose League Gazette*, 1 February 1901.

41. *Friendly Leaves*, March 1901.

42. See e.g. D. Thompson, *Queen Victoria: Gender and Power* (London: Virago, 1990), and K. Reynolds, 'Aristocratic Women and Political Society in Early and Mid-Victorian Britain', unpublished DPhil thesis, 1995, Chapter 6.

43. *The Imperial Colonist*. III/32. August 1904.

44. Victoria League Executive Committee Minutes, 18 July 1912 and 17 October 1912.

5 Women's Work for Empire

Female imperialists were sometimes congratulated by male platform speakers on their success in carrying out womanly work for the Empire, and they apparently relished this type of gendered compliment. Their organizational arrangements allowed only limited roles to male 'experts' because the women believed themselves to be the true experts in most of their chosen fields of work. This was the ultimate justification for separate ladies' imperialist associations, rather than merely the fact that women were excluded from power within male imperialist leagues. The process of defining womanly imperial work was part of broader contemporary debates over women's changing roles in British society, and the essential nature of women's work. There existed an extensive prescriptive literature on these subjects, much of it written by men. Alongside religious and social homilies that were designed to deter women from ambitions beyond their own homes and families, an increasing number of publications gradually appeared from women who were active in public life. In the year of the Victoria League's foundation, 'the Honourable Mrs Arthur Lyttelton' published *Women and Their Work*, no doubt with the support and approval of her sister-in-law and close friend Edith Lyttelton.[1] While Kathleen Lyttelton's text did not directly address imperial work, it did set out parameters of womanly work which, while respecting many established gender norms, could encompass a proactive and even political role for women. Chapters on 'The Family' and 'The Household' were seamlessly followed by chapters on 'Philanthropic and Social Work', 'Professions' and 'Friendship'. These aspects fitted closely together within a continuum of women's work which already demonstrably included female imperialism alongside other organizations and activities of the British women's movement.

Most imperialist ladies would have supported Kathleen Lyttelton's refusal to posit domestic and public life as alternative, and competing, priorities. Domestic virtues were imperial virtues too, as the late Queen had demonstrated, and the ladies' associations provided extensive opportunities to put them into practice. The notable convergence in the work of different imperialist organizations during the Edwardian period rested upon the shared outlook of their leaders concerning both social hierarchy and the special talents and duties of women. Basically conservative gender politics assumed a new and more assertive significance as women strove to fulfil their duties towards the Empire. While most leading ladies shunned feminist connotations, the organized female imperialists were inevitably caught up in the gender contestations of their times as they chose their own means of asserting female agency in public life.

They did so in ways which drew upon older upper-class traditions in politics and philanthropy, but which did not entirely separate them from the broader currents of the contemporary women's movement. Later chapters will illustrate female imperialist self-assertion in practice, and relate it to the Edwardian suffrage debates. Here, an attempt is made to generalize across the full range of organized women's work for the Empire in order to identify some of its characteristic traits.

The most frequently noted characteristic of women's imperial work was that it was 'practical'. Visible results, efficiency and attention to detail were qualities which were much prized by the lady imperialists across the full spectrum of their work. The emphasis on practicality could with hindsight be construed as a limitation, since it tended to steer women away from engaging in the debate on big ideas concerning Empire, and it sometimes left them overly complacent about the importance of small-scale achievements. However, during the late Victorian and Edwardian years practicality seems to have been regarded as an unmitigated and peculiarly feminine virtue. Emigration associations were to the fore in establishing this point. Writing in *The Queen* in 1886, Viscountess Strangford publicized the work of the Colonial Emigration Society by a lengthy account of the painstaking processes of selection and despatch.[2] 'The general idea is that you have only to wrap your Emigrants in paper, seal and stamp them, and they will get somehow to some place where they will immediately flourish,' she began, then proceeded to dispel this illusion. Detailed preparations started with hour-long interviews, perhaps repeated five or six times over for those who remained ignorant and uncertain, to be followed for the genuinely intending emigrant by hours of form-filling, 'the getting together of the required money', followed by 'endless directions, written and spoken, to the Emigrant to secure her being ready at the proper time and place for embarkation'. Nor was this the end of the emigrator's worries, for her responsibilities included ensuring that every emigrant's correct kit was on board and that the personalities inhabiting each cabin had been correctly mixed to ensure a bearable voyage. This account aimed to educate its readers both in the importance of detailed practicality and its cost implications for emigration societies. A further point of emphasis was the unique suitability of upper-class women as emigration organizers. 'The work of small personally worked societies is absolutely necessary,' claimed the Viscountess, offering only lukewarm approval to the newly established Government Emigration Office. The task of sifting applications demanded a woman's 'quicker and more searching' discernment and 'finer and readier' sympathies. Ellen Joyce's emigration methods twenty years later were based upon exactly the same assumptions. The South African Colonisation Society risked falling out with Lord Milner because it refused to cut corners in the interests of mass emigration. It also risked alienating South African collaborators by continually insisting on prescriptive detail in arrangements at both ends of the emigrant's voyage.

'Practical' and 'personal' were closely allied in the vocabulary of lady imperialists. The Girls' Friendly Society was constructed around belief in the value of personal contact between individual members and their middle- or upper-class associates. This belief related, in turn, to current views on the value of individual social service by cultivated, wealthy women, developed influentially in the late nineteenth century through the Charity Organization Society.[3] Personal contact would foster each individual GFS member's sense of her ability to make her small contribution to the Society's cause. As *Friendly Leaves* reminded its readers in July 1908,

> it is very important not to forget, in all the good and useful objects to which our attention is now directed, the simple personal foundation on which all the real value of the Girls' Friendly Society depends. Every Member, every Associate, is a weakness or a strength.

Most of the work of the branches was eminently practical, in the sense of being small scale, down-to-earth and (often) useful to others. The Society's journals perfectly capture the union of high religious and imperial idealism with advice on matters of tiny detail, from knitting patterns and recipes to common cures and tips on housework. No 'burden' was too small or too great to be shared. The formal linking of British and colonial GFS branches projected the same perspective on to a wider stage. Members were encouraged to correspond on a one-to-one basis, and to raise money for useful gifts for their colonial sisters. Diocesan reports in *Friendly Leaves* contain impressive lists of practical work, in which the local and the imperial rub shoulders. For example, in 1902 the Manchester GFS reported

> that one Branch keeps a boy in a Waifs and Strays' Home, and that others support a cot in the Cawnpore Hospital, a child in Zanzibar, and a little girl in the Rawstenstall Home. In one parish the girls have a blind friend to whom they are very kind, giving her orders for knitting and for tea.

Other branch activities included educating junior candidates, polishing church brasses, caring for the disabled and charitable garment-making. Clearly, Lady Bountiful ideals were being successfully transposed to a humbler setting.[4]

Returning to the social elite, it is interesting to note that the Victoria League was almost equally insistent upon the 'practicality' and 'person-to-person' nature of its work, despite the fact that it was rather silent about Christian ethics. Its original aims pledged to provide 'any practical work desired by the Colonies and tending to the good of the Empire as a whole'.[5] Though it kept in view its broader purpose of imperial unity, and devoted more energy to directly imperialist propaganda than the other associations, the League did in fact adopt a succession of 'practical' causes. Mention has been made of South African work for soldiers' graves, refugees and concentration camp victims. Later causes included promotion of individual correspondence, the sending of books and newspapers, support for a reduction in postage rates to Canada, collection of detailed information about industrial conditions (at Violet Markham's instigation), establishment of a London information bureau, and above all the encouragement of hospitality for colonial visitors. As the eleventh Annual Report put it, 'Politicians deal with institutions; the Victoria League deals with individuals.' Hospitality work was 'practical' and satisfyingly achievable, yet it was also linked to the highest imperial goals. It had the strong advantage of calling upon precisely appropriate qualities of gender and social class.

The area of 'entertainments' within the Primrose League drew upon some of the same qualities. We have observed the Ladies' Grand Council's tactical refusal to be pigeon-holed into such ladylike work. However, it is clear enough from the Habitations reports in *The Primrose League Gazette* that Primrose League Dames were much-approved hostesses, and (at humbler levels) poured a great deal of tea. They serviced the Conservative Party election machine by a lot of patient, 'practical' work on registrations and removals, as well as by canvassing. Such activity could be, and was, construed as womanly work for Empire, since the Conservatives believed themselves to be the party of patriotic imperialism. In September 1906 'a woman worker' contributed an unusually full exposition of this viewpoint to *The Primrose League Gazette*. 'Are the women of our country as a whole doing their duty for King and Country?' she asked, then answered in terms of a series of recommendations for expanding the scope of 'practical work'. Not only did mothers have 'the privilege of making future politicians' through the upbringing of their children, but they might also devote their leisure hours to the imperial education of poorer women. The repetitious use of the word 'practical' in this article suggests that it had a strong resonance both for the writer and her intended readership. However, her extension of its meanings into the realms of political education has more connection with female imperialism than with the customary outlook of the *Gazette*. Misogyny in its more patronizing forms characterized many of this journal's features concerning women. In August 1904 an article on 'The Great Ladies of Politics' dwelt extensively on the self-abnegation of Alice Balfour and Mary Chamberlain ('They act a simple, unobtrusive, womanly part, and yet they are great ladies of politics').[6]

Altruism was, of course, widely viewed as the finest and most feminine of all virtues by both men and women.[7] Prized across the spectrum of educated and comfortably off Victorian society, it was solidly built into the activities of female imperialism and firmly drilled into the psyche of individual imperialists as a moral imperative, if not a dominating code of daily life. Caring for others could be practised at many different levels, including the imperial one. Throughout her life Louisa Knightley subjected herself to intense self-criticism if she doubted that she was pursuing her organizational and political work for the sake of others. Her enjoyment of a GFS festival at Fawsley was dented when the local vicar 'spoke of the subtle temptation of doing the work for the gratitude and the "kudos" it brings. Such a temptation for me.' For Lent 1903 her prayer theme was 'I am so much too proud of what I do!'[8] The Girls' Friendly Society provided women with the ideal vehicle for exercising their caring nature and organizational talents upon a large scale without the need for guilt. The multiplicity of members' own charitable efforts merely reflected the wider aims of the GFS to serve as 'a great comfortable nest in a wide world',[9] a substitute or extended family for its members, and a source of comfort and support even for those beyond its boundaries. Assistance with job changes and protected travel was offered to girls whether they were in Britain or on their way to an imperial future. Among the earliest GFS departments were those for Lodges and Homes of Rest, headed from 1884 by Lord and Lady Meath respectively. In the 1890s and 1900s Lodges were promoted extensively in the Empire as a much-needed safe haven for girls between jobs, and a more permanent residence in such dangerous places as Johannesburg. Homes of Rest cared for sick and incurable members, or provided the possibility of convalescence and even cheap holidays. Practicality and caring also proceeded hand-in-hand through GFS missionary work overseas, characteristically focused on provision of schools and hospitals as much as on spreading the Christian message.

No other female imperialist association could match the breadth and scale of the Girls' Friendly Society's caring work. A similar rhetoric, however, did find its way into the emigration associations and even the Victoria League. Emigrators were not merely efficient and scrupulously thorough; they were also womanly carers. Emigration by suitable women to the colonies was very much in their interests, as well as those of the Empire, and the emphasis in publicity for the work swung back and forth between these dual aspects. The need for protection was usually even more strongly emphasized than was the availability of economic opportunities, since this was a major plank of emigration society work and a means of deflecting occasional hostile criticism. The philanthropic aspects of emigration work came strongly to the fore when the societies assisted distressed gentlewomen and unemployed factory workers; they were held in abeyance when servant girls were the issue, and moral surveillance rather than kindly protection was felt to be the main requirement. The Victoria League saw its caring role rather differently. The benefits of its example, its advice, and even its gifts in cash and kind were made available to the citizens of Greater Britain, particularly when they chose to visit London. The overriding aim was to strengthen the Empire, and educative, supportive hospitality was believed to be one of the best means of achieving this.

Helping the less fortunate was not merely a womanly and an imperialist virtue; it was also a Christian duty. Social historians of the Empire have made much of the associations between Christian militarism and imperialism. How far did female imperialists simply reinforce this ideal, and how far did they help to replace it with a feminized alternative version of Christian imperialism? The connections between gender, religion and Empire were complex and aroused varied responses among different associations and their individual adherents. A valid general answer to this question may therefore not be possible, but some relevant observations may be made on the basis of the evidence used in this study. First, it is clear from the journalism and diaries of lady imperialists that they were as much enthralled by the image of the heroic Christian soldier as any of their male contemporaries. Kitchener, Baden-Powell and particularly Lord Roberts took over where General Gordon had left off, and though the women were not immune to stories of concentration camp suffering, they voiced little criticism of military policies in South Africa once Britain was clearly on the path to victory. In this they merely followed the bellicose lead of the Anglican Church which was conspicuously committed to Empire-building during the early twentieth century. Certain constructive aspects of Christian imperialism were believed by at least some female imperialists to constitute their most important work for Empire. Their interventions in these areas (by both word and deed) did not amount to a rejection of masculine, militarist imperialism but did serve to reinforce existing female traditions of cultural imperialism developed through the work of women missionaries, teachers and medical personnel.[10] In turn, representations of such work were reimported into the British female imperialist associations. During the Edwardian years it was not uncommon for the Girls' Friendly Society, the emigration associations and even the Primrose League to project their work in both Christian and Christianizing terms. 'Why do we urge Imperialism?' asked Ellen Joyce at the GFS Imperial Conference in 1912: 'Not from selfish views, not from mere pride of race, but deep down in our hearts we believe that God has set us to be not only pioneers or civilisers, but evangelists.'[11]

Nor was gender lost sight of in the evangelism of women imperialists. Writing in the 1913 history of the Girls' Friendly Society, Agnes Money encouraged members to remember 'our true function as a handmaid of the Church'. She urged the Church itself to recognize more definitively 'our service as a real ministry of women' and the GFS colonial members 'to raise the standard of womanhood and fulfil the aim for which we are banded together – "not only to be pure but to purify"'.[12] In this appeal and others the GFS in fact sought to distinguish its Christian female imperialism from the normal expectations of missionary work among the heathens of the Empire. Much admiration for female missionaries was expressed in its journals, and there was a long tradition of fund-raising to support individual projects, but the Society's most important Christian work in Britain and Empire was to guide, protect and expand its own membership. 'I have always conceived of the GFS work as of the nature of a Mission, the Mission of Women to Women', wrote Mrs Townsend in 1897, before going on to suggest that GFS work in 'distant lands' should concentrate upon 'helping to sustain the work of the Church and *the work of the GFS as church work*'.[13]

Such advice was variously reflected in the 'practical' activities of the Girls' Friendly Society at home and abroad. The glamour of missionary work continued to enthuse British members, but the emphasis in journal coverage was mainly upon the philanthropic importance of medicine and education, and upon the value of missionaries as female role models rather than upon numbers of conversions achieved. The Christian faith upheld the missionary in her work as it might also uphold every other GFS member. The imperial expansion of the GFS itself was prominently reported in the journals, in ways which encouraged British members to feel closely involved. Their contribution to sustaining this work 'as Church work' consisted not merely of supportive prayer and the establishment of friendly links with individual branches, but also of fund-raising for new churches. The biggest efforts in this direction were made in 1912 to 1913 on behalf of western Canada, where eighty-four sites for churches were purchased by the GFS at prices varying from £25 to £42 10s. Louisa Knightley acquired an appropriate memorial when the chancel of St Peter's Church, Regina, was built in her memory in 1914.[14] Meanwhile, the emigration associations had also been using the Christian impulse within their work to practical purpose. The BWEA, then SACS, had a valued association with two of the leading Anglican women in South Africa: Sister Henrietta Stockdale, whose Kimberley Hospital contributed to founding the nursing profession, and Mother Cecile, whose Grahamstown Training School laid foundations for the country's teacher training.[15] The emigrators supplied nurses and teachers, receiving in return reports and visits which helped to publicize their own work in Britain. Though the emigration associations were not formally linked to the Anglican Church like the GFS, they relied upon its support and contributed to its growth in the colonies. Introductions to local clergy were among the indispensable papers carried by every departing emigrant.

The Pan-Anglican Congress of 1908 was a living embodiment of the worldwide power of the Church, and of Britain's leadership of Christian imperialism. It made a profound impact upon the Girls' Friendly Society and the Mothers' Union, reinforcing the growing emphasis on 'women's work for Empire' within both these large, all-female organizations, and spreading ripple effects into the other ladies' associations. Both the GFS and the Mothers' Union organized their own imperial gatherings alongside the main Congress, and sent many supporters to the sectional meetings on 'the Church's duty to her Colonists'. Laura Ridding was among them, a bishop's widow, a founder member of the National Union of Women Workers, and an enthusiast for female

Christian imperialism. Her diary recorded her own contribution in presiding over 'the Pan Anglican Congress Women's Recess Meeting on White Slave Traffic', as well as her general disappointment that '*women's* share in the work' was not given greater general prominence.[16] A few months later Laura Ridding set out to visit her brother and sister-in-law (Lord and Lady Selborne) in South Africa. Under the inspiration of the Congress, she used her visit to engage in a whole range of female Christian imperialist activities, starting with an investigation of church work in Cape Town and concluding with her pledge to become actively involved in emigration work. Her 1909 pamphlet, 'The Call of the Empire', was to be one of the fullest expositions of 'our special duty as women to be guardians of the moral standard of the Empire': a plea to Christian women to rise up and fulfil their responsibilities.

The organized caring undertaken by the ladies' imperialist associations cost a great deal of money, with missionary work, church-building and subsidized emigration being among the most expensive activities. The Girls' Friendly Society had extensive commitments to its charitable work at home as well as overseas, so it is not surprising to find it to the fore as a fund-raising body. To a certain extent, fund-raising can be considered as a distinctive, womanly activity in its own right. It took up a great deal of members' and associates' time, and provided them with pleasure and a sense of purpose. For the upper-class leaders of female imperialism, fund-raising had two different sets of connotations. On the one hand the Victoria League and emigration societies in particular were dependent upon voluntary (and irregular) contributions to sustain their day-to-day work. Their sporadic public appeals and private lobbying for money were often tinged with anxiety. On the other hand, aristocratic ladies had a particularly important role to play in the more enjoyable fund-raising for special projects. Frank Prochaska has described the nineteenth-century evolution of the charitable bazaar.[17] Lady imperialists were enthusiastic participants, both as patrons opening local events and sometimes as organizers of their own, socially exclusive fund-raising activities within the context of the London Season. Other genteel fund-raising events were semi-public concerts, art exhibitions and theatrical performances, all of which were employed by the emigration associations and the Victoria League.

The apotheosis of such efforts was undoubtedly the 'Great Sales' of the Girls' Friendly Society, which provided excellent imperialist propaganda as well as funds and fun. 'As we sit down to count up the results perhaps nothing strikes me more than the way in which the whole thing has testified to the solidarity of the G.F.S.,' wrote one of the delighted organizers in July 1905. Twin events were held on successive days, nicely reflecting the social divisions within the Society. Both the Sale and Loan Exhibition at Grosvenor House (opened by Princess Louise and the Duchess of Marlborough) and the Members' Imperial Sale at Pepys House (opened by Mrs Townsend and 'arranged by Members, managed by Members, carried through by Members') were held 'on behalf of the Colonial and Indian work of the G.F.S'. Goods for sale poured in from branches across the Empire, and the stalls at Grosvenor House were each named for a different colony or dominion and presided over by a great lady with appropriate imperial connections. Miss Lily Frere 'organised and arranged with untold effort and skill' the adjoining exhibition of 'souvenirs of upwards of 300 famous women of all times, including royalties, philanthropists, writers, artists, musicians and others'. At the Members' Sale, customers queued for 'delicious tea for 1d a cup' and enjoyed the musical performance of Members and 'short addresses on the Imperial work of the G.F.S.'.[18] The messages on Empire, gender and social class could hardly have been spelled out more clearly to those involved, and to the watching world beyond.

Most of the 'women's work' so far described was intended to spread the imperial ideal as well as to make a 'practical' contribution to Empire-building. There are, however, problems in deciding how far imperialist ladies believed themselves to be directly responsible for developing and spreading their own imperialist ideology. With a few notable exceptions, this was the Achilles' heel of female imperialism. Even associations with a clear propaganda mission, such as the Victoria League and the Primrose League, tended to allow (or encourage) lady members to revert to the 'practical' work in which they felt more confident, leaving publications and public platforms in the hands of men. This issue related as strongly to social convention as to personal self-confidence, but the evidence of diaries and letters shows the powerful influence of the former over the latter. Edith Lyttelton, and even Louisa Knightley, dreaded public speech-making; of the leading ladies, only Violet Markham and Ellen Joyce seem to have developed real enjoyment of the art, while Lady Jersey found herself more in demand for her 'silvery tones' and fine appearance than for the substance of her speeches. The most consistently successful female speakers for the imperialist associations were those educated women who were prepared to take on the task of paid lecturer, such as Miss Percy Taylor of the Victoria League. For the majority, drawing-room meetings were the summit of oratorical achievement.

At larger and more public gatherings the ladylike tradition lingered of 'saying a few words', either of introduction or of thanks, to a well-qualified line-up of male speakers. However influential within Society, or within the societies of female imperialism, no lady possessed the authority of a politician, a soldier, a church leader or an imperial administrator. The result was that a very high proportion of the words spoken and written directly about the ideals of womanly imperialism were in fact spoken or written by men. Many female imperialists genuinely believed that men could explain their cause better than they could themselves, and were influenced in their own view of their work by what they heard from the platforms of conferences and annual general meetings, or read from male contributors to the societies' journals. Thus even the ladies' own pronouncements on 'women's work for Empire' contained a great many 'borrowed' ideas and lengthy male quotations.

In these circumstances it seems sensible to conclude that lady imperialists did not prioritize the expression of a separate, feminine imperialist mission within their work. This accorded with their admiration for male imperialist rhetoric, which in turn related to their fundamentally conservative attitudes towards class and gender. Organized female imperialism was itself hierarchical, and it respected established external hierarchies. Respect for male leadership of the Empire should not be construed as a lack of initiative and determination, however. Within the female imperialist associations an inevitable undercurrent of tension existed between acceptance of the status quo regarding gender and Empire, and an active commitment to making a fuller, more valued contribution to imperial work. Despite some reluctance to mount the public platform or to proclaim independent viewpoints in print, the very existence of the ladies' associations in itself constituted an indirect challenge to male monopolization of imperial power. Female imperialists avoided criticism and confrontation, but nevertheless insisted strongly upon the importance of their own work. 'Women's work for Empire' was a vital complement to the admired achievements of male Empire-builders. Thus the imperialist ladies did contribute to framing their own and their supporters' view of Empire and women's work, but they usually tried to do so more by deeds than by words. Through their choice of activities and of organizational methods, and through their accounts of their work in minutes, reports, pamphlets, journals, correspondence and diaries, they expressed views on female imperialism which sometimes echoed those of male imperialists, but very often contained different emphases. The emphases of the ladies' associations emerged from the detailed practice of womanly work for the Empire. They can best be understood within that context, so the general characteristics outlined in this chapter will be explored through a study of selected aspects of the associations' work in the chapters which follow.

Notes

1. K. Lyttelton, *Women and Their Work* (London: Methuen, 1901).
2. Cutting from *The Queen*, 4 December 1886, in UBWEA press cuttings scrapbook 2.FL2B, 3/2. Fawcett Library.
3. See J. Lewis, 'Women and Late-nineteenth Century Social Work', in C. Smart (ed.), *Regulating Womanhood: Historical Essays on Marriage, Motherhood and Sexuality* (London: Routledge, 1992).
4. *Friendly Leaves*, April 1903.
5. Victoria League Executive Committee Minutes, 'preliminary meeting' on 2 April 1901.
6. *Primrose League Gazette*, August 1904.
7. See S. Collini, *Public Moralists: Political Thought and Intellectual Life in Britain 1850–1930* (Oxford: Clarendon Press, 1991). He analyses 'the culture of altruism' in largely ungendered terms, though making extensive use of certain female texts to demonstrate its prevalence. For a woman-centred perspective on altruism, see the Introduction to F. Prochaska, *Women and Philanthropy in Nineteenth Century England* (Oxford: Clarendon Press, 1980). He concludes that caring for others might lead towards a (sometimes unintentional) assertion of female power. These ideas are further developed in more recent work by Eileen Yeo.
8. Louisa Knightley's journal, 21 May 1901 and 1 March 1903.
9. *Friendly Leaves*, July 1908.
10. For discussion of this work, and its imperialist significance, see F. Bowie *et al.* (eds), *Women and Missions: Past and Present* (Oxford: Berg, 1993). *The Girls' Special Missionary Union Magazine, 1898–1908*, provides an informative source, alongside GFS journals, on the activities and attitudes of female missionaries and the ways in which they were publicized for a readership of British women. Ladies of the Curzon family contributed to its editorial committee. I am indebted to Judith Rowbotham for access to this source.
11. E. Joyce, 'Thirty Years of Girls' Friendly Society Work' (London: GFS, 1912).
12. A. Money, *The Story of the Girls' Friendly Society* (London: GFS, 1913), p. 52.
13. M. Heath-Stubbs, *Friendship's Highway* (London: GFS, 1926), p. 82.
14. *Ibid.*, pp. 87–88.
15. On the careers of Henrietta Stockdale and Mother Cecile, see C. Swaisland, 'Wanted – Earnest, Self-sacrificing Women for Service in South Africa: Nineteenth Century Recruitment of Single Women to Protestant Missions', in F. Bowie, D. Kirkwood and S. Ardener (eds), *Women and Missions: Past and Present Anthropological and Historical Perspectives* (Oxford: Berg, 1993), pp. 70–83. Their visits and correspondence are recorded in BWEA and SACS Minutes.

16. Laura Ridding's diary, 12 June and 17 June 1908. Hampshire Record Office.
17. See Prochaska, Part One, Chapter 2.
18. *Friendly Work*, July 1905.

6 Imperial Sisterhood?

The work of British female imperialists depended heavily upon successful co-operation with like-minded women overseas. Protected travel and colonial settlement could only be undertaken by the Girls' Friendly Society and the emigration associations if there were satisfactory reception arrangements and adequate channels for a two-way exchange of information with the colonies. The education and hospitality work of the Victoria League also rested upon the active willingness of colonial residents to take up the services offered by the League, and to reciprocate with similar services. At one level the establishment of links with organized female imperialism in the colonies was a straightforward matter. There was a clear perception of mutual need and benefit, and loyalty to the higher ideals of Empire and of womanhood could be tapped as effectively in the colonies as in Britain. From the 1880s onwards colonial GFS branches and female immigration committees sprang to life without an undue amount of British prompting. Under the influence of the South African War, women's patriotic associations took shape in Canada, Australasia and South Africa and rapidly cemented working alliances with the British Victoria League. However, the very fact that colonial female imperialism was its own creation, with its own historical roots and its own sense of organizational identity, presented British imperialists with certain dilemmas. Neither the rhetoric nor indeed the 'practical' realities of collaboration between Great and Greater Britain could diminish the latent inequalities of power and esteem underlying this imperial partnership.

The literary and artistic iconography of Empire depended heavily upon familial images. Britain and the 'white settler' Dominions were occasionally portrayed in terms of sisterly equality, but the overwhelmingly popular image, especially in Britain, was one of motherhood and daughterhood. The colonies (a term used indiscriminately by most female imperialists to include the Dominions) were Britannia's children. The native races of the colonies were her children's children, doubly infantilized by their manifest inequality with white settlers. Both male and female imperialists believed that a shared cultural heritage was indissolubly linked with still more powerful ties of British racial inheritance. This belief reinforced their fondness for family metaphors. Matriarchal power was an easy, even natural, attribute for the upper-class leaders of the ladies' imperialist associations. The very closeness of Britain's relationship to her colonies, the very tie of 'common blood', made the exercise of pre-ordained maternal control a sacred obligation. It is not surprising to find British female imperialists emphasizing their motherly role more insistently than any other. Nor, perhaps, is it surprising to find that the family imagery of Empire was also embraced with some enthusiasm by women in the colonies. Whether as sisters or daughters, their role in Empire-building was validated and given an aura of moral duty. The status of leading colonial women within their own communities was enhanced by the cultivation of visible interconnectedness with the British social elite. The tensions between inborn closeness and inevitably unequal status roles within the imperial family could be comfortably avoided for much of the time. Membership of the family, and its united strength and glory, was what counted. But the detailed work of joint organization by British and colonial female imperialist associations sometimes tested such uplifting abstractions. Sisterly working relations were expected by the organized women of the Dominions. Maternal superiority was frequently all that British lady imperialists had to offer.

One manifestation of superiority was a complacent ignorance of the developing Empire's diversity. British imperialists generally devoted less effort to educating themselves than to educating others, relying for their information upon their own and their acquaintances' very partial experience of Empire, and using such information to bolster universalizing concepts of imperial work. Most lady imperialists had little understanding of colonial nationalism and even less sympathy for it. Yet by the early twentieth century its impact was profound both upon gender relations within the emergent Dominions, and upon their perceptions of a shared imperial future. The colonial female imperialist associations were the outcome of a complex interplay of nationalism, imperialism and gender which was experienced differently in widely differing settings. Colonial women were both subjects and objects within the nation-building process signified (though far from completed) by the confederation of Canada in 1867, of Australia in 1900 and of South Africa in 1910, and by the granting of Dominion status to each of these new nations, together with New Zealand in 1907. Recent theoretical work on gender and nationalism has uncovered the key roles which women have played as repositories of national honour, as symbols of national aspiration, as guardians of national tradition and as the biological bearers of the nation's future.[1] Though the weight of such responsibilities has often cast women into the role of suffering victims, in the context of Dominion nation-building in the late nineteenth and early twentieth centuries the same responsibilities could evidently empower some women. Whether or not they became active agents of patriotism and imperialism, women of the Dominions led lives which were shaped by national (and nationalist) expectations of their gender role. All too frequently, British lady imperialists failed to grasp the national contexts of colonial imperialism, assuming instead that imperial loyalty was primarily a British export reinforced by universal moral ideals. There is clearly some danger of replicating these assumptions in a study based upon British evidence, and focused on the British female imperialists' outward relations rather than upon the colonial imperialists' own associations. Organized colonial imperialism is only now beginning to acquire its own published histories. There is abundant recent work on many other aspects of gender and nation-building in the former Empire, however, and readers are referred to this literature for a fuller discussion of the different Dominion contexts into which British imperialist interventions were received.[2]

Even the briefest glance at Dominion history reveals variety and contrasts. Yet it remains possible to identify certain shared historical characteristics which made feasible the development of organized female imperialism in every Dominion, and the further achievement of (usually imperfect) alliances with the British ladies' associations. The advance of British settlement and the imposition of new forms of British rule were generally influenced more strongly by the characteristics of the colonial setting than by the colonizing or imperializing will of the metropolitan power. Canada was Britain's first Dominion. It achieved self-governing status through a process begun in 1839, but the confederation of 1867 in fact preceded the nation-building challenges of northern and westward expansion, southern and eastern industrialization, and an inrush of settlers from Europe and Asia. The task of forging a national identity under the aegis of British rule, but through processes and experiences over which the imperial government exercised little control, was replicated in Australasia and eventually in early-twentieth-century South Africa. The nationhood of the Dominions was as much (or more) the outcome of their positive response to perceived combinations of economic opportunity, internal division and external threat as it was a result of any form of British cultural or political leadership. Idealism and pragmatism intertwined within emergent Dominion nationalism. An admired cultural heritage was one potentially useful ingredient within an imperial system which could also provide vital economic and strategic advantages for the foreseeable future. The South African War gave new meanings to the 'tie of common blood' as British troops fought alongside 16,000 Australians, 7000 Canadians and 6000 New Zealanders,[3] but imperial unity would only develop and flourish to the extent that its constituent nations continued to perceive reciprocal advantages. During the Edwardian gatherings of Dominion premiers, British imperialists were already encountering the limitations as well as the potential powers of a united Empire.

Meanwhile, gender relations in each of the Dominions intersected with issues of nationality, ethnicity and social class. There is strong evidence from Canada and Australasia of a late-nineteenth-century nationalist prescription of female roles which prioritized home-building and mothering duties. The white women of the Dominions, and especially those of British origin, played a full part in fostering this patriotic self-image, projected in new and empowering forms through national women's organizations centred on 'practical' women's work. The Women's Christian Temperance Union became an important organization in all the 'white settler' colonies during the 1880s, drawing together women around a broad programme of social and moral reform and instilling confidence in their ability to self-organize. Together with regional and local organizations, it provided the basis for the formation of National Councils of Women in the 1890s, to be followed by the gradual emergence of an international women's movement in which Dominion representatives played a prominent part. Social reform movements interacted with nascent suffrage and political organizations in each of the Dominions, drawing motivation and strength from women's broadening educational opportunities and the improved communications systems of gradually urbanizing, industrializing societies.

The links between women's organizations and patriotism were strengthened by their role in consolidating the racism inherent in the British colonial project, which is analysed more fully in Chapter 7. The exclusionary racial policies of the Dominions depended, at a fundamental level, upon white women's participation in the biological and cultural tasks of nation-building. Such participation was readily offered. Though there were debates and divisions among the white women of each of the Dominions, notably in relation to social class, recent feminist histories suggest that large numbers of women can justifiably be described as 'both colonised and colonising'.[4] They experienced the subordination, as well as the oft-proclaimed blessings, of British rule. At the same time they asserted gendered solidarity and power over 'inferior' and 'primitive' racial others through their embrace of white motherhood and their corresponding rejection of potential alliances with oppressed indigenous women. By the early twentieth century a growing minority were proudly conscious of themselves as both nation-builders and Empire-builders. The inherent contradictions and worries of this dual allegiance were as yet barely perceived. British lady imperialists looked to this constituency for their overseas allies. They did not look in vain, for the burgeoning middle-class women's organizations in the Dominions already included, in the early 1900s, several which were primarily devoted to advancing Dominion patriotism through appropriate branches of women's work for the Empire.

There was thus more than a purely idealistic basis for optimism that British and colonial women could work together successfully in the Empire's cause. But the terms of such a partnership remained to be negotiated anew between the organizations and the individual women involved in each separate initiative. It was at the point of detailed delivery that tensions sometimes emerged, and interesting evidence survives of the underlying reasons. First among these was the limited knowledge and the in-built sense of superiority of leading British ladies. When Empire visitors to London were described as 'colonials' the term was not usually meant, or taken, as a compliment. It ignored national identity and personal qualities, and strongly implied an absence of social polish. For the ladies of the British imperialist associations, social polish was important. Those who had spent periods of time in the colonies, usually in support of a husband's tour of imperial duty, seem to have developed a heightened sensitivity to its absence. Social etiquette was an important boundary marker in colonial settings as well as in London Society, and those occupying the status of 'Governor's Lady' had plenty of opportunity to comment upon solecisms. Lady Tennyson described to her mother the 'homespun' behaviour of the Lady Mayoress of Melbourne, who failed to curtsey to visiting royalty despite 'her importance and bliss over her position, and her attempt at grandeur, and absolute good nature with it all'.[5] Lady Jersey cut the New South Wales Premier, Sir Henry Parkes, smartly down to size as 'a remarkable character in his way. He was the son of a small farmer on my grandmother's property at Stoneleigh, where he attended the village school . . . I fear the education given him in Stoneleigh School had not altogether overcome a certain difficulty with his "h's".' Sir Henry filled Sydney's parks with 'statues and busts more notable for quantity than quality': a display of wealth and of aspiration to high culture which she considered reprehensible in a *nouveau riche* 'colonial'.[6] The large number of Governors' ladies on the Victoria League Council included, apart from Lady Tennyson and Lady Jersey: Lady Hopetown and Lady Northcote from Australia; Lady Onslow, Lady Ranfurly and Lady Islington from New Zealand; and Lady Minto and the Countess Grey from Canada. Maud Selborne dutifully filled the equivalent post in South Africa from 1905 to 1910, leaving a particularly full record of her scathing views on the outlook and behaviour of 'colonial' ladies. This did not, of course, disqualify her from a leading Victoria League role which she took up as soon as she returned to England. The finest achievement of such links was celebrated in April 1914, when the Victoria League threw a joint party for departing

Australian and South African Governors-General whose wives had both served for many years on the London executive committee.[7]

The British imperialists did not rely entirely upon such high-level appointments to develop personal communication with the 'colonials'. Emigration organizers were among the first to feel it their duty to establish firsthand knowledge through personal contact. Maria Rye blazed the trail with her 1862 voyage to New Zealand, to be followed twenty years later by Ellen Joyce's almost equally adventurous expedition across the Canadian West. Traditions of travel persisted into the Edwardian years, for by this date there were many overseas organizations which were willing to offer a hospitable welcome and (in the British view at least) likely to benefit from the travellers' advice. A considerable number of imperialist ladies undertook prolonged 'tours' on behalf of their associations, providing valuable journalistic copy as they did so. Canada was toured by Miss Vernon in 1904, Miss Saunders in 1906, Miss Lefroy in 1907 and Miss Williams in 1909 ('Miss Williams penetrating as far as Alaska').[8] Another emigrator, Miss Sykes of the Colonial Intelligence League, toured in 1911 and 1913. Meanwhile, for the Girls' Friendly Society, Miss Beckwith visited South Africa in 1904 and Lady Knightley in 1905. For the Victoria League, Mrs Fawcett revisited South Africa in 1903 (after her famous tour of the concentration camps two years earlier), while the 1901 Annual Report notes the semi-private visits of Violet Markham to Canada, Margaret Jersey to Australia and Mary Hervey to South Africa. In 1909 the League's Secretary, Meriel Talbot, began the meticulously diarized 'World Tour' which will be discussed later in this chapter. In between tours, resident British correspondents in the Dominions supplied contacts and information to supplement that obtainable from colonial visitors in London.

Despite the breadth of these contacts, it is inescapably true that most British imperialists followed the lead of Lady Jersey and Lady Selborne in regarding Britain as the yardstick both of good manners and of sound organizational methods. The very different perspective of the colonial imperialist associations is evident, even from the rather scant collection of their records which has survived in British hands. It was inevitable that the meeting points between British and colonial associations would become a site of conflict as well as of co-operation. Both conflict and co-operation are most fully revealed in the records of the Victoria League, whose inaugural aims had pledged collaborative work with 'such bodies of a similar nature as already exist, or as shall hereafter be formed, in other parts of the Empire'.[9] In contrast, the other female imperialist societies built and formalized their overseas relationships on a cautious, pragmatic basis. The Primrose League developed some overseas Habitations which were mere expatriate offshoots and of no particular significance for the organization as a whole. The emigration associations plainly had a strong need for colonial links, but were reluctant to take on direct organizational or financial responsibility for providing them. The result was a catholic choice of partners, including compliant government agencies and private patrons, and branches of loosely allied organizations such as the Girls' Friendly Society and the Young Women's Christian Association, as well as some specially constructed reception committees at the main ports of arrival. This approach did not preclude a certain amount of sniping between London committees (which knew best) and their overseas allies. The Girls' Friendly Society chose a different strategy as it moved with impressive speed into large-scale colonial organization linked initially to its emigration work. The Girls' Friendly Society system of treaties with colonial branches was intended to pre-empt conflict by establishing British-defined ground rules, and seems to have been fairly successful in doing so.

The Victoria League, on the other hand, suffered the consequence of issuing an open invitation to collaborators without clearly determining an acceptable basis for joint work. It found itself somewhat uncomfortably co-operating with colonial organizations which shared its wartime origins and purported to share its imperialist outlook, but which also prided themselves on independent national roots. The Canadian Daughters of the Empire, for example, originated in the mind of Margaret Polson Murray during a visit to England in 1899. On the one hand, as a long-standing Canadian resident, she was shocked and offended by English women's ignorance of 'the ways of the Western world – this lack of knowledge she felt, was a detriment to both British and Canadian women'. On the other hand, she noted that patriotic Canadian women 'were anxious to help on the home front but were handicapped by lack of channels through which to work'.

Organized female imperialism was clearly the answer, so 'upon her return to Canada she resolved to form an organisation based on the foundations of Patriotism, Loyalty and Service'.[10] Canadian women were to emulate the finest qualities of patriotic British women, while at the same time dispelling their ignorance of the colonies. From the outset the Imperial Order Daughters of the Empire (IODE) visualized an Empire-wide organization, to consist of multiple National Chapters linked to an Imperial Chapter which would be formed eventually in London. In the absence of the latter, the Canadian National Chapter willingly assumed responsibility as 'Head of the Order' for promoting organization at home and overseas. A constitution was drawn up in 1901 and a badge adopted which cleverly symbolized a relationship of united sisterhood:

> It is a seven pointed star on a dark blue ground and is encircled by the name of the Order in gold lettering on a white ground. The seven points of the star represent seven divisions of the British Empire: The British Isles, Canada, India, New Zealand, South Africa, Australia, and the British West Indies . . . The whole is surrounded by a white band which firmly binds all members of the Order in unity of purpose and in loyalty to the Crown which surmounts the Badge.[11]

It is not difficult to visualize the lack of enthusiasm which such plans aroused among the ladies of the British Victoria League. While they welcomed IODE as a prospective affiliate, they had no intention of surrendering their own prerogative for British and worldwide organization. The executive committee hastily consulted Lady Minto (as the Governor's Lady on the spot) about IODE's credentials, before deciding upon a strategy to outface Mrs Murray during her visit to London in June 1901. She was received at the Victoria League office by Margaret Jersey and Edith Lyttelton, flanked by two (loyal) South African delegates:

> Mrs Murray gave a full account of her work . . . and said she had come to England to form an important central committee in London, and at first did not seem disposed to work with the Victoria League in the matter. Lady Jersey made a statement as to the present position of the Victoria League in London, and that she hoped they might come to some arrangement of co-operation with Mrs Murray and her League.[12]

The South African ladies dutifully made it clear that their organization preferred alliance with the Victoria League to joining forces with Mrs Murray. At a second meeting Edith Lyttelton was joined by Violet Cecil, and Dorothea Fairbridge, founder of the South African Guild of Loyal Women. Mrs Murray had little alternative other than a nominal capitulation, recorded triumphantly in the Victoria League's Minute Book:

> Results: abandonment of Mrs Clarke Murray of her original idea to form a big London Committee. Willingness to propose the Daughters of the Empire League as an allied association of the Victoria League, and to co-operate in every possible way.[13]

This was only the beginning of a difficult relationship. The Daughters of the Empire continued to aspire to international organization and therefore to resent the steam-roller approach of the Victoria League executive. IODE Chapters were formed in Bermuda and the Bahamas, and a sister organization was launched for British citizens in the United States. Splits and conflicts within the Canadian Chapter were closely related to the London League's stance of superiority. In October 1901 Lady Jersey received a letter from Lady de Blaquière informing her that Mrs Murray had resigned as IODE Secretary; that she had misrepresented the Victoria League as 'hostile'; and that she now headed 'a committee of uninfluential people in Montreal *only*'.[14] However, the Victoria League failed to reach full agreement with either branch of the Canadian organization. In April 1902 the British ladies rejected the latest IODE proposals, and instead decided 'for the present no agreement should be signed, but that a friendly alliance should be entered upon'.[15] Lady Jersey's London meeting with Lady Minto in June 1902 failed to improve matters; not surprisingly, since the latter was by this time involved in her own fight with IODE over who should control fund-raising to protect the graves of Canadian soldiers in South Africa.

Nevertheless, the Victoria League remained somewhat shakily in contact with IODE over the next few years, and IODE itself was able to build a Canadian base which has lasted until the present day. When the Victoria League began to publish annual news from overseas allies in its reports, IODE was boastfully present. In 1907, 'The Imperial Order of Daughters of the Empire numbers 101 chapters, situated not only in the Dominion of Canada, where they extend from Prince Edward Island to British Columbia, but also in India, the West Indies, and the Bahamas.' Members were 'reading on Imperial topics', forming children's Chapters in schools, distributing Union Jacks, caring for war veterans, welcoming immigrants, and funding causes in Jamaica and India. Prizes had been offered in high schools for 'the best essay on "Queen Victoria: her life and reign"', and the Minister of Education had approved IODE 'Patriotic and Imperial programmes for use in schools on the last Friday of each month'.[16] Many of these activities were similar to work undertaken by the Victoria League, but the tone of the IODE reports remained proudly distinctive even after Meriel Talbot had encompassed Canada in her World Tour. Among the Order's distinctive policies were its enthusiasm for including India and the West Indies within its organization; and its insistence that women's work for the Empire should be undertaken by women-only societies, though with the ultimate purpose of strengthening and complementing the work of male nation-builders and imperialists.

The South African Guild of Loyal Women had as good a claim as IODE to have been first on the scene, and therefore to resist being taken under the Victoria League's wing. However, the League's formation was so closely tied to the South African War that there was much less probability of conflict, at least in the early years. We have noted that Violet Markham, Edith Lyttelton and Violet Cecil were all introduced to Dorothea Fairbridge during their Cape Town visits. As a third-generation British settler and daughter of a distinguished lawyer, scholar and Cape politician, Miss Fairbridge was widely respected as a pillar of the colonial establishment. Her decision to form the Guild of Loyal Women in 1900 was based upon her perception of women's prospective contribution to 'loyal' nation-building, as well as upon the evident need for their practical services during wartime. By September 1900 the Guild claimed 5000 members, half of them Dutch. When Miss Fairbridge entertained Edith Lyttelton to lunch, their conversation centred upon its work in schools where 'the most atrocious lies' were being taught by Boer teachers.[17] Violet Cecil paid tribute to Miss Fairbridge as 'fertile in ideas and tactful in suggestion',[18] and these qualities no doubt helped her to convince her visitors of the need for a London-based association. However, the gulf in social class status between the leaders of the League and those of the Guild soon threatened to become an obstacle. After the Downing Street inaugural ceremony, Violet Cecil commented in her diary on the over-familiarity of the South African delegate: 'She comes of missionary stock and addressed the assembled great ladies as "My loving sisters" and also spoke of my coming baby as a "loving link of Empire" to my confusion, and to the entertainment of my friends.' After the first executive committee meeting, 'the delegate came to tea. She is copious, impracticable, well-meaning and infinitely comic. She has suggested that we should all have red, white and blue visiting cards.'[19]

This colonial lack of poise had not, however, prevented the Guild from organizing several successful meetings in England before the Victoria League launch. It is interesting to discover that the Guild was able (and willing) to transfer its British members into the League's care; and that within six weeks of the launch 'Mrs Burridge of the GLW' had started a branch in Kent, raised £45 for the Guild at a meeting in Bexley, and was planning further meetings in Dartford and Bournemouth.[20] There was little danger of an attempted Guild takeover of the Victoria League's British work, however. The League was fully prepared to devote its energies in wartime to South Africa's cause, and its overwhelming advantages in terms of wealth and social and political prestige must have been very evident to Guild visitors. Co-operation over South African graves and refugee funds proceeded smoothly enough, despite the occasional snub. When a Guild representative suggested that 'some ladies of the League should go down as a deputation to meet Miss Fairbridge of the GLW at Southampton on her arrival from South Africa', the executive decided 'to express a wish that they might make the acquaintance of Miss Fairbridge at some future date'; and a Guild proposal to seek early royal patronage received an even blunter refusal.[21] There was also evident reluctance to trust the Guild with full oversight of the disbursement of the various South African funds. In June 1901 three executive members 'offered themselves to go to South Africa if thought advisable', and a few months later Georgina Frere did in fact depart there on a Victoria League mission of enquiry. She returned with praise for the Guild's work.[22]

The real test of the relationship between the League and the Guild came as the war receded into the past and the League began to develop new priorities. Meanwhile, the Guild continued to wrestle with the political and racial antagonisms of South Africa, rendered no less intractable by a destructive war which had been fought to a standstill rather than won or lost. Victoria League condescension was perhaps the least of the Guild's problems as its leaders and members struggled to carry out 'practical' patriotic work amidst a fast-changing political landscape. During 1903 heroic efforts were made to anticipate an imperial South African Union by drawing together Guild branches in the four colonies within a functioning federal organization. Representatives from Cape Colony, Natal, Transvaal and Orange River met at Pietermaritzburg to review the previous three years' achievements and to plan ahead. Debate centred on a federal constitution designed to relaunch the Guild as 'an organisation of women workers for the future, a power for good and usefulness when we have all ceased to be'. Delegates were urged to exercise 'self-control' and to attempt 'to see what is best, not for us or our Colony, but for South Africa and the Empire to which we belong'. Despite some suggestions that the whole federal attempt should be abandoned, a provisional agreement was eventually reached on a constitution and a 'Scheme of Work' covering patriotic education, benevolent work and the care of soldiers' graves.[23]

Gratitude was expressed for 'the channels of usefulness that are constantly being opened up for us by that excellent body in London the Victoria League'; but during the next few years the British organizations seem to have been unusually reluctant to intervene with direct guidance and advice. On at least one occasion the Victoria League executive turned down an invitation to take sides.[24] The dispute over a possible name change for the Guild was linked to ongoing South African debates over self-government, union, and relations between the British and the Dutch, and perhaps the British women felt reluctant to become involved in such divisive politics. Instead, they preferred to offer general support for the 'practical' work of the Guild, in the hope that such activities would indirectly strengthen its sense of imperial mission. A federal report of 1908 indicates both the modest success of philanthropic and educational projects (some of which were benefiting from Maud Selborne's patronage) and the scale of the political obstacles to effective joint work. 'South Africa is passing through a critical period,' wrote the Federal Secretary. 'There is a breathless pause experienced by individuals and organisations alike . . . We look forward to emerging from the turmoil and unrest a united nation eager to do a nation's work, fit to take our place in the civilisation and progress of the world.'[25]

Australian imperialist associations faced fewer obstacles, but also had fewer incentives to achieve a united approach to organization. During the 1900s there were various potential antipodean partners for the British Victoria League. A number of Australian women's organizations were committed to developing female forms of politics which would transcend old-style party politics, in the wake of the successful achievement of the (white) female vote. As Rose Scott, the leading feminist and suffragist, put it, 'We women must bring a new element into political life, an element which no sectional party can represent . . . Remember that a woman's mission is to inspire man and to help him build up our young nation upon all that is righteous.'[26] Such moral force politics could be appropriated to imperialism as well as to nationalism. Women were naturally an attractive target for all the political parties. In 1904 an Australian Women's National League was founded in Melbourne, mainly as a Liberal 'front', but stating its aims as 'To support loyalty to the throne and Empire', 'To combat socialism', 'To educate women in politics' and 'To safeguard the interests of the home, women and children'.[27] This organization rapidly achieved a membership of 10,000, but its priorities remained firmly focused on Australian politics.

The British Empire League, on the other hand, was as anxious to ally itself with the British Victoria League in Australia as it was in Britain. It was also more successful. Fears of a possible 'takeover' of Victoria League leadership in London did not apply to an organization on the other side of the world, and during the 1900s a number of Australian BEL branches were welcomed into friendly alliance with the British Victoria League. However, the Australian BEL was less than overjoyed to observe the gradual appearance of parallel organizations in both Australia and New Zealand bearing the Victoria League's own title. The Victoria League of Tasmania prided itself upon being the oldest such true ally. Its co-operation was noted in the Victoria League Annual Report of 1904, and three years later it claimed nearly 1000 members and the active patronage of the Governor and the Governor's Lady, Lady Edeline Strickland. The seventh Annual Report of the Victoria League carried accounts of branches in Wellington and Otago, New Zealand, as well as noting further progress in Tasmania and the formation of a Melbourne branch. The Victoria League of Victoria was founded on Empire Day 1908, and grew vigorously along lines close to the London organization. By 1912 to 1913 the doubly Victorian association was (appropriately) the largest in Australia, with a membership of 1200, a number of satellite branches, and a full range of education, hospitality and literature committees.[28]

Among the influences which produced this impressive outcome must be numbered Meriel Talbot's World Tour. 'The principal event of the year has been Miss Talbot's visit', noted the Melbourne Victoria League in the expanding 'Reports from Overseas' section of the London League's eighth Annual Report.[29] This sentiment was gratefully (and dutifully) echoed from around the Empire. Fortunately, we are not totally reliant upon such published reports for an account of the genesis, progress and outcomes of the League Secretary's marathon expedition. Meriel Talbot kept both official and private diaries during her tour. The latter provided an outlet for her less publishable views, while the former kept the Victoria League executive fully informed and formed the basis of monthly reports in the *Victoria League Notes*. The official aims of the tour were summarized in the League's eighth Annual Report:

> Miss Talbot's instructions were to confer with the Victoria Leagues and Allied Associations in those portions of the Empire; to explain to them the operations and ideas of the Central League and its Branches at home; and to place her services at the disposal of those whom she visited with a view to furthering the common cause.[30]

The gathering of firsthand information about the Empire was also regarded as an important duty. However, there could be little doubt where the balance lay between teaching and learning, advising and listening. As a later published account of Victoria League work put it, the tour 'helped to bring into the line the work of the Allied Societies overseas with that which is being done in the home country'.[31]

Meriel Talbot was well-equipped for such a task, both personally and professionally. A vigorous unmarried woman in her mid-forties, she combined determination, courage and a sense of humour with a range of interests which included social and health reforms, Anglicanism, music and cricket. Privately educated herself, though with many distinguished and intellectual relatives, she lacked any formal training for her responsible role but had already acquired a high level of diplomatic and administrative skills during eight years at the Victoria League Central Office. In the context of Edwardian Empire-building, her upper-class self-assurance was probably as valuable an attribute as any, coupled with the physical stamina to withstand endless journeys and meetings. At the Victoria League's Annual General Meeting in 1910 she described with gusto how

> she had been over 33,000 miles of sea and land, and had slept in sixty different beds during the thirty weeks on land, besides eleven nights spent on the train. Except for two days spent in Boston, USA, and one at Honolulu, the whole of the journey had been under the protection of the British Flag.[32]

This first nine-month epic from September 1909 to June 1910 took her round Australia and New Zealand and across Canada. It was to be followed by an almost equally gruelling second journey round South Africa from September 1910 to April 1911.

The Australian leg of the tour brought Meriel Talbot into contact for the first time with 'colonials' in their native surroundings. Eager to commence firsthand learning straightaway, she chafed at the 'quenching effect' of Government House hospitality on her arrival in Perth.[33] However, the advantages to her mission of such high-status patronage soon became apparent. The Governor and the Governor's wife were readily convinced of the Victoria League's importance; there was the opportunity to mingle with and proselytize among the Governor's many guests, and the Government House Ballroom was a splendid venue for the first of dozens of meetings. As the guest of Lord and Lady Carmichael in Melbourne, she was later to comment gratefully on 'the regal ease of every going out and coming in when one is attached to a Governor'.[34] Ambivalence over privileged social status became a sustained theme throughout the tour, and was reflected back into aspects of the British Victoria League's work over the following years. Meriel Talbot clearly prided herself upon her well-informed professionalism. For her, imperialism was more than mere sentimental patriotism linked with an aristocratic sense of feminine duty. It was above all a rational political choice, closely bound into social and educational issues which were integral to national greatness and a stable, prosperous world order. She often laughed at minor snobberies, even mildly ridiculing the majestic bearing of Lord and Lady Jersey on more than one occasion. Australian freedom from hidebound social customs was an enjoyable novelty. When she escaped from Government House on an initial foray to the mining town of Kalgoorie she revelled in 'seeing all sorts and conditions of people', visiting a state school, descending a mine shaft, and later lunching with potential leaders of a new Victoria League branch:

> We six women sat down to a homely meal and real sport in the way of friendly chaff among them all, and inimitable stories of the typical Australian in London . . . They were all Australian-born, never been home. With a strong feeling for it. With go, and pluck and humour. How the family would have laughed if they could have looked in on us. No servant in the house at all. It's quite a chance here apparently if you get them or not. It was a really refreshing atmosphere in many ways.[35]

To add to their virtues, a majority of these egalitarians were 'strong advocates of Woman Suffrage though disapproving of the extremists'. Such self-reliant, competent women would form the bedrock of the broad-based Australian Victoria League.

Nevertheless, Meriel also continued to benefit from the deference which her own social status inspired among many 'colonials'. In Tasmania a few months later she noted, 'I'm getting quite to take the "first lady" place as a matter of course now and to find all doors opening before me!' On the same evening she attended a Victoria League reception at the Masonic Hall:

> I was brought in late by Colonel Cameron, the sort of Kitchener of Tasmania, and led to a carpet where each guest was brought up and introduced – 'presented' to me – some of the dear dim little people almost curtsied! It was all very nicely done – the Hall decorated with red, white and blue flowers and hangings and a great Union Jack behind the little dais place.[36]

Despite her dislike of 'the Push' (as she nicknamed Melbourne's social climbers), Meriel's social class expectations remained deeply ingrained. Servants were essential to a comfortable life; ladies and gentlemen did not do their own cooking and serving; and both snobbery and deference were laughable largely because they were poor Australian imitations. Mingled admiration and condescension influenced Meriel Talbot's interventions into the organization of Australian female imperialism. Even before she left her ship at Fremantle she had received a letter from the Perth correspondent of *The Times*, warning her off interference with existing bodies such as the League of the Empire and the British Empire League in South Australia and New South Wales. Over the weeks that followed she certainly appears to have refrained from open criticism of existing arrangements, concentrating instead upon forming Victoria League branches in new areas, and supplementing those which already existed.

In New Zealand, however, the volume of her criticisms grew. The initial glamour of her encounter with colonial societies and with wide, 'unpeopled' spaces had perhaps worn off. In addition, her confidence in handling unfamiliar audiences and committees was growing. In February 1910 she arrived at Dunedin to a welcome from the Victoria League of Otago. Prominent local citizens appeared at an evening reception, including the Mayor:

> We went away arm-in-arm to the platform steps, the Mayoress, the shyest of little plumber's wives, following in her pathetic little Sunday gown with Sir Jas. Mills the great shipping man here . . . After the Mayor's somewhat hesitating words, I rose attired in one of my best evening gowns, and was touched by the round of applause – the Australians always waited till they had had something before doing that!

After her speech, 'various men spoke in praise of the Victoria League and in welcome to me . . . As usual no woman dared uplift her voice – No one need fear that the franchise makes women yearn to be on platforms – There are far fewer over here than at home.'[37] The substance of several later criticisms was reflected in this account. Social ineptitude allied to pretentiousness was becoming slightly tiresome. Prominent (male) citizens had their uses, but the Victoria League needed to reach beyond them to encompass a broader stratum of the public who had a more varied and interesting loyalty to the Empire. And, of course, women needed to be taught to make fuller use of their organizing powers. The warmth of the New Zealanders' welcome made such teaching a practicable task.

The following day, Meriel Talbot received cabled news of her father's sudden death, but she assuaged her grief in a flurry of meetings, mostly at her own request. A Labour member of the Upper House ('which sounds strange to English ears') was successfully persuaded 'that the Victoria League is interested in that side of things too'.[38] On 7 February 1910 a second large meeting was much more to Meriel's taste: 'We had been working up the Friendly Societies and Labour People and the general public, so as to get rid of the silly idea that the VL is a classy sort of thing.' An audience of 200 people filled the Early Settlers Hall, and were 'delightfully attentive' to a fifty-minute speech from Miss Talbot on 'the real purpose of the League and its practical work as it affects all classes'. Male bombast was absent and there was 'a nice business-like feeling about it all'. Two days later she attended a local Victoria League executive meeting: 'Got them to suggest men members on the committee and general reorganisation and broadening. All very nice and responsive, and harmonious altogether . . . Suggested the abolition of Vice Presidents in the presence of three of them!' Her diary entry ended with further reflections upon women's role: 'The *retiringness* of women and the want of nerve in anything like public speaking strikes me very much out here. Old-fashioned and conventional – very funny. It knocks one of the many fears about women's suffrage clean out.'[39] The solution was not to promote the Victoria League as a sheltered, all-female enclave. Male 'influence' was needed, the imperialist cause was one for both men and women, and women organizers could best be drawn out of their shells by working alongside able and sympathetic men.

During the remainder of her New Zealand visit, the same improvements were consistently advocated and generally welcomed. Meriel demonstrated her interest in 'broadening' by visiting factories, farms, clinics and schools, in the process developing the ideas which were to underlie the British Victoria League's own (slightly half-hearted) efforts to break down class barriers within imperialism between 1911 and 1914. At a Dunedin woollen factory she found a universal eight-hour day, a workforce of girls earning good wages, and an employer who responded to her account of the British Anti-Sweating campaign with the comment: 'We've none of that here – I sometimes wish they'd sweat more!'[40] She developed a strong admiration for the child health reformer Dr Truby King, after hearing him lecture on 'the uniform law governing the nutrition of plants, animals and babies. Deeply interesting . . . It's an imperial subject really and no mistake.'[41] Four years later Dr King was an important figure at the Victoria League's imperial health conference in London. Meanwhile, there were opportunities to put new firsthand knowledge to instant use during the train journey to Napier, when Meriel 'made friends with a nice baby, and urged the mother to give up the infamous "comforter"!'[42] Napier's Maori girls' school was another interesting experience:

> Their Maori teacher was persuaded to let them sing . . . I then spoke to them for a few
> minutes – just about the respect and affection felt for their race by our rulers, and of how
> we were all subjects of the same king, under the providence of the same God and Saviour.

Meriel was 'greatly struck by the seriousness and natural dignity of many of them', and by the fact that 'marriage with white people' was widely accepted.[43] But her own relatively liberal attitudes on this subject did not diminish her general willingness to go along with the attitudes of local white people towards the native peoples of Australia, New Zealand and Canada. She was unable to empathize at anything other than a very superficial level with the aspirations of those whom she clearly regarded (at best) as picturesque survivals from earlier history, rather than as future active citizens of the Dominions.

Another welcoming Governor awaited Meriel Talbot in Wellington:

> Governors are nothing new to me now! and we were soon deep in talk on the Victoria League and affairs of state . . . He was quite with me in wishing to get it into hands here other than the 'Push' – the class distinctions and prejudices in a place like this are very strong and quite ludicrous, for they are obviously artificial.[44]

This forthright conclusion on social class and leadership failed to diminish Meriel's own tendency to note class distinction at every turn. 'Well-bred' was a compliment merited by few New Zealand women; 'a pleasant enough woman, but no pretence of a lady' was kindly meant, since it absolved the person concerned from the sins of false snobbery; but in her heart of hearts Miss Talbot sympathized with her sister's castigation of Australia as the 'gigantic servants hall'.[45] The paradoxical shortage of real servants was of continuing concern to her, since their lack 'means real trouble in many otherwise happy homes'.[46] So, too, was 'the way men herd with men and women with women out here', though in Auckland she was delighted to find a Victoria League branch run by 'men and women, carefully planned committees, really excellent'. This was attributable to an Hon. Secretary who 'knows what business means unlike others of her kind in these countries'.[47] The Dunedin shipping magnate Sir James Mills proved his value to the Victoria League by securing the best cabin for the weary traveller during her voyage through the South Seas and on to Canada.

The Canadian leg of the tour was to prove in many ways the most testing. As Miss Talbot's nostalgia for upper-class creature-comforts grew, their availability further diminished. British government hospitality was thin on the ground, and there was no certainty of welcoming Canadian audiences to compensate. An interesting scene occurred at Vernon, where Meriel and her faithful attendant disembarked from the Canadian Pacific Railway only to find that 'A maid was clearly not expected, so C. went off rather gloomily to a Commercial Hotel hardby, which one driver assured me was quite respectable'. This turned out not to be the case, with the result that 'C.' later covered many miles on foot to rejoin her mistress. The following day Meriel mused in her diary about the possibilities of 'Victoria League hostels' in western Canada for intending servants: 'It would obviously be a real boon to the girls, bring many more of the right sort into the country, and do something to solve the pressing servant problem in the colonies.'[48] To add to her problems, Meriel Talbot coincidentally found Mrs Ord Marshall, Secretary of the rival British League of the Empire, 'ahead of me in Calgary and gulling many as usual'.[49] There were several farcical near-misses as the two imperialists strove to avoid sharing a platform and to justify the distinctiveness of their organizations to mystified Canadians. The business of putting across the Victoria League's methods and ideas recommenced in earnest when Meriel faced sixty school-teachers in a big public school: 'all Canadians, and experts in their own line, and I didn't a bit know their attitude towards imperial things'.[50] A tour of advice-giving gradually became more genuinely a tour of self-education by the Victoria League Secretary. Educational and church leaders were happy to provide her with information on their work, a tour of the Mounties' headquarters at Regina was enjoyed, and everywhere there were British settlers pleased to have an opportunity to tell their stories to a sympathetic listener.

The death of King Edward VII, as Meriel approached Winnipeg, served to heighten prevailing levels of patriotism and to warm the rather cautious welcome extended by local branches of IODE. However, even friendly Daughters of the Empire came in for the familiar criticisms:

> these good women who have banded themselves under the high-sounding name – Daughters of the Empire – have never thought out their work, and all I tell them of the VL practical things seems a new and wonderful revelation to them! Very funny. To find myself addressing Bishops' wives, and school teachers and wives and mothers of Ministers as if they were all children at the game, and I the teacher – makes me often laugh when it's all over.[51]

At Saskatoon the 'D of E people' were 'gloriously vague as usual about the work', and needed to be ticked off for unpunctuality.[52] At Regina, 'Talked with Miss Ross the acting D of E secretary. Given to trances! and I think was in one when I saw her.'[53] A meeting at Fort William turned out to be the epitome of 'Canadian casualness', with chairs unarranged, the Union Jack unhung, and local leaders reluctant to take the platform.[54]

Such minor inconveniences paled alongside the frosty reception awaiting Miss Talbot from the IODE leadership in Toronto. Seven years of sometimes hostile correspondence between the secretaries of the two organizations had paved the way for a face-to-face meeting: 'An important moment, for the VL has had many difficulties with this lady, and much of our future work in Canada depends on how I can make her see one or two things.' At first Mrs Nordheimer 'talked quite ceaselessly, and I think was somewhat nervous of my presence!' The following day other IODE ladies joined the pair for a luncheon:

> The atmosphere somewhat tense. After luncheon I talked a little of our VL work. Mrs N inflammatory – ready to suggest that D of E was doing all and more – and no apparent interest in hearing of any other society. Some of her colleagues obviously more interested. Felt inclined to be warlike every now and then.[55]

At this intriguing point Meriel Talbot's Canadian diary unfortunately comes to an abrupt halt. Published information suggests that civilities were more or less preserved, and that Meriel survived a week in Toronto before fleeing to the doubtless more congenial hospitality of Government House, Ottawa. After the briefest of visits to Montreal, Boston and Quebec, she sailed for home.

Less than three months later, Miss Talbot was on her way out to South Africa. Her enthusiasm for guiding 'sister' organizations along Victoria League paths remained quite undimmed. In fact the League's executive Minutes make it clear that her brief was to do precisely that. She was instructed to 'work closely' with the Guild of Loyal Women, but 'she should aim at securing the organisation of the work on a broad basis, in which men and women should join, independent of party politics, and do practical work such as is now undertaken by the Victoria League'.[56] Maud Selborne had joined the executive a few weeks previously, and the committee was close enough to South African affairs to understand that the launch of the Union was a make-or-break opportunity for the Guild. Meriel Talbot's arrival was eagerly awaited. The Guild's President was at the Cape Town docks to greet her at 9 o'clock in the morning: 'No breathing space was allowed me, and I was invited to a committee at twelve, and lunch at the Alexandra Club.' Introduced to a dozen waiting ladies at the Guild's office, Meriel 'felt a bit dazed, but said "a few words" and felt they were cordial'. This impression was reinforced over lunch, and the following day when she had a private meeting with Mrs Rawbone, known to be 'the ablest woman at the Cape'. Soon the Victoria League reorganization proposals were on the table, and the two ladies had reached agreement on the fundamentals, assisted no doubt by the discovery of common interests in 'Truby King work among the babies', in women's suffrage, and in various aspects of education.[57] Within a few days Meriel's diary had reached a high point of optimism: 'Nothing could be nicer than the way they take my suggestions and are willing to talk them out . . . It is at present incomparably easier than Canada.'[58]

But some setbacks were only to be expected, given the Guild's pride in its established traditions and the newly unified South Africans' inevitable resistance to over-direction from London. At a Claremont lunch party, 'Miss Fairbridge thawed gradually, but she is stiff with prejudices of all sorts, and I longed to throw bombs.'[59] Debate was lively at a specially summoned Cape Guild committee meeting the day after, a majority supporting Miss Talbot's plan, but 'one or two more sentimental people, and fearful of working with men, deprecated any change'.[60] In the longer term, 'racial feeling' (between Dutch and British) was likely to prove a stronger obstacle than mere sentiment. The Guild had failed to build upon its early success in bridging this divide, and Meriel found herself on hostile territory when she visited a Dutch church bazaar: 'I felt there was a lot of prejudice and misunderstanding, which if we all knew one another better and mixed up more would get far less . . . Oh for the Victoria League out here among them all.'[61] Unfortunately, this simple prescription had far from universal appeal even in Cape Province, and less so in the Orange Free State and Natal, where Meriel was soon travelling and encountering 'that feeling of the colonist at the English ignorance of their point of view'.[62] In November she returned to Cape Town for the royal opening of the new South African parliament, an imperial occasion which helped to sway the Guild in favour of her proposals. Public and private debates continued until a crucial Guild Federal Council meeting in March 1911 finally approved a reform plan along Talbot-inspired lines. The Victoria League's tenth Annual Report records the formal dissolution of the Guild of Loyal Women, and the establishment of a constitutional committee to formulate a new Victoria League of South Africa, based upon the principles of sound practical work, joint organization by men and women and a broad membership. The 'fundamental objects' of the new League were to promote 'a sense of comradeship as fellow-citizens of the British Empire', and 'a sense of comradeship amongst their fellow-subjects in South Africa'.[63]

Meriel Talbot left well-pleased with her success in promoting these changes, but also with a fuller appreciation of the obstacles to achieving an influential and united association. She would not soon forget the frank debates around her proposals (which at least showed South African women to be more articulate than those in other Dominions), nor encounters such as a January 1911 tea with 'five Dutch ladies':

> We all spoke our minds! I felt simply British to the core, as they obviously felt Dutch. It
> was refreshing to get away from the outside civilities and often shown sentiment to the

real feelings. It revealed many things: the sensitiveness of the Dutch in regard to what they conceive to be English contempt for them. Their very natural resentment, but also their unconscious realisation of inferiority in the stress they so often lay on the feeling.

Ignorance and narrowness were compounded by obstinacy over the 'artificial' maintenance of the Dutch language ('to go forward in the world today English happens to be the necessary language'); and if a 'South African nationality' was to emerge from such components it would be 'made as in America from much that is rather mongrel in the past . . . a hodge podge of things and a sorry result, with no distinction or literature'.[64]

Ultimately, therefore, Miss Talbot did complete her tour by reflecting upon nationalism as well as upon imperialism. She concluded that colonial nationalism should be subordinated within an imperialism having its genesis in the superior British (English) nation. This conclusion was most plainly expressed in relation to the South African Boers, but was also relevant to the emergent nationalism of Australians, New Zealanders and Canadians. After observing the 'colonials' at close quarters, the Victoria League Secretary was more convinced than ever of the need for British guidance. She was also more aware of colonial sensitivities. As a result, the British Victoria League spent the next few years facing in two directions: covertly centralizing and promoting common forms of organization among its Dominion allies, while at the same time loudly praising their autonomy. Male supporters of closer imperial federation faced similar dilemmas, and were, of course, intimately associated with the Victoria League ladies. The modest outcomes of the 1911 Imperial Premiers' Conference were paralleled by the Victoria League's detectable disappointment after its own ambitious three-day conference for 'Branches and Allied Associations' at the Imperial Institute in June 1911. As the tenth Annual Report commented: 'Perhaps the largest results of such a gathering are those which cannot be measured in precise terms, but are individually felt . . . It was widely felt that, so far as the formal discussions went, the area was somewhat too wide.' Among the more satisfactory achievements was a carefully qualified agreement on the importance of reciprocity: 'it is highly desirable that, as far as local conditions permit, each Branch and each League should be doing in their several ways the same definite pieces of Imperial work.' It was also agreed that all associations should attempt to broaden their social base; and 'from many parts came testimony to the value of mixed Committees of men and women'.[65]

British debates over imperial unity were heavily influenced between 1911 and 1914 by the looming crisis over Home Rule for Ireland. After the reform of the House of Lords in 1911, eventual Home Rule was widely seen as inevitable, and so threatening to the integrity of the Empire that many patriots and imperialists were prepared to support even military resistance. Here was 'colonial nationalism' at its most destructive. It was unavoidable that parallels should be made with other parts of the Empire, and that the Irish question should heighten general anxieties about achieving strong and lasting forms of imperial unity. Lord Milner led the collection of signatures to a 'British Covenant' pledging drastic action to prevent the implementation of Home Rule. Other diehard opponents with Victoria League connections included Rudyard Kipling, Lord Willoughby de Broke, Lord Selborne and the Cecil brothers.[66] Violet Cecil took up active organization and fund-raising on behalf of Ulster women and children alongside her Victoria League work. The issue was a stern test of the League's 'non-political' stance, since a minority of its Liberal members had come round to supporting the case for Home Rule, and others shrank from supporting incipient army mutiny over the issue.

There was no doubt relief in some quarters that the Victoria League had on several earlier occasions resisted the temptation to set up an Irish organization. However, other female imperialist organizations were less fortunately situated. The emigration societies had a limited Irish involvement (they had been advised by Lord Meath to keep it limited for fear of upsetting nationalists); and the Girls' Friendly Society had quite an extensive network of Irish branches in both the north and the south. Like the Victoria League, these associations seem to have concluded that caution was the better part of valour. Irish involvement in female imperialism was allowed to wither quietly as events in that country moved towards a climax. This was consistent with the female imperialists' enduring policy of centring their work and organizations heavily upon London and London Society. Apart from a small-scale assertion of independence by Scottish emigrators, and a judicious concession of slightly altered rules to the Scottish GFS, there is little evidence of internal dissent from this policy. Prominent Scottish ladies such as Alice Balfour, Helen Munro-Ferguson, Mary Jeune, Elizabeth Haldane and Frances Balfour exercised their influence upon organized female imperialism primarily from their London residences. Though London 'colonization' of the movement undoubtedly grated occasionally, there was little likelihood of Scottish, Irish or Welsh lady imperialists making common cause with the colonial nationalists of the Empire. Socially and politically, they had thrown in their lot with the London-based British establishment.

This option, of course, was never fully on offer to the imperialists of the Dominions, who were invited to identify closely with the British Empire but not to lead it. A 'model' association in the Dominions was one which conformed to dutiful daughterhood by working closely with London and following London's organizational example. How extensively was this relationship achieved, in the wake of Miss Talbot's tour? Once again, over-reliance upon the British Victoria League's own records is likely to be misleading, but the annual reports leading up to the First World War contain extensive reports from the Dominions which provide at least an indication of what Miss Talbot had and had not achieved. Some reports paid her fulsome tributes, while others paid the indirect compliment of describing improvements in organization subsequent to her visit. In several cases Dominion organizations reported very directly the detailed advice she had given and which they were following. A large proportion of the new overseas branches formed between 1909 and 1911 attributed their origins to Miss Talbot, especially in Australia and New Zealand. From South Africa came circumspect progress reports on the wholescale reorganization of 1911, exaggerating the unity of support for the new scheme but omitting to give Miss Talbot's intervention the prominence it deserved. Only from Canada did the Victoria League visitor receive no credit at all. IODE reports continued to record a history of uninterrupted success achieved in the Empire's interests, but on thoroughly Canadian terms. It is interesting to note, however, that a new bout of IODE infighting in December 1911 once again had Victoria League overtones. Mrs Nordheimer and her Secretary resigned after disagreements over constitutional matters and over a hostile report on the Victoria League's London conference. The reconstituted executive passed a 'spontaneous resolution' regretting 'unjust criticisms' and pledging a more harmonious future.[67] The hope remained that IODE members could reconcile their loyalties to nation and Empire, and that they could both follow their own trajectory and sustain a mutually respectful relationship with the ladies of the British Victoria League.

Ultimately, the existence of partnerships (even unequal partnerships) depended upon their usefulness. By 1914 a number of areas of genuinely reciprocal 'practical' work had been developed by all the female imperialist associations in Britain and overseas. Whether the work concerned emigration, education or hospitality, it required close co-operation. The emigration associations and the Girls' Friendly Society were as conscious of this as the Victoria League. From the Dominion viewpoint, such co-operation brought tangible benefits as well as political satisfaction. The 'right sorts' of emigrants were truly welcomed; Canadian or Australian girls were as much in need of the GFS's steadying moral influence as those in Britain; 'Britons' everywhere enjoyed enhanced imperial education; and Victoria League hospitality was a treasured asset, especially when it came from Society's upper crust. A genuine appreciation of mutual benefit helped to hold together overseas alliances as much as shared faith in the Empire's glorious future. The power of imperial sentiment should not be underestimated, moreover. A fair proportion of what was said and written about the Empire's united moral purpose, and its power to achieve peace and prosperity for all its citizens, was deeply believed.

On New Year's Day 1913 Violet Markham was in Bloemfontein, helping to complete the task of shepherding reluctant Guild members into the new South African Victoria League. She took 'the League and its ideals' as the subject of her speech, and directly addressed the relationship between nation and Empire:

> it was a source of pride to the organisation that the Leagues in different countries were self-governing bodies, following the lines of their own individuality. The Empire was a curious and unique development. It was an extraordinary tie that bound five nations together . . . Membership of the Empire gave a wider citizenship and horizon than could be possible to individual nations. There was absolutely no conflict between the spirit of Empire and nationality, for nationality was inseparable from Empire. It was because the nations were so different that they were so strong. But their nationality must stretch out – not look in on itself. They must stretch out the hand of their friendship to the other members of the family.[68]

This was a speech carefully tailored to its audience. It implied an equality between imperial nations which, in practice, the British female imperialists did very little to promote. Had it existed, the South Africans might have been less slow to give up their Guild, and Mrs Nordheimer might not have stormed out of the Canadian IODE. There might also have been less reluctance at Victoria League headquarters to put Dominion branches in touch with each other, rather than merely in touch with British branches. In actuality, the British lady imperialists seldom wavered in their determination to build a worldwide web of daughter associations with the Mother Country's own societies in the leadership position for which social status and imperial destiny had qualified them.

Notes

1. See S. Allen, Chapter 5, 'Race, Ethnicity and Nationality', in H. Afshar and M. Maynard (eds), *The Dynamics of 'Race' and Gender: Some Feminist Interventions* (London: Taylor & Francis, 1994); *Gender and History*, 1993, 5, 2. Special Issue on Gender, Nationalisms and National Identities; M. Maynard and J. Purvis (eds), *New Frontiers in Women's Studies: Knowledge, Identity and Nationalism* (London: Taylor & Francis, 1996); D. Stasiulis and N. Yuval-Davis (eds), *Unsettling Settler Societies* (London: Sage, 1995); N. Yuval-Davis and F. Anthias (eds), *Woman-Nation-State* (London: Macmillan Press, 1989).

2. See B. Brookes, 'Nostalgia for "Innocent Homely Pleasures"', *Gender and History*, 1997, 9, 2; A. Curthoys, 'Identity Crisis: Colonialism, Nation and Gender in Australian History', *Gender and History*, 1993, 5, 2; A. Else (ed.), *Women Together: A History of Women's Organisations in New Zealand* (Wellington: Daphne Bresell Associates Press, 1993); R. Fry, *Maud and Amber: A New Zealand Mother and Daughter and the Women's Cause 1865–1981* (Canterbury, NZ: Canterbury University Press, 1992); N. Grieve and A. Burns, *Australian Women: New Feminist Perspectives* (Australia: OUP, 1986); P. Grimshaw, M. Lake, A. McGrath and M. Quartly, *Creating a Nation 1788–1990* (Victoria: McPhee Gribble, 1994); P. Grimshaw, *Women's Suffrage in New Zealand* (Auckland: Auckland UP, 1987); M. Lake, 'The Inviolable Woman: Feminist Conceptions of Citizenship in Australia, 1900–1945', *Gender and History*, 1996, 8, 2; A. Oldfield, *Woman Suffrage in Australia: A Gift or a Struggle* (Cambridge: Cambridge University Press, 1992); A. Prentice, P. Bourne, P. Brandt, B. Light, W. Mitchinson and N. Black, *Canadian Women: A History* (Toronto: Harcourt Brace, 1988); A. Summers, *Damned Whores and God's Police* (Victoria: Penguin, 1975); D. Stasiulis and N. Yuval-Davis (eds), *Unsettling Settler Societies* (London: Sage, 1995). Chapters by W. Larner and P. Spoonley (Aotearoa/New Zealand), J. Pettman (Australia) and D. Stasiulis and R. Jhappan (Canada); C. Walker, *Women and Gender in South Africa to 1945* (Claremont: David Philip, 1990); *Women's History Review*, 1993, 2, 3. Special Issue on Australian Feminisms, including articles by P. Grimshaw, B. Caine and M. Lake. On organized colonial imperialism, see forthcoming work from Catherine Pickles (history of IODE) and Peter Merrington (Dorothea Fairbridge and South African imperialism).

3. See C. Miller, *Painting the Map Red: Canada and the South African War, 1899–1902* (Quebec: Canadian War Museum, 1993); B. Penny, 'Australia's Reactions to the Boer War: A Study in Colonial Imperialism', *Journal of British Studies*, 1967, 7, 1–2: 97–130.

4. See M. Lake, 'Colonised and Colonising: The White Australian Feminist Subject', *Women's History Review*, 1993, 2, 3: 377–86.

5. Quoted in B. Kingston, 'The Lady and the Australian Girl: Some Thoughts on Nationalism and Class', Chapter 2 in N. Grieve and A. Burns (eds), *Australian Women: New Feminist Perspectives*, 1996, 31–2.

6. M. Villiers, Countess of Jersey, *Fifty-one Years of Victorian Life* (London: John Murray, 1922), pp. 249–50.

7. Victoria League Twelfth Annual Report, 1913 (1914). Lady Helen Munro-Ferguson and Lady Buxton were the Governors' Ladies-to-be.

8. *The Imperial Colonist*, VII/94, October 1909.

9. Victoria League Executive Committee Minutes, record of 'preliminary meeting' on 2 April 1901.

10. The Imperial Order Daughters of the Empire (1950). *Golden Jubilee 1900–1950*. Toronto: IODE. Front page.

11. *Ibid.*, p. 11. See also the early chapters of C. Pickles, 'Twentieth Century Canadian Colonial Identity: The Imperial Order Daughters of the Empire (IODE)'. PhD thesis, McGill

University, Montreal, 1996. She concludes that 'in twentieth century Canada, colonial identity has been imposed not directly by a British imperial centre, but by their descendants in Canada, who have supported, yet at the same time changed, imperial institutions' (p. 42).

12. Victoria League Executive Committee Minutes, 21 June 1901.
13. Victoria League Executive Committee Minutes, 27 June 1901.
14. Victoria League Executive Committee Minutes, 31 October 1901. Catherine Pickles concludes, from Canadian evidence, that Toronto IODE members were possibly acting opportunistically in siding with the Victoria League in opposition to Mrs Clark Murray. The simultaneous change of name from 'Federation of Daughters of the Empire' to IODE was intended to demonstrate to the British organization that the Canadians had curbed their initial aspirations. Letter to the author, 21 February 1998.
15. Victoria League Executive Committee Minutes, 10 April 1902.
16. Victoria League Sixth Annual Report, 1907 (1908).
17. Edith Lyttelton's diary, 10 September 1900. Chandos I, 6/3. Churchill College, Cambridge.
18. V. Milner, *My Picture Gallery 1886–1901* (London: John Murray, 1951), p. 153.
19. Violet Cecil's diary, quoted in Milner, pp. 237–8.
20. Victoria League Executive Committee Minutes, 15 May 1901 and 21 May 1901.
21. *Ibid.*
22. Victoria League Executive Committee Minutes, 27 June 1901 and 24 October 1901.
23. The Guild of Loyal Women of South Africa. Report of Federal Conference, April 1903. Milner papers, 340/13. Bodleian Library. The carefully balanced representation included eight delegates each from Cape Colony, Natal and the Transvaal, and two from Orange River (with four votes each!). Milner's papers also contain an undated copy of 'Principles, Constitution and Rules of the Guild of Loyal Women of South Africa', published in Wynberg. 338/8.
24. Victoria League Executive Committee Minutes, 28 October 1902. Lady Hely-Hutchinson, the Cape Town Governor's wife, appealed to the League to support efforts to rename the Guild in order to attract a larger Dutch loyalist membership.
25. Victoria League Seventh Annual Report, 1908 (1909).
26. Quoted in Summers, p. 347. Rose Scott was writing in *The Australian Woman's Sphere*, December 1903.
27. Quoted in Oldfield.
28. See the Victoria League Fifth Annual Report, 1912–13 (1913). Royal Commonwealth Society Archive. Cambridge University Library.
29. Victoria League Eighth Annual Report, 1909 (1910).
30. *Ibid.*
31. Royal Colonial Institute, *United Empire*, VI. 'Kindred Societies – Past and Present. V. The Victoria League', 1916, p. 589.
32. *Victoria League Notes*, 15 July 1910.
33. Meriel Talbot's private diary, 9 October 1909. Centre for Kentish Studies, Maidstone, Kent.
34. *Ibid.*, 28 October 1909.
35. *Ibid.*, 14–16 October 1909.
36. *Ibid.*, 21 January 1910.
37. *Ibid.*, 1 February 1910.
38. *Ibid.*, 5 February 1910.
39. *Ibid.*, 9 February 1910.
40. *Ibid.*, 8 February 1910.
41. *Ibid.*, 10 February 1910.
42. *Ibid.*, 3 March 1910.
43. *Ibid.*, 4 March 1910.
44. *Ibid.*, 26 February 1910.

45. *Ibid.*, 5 March 1910.
46. *Ibid.*, 13 March 1910.
47. *Ibid.*, 12 March 1910.
48. *Ibid.*, 22 and 24 April 1910.
49. *Ibid.*, 25 April 1910.
50. *Ibid.*, 28 April 1910.
51. *Ibid.*, 29 April 1910.
52. *Ibid.*, 4 and 5 May 1910.
53. *Ibid.*, 6 May 1910.
54. *Ibid.*, 14 May 1910.
55. *Ibid.*, 17 and 18 May 1910.
56. Victoria League Executive Committee Minutes, 21 July 1910.
57. Meriel Talbot's diary, 27 and 28 September 1910.
58. *Ibid.*, 30 September 1910.
59. *Ibid.*, 2 October 1910.
60. *Ibid.*, 3 October 1910.
61. *Ibid.*, 8 October 1910.
62. *Ibid.*, 22 October 1910.
63. Victoria League Tenth Annual Report, 1911 (1912).
64. Meriel Talbot's diary, 16 January 1911.
65. Victoria League Tenth Annual Report, 1911 (1912) and *Victoria League Notes*, June 1911.
66. See G. Phillips, *The Diehards: Aristocratic Society and Politics in Edwardian England* (Cambridge, MA: Harvard University Press, 1979); and A. Gollin, *Proconsul in Politics: A Study of Lord Milner in Opposition and in Power* (London: Anthony Blond, 1964).
67. *Victoria League Notes*, December 1911.
68. *Ibid.*, March 1913.

7 'Race' and Empire

By the end of the nineteenth century, 'race' had become a central concept within British imperialism. It was of corresponding importance to female imperialists, who both adopted and adapted current 'race thinking' to serve their cause. Essentially, the superiority of the white Anglo-Saxon race was held to provide both an explanation and a justification for the entire colonization project. Racial superiority was a major incentive to continue the task of Empire-building, by now construed as both a natural, inevitable process and a moral duty. All mankind would benefit from a peaceful world future in which British imperial citizens dominated over lesser races.[1] Thus Rudyard Kipling's emphasis was upon responsibility rather than glory, when he urged his fellow-countrymen to

> Take up the White Man's burden –
> Send forth the best ye breed . . .[2]

Definitions of 'race' remained somewhat hazy as the term entered increasingly common usage during the late Victorian period. Scientific interest in racial differences extended back into the eighteenth century, when classification of natural specimens developed alongside a growing curiosity about the biological origins of life, and an earlier phase of European colonization received *post hoc* justification from the widespread belief in polygenism.[3] A common human ancestry was denied and it was asserted that the enslaved black peoples of Africa derived their inferiority from their ape-like relatives. Darwin's *Origin of the Species* (1859) put paid to this theory, but nineteenth-century acceptance of a single ancestry was soon accompanied by invidious new theories. European economic and political ambitions were rationalized into scientific 'truths' as Herbert Spencer and other Social Darwinists sought to demonstrate that human societies and nation states mirrored the processes of biological evolution. Social commentators placed new emphasis upon the inevitability of struggle, and the necessity for the 'survival of the fittest' in order to advance human civilization.[4] British conquerors and colonizers were fulfilling the beneficial tasks of social evolution. Public debate opened up when Governor Eyre, himself a leading proponent of scientific race theory, put down the 1865 Jamaican rebellion with brutal disregard for black lives.[5] His critics included distinguished liberals and some scientists (among them Darwin himself), but they were eventually outweighed in public and governmental esteem by the combined forces of the literary establishment. Dickens, Tennyson, Kingsley, Arnold and Ruskin rallied to the Governor's defence. Patriotic race-thinking won the day, and was soon being more widely transmitted than ever before through the popular press, fiction, poetry, school texts and juvenile magazines.

By the end of the nineteenth century Social Darwinism had itself evolved, and was increasingly linked to the related doctrines of eugenics. Francis Galton was an early proponent of the view that human societies could manage their own evolution through a scientific programme of racial breeding which would foster the birth of desirable future citizens, while suppressing the reproduction of racially unfit 'degenerates'. His pupil, Karl Pearson, became the first Professor in Eugenics in 1911, and was also a well-known feminist sympathizer. A large number of women were attracted to the eugenist cause, including many female imperialists.[6] The Eugenics Education Society (1907) was open to both sexes, and appointed Arthur Balfour to its presidency after giving evidence to successive Edwardian government enquiries into social issues. The appeal of eugenics to middle- and upper-class women may be explained by its emphasis upon the status and responsibilities of motherhood.[7] The potential for maternal improvement was also emphasized. Philanthropic and racial aims combined in Edwardian child and maternal welfare campaigns which were closely allied, in their turn, to the cause of emigrating 'the right sort of woman' to populate white settler colonies. Eugenics associations spread rapidly to these same colonies, where scientific theory reinforced existing government policies of racial oppression and exclusion.[8] While learned debates continued over whether social and cultural attributes were truly hereditary, it was almost universally accepted by the imperial intelligentsia that such qualities existed in higher and lower forms, and that varied levels of culture were linked with racial difference. It was the destiny and duty of the higher to triumph over the lower, and many women believed their patriotic female agency to be a central part of the process.

Among the significant meanings attached to 'race' by the Edwardians was a gradual elision of racial and national identities. 'Anglo-Saxons' were assumed to be British, and indeed usually English. The fount of racial superiority was also the fount of political power. The bid for British racial superiority in a global context was a bid for supremacy among competing nation states, as well as an assertion of the right to rule those deemed incapable of nationhood. Within Britain itself, national identity required strengthening against threats of social and political turmoil. Reference to a shared racial inheritance could prove a useful unifier. Far from being merely a celebration of an illusory common past, it became a plank in current policy-making.[9] The looming Home Rule crisis made it increasingly important to justify Anglocentric rule within the British Isles. Hostile racial stereotyping was more than ever part of the stock-in-trade of opponents of Irish nationalism.[10] Interventionist social policies emerged out of social enquiries, and in response to labour unrest. Anxieties over unfit recruits for the South African War and over drunkenness, venereal disease, falling birth rates and the operation of the Poor Law were all bound into a general concern to ensure racial fitness, linked in turn with Britain's national and imperial destiny. On the one hand, the innate superiority of the British race was loudly trumpeted. On the other hand, commentators from across the political spectrum voiced the urgent need to ensure that national greatness was not being undermined by an insidious weakening of racial fibre. Whether in domestic or imperial settings, the future of the dominant race must be striven for rather than taken for granted.

The race-thinking of British imperialists was essentially concerned with linked hierarchies of value and power. The Anglo-Saxon 'race' was believed to merit worldwide supremacy because of its manifest superiority, first, to European competitors, then (in descending order) to Asians, Africans, and the Aboriginal peoples of Australasia and America, who were conveniently declining towards the point of racial extinction.[11] The Dominions occupied their own racially defined place within this hierarchy. Canada, Australia and New Zealand contained majority populations of British descent, and were engaged in a process of nation-building which was designed to strengthen their racial affinity with Britain. The unanimity of British imperialists and colonial nationalists on this point is very striking, given the divergence of other attitudes and aspirations noted in Chapter 6. An emphasis upon 'race' within imperialist propaganda was accepted as a vital means of drawing together the most valued people of the British Empire. 'Greater Britain' was an expression which perfectly encapsulated British hopes of securing an uncertain supremacy into the twentieth century by combining forces with distant countries proclaimed to be part of the same racial whole.

Organized female imperialists were enthusiastic participants in the process of racializing imperial rule. As we have seen, they moved in the same social circles as imperial statesmen, soldiers and administrators, and were influenced by the same intellectual currents despite their lack of public school and university education. It is not surprising to find them using what had become by the 1900s a common currency of racial language and ideas, extending its influence into every area of British society. But it is worth considering in some detail how and why such ideas were assimilated into organized female imperialism. The evidence on this point adds significantly to our understanding of these women's evolving outlook. On the one hand, they saw themselves (and were seen) as useful agents transmitting general imperialist ideas in both Britain and the colonies. On the other hand, the female imperialist associations were distinguished by their consciousness of gender, in both their modes of organization and their chosen activities. The advancement of 'women's work for Empire' required imperialist ladies to be more than mouthpieces for masculine ideas. They extended and adapted male views on race and Empire in ways which suited their own viewpoints and public work. For a variety of reasons, 'race-thinking' proved to be a particularly congenial aspect of imperialism for many upper-class British women. This chapter outlines the 'race-thinking' of some leading male imperialists, before investigating the translation of their ideas into the propaganda and practice of the female imperialist associations.

The leaders of the female associations were deeply impressed by their personal encounters with Cecil Rhodes, Joseph Chamberlain and Alfred Milner.[12] These were imperial heroes whose decisions and charisma had visibly shaped the Edwardian Empire. They were also among the leading ideologues of Empire, and their speeches and writings gave forceful endorsement to the view that imperialism was a racial mission. Rhodes and Milner both arrived at this conclusion during their Oxford careers in the 1870s, under the influence of Dilke, Ruskin and the Cambridge Professor J. R. Seeley, whose 1883 book *The Expansion of England* is also credited with Chamberlain's conversion to what has been subsequently labelled the New Imperialism.[13] Already fired by his first visit to South Africa between 1870 and 1873, Rhodes summed up their shared 'race-thinking' in a typically uncompromising early statement:

I contend that we are the first race in the world and that the more of the world we inhabit the better it is for the human race. I contend that every acre added to our territory provides for the birth of more of the English race who otherwise would not be brought into existence. Added to which, the absorption of the greater part of the world under our rule simply means the end of all wars.[14]

Neither the scholarly Milner nor the radical politician Chamberlain would have expressed himself in quite the same terms in the late 1870s. But the essence of Rhodes' words proved prophetic. Milner had already cemented a close friendship with the visionary Canadian imperialist George Parkin, who during the 1880s devoted several years to organizing the first Imperial Federation League. A few years later Milner departed for a period of administrative duty in Egypt which confirmed both his conviction of British racial superiority and his confidence in Britain's ability to rule lesser races more fairly and efficiently than they could rule themselves. Imperialism was a movement of social and political reform on the grandest scale. Violet Markham asserted in her autobiography that Milner's book *England in Egypt* (1892) had made her 'a convinced Imperialist'.[15] In a chapter titled 'English and Egyptians', Milner wrote of the latter: 'Such a race will not of itself develop great men or new ideas, or take a leading part in the progress of mankind. But under proper guidance it is capable of enjoying much simple content,' adding, 'their ignorance, and their lack of independence, increase enormously the responsibility resting on their governors.'[16] Here, then, was the fully developed concept of the white man's burden which could ultimately, by different means, become the white woman's burden. The development of the racially inferior 'dependent Empire' was a task which complemented the separate task of spreading 'the English way of life' throughout the Dominions, but which combined together with it in South Africa and in circumstances where majorities of British settlers found themselves 'responsible' for minorities of indigenous Maoris, Aborigines or Canadian 'redskins'.

Milner regarded British geopolitical control of southern Africa as equally a matter of racial duty. Despite the post-war talk of imperial harmony, the essence of his South African reconstruction policy was an attempt to ensure that effective self-government was postponed until immigration, language and education policies had achieved a reliable degree of anglicization.[17] Chamberlain was his chief accomplice in both the war and the reconstruction. Alfred Lyttelton and William Selborne, who succeeded Chamberlain and Milner as Colonial Secretary and High Commissioner respectively, revealed in their private correspondence that they shared the same aims, though they sometimes differed over the best means to accomplish them. These men's influence stood at the heart of Edwardian female imperialism. Their close personal and family relationships are inseparable from the developing web of their political ideas, within which South Africa and 'race-thinking' were central. For Milner, and still more for Selborne, economic reconstruction was the indispensable basis for successful anglicization. However, for the South African Colonisation Society, the Victoria League and the Girls' Friendly Society the assertion of imperial rule was more readily comprehended in terms of 'the English way of life'. The assertion of racial superiority through anglicizing religious, educational and social projects was very much within the sphere of womanly imperialism. So too was the task of transplanting much-needed female settlers to ensure longer-term British racial predominance. 'A British population is our only ultimate safeguard' wrote Milner to Chamberlain in June 1902.[18] With the deathbed support of Cecil Rhodes, he had secured government and private backing for a land purchase scheme designed to counterbalance Boer rural predominance and to introduce 'well-selected settlers' who would 'raise large families'.[19] A genuine partnership with British female emigrators was temporarily possible. It was signalled privately by Milner's eagerness to consult their leaders both in London and South Africa, and publicly by his endorsement of their work through the pages of *The Imperial Colonist*.[20]

During the years after his return to Britain, Milner continued to develop his race-centred ideal of imperialism. Many of his South African projects foundered due to the reluctance of a Liberal government, the impatience of Dutch and British South Africans to achieve self-rule, and the impact of economic recession. However, his frustration with politicians deepened his determination to work for Empire in arenas beyond their interference. The female imperialist associations, as well as the Round Table group established in 1910, were the beneficiaries of this decision. As a leading member of the Rhodes Trust, Milner arranged funding on a generous scale both for the South African Colonisation Society and for the Victoria League. In return, he himself enjoyed, and hoped to benefit from, the close personal friendship of the leading ladies whom he had befriended in South Africa. Violet Cecil was an active ally in promoting the National Service League and resistance to Home Rule. He received from Violet Markham the benefits of an expert journalist's talents as well as the devotion of an admiring friend. Both qualities proved useful during the 'Chinese Slavery' debate in 1905, which resulted in a Commons vote of censure followed by a public rehabilitation campaign.[21] Equally valued, from Milner's viewpoint, was Violet Markham's ability to lobby her wide Liberal acquaintance, and her willingness to tap her private fortune at his request. South African newspapers and Milner's favourite imperial propagandists were among the beneficiaries of what he referred to as her 'secret service' donations.[22]

Milner's biographers have demonstrated that his views on race and Empire remained remarkably consistent from the 1880s onwards. A semi-religious 'Credo' on British Race Patriotism was found among his papers after his death in 1925.[23] It provides a useful summary of views which had already been published in a 1913 collection of speeches entitled *The Nation and the Empire*, and presaged in his earlier writings on Egypt. In the 'Credo', Milner justified the pursuit of national self-interest as 'the law of human progress', but simultaneously embraced the 'practical necessity' of imperial unity. Throughout his later life he had sought the most effective means of drawing together the Dominions into closer economic, military and political union, believing this to be essential for the preservation of a national greatness in which all Britons could share. A common British and imperial citizenship would embody full respect and tolerance for diversity, while guaranteeing the predominance of moral and political values which were the birthright of the British race worldwide. At the same time, Milner stated unambiguously his pride in belonging to the country which was the well-spring of that race:

> I am a British (indeed primarily an English) nationalist. If I am also an Imperialist, it is because the destiny of the English race, owing to its insular position and long supremacy at sea, has been to strike fresh roots in distant parts of the world. My patriotism knows no

geographical but only racial limits. I am an Imperialist, and not a Little Englander, because I am a British Race Patriot.

The same pride in both country and Empire, and the same insistence on their indivisibility, had sustained Milner throughout his political career. In *The Nation and the Empire* he developed two aspects of his imperialist faith. Britain's talent for social administration was required at home as well as in the dependent Empire if the quality of the imperial race was to be preserved. In a speech made in 1906, Milner denied the existence of a conflict between the priorities of imperialism and of social reform.[24] His summons to serve an Empire based on 'the strength of the whole people' found an echo among those imperialists whose patriotism was already linked to philanthropic concerns over poverty and unemployment, and those whose maternal imperialism extended into concerns over child welfare and the threat of physical degeneracy to an over-urbanized British population. Female imperialists were by no means unanimous on social reform issues, but in the later Edwardian period Milner's views helped to impel them along the path which led to a Victoria League industrial committee, the Imperial Health Conference of 1914 (focused on child welfare and town planning), and of course the League's 'democratization' impulse of the pre-war years.

Racial health was essential to the preservation of racial kinship. However, despite the strong tendency of Milner and his female imperialist acolytes to focus primarily upon British kin within the Empire, there was a general recognition of the need for an imperialism which could accommodate racial 'others'. This was one of the least developed aspects of Milner's own outlook. At the philosophical level, Milner echoed Rhodes' belief in 'equal rights for all civilized men', and cautiously emphasized the possibility of change and development and the need to adapt policies accordingly. He made some efforts in South Africa to improve black education and to secure limited personal rights for 'natives',[25] but his defence of these racial inferiors remained contingent upon his calculation of its political and economic impact, acceptability to white South Africans proving the touchstone.

Back in London, Joseph Chamberlain was equally attentive to political pressures, and equally unprepared to set any abstract belief in human equality above his fundamental conviction that all African races would remain deeply unequal for the foreseeable future. As an imperialist, he had sometimes used visions of the needy natives to spur on British commitment to Africa. 'Who is to undertake their protection, and to secure that they peacefully continue their progress in civilisation and in orderly government?' he demanded rhetorically in an address to the London Chamber of Commerce in 1888; but this merely led to a far more important question: 'In other words, who is to be the dominant power in South Africa?'[26] Concern for British interests could rapidly diminish any protective impulse which underlay imperial rule. In private correspondence with Milner during 1901 Chamberlain was sympathetic to the latter's complaints about ill-informed criticisms from the London-based Aborigines' Protection Society. His reply to Milner's attack upon 'Negrophilists' soothingly suggested that he should concentrate instead upon 'the larger work of settling principles'.[27] The domination of blacks by whites in South Africa, and throughout the Empire, was not a matter of general principle which either man wished to open up for debate.

The same fundamental viewpoint was shared by virtually every supporter of the female imperialist associations. So unanimous was the belief in racial hierarchy that the subject seldom required discussion. British duty to protect and to civilize could also be taken as read. However, this was not the end of the matter, for different lady imperialists encountered current racial orthodoxies in different ways. Though they seldom questioned the basic premise of black inferiority, they thought about it and formed related policies in ways which inflected female imperialism with a racial outlook subtly different from that of Rhodes, Chamberlain or Milner. As white British women, they had distinctive racial duties to perform. Caring, educating and childbearing within the Empire all bore a racial message, as too did most forms of female colonial employment. Even those lady imperialists who never left British shores were conscious of playing their part in sustaining racial superiority through their own efforts, and their support for 'sisters' overseas. Racial solidarity was both implicit and explicit within virtually all the female imperialist work which linked Britain to the Dominions. Perceptions of racial difference were an equally inescapable part of the same work, especially in South Africa, and deeply influenced the imperialists' individual experiences and their collective decisions.

Like other aspects of female imperialist ideology, 'race-thinking' is expressed in a somewhat fragmentary way in the surviving records. Violet Markham was a rare exception as an imperialist lady who plunged boldly into the 'masculine' world of political controversy with her two books on South Africa published in 1900 and 1904.[28] Her lengthy first defence of Britain's right to rule South Africa was strongly infused with Social Darwinism. Despite the military conflict, the British and Dutch were 'two closely allied branches of the great Teutonic family . . . By every natural law, two peoples so akin should long since have been fused into one race with common aims and ideals.' There was therefore every prospect that 'when we have proved our strength, and the balance has been restored between the two nationalities, racial animosity will subside', and she held forth the prospect of welcoming Dutch cousins into the protective embrace of a familial Empire.[29] The next section of her argument encompassed the contrasting threat of racial difference:

> The present racial struggle is a dwindling factor, but the great racial struggle of the future is one which every additional year is bound to render more formidable. There are many reasons urged why Boer and Briton should bury their feuds and dwell in peace together, but the most powerful of any is the argument that they are a White brotherhood in a Black continent, and it is as brothers and allies they must face a future problem, the difficulty of which affects them equally.[30]

An insistence upon 'The African Colour Problem' as 'the great rock which looms ahead in the path of Africa' formed Violet's most important departure from the imperialist patriotism framed by Alfred Milner.[31] It is impossible to be altogether certain why she took this stance. Much of her book consisted of a determined effort to conduct a masculine-style analysis of facts and figures, and even her choice of family imagery appeared slanted towards a male rather than a female audience. Yet her diary and letters reveal how her subjective experience as a white woman visitor to Africa also contributed to her conclusions. 'People who have never been brought into personal contact with natives entirely fail to grasp the meaning of the words racial feeling,' she wrote.

It is sometimes supposed that racial hatred goes hand in hand with a wish to oppress. This is by no means the case, for the feeling often springs more from a sense of physical repulsion than any other impulse. At the same time an element of intolerance for the limitations and stupidity of the kaffir undoubtedly enters into the matter.[32]

So, too, she might have added in her own case, did an element of physical fear. Her diary recounted the loathsomeness of physical contact with 'natives' who jostled white people on the streets of Cape Town; the unpleasant details of black appearance; and, at the Lovedale missionary school which was well known as a high point of black education and Christianization, the sense of incongruity experienced by a lonely white woman eating her evening meal 'surrounded by savages'.[33]

Violet Markham evidently intended her book to be taken seriously as a well-researched contribution to knowledge rather than a mere polemic. 'By Jove – what a clever girl she is!' was Milner's reported comment when he read her detailed analysis of Cape politics.[34] However, in the absence of reliable information on the 'natives', the long section on relations between blacks and whites contained a great deal of apocalyptic speculation. Using the weapons of both fear and ridicule, she attempted to demonstrate the dangers of applying European theories of human equality and natural rights to innately inferior races. 'The cleavage between the blacks and whites is complete and absolute,' she concluded.

> It seems most unlikely that sympathy and intercourse, in our sense of the words, will ever exist between them. The ordinary social and domestic ties which unite Europeans of different nationalities are, of course, wholly impossible. Time, which softens so many animosities, will be unable, as far as we can judge, to bridge in the faintest degree this great gulf of racial repugnance. Pity, toleration, and kindness: these things are possible, but nothing more.[35]

Lord Milner was anxious to provide some form of native education with the intention of inculcating habits of steady labour; but Violet's experience of the most successful black school in South Africa led her to different conclusions. Education was simply making black Africans unhappy, discontented and even less suited to the manual labour for which they were predestined.[36]

A second South African volume defended Milner's Chinese Labour scheme, and showed no appreciable change of heart on 'race' issues. However, a third book, published in 1913, marked the reawakening of a troubled liberal conscience.[37] A return visit to South Africa had included a shipboard encounter with a highly educated Indian reformer who 'wanted to see his countrymen trained to bear the burthen of government', and who was visiting South Africa to investigate 'the disabilities of Indian subjects'.[38] Violet's own investigation of race relations subsequently took on a less censorious approach. In *The South African Scene* she reconsidered 'the ethics of Imperial responsibility' in relation to 'the coloured races within the Empire', acknowledging that 'the arrival of the educated native throws a new counter on to the board'. Her conclusion was that white imperial rulers must in future give more attention to their responsibilities for the 'weaker brethren' of other races; but that ultimately 'The white races have white civilisation to guard and uphold – a trust and heritage of the first magnitude'. Eventually 'the test of civilisation' must supersede that of race or colour alone. However, the manifest inequality between 'the black man and the white' would prevent, for the foreseeable future, 'an indiscriminate handing out of roles and political privileges to a race unfitted to use them'.[39] The more open-minded commentator of 1913 thus continued to assert the reality of racial division and potential conflict, and to uphold the duties of racial hierarchy.

It is difficult to estimate how far Violet Markham's views on racial difference were shared by other female imperialists. There is no reason to believe that her strongly expressed views on race would have been unpalatable to the majority. It is possible to draw some tentative comparisons with the views of other leading ladies, though in every case the record is indirect and incomplete. Violet Cecil perhaps came closest to Violet Markham's categorical and alarmist condemnation of racial inferiors. She displayed no particular interest in 'the native question' while in South Africa, but took the lead within the Victoria League in resisting any extension of the League's hospitality to male Indian visitors in London. Her very apparent sense of a sexualized racial threat on this occasion echoes some of Violet Markham's writings. Like the latter, she often dispelled the tensions of serious aversion by recounting tales which ridiculed 'native' stupidity. More forthcoming, and more genuinely interested in 'native' life, were Laura Ridding and Louisa Knightley. Both paid extended visits to South Africa during the 1900s, though neither lived there for long enough to acquire the complacent and incurious attitude towards black people which characterized so many long-term expatriates. Both, moreover, were motivated to record their views by their involvement in women's organizations and their commitment to associated journalism.

Laura Ridding travelled to South Africa in 1908 as the guest of her brother, Lord Selborne. Her family visit was inevitably full of the politics of the nascent Union, but was also deeply influenced by her own enthusiasm for moral reform, Anglicanism and social welfare. Within two days of her arrival, she began to record in her diary the evidence which confirmed her worst fears of the racial 'other':

> Col. Fortescue warned us that we should not walk alone on any part of Table Mountain out of reach of houses because of the bad number of assaults on white women by coloured or black people that had recently taken place . . . He says nowadays white people will have one servant, a 'black boy', who will bang on their bedroom door – bring in their cup of coffee to them in bed – bang again to come in to clear it away and be allowed to come in even if they were in their baths – (women or men) – So 'familiarity breeds contempt' . . . Another awful cancer is the lowest type of white prostitute, who prefers soliciting coloured men because they pay better.[40]

Images of sexual assault by black men on white women were deeply ingrained within late Victorian and Edwardian 'race-thinking'. To the extent that they had any historical basis, such images were drawn particularly from the Indian Mutiny of 1857 and the Jamaican uprising of 1865, but had been reinforced by hysterical allegations from elsewhere in the Empire and fuelled by the expectations of sexual excess and depravity which were integral to popular stereotypes of 'savages'. Between 1893 and 1913 South Africa was swept by a series of 'black peril' scares. A limited number of assaults, including some attacks by 'houseboys' on their mistresses, spread into a generalized wave of fear which was exacerbated by economic and political uncertainties during the years preceding the Union.[41] In mid-1907 a group of Transvaal women's organizations appealed to the government for the enforcement of complete social segregation between blacks and whites. Laura Ridding would certainly have known about this campaign. She arrived in South Africa with her own sensitivities about male sexual behaviour heightened by her involvement in 'social purity' campaigns in Britain against prostitution and abuse of minors, and with a strong commitment to the Girls' Friendly Society and Mothers' Union codes of pure living. It is not surprising that she was easily frightened. Two months later she endured the worst shock of her visit while staying in the home of Archbishop Carter. After an afternoon discussing 'Soul Training' with the local Mothers' Union, she sat up late reading in her ground-floor bedroom. The strong scent of a vase of honeysuckle began to trouble her, so she opened the window to place it outside on the sill: 'When I opened it, I saw a pair of naked brown feet standing on the sill. The man had been looking through the curtains which did not meet, watching me. Mercifully I had not begun to wash.' The Archbishop was hastily summoned 'and showed himself at my window, in order that it might be seen that a man was in the house'. Then Laura spent a sleepless night cowering behind the combined defences of 'a very weak bolt' on the window, a carefully balanced slop pail ('so that if he tried to force the windows or door, the rattle would awake me') and a sunshade and umbrella 'by my bed to fight with'.[42]

Alongside her diary, Laura Ridding kept a detailed notebook of her South African visit in which she recorded facts, opinions and summaries of her reading and conversations, presumably with a view to resourcing future talks and articles. She was very much the 'working' lady imperialist rather than a mere tourist. A substantial part of her record was devoted to what she referred to as 'the Native problem' – 'as crushing a one as white races ever in their existence have had to tackle'.[43] Like Violet Markham, she visited schools and discussed the educability of black people. From Cape Town women involved in church work she learned of the failure of the Mothers' Union and the Girls' Friendly Society to help 'native or coloured girls', both because of white women's refusal to 'mix' and because of black women's inability to meet the necessary moral standards. From Deaconess Julia in Johannesburg she heard about controversy over whether native girls should or could be trained as domestic servants. From Mr Gore Browne, Rector of Pretoria and 'a Saint', she heard that 'the black man is unspeakably provoking' if treated too philanthropically.[44] Drawing upon her own extensive experience of philanthropy and Poor Law work in Britain, she paid inquisitorial visits to mine compounds and hospitals in order to inspect 'native' living conditions. Resident white officials sometimes quailed before her determination to uncover the truth. At Sir John Robinson's Crown Deep compound she recorded the details of buildings, behaviour, clothing and food: 'The smell was strong – but as natives prefer as a delicacy *all* the intestines . . . the coarse knock-you-downness may be to them attractive. It was much nastier than workhouse messes.' A visit to the hospital was next insisted upon, where Laura found 'barely decent provision' and a single doctor supported by something vaguely referred to as 'tribal nursing'.[45] A visit to a far more orderly Chinese labour compound followed later, together with visits in Deaconess Julia's company to 'native' homes and chapels outside the grip of the mine owners. Finally, publication of the new Draft Constitution provided opportunities for observation of South African attitudes towards black participation in politics. Laura noted with approval the cheers which greeted Patrick Duncan's support for 'a white

1. Susan Grosvenor

2. Louisa Knightley

3. Margaret Jersey (right) with Lady Northcote

4. Ellen Joyce

5. Edith Lyttleton

6. The Cecil family in 1896

Back row, left to right: Earl of Selborne. Lord Hugh Cecil, Lord William Cecil, Marquess of Salisbury, Lord Edward Cecil.

Middle row: Countess of Selborne, Viscount Cranborne, Marchioness of Salisbury, Lady Robert Cecil, Lord Robert Cecil.

Front row: Vicountess Cranborne, Lady Gwendolen Cecil, Lady Florence Cecil, Lady Edward Cecil.

7. Drawing from the *Victoria League Notes*: 'Britannia welcoming her daughters' (October 1911)

8. Drawing from the *Victoria League Notes*: 'Unity is Strength' (May 1910)

man's country' during a Johannesburg meeting: 'It is our duty as well as profit to act
for an unknown number of years to come as trustees for the Native Races (ie that would
keep Natives from having a share in Government).'[46]

For a devout Christian such as Laura Ridding, one of the most troubling aspects
of 'the Native problem' was the issue of whether black people had equal status before
God, since this might logically imply other rights to equality. Maud Selborne's
correspondence contains a number of references to the social unease caused by the
appearance of black clerics in Anglican churches. She herself seemed less beset with
fears than her sister-in-law, and more inclined to share Milner's private leaning
towards acceptance of some degree of common humanity between black and white,
though white interests and white unity must not be jeopardized by such admissions.
Maud's views appear as a sort of counterpoint to Laura's own in her diary and
notebook. 'Maud says . . .' usually prefaced a relatively liberal opinion spoken with
authority. For example, 'Maud says when a "professing Christian" refuses to admit
the desirability of making Christians of the natives, she always fights the question
out with him'; 'They say missionaries ruin the blacks. Maud says missionaries
probably tell the black man his rights'; and, with regard to education, 'Maud believes
that one secret of getting more justice and respect for natives is to teach them all
English. So long as they talk "gibberish" and don't understand English, so long a
majority of whites consider them like animals.' Maud also supported the training of
black domestic servants ('Maud says . . . that the Kaffir is naturally very clean'), but
strongly disapproved of an Anglican native school where 'the children were eating
their dinner seated at a table with a table cloth. This is the blunder. When such go
out to service, they expect to be treated and count themselves on an equality with
white servants.'[47] Acceptance of black humanity did not in fact imply much prospect
of equality upon Earth, though it might open the gateway to a future Heaven.
Neither should Laura Ridding's insistent use of Poor Law comparisons be taken as
evidence of a departure from belief in racial hierarchy; rather, it reflected the rigidity
of her own and her sister-in-law's views on social class. Both Kaffir and pauper
children could be improved by education, but in each case there was a clear (and
different) ceiling upon what was possible and desirable.

Louisa Knightley's diary contains a longer history of the evolution of her views on
'race', alongside the history of her growing involvement in female imperialism. She
had no firsthand experience of 'Greater Britain' before her tour of South Africa in 1905.
Nevertheless, she developed into an imperialist 'race-thinker' through a range of
experiences and encounters rather than through systematic study of the subject. Her
conversion to imperialism coincided with the splendours of Queen Victoria's Diamond
Jubilee, her funeral, and the Coronation of her successor. Louisa admired 'wonderful
dark faces' in processions, and exotic Indian troops who were 'a picture book alive'.[48]
At the same time the Boer War was bringing the African experiences of soldiers and
settlers to London's dining-tables. Alongside tales of military heroism, she heard 'some
queer views . . . [he] approves of polygamy for the natives and thinks they need not be
Christianised!!'[49] A visiting researcher from the Victoria County History came to
examine deeds at Fawsley, and added to her limited store of knowledge by explaining
'about neolithic and paleolithic man – and how even in those remote ages there was
always a white race and a dark race and the dark race was always conquered'.[50] At the

same time she was beginning to wrestle with the practicalities of emigrating British girls for domestic service in South Africa:

> It is all so complicated by the Kaffir question. I wonder if it is true, as Mrs Phillips says, it is impossible to treat Kaffirs otherwise than very strictly. All white people seem to concur in disliking them so much. These race questions are so frightfully difficult.[51]

'Race' was high on her investigative agenda when she set sail for South Africa. As an emissary both of the South African Colonisation Society and of the Girls' Friendly Society she had a busy schedule of meetings and of tourism, but nevertheless insisted on visiting both Kaffir and Chinese mine compounds, where she gathered together favourable impressions to relay back to Lord Milner's critics in Britain. Her comfortable conclusion was that 'it is all a question of management. Where the management is at once fair and kind – all goes well.'[52] Other aspects of the visit confirmed her acceptance of the basic orthodoxies of racial difference. In Bulawayo 'we were shown the tree under which Lobegula used to sit and order the indiscriminate slaughter of his subjects'; the same evening an archaeologist failed to either interest or convince her with an unlikely new theory that 'natives' (rather than Phoenicians) had constructed the ruined city of Zimbabwe.[53] Meanwhile, her solicitous visits to 'native' settlements revealed 'disappointing' tin shacks alongside the 'picturesque' squalor of the huts she had expected.[54] Most satisfying of all was 'a real native dance on a very large scale':

> The Governor sat in the centre and first one tribe and then another of warriors in full war dress defiled on to the ground below and began their performances by a royal salute, bending down, shaking their sticks (they are not allowed spears or clubs for fear of a fight between their tribes – which hate one another).[55]

At the end of a five-week visit, Louisa Knightley's existing views on 'race' seem to have been reinforced by her experiences of white and black South Africa. Even the unpleasant experience of an attempted robbery on Table Mountain (presaging the advice so fearfully received by Laura Ridding) does not seem to have undermined her basic confidence that 'the Native question' could be solved by firm management. The main dangers lay in mistakened leniency and a failure to defend racial boundaries. During the voyage home she read Baden-Powell's *Matabele Campaign of 1896* and wrote in her diary: 'for the future welfare of the whole country it is essential to solve the native question in the right way.'[56]

Violet Markham, Violet Cecil, Laura Ridding and Louisa Knightley shared a conviction that the relationship between black and white races in South Africa and the wider Empire was of supreme long-term importance. Other female imperialist travellers in Africa and India, including Maud Selborne, Meriel Talbot and Margaret Jersey, laid less stress upon this issue but appear to have accepted the same basic premises. Insofar as the lady imperialists held a collective view on 'race', they were committed both to fostering British racial solidarity and to a recognition of the potentially threatening inferiority of all lesser races. The 'dependent' peoples of the Empire required not merely guidance, but firm and kindly control. These beliefs added extra dimensions of responsibility to the tasks of a caring and educative womanly imperialism. When racial issues came to the forefront in the associations' work, policy-making was influenced by the leading ladies' personal experiences as well as by the wider inculcation of 'race-thinking' to which they themselves contributed.

The gendered significance of white women's racial duty was frequently spelled out to them by male speakers upon Emigration Society and Victoria League platforms. At the SACS Annual General Meeting of 1904, Sir Henry McCallum dwelt upon South Africa's need:

> Imagine a home in the veldt far away from neighbours; the lady of the house, with a family of young children, immersed in household duties, and little or no time to look after them; the only servants kaffirs, and without the companionship and help of white servants. What then happened? The children were brought up with natives and by natives, with unsatisfactory results, for daily contact with a lower race must induce a familiarity with lower ideals. Did not humanity, did not pride of race, dictate a measure of self-sacrifice for the amelioration of the lot of that poor lady and her children?[57]

In the following year George Parkin, Milner's long-time associate, took up the same theme in grander terms:

> They had a greater problem to solve in connection with the colonial population, which had existed for six thousand years, and in all that time had never written a book, painted a picture, built a bridge, or done anything else that could be reckoned among the accomplishments of civilisation. The task of civilising the black population of South Africa gave the British people for the next ten centuries the hardest job that any nation had ever undertaken in the world's history.[58]

Female speakers and writers less frequently engaged in direct racial exhortation, but when they did so, their emphasis upon women's particular contribution gave an original slant to standard imperialist rhetoric. British women's racial duty was also their unique opportunity. Through their work for the Empire they could 'slough off the pettiness of the past and rise to the height of Imperial womanhood', as Lady Susan Malmesbury put it in a posthumous tribute to Cecil Rhodes published in *The Imperial Colonist* in May 1902. Writing under the somewhat grand title 'The Ethics of Emigration', Mrs Chapin outlined a racial history of Britain, first to a GFS audience, then to *The Imperial Colonist*'s readers.[59] The definitive role of Christianized Anglo-Saxons led inexorably to the conclusion that 'England must be the Kindergartener to teach South African faith and self-activity'. Metaphoric and literal meanings intertwined as she went on to explain the concept of an 'imperious maternity' which would reconcile the Boers to voluntary allegiance to the Empire. The essence of 'England's spirit' lay not in military conquest, nor even in political control, but rather in developing 'the three great institutions of life – the family, the Church and the State':

> What *is* England in South Africa? Is it the Government? To a certain extent, yes, but to a greater extent it is every English individual who goes out there . . . the result of any ideal is responsibility, and the responsibility lies with those who go out, for they should be the bearers of the torch that kindles and lightens. And in presenting the possibility of emigration to members of the GFS, are we not offering them a great opportunity and laying upon them a great responsibility? But they need not hesitate if their purpose is high enough.

Mrs Chapin concluded with a ringing call to feminine racial service: 'the impulse is one of *imperious maternity* – I like the words imperious maternity much better than Imperialism.'

Inspiring and self-reinforcing though it might be, the racial mission of female imperialism was not without its complications. These are best understood through a study of the day-to-day practice of the imperialist associations rather than from statements of abstract principle. The emigration societies offer multiple examples of race-thinking moving from theory into practice, and their work will be considered in detail in Chapter 9. There follows here a discussion of some organizational dilemmas which faced the Girls' Friendly Society and the Victoria League. In each society the leading ladies shared the basic racial outlook of Rhodes, Milner and Chamberlain and gratefully adopted the embellishments to their ideas supplied by the female imperialist press. But the differing 'practical' work of each society, and the differing experiences and emphases of individuals, sometimes led to uncertainty and disagreement. The resolution of policy difficulties was itself an important part of the development of 'race-thinking' within female imperialism. It provoked debate and discussion, with consequences which spread beyond the elite circle of leaders.

The Girls' Friendly Society moved confidently into the work of establishing overseas branches from the 1880s onwards. By the early 1900s 'twinning' arrangements linked individual branches, and gifts and correspondence were exchanged between Thirsk and Johannesburg, Bournemouth and Toronto, Newbury and Wooloongabba, Queensland. A list published in *Friendly Words* in 1908 recorded nearly a hundred such linked branches; among them were twelve in the Indian Chain and six in the Ceylon Chain.[60] But who were the Indian members? Should the Christian sisterhood of the Girls' Friendly Society extend across racial boundaries? There is no doubt that this issue posed some difficulty for GFS imperialists. In 1905 the Society's colonial committee approved the establishment of whites-only Jamaican branches. Miss Brewin had been granted £10 towards the expenses of Jamaican work a few months earlier, and there was enthusiastic endorsement for her recommendation that work should progress through Sister Madeline and selected girls' day schools since 'You could not start the GFS amongst the natives' and 'there are not enough of the quite upper white class to keep the GFS flourishing' outside the schoolroom.[61] An even more exclusive white branch was soon formed in Bridgetown, Barbados,

> practically composed of 'leisured' Members for there it was deemed advisable to begin in this way . . . They are doing much good and self-denying work, visiting the alms-houses and hospitals and cheering the inmates. They have an Annual Sale for Missions held at the Church House, and this year they sent the proceeds (£10) to the GFS medical Mission at Cawnpore.[62]

By the same date the Jamaican Spanish Town branch was also donating £3 10s each year towards the upkeep of an orphan girl in Tokyo, underlining the point that charity towards (distant) sisters of inferior race was considered commendable, while racial mingling within GFS branches was probably not. In the 1920s a photograph of the GFS holiday home in Barbados shows a group of 'quite upper white class' girls (seated) accompanied by three black maids in caps and aprons (standing and kneeling).[63]

However, not all colonial branches remained oblivious to possible sisterhood in relation to 'natives' nearer home. Laura Ridding's South African notebook suggests that some effort had been made to enrol black girls in Cape Town, though it had apparently ended in failure. During the 1880s the GFS suffered a split among its British members over the rigid and self-defeating enforcement of the 'purity' rule within branches in factory towns. A separate organization, the Women's Help Society, resulted. It is interesting to discover that Deaconess Julia found it more appropriate to enrol black girls in this smaller, more tolerant society in the 1890s rather than in the GFS in Johannesburg.[64] A differently nuanced racial problem faced the GFS in India. It is recorded in the Society's journals, though not debated by its London committees, that Indian branches significantly compromised racial boundaries by admitting Eurasian members during the 1900s. The 1913 GFS history applauded this decision: 'We rejoice to welcome them to our Society which is for girls of the English Empire everywhere.' However, the author pointedly noted the Eurasians' impeccable 'English' credentials of Christianity, language, dress and education: 'They have the greatest love for England and for all that belongs to it, and will speak of England as "home", though they have never seen it and many can never expect to do so'; and strongly implied that Eurasian girls were particularly in need of education from childhood onwards towards a purer lifestyle. Eurasians were described euphemistically to the GFS readership as 'the children of marriages in times past between Europeans and natives, such marriages being much less frequent now than they used to be'.[65] No doubt the new members were used to such implicit denigration. One wonders what they made of Mrs Joyce's speech in the same year to the GFS Imperial Conference on the indissoluble union between British culture and British heredity.

Meanwhile, an even more daring experiment was attempted by Miss Townend, the GFS Vice-president, when she toured India in 1904. 'Native Christians' were admitted to membership in Delhi, the very first of these being the 'daughter of a high-class Mohammedan'.[66] Class status and Christianity helped, but the barriers to integration remained formidable. Separate 'native' branches are implied by the 1926 GFS history's report of 'Branches for Sinhalese girls' in Ceylon. The same history described India's 'three spheres of work . . . each has its own importance and its own claims'. These were 'first, the work among the European communities . . . Secondly, there are the Anglo-Indians . . . Lastly, there is the native population itself, with whom the Society has chiefly come into touch through Mission work.'[67] Despite some slight ambivalence, it is not unexpected to find that GFS work remained segmented, and largely supportive of established racial hierarchy. Antoinette Burton has demonstrated the importance of the trope of 'the Indian woman' within British feminist discourse.[68] For non-feminists, too, imperialism implied an assumption of responsibility for Indian 'sisters', but ultimately a distancing through self-defining contrasts between Indian women and their racial superiors. Accounts of Indian missionary work in the GFS journals were full of such statements, conveyed in pitying tones. The 'oppressed' Indian woman of the zenana or the hill village was more readily embraced than the Indian GFS fellow-member.

The Victoria League faced up to Indian race issues by first ignoring them, then deliberately attempting to exclude them from its work. The League's origins lay in South Africa, as we have seen, and its work was firmly focused upon a vision of racial and imperial unity between 'white settler' Dominions. Where the 'dependent' Empire was acknowledged, it was conceived mainly in terms of darkest and most utterly dependent Africa. Though Indians made a fine showing at imperial ceremonies, the League had difficulty in accommodating India's political and social complexities to its female imperialist world view. The size and importance of India within the Empire, and the growing support for an educated Indian nationalism, made it difficult to foresee an indefinite future of imperial unity centred solely on white-ruled Dominions. But the 'race-thinking' of many male and female imperialists made an Indian Dominion still more unthinkable. The Victoria League resolutely refused to accept Indian members or to set up Indian branches in the 1900s, despite an increasing number of overtures by and on behalf of wealthy, educated Indian loyalists who considered such admission to be a legitimate (and legitimating) privilege. The issue was a genuinely divisive one, for even the most prejudiced 'race-thinkers' among the female imperialists believed that Asians occupied a higher place on the scale of civilization than Africans – especially if they were 'westernized' and of high social rank. Indian gentlemen, and even Indian princes, were far from uncommon in London's drawing-rooms, and had sometimes found favour with Queen Victoria herself. Should such people be received by the Victoria League? As early as May 1903, a request arrived for help in entertaining an Indian Rajah: 'The Committee argued that his name should be sent to Mrs Wernher, but that such visitors should not be offered Hospitality with the compliments of the Ladies' Committee.'[69]

Four years later a major argument developed within the executive committee over the India issue, following a meeting held at the request of Anglo-Indian organizations to discuss how the Victoria League might alleviate the loneliness of Indian students in Britain. Lady Helen Munro-Ferguson agreed to support the establishment of a club for Indian students at Edinburgh University. However, Lord Ampthill insisted that 'personal rather than corporate hospitality' was required. Cautiously, and in terms which made it absolutely clear that sexualized 'race-thinking' underlay the decision, the executive agreed 'they would be willing to offer personal hospitality through their members to Indian girls and ladies coming to England'. Even so, 'Lady Edward Cecil wished it to be recorded that she greatly deprecates the Victoria League taking up this Indian work.'[70]

Over the next few months the issue festered uncomfortably. A special all-male consultative committee was set up to look further into the issue of 'Indian men students', but failed to agree on safety-proof procedures for introducing Indian males into British homes. Meanwhile, Violet Cecil had conducted a private canvas of leading imperialist men. Her estranged husband, by then a senior administrator in Egypt, received a straightforward request:

> I wonder whether you would be so good as to send me your *unvarnished* opinion of the desirability of mixing Eastern men with English families. I know your views. They are mine, but I want them *in writing*. Never mind mincing language and put in all spades by their proper names and tell as many illustrative anecdotes as you can. I should like to be able to send your letter to Lady Jersey and one or two others . . . the dear, nice, innocent women all think that Mohammedan men have only got to see them to become Westernised.[71]

A similar request obviously went to Lord Curzon, for his lengthy reply survives among Violet Cecil's papers. He sympathized with her dilemma and, after an analysis of the relative dangers of long and short stays, Moslems and Hindus, and the educated nobility as opposed to 'the *average* Indian student', he concluded that 'the experiment should not be undertaken except with great caution and the most stringent guarantees'.[72]

The executive committee was divided and unhappy. The views of all the ladies present at its next meeting were canvassed by Lady Jersey and recorded individually, with Violet Markham predictably lending her support to the opposition. Violet Cecil threatened to resign if the Asiatics were admitted. Conflicting proposals were tabled; on the one hand, holding open the option of entertaining Indians who had been vetted by two Anglo-Indian societies as well as by the League itself; on the other, closing down even that option. It was noted that 'Mr Rudyard Kipling, having been invited to become a Vice-President, had written to say that should the League undertake to offer hospitality to young Asiatics residing in England he could not accept any connection with the League.' The meeting concluded, at Edith Lyttelton's suggestion, with a decision to drop the whole proposal 'owing to the widespread feeling against it which exists among friends and well-wishers of the Victoria League'.[73] A sad little postscript was added two years later by an executive decision to ban pen-friendships, under the League's auspices, between British and Eurasian children. More significantly, the executive also rejected offers from Indian imperialists to set up branches of the Victoria League in their own country in 1909 and 1911. 'It was resolved not to invite Indian Societies' to the League's 1911 Imperial Conference, but a Mrs Faridoonji nevertheless turned up and 'expressed a strong desire that the women of India should be brought into the movement'.[74] No response is recorded, and no action was taken. There was another moment of embarrassment in 1910 when the Archbishop of the West Indies queried 'whether the Hospitality Committee would be prepared to offer some form of hospitality to less educated coloured people who visit this country from Jamaica'.[75] This proposal, too, was shelved, then quietly dropped.

Despite the fracas over hospitality for Asiatics, the Victoria League seems generally to have been more comfortable and more consistent in its race policies than the Girls' Friendly Society. The absence of an overtly Christianizing strand within its imperialist faith probably helped. The Canadian Daughters of the Empire took a bolder position on links with the 'dependent' Empire by establishing Chapters in both the West Indies and India, but it is likely that this evidenced their ambition to head a worldwide organization rather than any fundamentally different 'race-thinking'. Though Dominion imperialists sometimes resented the snobbish and controlling behaviour of their British 'sisters', they had a strong vested interest in preserving the racially based family tie. Support for Empire was largely synonymous with self-identification as British in origins, culture and aspirations. Emergent Dominion nationalism drew heavily upon this perception of common heritage, shared by dominant ruling groups and, in Canada, Australia and New Zealand, indicative of the boundaries which defined them as such. The process of nation-building involved both inclusion and exclusion and, in the Dominions as well as in Britain, 'race-thinking' helped to establish hierarchies of power. Leadership, and even membership, of the newly self-governing colonial nations was determined by biological and cultural birthright. These signifiers justified the exclusion from full citizenship of the indigenous races of the Dominions, for the strength of the nation was judged to lie in its unity and affinity with the dominant 'race' of the British Empire.[76] The female imperialist organizations of Canada, Australia, New Zealand and South Africa were largely silent on the subject of indigenous peoples. So powerful was the consensus on this matter that it did not require discussion. They were vocal, on the other hand, in their protestations of allegiance to a British past and an imperial British future. The fostering of this allegiance was the main reason for their existence. Until 1914 at least, it seemed perfectly possible (and indeed necessary) to combine love of country with a wider imperial loyalty based upon racial belonging.

'Race-thinking' served important purposes within Edwardian imperialism. It shaped a scientific and historical explanation of the Empire, and by so doing provided confidence and eloquent arguments for its supporters. The contingent nature of racial identity was not evident to those who needed to believe in its permanence, including the organized female imperialists of Britain and the Dominions. Though racial ideas were integral to imperialism at every level in this period, there were particular reasons why 'race-thinking' appealed strongly to these women. Their chosen work for Empire lay in areas which linked biological and cultural reproduction. Imperial motherhood and imperial education were construed as inherently feminine duties. By assuming these responsibilities, and encouraging others to do so, imperialist women enhanced their gendered racial role as citizens of Empire. At the same time there were important continuities with aspects of late Victorian philanthropy to which many upper- and middle-class women were already committed. Healthy minds and bodies were fundamental to the racial future. Maternal and child welfare and the social purity campaign were major social reform movements at the turn of the century. They drew upon the language and concepts of race-thinking, and in turn contributed to the enthusiasm which many women reformers developed for imperial work.

The emphasis of the female imperialists' 'race-thinking' was upon nurture rather than conquest. Nevertheless, a deep fear of racial threat and sexual violence also lay at the heart of their gendered racial attitudes. Such fears were fostered by male rulers and propagandists in various parts of the Empire as a means of asserting new controls over indigenous peoples.[77] This process was accompanied by an internalization of fear and a reinforcement of existing negative racial stereotypes. British women contrasted their own superiority with the degraded lower races' inferiority, embodied in both their victimhood and their potential threat. Personal knowledge of the Empire rarely shook such certainties. On the contrary, the imperialist ladies who visited distant parts of the Empire tended to see what they expected to see. They returned to their British associations with fresh vigour for the task of firm but benevolent rule over 'dependants', and with renewed determination to build the racial alliances which underpinned 'Greater Britain'.

Notes

1. See P. Rich, *Race and Empire in British Politics* (Cambridge: Cambridge University Press, 1986), for an account of Anglo-Saxonism and of the gradual undermining of 'the simplicities of Victorian racial theory' (p. 26). On Victorian 'race thinking', see C. Bolt, *Victorian Attitudes to Race* (London: Routledge and Kegan Paul, 1971); M. Biddiss, 'Racial Ideas and the Politics of Prejudice, 1850–1914', *Historical Journal* (1972), **15** (3): 570–82; P. Fryer,

Staying Power: The History of Black People in Britain (London: Pluto Press, 1984*)*; D. Lorimer, *Colour, Class and the Victorians* (New York: Holmes and Meier, 1978).

2. R. Kipling, 'The White Man's Burden'. Printed for private circulation in 1899, then published in *The Five Nations* (London: Methuen, 1903), p. 79.

3. See Fryer, *Staying Power*, Chapter 7.

4. See L. Bland, *Banishing the Beast: English Feminism and Sexual Morality 1885–1914* (London: Penguin, 1995), Chapter 6.

5. See C. Hall, *White, Male and Middle Class: Explorations in Feminism and History* (Cambridge: Polity Press, 1992), Chapter 10.

6. Bland considers in detail the appeal of eugenics to women.

7. See also A. Davin, 'Imperialism and Motherhood', *History Workshop Journal* (1978), 5: 9–65.

8. For details of these policies, see M. de Lepervanche, 'Women, Nation and the State in Australia', in N. Yuval-Davis and F. Anthias (eds), *Woman-Nation-State* (Basingstoke: Macmillan Press, 1989); also W. Larner and P. Spoonley, 'Post-Colonial Politics in Aotearoa/New Zealand', and D. Stasiulis and R. Jhappan, 'The Fractious Politics of a Settler Society: Canada', both in D. Stasiulis and N. Yuval-Davis (eds), *Unsettling Settler Societies: Articulations of Gender, Race, Ethnicity and Class* (London: Sage, 1995).

9. For a summary of factors contributing to national uncertainty and its imperial and racial manifestations, see L. James, 'The Mission of Our Race: Britain and the New Imperialism, 1880–1902', in *The Rise and Fall of the British Empire* (London: Little, Brown & Co, 1994), pp. 200–16.

10. See L. Curtis, *Nothing But the Same Old Story: The Roots of Anti-Irish Racism* (London: Information on Ireland, 1984). In a notorious 1886 speech, Prime Minister Salisbury compared the Irish to Hottentots; see J. Smith, *The Taming of Democracy: The Conservative Party, 1880–1924* (Cardiff: University of Wales Press, 1997), p. 94.

11. This racial hierarchy is depicted in detail in B. Putnam Weale, *The Conflict of Colour* (London: Macmillan, 1910). It reappears, in varying forms, in most contemporary texts concerning race, including school textbooks.

12. See Chapter 3.

13. See J. Marlowe, *Milner: Apostle of Empire* (London: Hamish Hamilton, 1976); P. Marsh, *Joseph Chamberlain: Entrepreneur in Politics* (Yale: Yale University Press, 1994).

14. Quoted in J. Marlowe, *Milner: Apostle of Empire* (London: Hamish Hamilton, 1976), p. 5. Rhodes wrote this statement in 1877 while an undergraduate at Oriel. Milner was elected to a New College Fellowship in the same year, but had not yet made Rhodes' acquaintance.

15. V. Markham, *Return Passage* (Oxford: Oxford University Press, 1953), p. 48.

16. A. Milner, *England in Egypt* (London: Edward Arnold, 1904, 11th edn), p. 314.

17. See the evidence of Milner's published papers concerning reconstruction, in C. Headlam, *The Milner Papers, South Africa* (London: Cassell, 1933). On 27 December 1900 he wrote confidentially to Major Hanbury Williams, 'If, ten years hence, there are three men of British race to two of Dutch, the country will be safe and prosperous' (p. 242).

18. Alfred Milner to Joseph Chamberlain, 9 June 1902, in *ibid.*, p. 370.

19. *Ibid.* Milner composed a long, passionate memorandum on this theme.

20. The first issue of *The Imperial Colonist* contained a 'Letter from Lord Milner' expressing warm support. *The Imperial Colonist*, 1 (1), January 1902.

21. Milner's political enemies campaigned effectively against his policy of sanctioning the employment of indentured Chinese labour in South African mines in order to stave off a critical labour shortage.

22. Violet Markham's donations to Milner's work are chronicled through his grateful letters of acknowledgement to her on 15 November 1902 ('I *just jump* at your most generous gift . . .'), 20 September 1903 and 2 August 1905. On 6 April 1906 he wrote to solicit a contribution towards a fund to support the imperial propagandism of Sir Frederick Pollock, and on

12 April 1912 he thanked her for a £100 donation ('I shall grow shy of "bleeding" you if you *always* give me more than I ask'). VMar, 25/56. BLPES.

23. '"Credo". Lord Milner's Faith', in *The Times*, 27 July 1925.

24. A. Milner, *The Nation and the Empire* (London: Constable, 1913), p. 139.

25. See Headlam, pp. 153–4, 307, 312–14. On 6 December 1901 Milner outlined his plans for the 'natives' to Joseph Chamberlain, emphasizing 'the impracticability of governing natives, who, at best, are children, needing and appreciating a just paternal government, on the same principles as apply to the government of full-grown men' (p. 312).

26. J. Chamberlain, *Foreign and Colonial Speeches* (London: Routledge, 1897), p. 196.

27. Joseph Chamberlain to Alfred Milner, 30 December 1901. Chamberlain Papers. JC13/1/205. Birmingham University Library.

28. V. Markham, *South Africa, Past and Present* (London: Smith, Elder & Co, 1900); V. Markham, *The New Era in South Africa* (London: Smith, Elder & Co, 1904).

29. Markham, *South Africa*, pp. 4 and 231–2.

30. *Ibid.*, p. 234.

31. *Ibid.*, p. 231.

32. *Ibid.*, p. 244.

33. Violet Markham's diary, 5 September 1899. VMar, 17/5.

34. Annie Hanbury Williams to Violet Markham, 4 July 1900. VMar, 25/56.

35. Markham, *South Africa*, p. 245.

36. *Ibid.*, p. 248: 'It is impossible not to feel as regards the Kaffir that the feeble educational efforts of one generation will scarcely suffice to stem that devastating flood of savagery which may suddenly rise and overwhelm his little growth of civilisation.' Immediately after her visits, she noted in her diary her dissent from 'the spirit of Lovedale', and pondered at length on the depth of inequality between black and white (5 September 1899).

37. V. Markham, *The South African Scene* (London: Smith, Elder & Co, 1913). Most of the book was first published as a series of articles in *The Westminster Gazette* during the spring of 1913.

38. V. Markham, *Return Passage* (London: Oxford University Press, 1953), p. 106.

39. Markham, *South African Scene*, pp. 359, 376, 382, 236 and 269.

40. Laura Ridding's notebook, 26 November 1908, 9 M68/61. Hampshire Record Office.

41. See C. Van Onselen, *Studies in the Social and Economic History of the Witwatersrand, 1886–1914. Volume Two. New Nineveh* (London: Longman, 1982), pp. 50–4; M. Strobel, *European Women and the Second British Empire* (Bloomington: Indiana University Press, 1991), Chapter 1.

42. Laura Ridding's diary, 4 February 1909. 9M68/62. This vivid account was adorned by a sketch of the offending African feet at the window – but is characterized by fear rather than humour.

43. Laura Ridding's notebook, December 1908, p. 33. 9M68/61.

44. *Ibid.*, November 1908 to February 1909, pp. 33, 20 and 126. 9M68/61.

45. *Ibid.*, January 1909, p. 79. 9M68/61.

46. *Ibid.*, February 1909, p. 140. 9M68/61.

47. *Ibid.*, December 1908 to February 1909, pp. 34, 102, 40 and 37. 9M68/61.

48. Louisa Knightley's journal, 7 August 1902. Northamptonshire Record Office.

49. *Ibid.*, 6 August 1902.

50. *Ibid.*, 21 June 1902.

51. *Ibid.*, 19 June 1901.

52. *Ibid.*, 28 August 1905.

53. *Ibid.*, 9 September 1905.

54. *Ibid.*, 21 August 1905.

55. *Ibid.*, 25 August 1905.

56. *Ibid.*, 18 September 1905.
57. *The Imperial Colonist*, III/30. June 1904.
58. *Ibid.*, IV/43. July 1905.
59. *Ibid.*, II/8. August 1903.
60. *Friendly Words*, July 1908.
61. GFS Colonial Committee Minutes, 20 November 1905.
62. A. Money, *The Story of the Girls' Friendly Society* (London: GFS, 1913), p. 82.
63. M. Heath-Stubbs, *Friendship's Highway* (London: GFS, 1926), p. 156.
64. I am indebted to Deborah Gaitskell for this information.
65. Money, p. 44.
66. Heath-Stubbs, p. 147.
67. *Ibid.*, pp. 146–7.
68. A. Burton, *Burdens of History: British Feminists, Indian Women and Imperial Culture, 1865–1915* (Chapel Hill: University of North Carolina Press, 1994).
69. Victoria League Executive Committee Minutes, 28 May 1903.
70. Victoria League Executive Committee Minutes, 27 June 1907.
71. Violet Cecil to Edward Cecil, 10 November 1907. VM60, C705/23. Bodleian Library.
72. George Curzon to Violet Cecil, 11 November 1907. VM38, C251/9.
73. Victoria League Executive Committee Minutes, 5 December 1907.
74. Victoria League Executive Committee Minutes, 19 January 1909; *Victoria League Notes*, June 1911 (conference report).
75. Victoria League Executive Committee Minutes, 20 October 1910.
76. Aboriginal Australians were not enfranchised until the 1960s: see M. de Lepervanche, p. 37. Admission to citizenship should not be measured, however, solely in terms of voting rights. New Zealand Maori men and women achieved votes in 1893, but this did not end their economic, cultural and political marginalization: see W. Larner and P. Spoonley, pp. 43–4. Canadian 'Indians' underwent a process of 'enfranchisement' from 1876 onwards which was designed to deprive them of their distinctive status and the minimal rights attached to it. They were excluded from voting in federal elections until 1961: D. Stasiulis and R. Jhappan, pp. 114–15. All the newly formed Dominions enacted racially exclusive immigration policies which have variously endured into the late twentieth century.
77. This issue is considered in M. Strobel, *European Women and the Second British Empire* (Bloomington: Indiana University Press, 1991), Chapter 1.

8 Education

When Edwardian women committed themselves to imperialist education they entered a crowded field. In some ways education lay at the heart of female imperialism. Unless sufficiently widespread enthusiasm was generated, practical schemes of womanly work for the Empire would fail. No clear line could be drawn between education as propaganda, promoting essential levels of interest and support, and the more systematic, sustained imperialist education designed to provide a deeper understanding of the Empire. Female imperialists engaged in both, as well as equipping themselves (and others) with specialist knowledge in their chosen fields of work. In terms of their general propaganda work, imperialist women undoubtedly benefited from the fact that they did not act alone. On the contrary, an enthusiasm for Empire was being widely inculcated in British society during the 1900s. Imperialist education extended its range from university professors, archbishops and government ministers, throughout the formal educational system, across into the worlds of literature, the press and entertainments, and thence down to the levels of popular consumption, packaging and advertising. Whether through textbooks, sermons, art exhibitions or the music-hall, Britons found themselves to be participants in a process of education and socialization which increasingly equated citizenship and self-worth with love of nation and Empire.[1]

The core ingredients of the late Victorian and Edwardian imperialist message were patriotism, belief in racial hierarchy, respect for the monarchy, Christianity and the armed services, and admiration for the past and present British 'heroes' who exemplified these values. As we have seen, most female imperialists were happy to endorse such a faith. The distinctive nuances of female imperialism evolved out of its gendered and class-bound choice of particular fields of work rather than from any consciously formulated challenge to existing ideals. On the other hand, fortunate though the women's associations were to find support, finance and collaborators from within the surge of imperialist sentiment, the very popularity of Empire-building education posed certain dilemmas. Could general propaganda and the tasks of formal education be safely left to others? How far was this work integral to womanly imperialism, and how well-equipped were the leading ladies to undertake it? Each association found its own answers to these questions. Female imperialists did contribute to the large-scale Edwardian project of imperialist education, but not without setbacks. They resisted the submergence of their own perspectives on organizational methods and the grander purposes of Empire, and by so doing restricted the scope of their educational achievements. Ultimately their most successful educational work was to be undertaken in the specialized context of those imperialist activities best suited to their upper-class feminine abilities.

Selective achievement in the field of education was as much the result of the pressures of competition as of deliberate organizational policy. It is important to grasp the full extent and complexity of the contemporary educational onslaught in Empire's name. In the first place, the women's associations were forced to choose between tactics of rivalry, co-operation or avoidance in relation to the many male-led voluntary societies which existed to promote imperialism. Such societies were generally larger, better resourced and more influential than their female equivalents, and attached a higher priority to education and public propaganda. The Royal Colonial Institute had occupied a high-status position since 1868, with its gracious premises, fine library, annual lecture programme, expensive publications and distinguished membership. The Imperial Institute followed some way behind, despite the royal patronage which linked its foundation to Queen Victoria's 1887 Jubilee. Its imposing building proved to be a financial liability, compounded by a diffuse set of aims in which popular education rubbed shoulders with the dissemination of technical expertise and a range of social purposes. It was to these two institutes that Joseph Chamberlain first turned in 1902 when he decided to foster mass imperialist propaganda through a Colonial Office Visual Instruction Committee. British pressure upon colonial governments eventually secured funding for a worldwide scheme of published lectures supported by lantern slides, devised and administered by the institutes' London-based experts.[2] Leading figures from the two institutes were also to the fore in establishing large-scale unofficial propaganda through the British Empire League (1894), the Navy League (1895) and the National Service League (1902). By 1914 the two latter organizations boasted memberships of 100,000 and 220,000 respectively, and the former had achieved an extensive network of overseas branches. As well as campaigning for stronger imperial defence, the male leagues reached a wide audience with their general propaganda on the ideals of Empire. These societies' failed attempts to woo the Victoria League have already been described in Chapter 4. In this chapter we will examine the Victoria League's more directly competitive relationship with the League of the Empire, whose activities were far too close for comfort, partly because they determinedly linked adult propaganda to the imperial education of children.

A great deal of voluntary imperialist education was inevitably aimed at the nation's youth. Among the largest male-led associations were the Boys' Brigade (1884), the Church Lads' Brigade (1891) and the Boy Scouts (1908), all three linked once again to militarism, but also shaped around broader ideals. Baden-Powell believed that imperial citizenship was not the sole prerogative of those who fought, traded or settled in the distant Empire. It required development nearer home if Britain was to preserve its world leadership. On this basis he grudgingly accepted that girls too should receive imperial training, but insisted that it must be conducted differently and separately so that the boys' training should not be prejudiced. From 1910 his sister Agnes headed the much smaller Girl Guides association. Its handbook was entitled *How Girls Can Help Build up the Empire*, but its initial activities have been described by John Springhall as 'tepid and uninspiring', and were hampered by Victorian conventionality.[3] Similar gender inhibitions prevented the development of successful female equivalents to the

Boys' and Church Lads' Brigades, let alone the Army Cadet Force (with over 40,000 members by 1914) or Lord Meath's Lads' Drill Association, formed in 1899 and eventually merged into the National Service League. The women's imperialist associations faced various dilemmas in relation to such youth movements. Should they attempt to appropriate juvenile education as a 'feminine' branch of imperial work? Should they co-operate with existing organizations, or establish their own? The established links between female imperialism, maternal caring and the transmission of moral and cultural values appeared to suggest a field of womanly duty. There seemed to be little doubt that the imperialist education of youth must be appropriately gendered, and it was clear that the male-inspired youth movements would privilege the education of boys.

The needs of girls were proving less easy to ignore within the formal education system, however. Elementary schools increasingly provided girls as well as boys with some superficial knowledge of Empire history and geography, and with a diet of reading material, songs and prayers designed to foster imperial patriotism. The voluntary associations, both male and female, found themselves pushing at an open door as they strove to influence teachers and textbook writers towards the provision of a strongly imperial school education.[4] Their efforts were reinforced, and in some ways superseded, by the prestigious academic guidance issuing from the universities. This supplemented the influences of an increasingly imperialist (as well as cheap and plentiful) supply of leisure reading for adults and children alike.[5] Kipling was the unchallenged bard of Edwardian imperialism. Its novelists were Ballantyne, Stevenson and Henty, together with Bessie Marchant and Evelyn Everett Green (for girls) and innumerable imitators among popular biographers and magazine writers. The style and content of such literature permeated the fictional and poetic offerings of the female imperialist journals, and rubbed off on the rhetoric of published speeches and reports. Meanwhile, the influences of the schoolroom and of leisure reading were compounded by a vast range of adult and juvenile entertainment with an imperialist message. From the exhibitions of the Royal Academy to penny peepshows on the pier, visual imagery was harnessed to the cause. So too was dramatic and musical performance, another form of propaganda that had been gratefully borrowed by the female imperialist associations for their own educative and fund-raising purposes.[6] The boundaries between entertainment and propaganda, and between propaganda and imperial education, were increasingly difficult to draw. Each form of communication fed off the others and contributed to a discourse of Empire which drew in participants of all ages and at every social level.

Inevitably, the female imperialists were drawn by the prospect of building upon such mass educational influences. Even the least populist of their leaders were conscious of the advance of democracy and the importance of influencing the British public, as well as the upper echelons of Society; but where should their efforts be directed? The precise choice of medium and audience was by no means so obvious, and varied considerably between the different associations. Helped by their shared leadership, the associations successfully avoided the problems of additional competition among themselves. Their educational activities related to their chosen fields of work, and seem to have been regarded as mutually reinforcing. There was a generous exchange of space within the female imperialist journals as different associations publicized each other's work and published or republished each other's articles. Many leading speakers were also shared between the societies, offering their imperialist wisdom to the audiences of each in turn. Beyond this general level of reciprocity, each society evolved its own pattern of educational work. The Primrose League and the Girls' Friendly Society addressed mass memberships, but very differently. The emigration societies chose to confine themselves mainly to the 'practical' and specialized task of providing a realistic picture of colonial opportunities for women, and a down-to-earth preparation for those selected as suitable emigrants. Sporadically, they were drawn into more widespread propaganda work by the demands of fund-raising, the need to silence critics, and the urgency of their operations at the end of the South African War. The Victoria League wavered between 'specialized' intentions and broader imperial propaganda. The development of its educational work is particularly interesting since it provides a clear reflection of the weaknesses (as well as some strengths) of upper-class female amateurs operating in an increasingly professional and competitive field. The one area in which they achieved incontrovertible success was in the heavily gendered niche of educative colonial hospitality.

Though educational strategies varied, all the main female imperialist associations devoted much effort to the production of literature for organizational and propaganda purposes. Voluminous annual reports were an important means of communicating with supporters and establishing public credibility. The patronage of the Rhodes Trust and other donors enabled even the smaller societies to produce monthly journals. It seems unlikely that either *The Imperial Colonist* (1902) or the *Victoria League Notes* (1910) fully recouped their costs, but the mass-circulation papers of the Primrose League and the Girls' Friendly Society made the breakthrough to profitability and were central to the achievement of propagandist aims. Publication policies reflected the priorities, as well as the relative size and wealth, of each society. Should published literature be addressed mainly to existing members, or to a wider public? Should it aim to organize 'practical' work, or aspire to more ambitious educational heights? There is evidence of some ambivalence within each of the female imperialist associations, as well as of divergence between them. Added to the competitive pressures of the male leagues, and of mass imperialist education from other sources, were the uncertainties generated by awareness of publication as a public platform. To trespass boldly upon it might be to transgress conservative class and gender boundaries. On the other hand, to refrain from addressing a wider public might be to forfeit organizational growth and to neglect the imperial value of a potential mass audience. In the field of publication, as elsewhere in imperialist education, the leading ladies of organized imperialism sensed both their opportunity and their duty to offer new forms of service, but their decisions on forms of action were circumscribed by the existing duties and expectations of upper-class female behaviour.

At one end of the spectrum, the emigration societies seemed genuinely reluctant to move into the arena of public propaganda. These societies had originated in private philanthropy, and they clung to their traditions of selective, individualized work even after *The Imperial Colonist* had begun to publicize official links and to promote broader imperial service by and for women. The BWEA's subcommittee for diffusing information, formed in 1903, turned out to be a half-hearted affair. At its inaugural meeting Ellen Joyce explained 'the desirability of a special department to undertake the work of making known the openings which could be found for women in the colonies and the facilities offered by the Association for their protection'.[7] However, the ambitions of the new publicity drive were soon qualified by the committee members' emphasis upon the need for carefully chosen channels of communication. BWEA leaflets might safely be dispensed through contact with 'the heads of Governesses' Homes, Technical Schools, Ladies' Settlements, Clubs and Homes, and Clubs for business girls', but the Letter Writing Guild was rejected as 'connected chiefly with factory girls'. When the insertion of female emigration press notices was discussed, a suitably ladylike list was compiled of the journals with which the committee members had personal contact: *Hints, Church Monthly, The Gentlewoman, Treasury, The Churchwoman* and *The Queen*. Lack of funds compounded intentionally modest publicity aims. Each lady committed to 'diffusion of information' paid a small voluntary subscription towards costs of printing and postage, and at the meetings which followed reported upon her contacts with institutions and editors, and her approaches to vicars and parish magazines.[8] The impression remains of a society working to old-fashioned methods, and as determined to exclude some applicants as to encourage and educate others.

The Victoria League was less inherently hostile to the concept of mass propaganda, despite the social exclusivity of its leadership. It saw its duty as not merely to publicize its own activities but also to educate an increasingly wide sector of the public into a fuller appreciation of the Empire. For reasons which are not entirely clear, its initial propaganda vehicle was the public lecture with lantern slides rather than the publication of literature. Leaflet production remained small scale and largely confined to organizational matters. Did the Victoria League ladies feel that other organizations' publicity material served the purposes of political education equally well? The literature committee of the League devoted itself to the alternative work of selecting and dispatching suitable books, magazines and newspapers to grateful colonists. The education committee, as we shall see, became deeply involved in work with schools. Its efforts to establish professional credibility led it to become the only committee of the League with a male majority, so that its adoption of external imperialist literature is not unexpected. The Victoria League's most ambitious independent publication (apart from its journal) was its *Industrial Handbook*, the rigorously informative product of a subcommittee headed by Violet Markham and May Tennant.[9] The absence of a substantial body of Victoria League literature reflects the ambiguity of this society's position in relation to imperial education, as well as its restricted funds. In abstract terms, it was committed to the widest possible education. In practice, it made only limited attempts to enter the arena of public propaganda where so many others were already at work.

The Primrose League was in the forefront of popular imperialist education in the late Victorian and Edwardian years. As a well-funded organization supported by many wealthy and influential men, it pursued its joint social and political role through a wide variety of public activities and entertainment. Britain's imperial mission was deeply embedded in Primrose League propaganda and developed an appeal which was none the less powerful for being somewhat vaguely defined. According to Martin Pugh, the key ingredients of rank-and-file interest were 'sheer curiosity, the cult of the hero, patriotism, and militarism'.[10] Each of these opened up channels for educative imperialist propaganda, including lantern lectures and literature. At times of crisis such as during the South African War or at the outbreak of the First World War, the League was prepared to finance tens of thousands of leaflets on the issues of the day alongside its regular journals and pamphlets. There is evidence to suggest that the Ladies' Grand Council was eager to place its energy and resources into propaganda work. The ladies' educational initiatives led directly to the establishment of a joint literature committee, providing a formal link to the male Ruling Grand Council and in receipt of a sizeable annual grant voted by the Ladies' Grand Council. In addition, the ladies continued to finance some educational activities of their own, such as a 'van tour' in 1891.[11] However, despite the importance of female support for the educative work of the Primrose League, it would be difficult to demonstrate any distinctive femininity of form or message. To all intents and purposes, the efforts of the Dames were submerged within the larger organization of the League. Indeed, when the Ladies' Grand Council ventured independent criticism of the quality of the *Primrose League Gazette* in 1889, they received a scarcely concealed rebuke ('The Grand Council are of the opinion that as an official organ it served a business-like purpose, though it is admittedly not an attractive or entertaining paper').[12] During the 1900s the *Gazette* made limited concessions to the widening spectrum of potential readers, but remained under the heavy hand of an anti-feminist male editor.[13]

The centrality of a distinctive mass literature within the Girls' Friendly Society is in marked contrast to its absence from the emigration societies and the Victoria League, and the lack of feminine influence upon the publications of the Primrose League. By the 1900s imperialism was prominent within GFS work, but the Society remained true to its initial aims of religious and moral training and practical assistance for young working women. Both directly and indirectly, the Empire's needs had come to permeate these aims. The essentially educative nature of GFS work created multiple opportunities for imperialist propaganda directed at a large and varied audience. In the first year of its existence the Society established its *Members' Magazine* and a circulating library designed to promote moral education. In 1879 a literature department was created which encouraged educational initiatives at both central and local levels. Diocesan lending libraries and a central postal library ensured that good literature lay within reach of every member, and reading unions at both elementary and more advanced levels provided inexperienced readers with encouragement to take up the opportunities thus provided. From 1895 onwards a monthly Reading Union leaflet offered diligent girls a winter plan of reading which culminated (for the lucky few) in a residential week of study and prayer shared by members and associates. Less ambitious readers often formed local study circles devoted to particular topics, or particular works, and guided by any moderately educated associate.

At Fawsley, Louisa Knightley led a reading circle which considered 'the beginning of Colonial Enterprise' through the summer of 1902.[14] Other evidence confirms that GFS reading was strongly patriotic and imperialist as well as religious in tone. Shakespeare's histories were a particular favourite, as were the poems of Wordsworth and Tennyson and the novels of Scott, Kingsley and Dickens. The Girls' Friendly Society's own publications list had become very varied and extensive by the 1900s. A hierarchy of GFS journals extended from the *Associates' Journal* through *Friendly Work* and *Friendly Leaves* down to the juvenile candidates' paper, *Our Letter*. Though leaflets and journals served an organizational purpose, they maintained a strongly didactic flavour as well.

Articles, stories and letters from Empire settings were a mainstay at every level, and this was no doubt a consideration when the GFS Colonial Committee decided against the establishment of a specialized imperialist journal in 1906. Instead, 'The Flying Post' was established as a regular extra supplement within the highly successful *Friendly Work*, under the byline of 'Friendly News for Friendly Workers throughout the Empire'.

Travelling GFS emissaries were ideally placed to provide home readers with a congenial imperial education. In autumn 1906 the *Associates' Journal* carried a lengthy series entitled 'With Miss Peacock in Australia'. In the same year *Friendly Work* relayed instalments of 'News from Miss Whitley' in Canada. Her letters to members were intimate and educative in turn. When she visited Newfoundland, readers learned that Newfoundland's GFS Treaty was framed alongside a portrait of Queen Victoria in the members' meeting room at St John's. A forty-nine-hour journey from Nova Scotia had been endured by night steamer and then through a heavy snowfall, cleared from the railway tracks by a 'cow-catcher'. In St John's the children were 'busy with their toboggans', and Mr Stewart, the 'Eskimo Missionary' sponsored by the East Molesey GFS branch, was busy 'pursuing his heroic work, having lately baptized twenty-four Eskimos'. The St John's GFS members received a letter from their Oxford 'link' branch, read aloud by Miss Whitley – 'such a delightful way of realising the bond between the Old Country and the Colony'.[15] These accounts carried the adventurous, patriotic flavour of much Edwardian imperialist leisure reading, but with the added enjoyment, for British GFS members, of feeling themselves to be active and valued participants.

Even the chattiest of colonial members' letters invariably related to GFS organization and GFS values, in which Empire, patriotism and Christianity had become so closely entwined. From British Columbia, a married emigrant described the beauties of autumnal forests, the roar of bears and the perils of winter journeys, before setting out her own exemplary record of womanly work for the Empire:

> My days are filled up with my little duties, as we have all our own baking of bread and everything to do, and I enjoy doing it, and love my Canadian home and make it as homely and *English* as I can . . . We enjoyed our Christmas very much: we had eight of us to dinner, and five to tea and supper, and it was most touching, the lads thanking us for letting them come and enjoy a real English Christmas out here. We had for dinner, two turkeys, sausages and potatoes, and cabbage (25 cents=1s, what price cabbage here!) . . . We were asked out to three different places for the New Year, but preferred spending it cosy together as our first one, and so we have started another year, and everywhere is several feet deep in snow, and just now a blizzard is blowing it in all directions . . . It is so difficult to get to Church very often, so we have our service to ourselves of a Sunday evening, so as to keep in touch with our dear ones in prayer and praise in the dear old England we love, and I do hope to start the GFS work in the spring if I possibly can.[16]

This letter was followed by a practical message of advice from Mrs Joyce 'To Members Emigrating'. Longer and more directly educational articles were frequently published on emigration and mission work, but there can be little doubt that the firsthand, personal records of GFS travellers and settlers held a unique appeal for a youthful female readership.

Lady imperialists in Britain were sometimes fortunate enough to be able to call on firsthand colonial experience when they organized public meetings and lectures.

However, the intimacy of GFS journalism did not often survive the transition to a public stage. Mrs Joyce was herself a travel veteran and a champion of 'the personal' in emigration work, but she tended to become bombastic in public. Many of the leading ladies of female imperialism were reluctant to mount the platform at all, and happy to leave this sphere to male visitors who were not interested in the price of cabbages and the details of children's games. The education offered at public meetings was usually general and rhetorical. When an address was billed as a 'lecture', on the other hand, it was often heavily informative. Public lantern slide lectures on aspects of the Empire were presented regularly by both the Primrose League and the Victoria League, to audiences of mixed sex and varied social class. Most Primrose League lecturers were male, and preferred topics included the Army, the Navy and the South African War alongside familiar tales of imperial 'heroism'. The Victoria League, on the other hand, developed a lecture programme closely related to that of Chamberlain's Colonial Office Visual Instruction Committee. It seems likely that the Victoria League Education subcommittee drew up its own comprehensive lecture scheme before the official government scheme was launched, whether in response to official prompting or as an independent prompt related to perceived need. A copy of the Victoria League scheme survives among Milner's papers in the form of a 'Plan for Imperial Education' submitted unsuccessfully to the Rhodes Trust during 1902. No doubt the appeal was at this point rejected as over-ambitious, coming as it did from a newly formed female-led association. Its scope was certainly impressive. A two-pronged approach was designed to provide imperial instruction both 'throughout the chief self-governing Colonies and in this country, on subjects bearing on the unity of the Empire'.[17]

The Victoria League was compensated for the rejection of its own scheme by a seat on the Colonial Office Visual Instruction Committee's advisory board, where its representative joined the most distinguished male imperial educators in Britain. Nevertheless, a decision was taken to persist with independent education projects. 'A beautiful magic lantern' was presented by Lady Jersey to the Victoria League during the first year of its existence, and various sets of slides were soon in preparation. Mrs Fawcett was among the early users, and donated eighty 'beautiful coloured slides' after lecturing in South Africa on 'The Life of Queen Victoria', 'A Visit to London', 'The Country Houses and Gardens' and 'The Institutions of England' during 1903.[18] Over the next few years a British lecture programme and the formation of local branches progressed side by side. There was also a growing demand for Victoria League speakers from other, mainly male, organizations. Eleanor Percy Taylor proved an inspired appointment as secretary to the education committee, then as a travelling lecturer. Between 1906 and 1907 she gave twenty-six out of fifty-two public League lectures. Other speakers included Violet Markham and Maud Pember-Reeves, wife of the New Zealand Agent-General in London and well-known Fabian social investigator and suffragist.

The 1906 Victoria League Annual Report recorded that lecture attendance had ranged from industrial artisans and agricultural labourers to the youth of high schools, elementary schools and boys' clubs, as well as 'mixed audiences both in town and country'.[19] No wonder stalwart professional lecturers were sometimes judged necessary to undertake the work rather than aristocratic ladies. Subjects in 1906 included 'How the British Government fights a Famine in India', 'Our Mediterranean Possessions' and

'The British Empire: Its Problems and Ideals', as well as 'general lectures' on India, Ceylon, Australia, New Zealand, Canada, Rhodesia, Egypt and the Sudan. When the Victoria League began its democratization attempt in 1911, it entered into friendly relations with the Workers' Educational Association, and its General Secretary was invited on to the League's executive. Meanwhile, male 'experts' were beginning to outnumber Victoria League women both as public speakers and as education committee members. By 1914 the committee contained male representatives of the Working Men's Clubs and Institutes Union, the National Union of Teachers, the Headmasters' Conference and the London Teachers' Association, as well as a scattering of professors and MPs. The very success of the Victoria League's educational programme had undermined its distinctiveness. The education committee had been virtually abandoned by titled ladies, who instead moved over to the literature committee and the hospitality committee, where their aristocratic attributes were more appreciated.

The Victoria League's literature committee was closely associated with its lecture programme. The patronage of Alfred Beit, South African mining magnate and colleague of Cecil Rhodes, enabled the League to set up a lending library which despatched book boxes to British branches to supplement the education provided by meetings and lantern lectures. This work was soon overtaken by the task of supplying colonial readers with books, newspapers and magazines. It had always been expected that the imperial education of the British and the colonial public would proceed hand-in-hand. They might exchange slides, lectures and lecturers, but in the field of literature provision the British benefactors were able (not for the first time) to display philanthropic superiority. The development of English-language school libraries in South Africa was seen as an urgent patriotic duty as the war ended, and the needs of lonely Canadian loggers or Australian bush-dwellers were soon arousing equally generous sympathy. Though much of the colonial education undertaken by the Victoria League and its overseas allies was directed towards schoolchildren, the leading ladies were enthusiastic proponents of adult distance-learning which fostered 'person-to-person' contacts between Britain and its Empire. During 1909 and 1910 the literature committee sent out over 14,000 books and magazines, but particularly prided itself upon having stimulated individuals to despatch 72,000 newspapers. Sending newspapers was labour-intensive work, for the Victoria League insisted upon careful matching of donors and recipients and systematically monitored the acceptability of what was sent. The majority of senders were certainly female, and though the initial recipient was often a male householder, pen-friendships which followed sometimes linked women imperialists across the oceans in a process of mutual education.[20]

Undoubtedly the most successful single aspect of Victoria League 'person-to-person' education was the work of its hospitality committee. Here the leading ladies ruled unchallenged until the First World War, when the needs of massed colonial troops forced them to broaden their schemes. The hospitality committee of 1902 was set up in anticipation of the opportunities afforded by Edward VII's Coronation for welcoming colonial visitors to London. Chaired by Lady Jersey, the committee's original members included Violet Cecil, Edith Lyttelton, the Duchess of Marlborough and the Viscountess Cranbourne. Frances Balfour proved a mixed blessing as Honorary Secretary, but was well placed for the task of approaching English hostesses 'with the result that nearly every well-known house in London extended a warm personal welcome to all visitors introduced by the Victoria League'. During May, June and July 'forty parties of various kinds were given and about 4,600 invitations sent out to visitors . . . from every corner of the British Empire'.[21] The ladies' political and social connections also secured seats for colonial guests at the Solemn Intercession Service in St Paul's Cathedral, at the Royal Review of the Colonial Troops, and along the route of the Coronation Procession.

In April 1902 a group of forty Canadian teachers on their way to concentration camp schools in South Africa were greeted by an avalanche of hospitality which they were still remembering eight years later when Meriel Talbot met them during her World Tour. Rather than simple enjoyment, the aim of the Victoria League was 'to put them in the way of seeing something of the historical and social life in England'. During a stay of just over a week they were entertained by Princess Louise and her husband (Frances Balfour's brother) at Kensington Palace, by Lady Gough at the Tower of London, and at four other ladies' homes. Visits were made to the Houses of Parliament, Oxford and Hatfield, and at Miss Balfour's Downing Street party the teachers were introduced to 'some of our leading Englishmen', including Lord Roberts and Joseph Chamberlain.[22] The patriotic education of colonial educators was a priority for many imperialists, and the Victoria League found its services in demand once again when 165 Canadian teachers spent six weeks in Britain during the summer of 1910. The Board of Education 'invited the Central Executive to undertake the social arrangements', and 'a delightful programme' was soon on offer, including more receptions at the house of leading London hostesses, tea at the House of Commons, tours of St Paul's, Westminster Abbey and Canterbury Cathedral, and visits to Hatfield and Warwick Castle.[23]

Meanwhile, the League's regular pattern of colonial hospitality had emerged from somewhat haphazard beginnings. The personal contacts of League members with colonial visitors were supplemented by information from the Colonial Office, where Alfred Lyttelton presided from 1903 to 1905. As his wife recounted in his biography:

> The efforts of the Victoria League . . . received great encouragement from the new Colonial Secretary: he made arrangements by which, through the League, the arrival of distinguished visitors from the Colonies was communicated to a few people who undertook to direct hospitality. The desire to meet and to make friends was keen on both sides, it needed only to bring the hosts and the guests together . . . These efforts were, of course, only an attempt to carry into the social sphere the great impulse towards Union between Great Britain and the Dominions, which had been given by Mr Chamberlain's imagination and statesmanship.[24]

The League's efforts to organize social recognition for visitors were undoubtedly much appreciated by colonials who were sensitive to metropolitan snobbery. The political dimensions of hospitality were hinted at in the hospitality committee's careful investigation of occasional complaints from the neglected, and directly addressed in a private letter from Earl Grey (Canadian Governor General) to Violet Markham in November 1906:

> Canadians of influence have had their white hearts towards England turned black by C[olonial].O[ffice]. neglect. The Ladies Organisation has done splendid work in this direction, and the enthusiasm with which Canadians have spoken on their return of the kindness they have received, and especially of Mrs Alfred Lyttelton, is very pleasant to

witness. A little attention is so tremendously appreciated, and conversely a want of attention excites all sorts of disappointed and angry feelings.[25]

There was some concern in Victoria League circles that this useful relationship between male official and female voluntary effort would cease when the Conservatives lost office in 1906. However, the League's non-party stance and social exclusiveness stood it in good stead, and Liberal Colonial Secretaries were soon not merely requesting its assistance, but adding their wives to its hospitality committee. The Imperial Conferences of 1907 and 1911 afforded the Victoria League semi-official status as the preferred channel for hospitality to visiting premiers, their wives and leading staff. Entertainment and education merged seamlessly together in 1911 as the Victoria League's own Imperial Conference offered expert hospitality to visiting delegates, culminating in one of Lady Jersey's famous Osterley garden-parties. Among the outcomes of this conference was a decision to 'channel' hospitality more deliberately in future so that colonial visitors might benefit from introductions to British hosts who shared similar interests or professions. During 1911 the League hosted more than 1500 visitors. The private generosity even of the wealthy was stretched to its limits. Efforts were made to reproduce an upper-class drawing-room atmosphere within the League's own Millbank House headquarters, where eight special parties were held.[26] Another means of spreading the demands of hospitality was the establishment of the Ladies' Empire Club in London from 1902 onwards. Victoria League women were in the vanguard of this scheme, which enabled their executive committee to be 'at home' to members on Tuesday afternoons and 'soon proved to be a great help in promoting that friendly intercourse and interchange of hospitality, which was the object of its founders'. Permanent premises were obtained in Grosvenor Street, Joseph and Mary Chamberlain took a friendly interest, and before long it was evident that the Club could become a profitable independent enterprise. By 1904 it had over 900 members ('of whom nearly 300 are Colonial Ladies'). The Victoria League retained the right to nominate one-third of the Club's central committee, and made extensive use of its facilities.[27]

The success of the Ladies' Empire Club was part of the wider success of Victoria League hospitality, and underlines the connections between its chosen activities and the wealth and social status of its female leaders. Social exclusivity proved to be both an asset and an obstacle in the tasks of imperial education. Many colonial visitors were deeply impressed by the League's hospitality, as much because it provided opportunities to rub shoulders with the aristocracy as because it made them 'feel at home in England in every sense of the word', as the League's third Annual Report put it.[28] In fact, the social attractions of the British association were so strong that its executive committee felt obliged to erect barriers to prevent over-eager visitors from deserting their own colonial imperialist organizations. In July 1902 they decided that no 'colonial' should be admitted who was not already a member of the relevant allied association overseas. In July 1906 this decision was reinforced, on Violet Markham's suggestion, by a resolution that long-term colonial visitors should complete a year of British residence before applying to the Victoria League. The only sweetener offered by the committee a year later was the opportunity for long-stay colonials to pay reduced Victoria League subscriptions.

These decisions undoubtedly caused some offence. Though many visitors had social aspirations, not all were prepared to merge their pride in shared British race into an attitude of social deference. It is no coincidence that the complaints which reached the hospitality committee sometimes came from leading ladies of the Dominions' imperialist associations who were deeply conscious of a wider range of contested issues around colonial nationalism and imperial sisterhood. In October 1910 Meriel Talbot relayed to the committee a complaint from Mrs Rawbone in South Africa who was 'offended at no notice having been taken of her by the Hospitality Committee when she was in England five years ago'.[29] Still more predictably, Mrs Nordheimer of the Canadian Daughters of the Empire also complained that 'although 30 introductions had been given to Canadian visitors coming to London, none had been made use of'.[30] After investigation, both complaints were dismissed as groundless. The mingled issues of social class and imperialist politics became increasingly complex as the Victoria League endeavoured to 'democratize', and as the growing size of its overseas affiliates further fuelled the demand for British hospitality. Perhaps in consequence, the League seems to have been unusually responsive to the overtures of a new 'rival' in the imperial hospitality field in the years before the war. Evelyn Wrench and his daughter received League introductions to Dominion imperialists as they toured the world in 1913 drumming up support for the Overseas Club, a loosely defined but determinedly democratic association of imperialists pledged 'to draw together in the bond of comradeship British people the world over'.[31]

Victoria League hospitality remained an almost exclusively feminine venture up to 1914. The women's expertise in such work was flatteringly acknowledged by successive governments and was, of course, an extension of a well-established and respected female role in upper-class Society. From the perspective of the League's leading ladies, there was no doubt about its educative importance. As one Annual Report summarized it, 'Such mutual intercourse is sure to be of benefit to both sides, removing misunderstanding and prejudices founded upon ignorance, and opening the way to that wider and more intelligent sympathy which should be the aim of every true citizen of the British Empire.'[32] There was, however, some danger that the role of hospitality would not be taken as seriously by external male sympathizers. With good reason, Primrose League ladies had earlier rejected their male leadership's efforts to typecast them into the management of 'entertainments'. As a high-profile aspect of female imperialism, hospitality work enhanced the status of 'women's work for Empire' as a distinctive, but in this case distinctly subordinate, complement to the male tasks of military, economic and political Empire-building. There were few male challengers in the field of hospitality partly because it was regarded as a relatively unimportant aspect of imperial education.

The imperial education of schoolchildren, on the other hand, was one of the most congested areas in a crowded field. When formal education moved to the forefront of the Victoria League Education Committee's work, the leading ladies found themselves rapidly marginalized by male professionals. Schoolteaching was a career increasingly open to women, but the education system as a whole was controlled by a male hierarchy of local and national politicians, officials and university-educated experts. The task of imperializing school education was already underway, and the initiative in this area was not likely to be surrendered to untrained female volunteers, however nobly born.

Nevertheless, all the women's imperialist associations maintained a strong belief in their particular, gendered contribution to the nurture and upbringing of the Empire's youth. With the exception of the emigration societies, the associations developed their own forms of junvenile propaganda activity which resisted submergence within the wider imperial studies movement centred upon the schools, and also avoided takeover by the large-scale voluntary youth movements. Achievements were relatively small scale, but provide further evidence of the underlying ideals of organized female imperialism.

The Girls' Friendly Society led the way in juvenile education. The vast majority of its membership consisted of young women aged between 12 and 25 years, but it was decided as early as 1879 that there was an important place within the Society for still younger candidates aged between 8 and 12 years. Mrs Townsend herself became head of a special candidates' department in 1896, and encouraged the spread of its work through every diocese in Britain.[33] *Our Letter* was founded as the candidates' journal in 1901, and gradually came to carry its share of the imperial message. By 1906 it was 'Our Letter for GFS Candidates all over the World'. The Christmas edition of that year carried the first of a new series entitled 'Stories of Brave Girls'. It was introduced with the slightly startling claim that

> as it is the possible fate of every English girl to go and live her life at the ends of the world, perhaps among wild animals and wild men, any one may some day find herself in a 'tight corner', with a home to defend, and but few to help . . . In that day, perhaps, nothing will cheer more than the recollection of the brave deeds of real girls in the olden days, who, all unprepared, fought and even died for their country.

An article on Empire Day recommended that candidates should learn 'The Flag of Britain' and quoted from the Earl of Meath's letter commending GFS patriotism. A pleasing vision of girls leading the way in imperial education was reinforced by details of the candidates' central examination in an adjoining column. Girls aged 10 to 12 years were asked, 'Suppose you were going to Canada, how could you continue to be a Member of the GFS?', while more advanced candidates aged 13 to 14 years faced a battery of questions on 'The GFS in the Colonies', including 'Draw a map of any one Colony, and mark on it any places where you know the GFS is at work. (This may be done with the aid of an atlas and tracing paper.)' and 'In what ways are some of the Branches in England specially interested in those of other countries?'[34]

In 1911 the Girls' Friendly Society reported over 80,000 candidates, alongside 194,000 members and 38,000 associates. This compared favourably with the Primrose League's total of 65,000 juvenile members (1913) alongside an adult 'live' membership of 656,000 (1912). Interestingly, the task of organizing the young seems to have been automatically passed on to the Primrose League's Dames when the first juvenile branches were acknowledged in the early 1890s. Children aged from 7 to 16 years were to be recruited with their parents' consent, and engaged in a range of activities which included sport, singing and first aid, as well as instruction in citizenship and the politics of the Primrose League. A close association with the Boy Scouts movement developed after 1908, probably reinforcing a gender imbalance among the junior membership. However, women retained an important organizational role, and reports in the *Primrose League Gazette* suggest that this was one area of the League's work where their strengths were acknowledged. The content of Dames' addresses to the juveniles (or 'buds' as they were sometimes known) was occasionally reported. In January 1901 Mrs Sympson urged the Lincoln Juvenile Branch 'to stick fast to our United Empire, dear old Great Britain and Ireland, and our Colonies – one great family under one good Mother Queen'. In November 1904 the Countess of Darnley summarized juvenile imperial duty in terms of 'being good' and 'knowing the King and Queen'. While boys might become soldiers, 'You girls can do just as much, for it is the girls' influence in the home, as in later years the woman's influence, that makes and keeps men good and straight.' Examinations in Empire knowledge were a feature of the Primrose buds', as well as GFS candidates', annual calendar. Juveniles of the Grantham Dames Habitation answered a formidable list of questions in December 1900 which included 'What is meant by the phrase "Britannia rules the waves"?' and 'Give a short sketch of the war in South Africa, its cause and progress. What good is expected to result from it?'[35]

Like the Primrose League, the Victoria League acquired its junior members as a result of spontaneous activity at branch level rather than as a result of central policy. In this case the initiative had more to do with the enthusiasm of individual schoolteachers than with female imperialist nurturing of the young, though there was a certain amount of overlap between these categories. The hero of the Victoria League Junior Associates was Mr George Hallam, who by 1908 had 'organised a gallant band of 700 young Victoria Leaguers at Harrow'[36] and, after securing the executive committee's approval, devoted an increasing amount of time to founding branches in schools elsewhere. He was recruited to the League's organization committee, and was the inevitable choice to edit a boys' and girls' page in the new *Victoria League Notes* of 1910. Two years later the Victoria League's Annual General Meeting debated a proposal to lower the minimum entry age for junior associates from 10 to 7 years. On Mr Hallam's advice, this suggestion from a lady member was rejected, though a compromise category of 'Junior helpers' was permitted. Mr Hallam 'feared that the standard of achievement might be seriously lowered' by the admission of younger children: a reflection of his own determination to use the Victoria League as a channel of supplementary imperialist education rather than merely as a focus for socializing and entertainments.[37] Most of the junior associate branches which reported their work during 1911 were based in individual public schools, high schools and grammar schools, though some drew upon a wider catchment area. In Harrow itself, Mr Hallam organized members from fourteen different schools. The activities pursued by this varied membership were largely educational: 186 children were engaged in colonial correspondence; 177 were sending newspapers to the Dominions; and hundreds more had attended lectures on Canada and India which culminated in the singing of appropriate Victoria League songs ('Copies of the words can be supplied by the Harrow Branch for a small payment').[38]

Most other junior Victoria League branches were considerably smaller, but modelled their activities around the successful example of Harrow. Overseas junior branches also developed, and their members were welcomed into a world of essay competitions on stirring imperial themes, made attractive by the publicity of the *Victoria League Notes* and by the prospect of some glamorous prizes. Sets of Mafeking stamps were competed for in 1904 – 'one to be given in Great Britain, one in Canada, one in South Africa and one in Australia'[39] – and twenty MPs, led by the Prime Minister and Colonial Secretary, donated signed volumes for presentation in South African schools. As a grateful education official wrote to the League, 'Nothing can help us more in our work in this Colony than the practical evidence afforded by the gift of these prizes of the interest of the leading public men at home in the welfare of the Transvaal children.'[40] Lady Darnley's prize of six guineas' worth of books for an essay on Australia was somewhat predictably won by Miss Amber Reeves, daughter of a New Zealand Agent-General and a Victoria League lecturer. In later years the volume of donated prizes caused a positive glut of essay competitions, some of which attracted disappointingly few entrants. It took a Balliol scholarship-winner from Harrow to successfully 'Describe the leading principles of the various systems of Government in operation within the British Empire' in 1909; in the following year judges could find no worthy first prize-winner from among those attempting to 'Discuss the best means of promoting "The True Temper of Empire" in a Great Democracy'. More successful were simpler titles such as 'Tasmania', for which the Tasmanian Victoria League offered prizes to be competed for among the elementary schools in Oxford and Southport, where juvenile branches were strong.[41]

The menu of competitions sometimes extended to include drawings and poems. Two successful entries are reproduced in Plates 7 and 8. Under the auspices of the Victoria League, talented juveniles rendered the imperialist message in ways that were highly congenial to their elders. Among the lessons successfully learned were those of race and gender. The Empire could be visualized, and portrayed, in both male and female forms and in terms both of conquest and nurture. It is interesting to find female contestants opting mainly for the latter, and notable that feminized versions of imperial duty remained strongly to the fore within what had become (particularly in its educational work) a mixed-sex association. The Victoria League had its heroes, but generally lacked the militarist emphasis which was so pronounced in other juvenile and adult imperialist societies during the Edwardian years. Though individual enthusiasts might promote rifle-shooting or supplement Victoria League membership with support for the Navy League or National Service League or Boy Scouts, the predominant political ethos remained one of 'sane', non-aggressive imperialism. Neither imperial defence nor imperial economics was prominent in the propaganda and educational work of the Victoria League, except insofar as these were linked to 'human interest' stories of soldiers' and settlers' lifestyles and family ties to the Motherland. The shared racial inheritance of the British Empire, on the other hand, was a subject close to the Victoria League's heart. Endlessly symbolized through family images and the icons of royalty, it inflected most of the work produced by juvenile members. Sidney Griffin's prize cartoon (Plate 8) is a particularly crude (and powerful) portrayal of racial hierarchy in South Africa. Isabel Field's 'Britannia welcoming her daughters'(Plate 7) is slightly more subtle. Sturdy white daughters, led by New Zealand and providing a classical ideal of European beauty, occupy the foreground of the procession. Ceylon and India huddle shyly behind. Jamaica and Mauritius have sent white representatives, while Africa seems to have got lost altogether within the throng. Beyond the elegant, helmeted figure of Britannia, with her garlanded attendants and her feminized royal lion, an inexpertly drawn battleship guards the white cliffs of England.

The Victoria League had perhaps 2000 signed up junior associates by 1914, but its educational influence reached beyond this number into all the schools where there were adult sympathizers. The success of educational work depended heavily upon the co-operation of teachers. This point was accepted more willingly and completely by the

League of the Empire than by the Victoria League, and largely accounts for its substantial achievements. The two Leagues became long-standing irritants to each other, despite frequent and time-wasting attempts to mend fences and to negotiate alliance or merger. Curiously, the best chance of success probably occurred in the opening weeks of the Victoria League's existence. The League of the Empire had narrowly preceded it, but was conscious of the advantages attached to the social status of the rival body. The first executive minute book of the Victoria League carries a carefully amended account of an exploratory joint meeting in May 1901. The amendments and content of this report indicate clearly enough how the land lay. The Victoria League had reacted with conscious .superiority to the other League's overtures, and insisted upon asserting its own higher authority.[42] Unfortunately, the League of the Empire was also headed by a determined woman, of upper-middle-class rather than aristocratic background. Mrs Ord Marshall was the Honorary Secretary and inspiration of her League from 1901 until her death in 1931. She was not prepared to submit deferentially to aristocratic Victoria League leadership, and was soon successful in supplementing her limited social connections with a powerful phalanx of representatives from professional interest groups concerned with imperial education. Academics, teachers and education officials joined her committees, further supplemented by colonial representatives who were rather tardily drawn into the Victoria League's own structure.

The League of the Empire's biggest successes were its imperial education conferences in London in 1907 and 1911, and its organization of the first conference for imperial teachers' associations in 1912. A monthly journal boasted of 'official recognition' from the Colonial Office and the Headmasters' Conference, and by 1913 the League also claimed credit for the Hyde Park Empire Day parades of schoolchildren and for 26,556 happily linked juvenile imperial correspondents.[43] Milner commented privately to Violet Markham on Mrs Ord Marshall's 'Bismarckian personality',[44] and the Victoria League's own record of negotiations suggests that some of her claims were matters of show rather than substance. The personal clash between the two Leagues' secretaries must have been formidable and may (as Milner and other weary onlookers believed) have been in itself an insuperable obstacle to amalgamation; but the failure is also of some interest as a reflection upon the strengths and weaknesses of the Victoria League. Ultimately, the League of the Empire was more successful in cornering the support of education professionals. The Victoria League was less whole-hearted in its attempts to reach out to middle-class allies and colonial supporters under terms which suggested an acceptable degree of equality. Its educational work continued to reflect the dominance of an aristocratic female leadership, despite the broadening membership of its education committee.

The celebration of Empire Day, on Queen Victoria's birthday, was in many ways the apotheosis of juvenile imperialist education. No single organization could monopolize credit for the escalating success of this event from 1904 onwards. The first such celebrations apparently occurred in Canada, where 24 May was made a national holiday in 1901. The Earl of Meath, who was the key British instigator of Empire Day, unsuccessfully urged Joseph Chamberlain to place a similar proposal on the agenda of the 1902 Colonial Conference. From Meath's Social Darwinist perspective imperial education was indissolubly linked to racial hierarchy and racial improvement. Both he and his wife were heavily involved in the work of the Girls' Friendly Society, and many of his appeals were directed particularly to women. 'My appeal to British mothers is to consider themselves the trustees of the Empire in the training of their children,' he wrote in 1908.[45] The undertone of anxiety in Meath's passionate imperialism helped to make him an effective advocate. He lacked any possessiveness about his Empire Day scheme, and begged every available organization and individual to join in its success. Such appeals were sympathetically received by all the female imperialist associations, which he visited in turn in order to press home the case in person. The Victoria League showed its customary reluctance to commit to unconditional alliances, but reports from its adult and juvenile branches show how enthusiastically its membership entered into the spirit of an occasion which held open limitless opportunities for both education and mass enjoyment.

Empire Day was perhaps the most structured occasion during the year when the Victoria League, the Primrose League and even the Girls' Friendly Society merged cheerfully with each other's activities and with those of other juvenile imperialist groups. Patriotic schoolteachers determined the order of ceremonies, and drilled their classes accordingly. However, there is copious evidence to suggest that voluntary imperialist associations encouraged this to happen. As early as 1905, the Cheltenham Branch of the Victoria League 'promoted the observance of Empire Day in co-operation with the Town Committee':

> A half-holiday followed a morning of patriotic lessons. More than a thousand children assembled at the Town Hall to hear a message from Lord Meath, to sing patriotic songs, and to watch the award of Victoria League prizes.

A souvenir booklet was presented to every child 'by the Deputy Mayoress representing the town, and one of our Committee representing the Victoria League'.[46] Mr Hallam's branch was naturally not to be outdone, and reported proudly in the same year that 'Owing to the efforts of the League, Harrow on Empire Day was quite en fête'.[47] In London, Lady Jersey engaged in a mild dispute with the London County Council's Education Committee before eventually obtaining permission 'to present the National flag to the Council Schools in Chelsea'.[48] A heavyweight ceremony followed on Empire Day 1907. In the grounds of Chelsea Hospital, and in the presence of most of the League's leading ladies, 'Lord Methuen made the presentation and Sir Frederick Lugard addressed the children'. Two thousand children then joined in 'the combined singing of Kipling's Recessional and the Children's Hymn' to the strains of the Duke of York's school band.[49] By 1914 accounts of such events filled many columns of the *Victoria League Notes*, the *Primrose League Gazette* and the GFS papers. The fact that Empire Day was truly pan-imperial added to its attractions, and of course to its educative potential.

The educational work of the female imperialists was naturally recorded by them in terms of its successes. There were some impressive achievements in the fields of both adult and juvenile education. The fact that the ladies' associations joined a rolling bandwagon should not deny them a share of any credit due for the escalation of popular imperialism, and of an imperialist school curriculum, during the Edwardian years. However, from a longer-term perspective it is evident that their share in these developments was relatively modest. Both the emigration societies and the Girls' Friendly Society preferred to work towards their own selected, gendered aims. The

Primrose League deliberately swamped the potentially distinctive contribution of its female leadership in this area of work as in others. Neither the emigration societies nor the Victoria League were large enough organizations to mount a truly effective mass propaganda drive. More significantly, neither really aspired to do so. The emigration societies successfully supported small-scale practical training and informational work among intending emigrants. The ladies of the Victoria League successfully developed colonial hospitality and other 'person-to-person' methods of extending imperial knowledge and mutual understanding. The Girls' Friendly Society successfully added imperialist overtones to its moral message. But the upper-class female leaders of all these associations recoiled from the whole-hearted engagement with the media, the academics and the teaching profession which would have been required if they were to enter into genuine partnership with the true educators of the British public.

Notes

1. In the past two decades an extensive literature has developed around the themes of education, socialization and Empire. John Mackenzie led the way with *Propaganda and Empire* (1984) and an edited volume, *Imperialism and Popular Culture* (1986), to be followed by James Mangan, *Benefits Bestowed: Education and British Imperialism* (1988) and *The Games Ethic and Imperialism* (1989) (all Manchester: Manchester University Press). More theoretically nuanced recent works include K. Tidrick, *Empire and the English Character* (London: I.B. Tauris, 1992); and A. McClintock, *Imperial Leather: Race, Gender and Sexuality in the Colonial Contest* (London and New York: Routledge, 1995). The resistance to imperialist soft-soaping has also been addressed by several authors, notably in H. Pelling, *Popular Politics and Society in Late Victorian Britain* (London: Macmillan, 1979); and in E. Hammerton and D. Cannadine, 'Conflict and Consensus on a Ceremonial Occasion: The Diamond Jubilee in Cambridge in 1897', *Historical Journal* (1981), **24**: 111–46.
2. See J. Mackenzie, *Propaganda and Empire*, pp. 162–6; also T. Reese, *History of the Royal Commonwealth Society 1868–1968* (Oxford: Oxford University Press, 1968).
3. J. Springhall, *Youth, Empire and Society* (London: Croom Helm, 1977), p. 132. See also the chapter on Scouting and Guiding by A. Warren in Mackenzie, *Imperialism and Popular Culture*.
4. On school education, see J. Mangan, *Benefits Bestowed*, and Chapter 8 in Mackenzie, *Propaganda and Empire*. See also V. Chancellor, *History for Their Masters* (Bath: Adams and Dart, 1970); and P. McCann (ed.), *Popular Education and Socialisation in the Nineteenth Century* (London: Methuen, 1977).
5. Imperialist leisure reading has also been well served by historians recently. See J. Bristow, *Empire Boys: Adventures in a Man's World* (London: HarperCollins Academic, 1991); P. Dunae, 'Boys' Literature and the Idea of Empire, 1870–1914', *Victorian Studies* (1980), **24**: 105–21; M. Green, *Dreams of Adventure, Deeds of Empire* (London: Routledge & Kegan Paul, 1980); J. Rowbotham, *Good Girls Make Good Wives* (Oxford: Basil Blackwell, 1989); K. Castle, *Britannia's Children: Reading Colonialism through Children's Books and Magazines* (Manchester: Manchester University Press, 1996).
6. Musical and dramatic female imperialism is exemplified by performances at the GFS Great Sales (see Chapter 5) and numerous Victoria League entertainments, including an ambitious pageant which originated with the Newlands Corner branch and eventually found its way to a West End stage (Victoria League Seventh Annual Report, 1908). Empire Day concerts also became a feature of the Victoria League calendar, acting as a show-case for imperial composers and performers as well as gratifying imperialist audiences.

7. Minutes of the BWEA subcommittee for diffusing information, 5 June 1903. Fawcett Library.

8. Minutes of the BWEA subcommittee for diffusing information, 5 June 1903, 12 June 1903, 8 October 1903 and 6 January 1904.

9. The Victoria League's *Industrial Handbook* was eventually published in 1907. It detailed labour conditions and protective legislation across the Dominions, presumably for the benefit of prospective emigrants but also as an indirect means of influencing imperial legislators. Victoria League Sixth Annual Report, 1907 (1908).

10. M. Pugh, *The Tories and the People 1880–1935* (Oxford: Basil Blackwell, 1985), p. 91.

11. Primrose League Ladies' Grand Council Executive Committee Minutes, 12 and 25 June 1891. Bodleian Library.

12. Primrose League Ladies' Grand Council Executive Committee Minutes, 27 July 1889. Louisa Knightley was among the critics of the *Gazette*.

13. See e.g. the frequent inclusion of anti-feminist 'humour' in the *Primrose League Gazette*, especially in its 'After Office Hours' column.

14. Louisa Knightley's journal, 18 July 1902. Northamptonshire Record Office.

15. *Friendly Work*, February 1906.

16. *Ibid.*, May 1908.

17. Milner Papers, 467/240. Bodleian Library. The education scheme was accompanied by a letter from Jane Lathan, Hon. Secretary to the Education Committee of the Victoria League, dated 27 November 1902. In the same year the Rhodes Trustees had already granted £1000 towards the emigration of women to South Africa, care of Miss Balfour, so the Trust was seen as a promising source of funds.

18. Victoria League First Annual Report, 1902 (1903).

19. Victoria League Fifth Annual Report, 1906 (1907).

20. Victoria League Eighth Annual Report, 1909 (1910). The 'practical' process of matching newspaper donors to recipients was described in exhaustive detail in the *Victoria League Notes*, 15 May 1911.

21. Victoria League First Annual Report, 1902 (1903).

22. *Ibid.*

23. Victoria League Ninth Annual Report, 1910 (1911).

24. E. Lyttelton, *Alfred Lyttelton* (London: Longmans, 1917), pp. 314–15.

25. Earl Grey to Violet Markham, 17 November 1906. VMar, 25/33. BLPES.

26. Victoria League Tenth Annual Report, 1911 (1912).

27. Victoria League Second Annual Report, 1903 (1904).

28. Victoria League Third Annual Report, 1904 (1905).

29. Victoria League Hospitality Committee Minutes, 21 October 1910.

30. Victoria League Hospitality Committee Minutes, 20 January 1911.

31. For details of the Overseas Club, see 'Kindred Societies—Past and Present VII' in *United Empire*, 6 (1915), journal of the Royal Colonial Institute.

32. Victoria League Third Annual Report, 1904 (1905).

33. M. Heath-Stubbs, *Friendship's Highway* (London: GFS, 1926), p. 30.

34. *Our Letter*, Christmas 1906.

35. *Primrose League Gazette*, 2 September 1901.

36. Victoria League Seventh Annual Report, 1908 (1909).

37. Victoria League Annual General Meeting, 1912.

38. Victoria League Tenth Annual Report, 1911 (1912).

39. Victoria League Second Annual Report, 1903 (1904).

40. *Ibid.*

41. Victoria League Ninth Annual Report, 1910 (1911).

42. Victoria League Executive Committee Minute Book, 20 May 1901.

43. *League of the Empire Monthly Record* and Annual Report, 1912–13.

44. Alfred Milner to Violet Markham, 1907. VMar, 25/56. As Milner observed, 'Empire Education is too big a thing to remain a "one man" or even a "one woman" show.'

45. Earl of Meath, *Brabazon Potpourri* (London: Hutchinson, 1928), pp. 68–9. In 1910 Lord Meath presided over a conference of ladies on 'Domestic Hygiene, Child Study and Social Economy', again with a strongly imperial theme: 'If the British Empire is to be maintained it must be through the strenuous wills, the active brains, and the virile bodies of the 55 million of white men and women who are to be found within its extensive borders' (p. 72).

46. Victoria League Fourth Annual Report, 1905 (1906).

47. *Ibid.*

48. Victoria League Executive Committee Minutes, 3 and 11 May 1906.

49. Victoria League Sixth Annual Report, 1907 (1908).

9 Emigration

In the Edwardian years there was a widespread belief that a steady flow of British emigrants to the Empire would provide the most solid guarantee of its future prosperity, loyalty and moral worth. Empire was a civilizing mission because the special qualities of the British character made it so. Reproduction of both British children and British culture within settler communities depended crucially, in turn, upon well-managed female emigration. From the 1860s onwards voluntary societies developed in Britain to select and protect 'the right sort of woman' for this Empire-building role. Feminist and philanthropic in origin, they took on an increasingly imperialistic hue as the Empire gained in popularity and political importance. Women continued to emigrate in search of a secure future, and possibly a freer and more adventurous one too. Those who organized and assisted them did so with mixed motives, but generally in the hope that the lure of individual opportunity would coincide happily with the Empire's need for female workers, wives and mothers.[1]

On many counts, organized emigration was one of the success stories of female imperialism. Already solidly established by the turn of the century, the British Women's Emigration Association retained respect for its 'specialist' expertise as other imperialist societies expanded and diversified around it. This achievement compares favourably with the relative failure of the Victoria League to keep abreast of male-led competitors in the field of imperial education. The BWEA not only defended its established territory but also achieved the accolade of government recognition to a more significant extent than any other female imperialist society. Milner and Chamberlain sought to adapt its services to the task of South African reconstruction between 1902 and 1903. The obstacles to organized mass emigration proved insuperable, but a range of Dominion governments continued to welcome the constructive work of the female emigrators during the following years. The women's emigration societies were leading participants in the Royal Colonial Institute's joint emigration committee from 1910 onwards and Ellen Joyce and Louisa Knightley were summoned as expert witnesses to the 1911 Royal Commission on the Dominions. The First World War brought emigration temporarily to a halt, but its outcomes included a further reinforcement of the relationship between the government and the female emigration societies. The Dominions' Royal Commission Final Report (1917) signalled the need for closer government involvement in emigration. Under the ministerial authority of no lesser imperialist than Alfred Milner, as Secretary of State for the Colonies, the government decided at the end of the war to combine official support and voluntary emigrators' efforts on a larger scale than ever before. Funded by an annual government grant, the new Society for the Oversea Settlement of British Women (1920) drew together the older female emigration associations and perpetuated their efforts to achieve the selected, protected emigration of 'British women and girls of good character and capability'.[2]

However, it would be misleading to dwell exclusively upon the continuities and successes of the female emigration societies. Their history was less straightforward than it may appear in retrospect. The evolution of women's emigration associations from Victorian feminism and philanthropy into Edwardian imperialism, and thence into a post-war semi-official role, was littered with both internal and external controversy. These debates centred not only upon women's role in Empire-building, but also upon other fundamental gender issues troubling late-nineteenth- and early-twentieth-century British society. How could women's need and desire for paid employment be reconciled with their family duties? How could they be best prepared for employment, for motherhood, and for emigration which might commit them to both? How could the colonies' needs be linked to those of unemployed and unmarried middle-class women without offending deeply ingrained social prejudices? How could the respectability of all women, as well as the gentility of some, be protected by emigrators alerted to the dangers of sexual predators through current social purity campaigns? The female emigrators themselves were less confident, and less unanimous, about such matters than their public pronouncements seemed to suggest.

Though female emigration was in many ways a clearly demarcated field, its organizers' discussions reflected wider exchanges within the contemporary women's movement. Chapter 10 examines in detail the complex relations between organized female imperialism, suffragism and the British women's movement. This chapter approaches key issues within this relationship through an investigation of the mixed motives of female emigrators. Their organized work was shaped by their evolving views on employment, marriage, home-building, self-fulfilment, moral guardianship, and imperial and racial duty. Perhaps the most difficult question of all was how female Empire-building could resolve dilemmas around these issues by relegating gender to a level of lesser significance. Should women emigrants merely replicate idealized but subordinating feminine roles conceived in a British context, or should they (as some imperialists and many feminists believed) use the Empire's needs as a platform for asserting a new, elevated role for British womanhood? In colonial settings even the most conservative prescriptions concerning women's social and familial role could be reinterpreted into a bolder and more egalitarian vision of the female future. Sometimes deliberately, but often without any such conscious intent, the organized supporters of female emigration played their part in this translation.

The Female Middle Class Emigration Society, founded in 1862, was a direct antecedent of the British Women's Emigration Association (1884) and its Edwardian offshoots, the South African Colonisation Society (1902) and the Colonial Intelligence League (1910). In its turn, the FMES owed its origins to the feminist Society for Promoting the Employment of Women, which was founded three years earlier to train women for employment and to act as a genteel labour exchange. The inspiration for these linked enterprises came from the ladies of Langham Place, a distinguished group of women headed by Barbara Bodichon and Bessie Rayner Parkes which drew such important figures as Millicent Fawcett, Emily Davies and Josephine Butler into collective debate over the position of women. Lack of female employment opportunities was a central feminist concern, but was never viewed as an isolated issue, nor merely in philanthropic terms. In *The English Woman's Journal*, Bessie Parkes described the flood of surplus applicants to her business enterprises, before advocating imperial solutions:

> While endeavouring to relieve the strain of female necessities, we must not forget that our colonies are eminently in want of women of every rank, and that they are the natural destination of the great surplus which exists in England. If it were possible to plant those who are suffering and struggling at home . . . in useful independence or happy marriage over the broad fields of Australia and New Zealand, who among us but would say that it was by far the best solution of our difficulty?[3]

Her views were forcefully echoed in the same journal by Maria Rye, future FMES Secretary, who lamented the 'fatal indifference and most disgraceful supineness' of governments who left unpeopled 'the fertile plains and valleys of our colonies, quite as much our own though they are thousands of miles away'.[4] Both writers viewed colonial prospects with positive enthusiasm. They also rejected the polarized choice between paid employment and marriage which was already part of the stock-in-trade of anti-feminists. 'Useful independence' and 'happy marriage' might complement rather than contradict each other, whether in British or overseas settings. 'Marriage will be found to be best promoted by aiding and not by thwarting the efforts of single women to improve their condition', wrote the conservative feminist Frances Power Cobbe in November 1862.[5] Though herself determinedly unmarried, like Maria Rye, she accepted the benefits for many women of a marriage freely entered into. This view was entirely compatible with rejection of matrimony as a refuge from female penury, or indeed as a primary goal of female emigration. William Greg's notorious article 'Why Are Women Redundant?', published in 1859 and republished many times, helped to set the terms of the feminist emigration debate by claiming that only assisted emigration could correct the imbalance of the sexes in Britain and the colonies, thus enabling women to fulfil their sole natural destiny of marriage and motherhood.[6] The emphasis of the FMES and its successor organizations upon women's paid employment opportunities was as much a refutation of the accusation of 'matrimonial colonization' as an acknowledge-ment of the economic necessities driving most middle-class emigrants. The same derogatory accusation, and the same employment-focused refutations, lingered on into the twentieth century.

As the FMES got down to work in the 1860s, it proved impossible to live up to supporters' rosy expectations. The only means of matching potential emigrants with genuine colonial work opportunities was to narrow their numbers down to those who were qualified governesses, and who in addition had sufficient knowledge of housework (and willingness to undertake it) to make themselves welcome in colonial households. The society's archive records early failures as well as successes, and its letter books are an eloquent testimony to the suffering of emigrants who found themselves mismatched in terms of outlook and training. Maria Rye herself soon moved beyond exclusively middle-class female emigration, perhaps in tacit recognition of the difficulties which she observed at first hand during voyages to New Zealand, Australia and later Canada.[7] However, the FMES remained true to its title and by the early 1880s had sent out a total of 302 educated lady settlers. Moreover, it had established careful systems of selection, escort and protective reception upon arrival which were to be adopted and further expanded by the BWEA.

Over the next thirty years the emigration associations assisted approximately 20,000 women who chose to settle in the Empire. This was a small proportion (less than 10 per cent) of the total number of female emigrants in the same period.[8] It is safe to assume that a majority of both assisted and unassisted emigrants left Britain for reasons of their own, and primarily for economic opportunity. However, the records of the emigration associations provide a valuable insight into the ideas as well as the activities of the promoters of female emigration. Their self-appointed task was ideological as well as practical. As the nineteenth century drew to a close their work positioned them firmly within the swelling ranks of female imperialism, and an ever-increasing overlap developed between the leadership of organized female emigration and that of the Primrose League and the Victoria League. Within the Girls' Friendly Society, emigration work also served to cement broader political and organizational alliances with fellow-imperialists, constructed initially at leadership level by Ellen Joyce and Louisa Knightley and reflected outwards into the movement's choice of activities and propaganda during the 1900s.

The Edwardian emigration societies retained a strong commitment to the interests of middle-class women seeking employment, with or without the goal of eventual marriage. In the first issue of *The Imperial Colonist* (January 1902) Ellen Joyce wrote buoyantly of their prospects in post-war South Africa:

> The large influx of British population, the great progress of trade, commerce, agriculture – all of which will spring into life when matters have settled down – will provide occupation of various sorts for many hundreds of our countrywomen. It will require British women's energy to assist in all these developments. Womenkind are adepts at many forms of business, they can promote and practice all the small agricultural industries of poultry-farming, fruit-growing, jam-making, bee-keeping; besides this, education, with its widespread influence on mind and manners, will be greatly in the hands of women of culture. Nurses and mother-helps will form part of the contingent required.[9]

This vision of prosperous usefulness was supported in the same edition by General Baden-Powell, grilled by Mrs Joyce on the subject of female employment before he sailed for South Africa in December 1901: 'He especially mentioned *small* poultry business as likely to pay well, and said that by-and-large, though he could not say when, there would be many opportunities for useful women to practise such callings. There would certainly be a good chance for bee-keeping.' The General also added a commentary on 'the importance of selecting the right sort of women'. Gentility, 'character' and usefulness were closely associated in the female emigrators' depiction of the ideal emigrant. Writing in March 1902 on 'Prospects in the Transvaal', Alicia Cecil promised a range of employment for those 'above the servant class', but re-emphasized the dual responsibilities of emigrants for 'a high standard of moral worth and efficiency'.[10]

Nowhere was this more important than in the teaching profession, the first enthusiasm of many Victorian and Edwardian emigrators. Qualified teachers rather than helpless, impoverished governesses were required, but emphasis upon ladylike qualities remained strong. The South African Expansion Education Committee pledged itself to recruit 'superior women of all classes . . . For the arts, and all that pertains to the riper cultivation, everything, almost, remains to be done in South Africa. Musical talent will be specially valuable.'[11] Under the influence of Philippa Fawcett, an increasing number of 'experts in education' eventually joined the committee and endeavoured to steer it towards professional relevance and an acknowledgement of the colonists' perception of their own needs. However, the decision to establish a separate Colonial Intelligence League in 1910 is an interesting commentary upon the reluctance of the BWEA and SACS to move beyond older traditions of genteel, philanthropic emigration. The CIL set itself the clear task of professionalizing the business of job-hunting in the Dominions by 'educated women'. Its vice-presidents were mainly aristocratic, and included the distinguished figures of Milner, Curzon, Lady Knightley, Lady Talbot and the Countess of Selborne, but its all-female executive was notable for the presence of six headmistresses from girls' high schools. Strenuous efforts were made over the next few years to establish 'an Intelligence Office which shall estimate the demand for Women's Work in the Colonies, and bring it into relation with the supply in this country'.[12] Despite the employment of 'expert Agents', and the offer of on-the-spot training in western Canada, outcomes were less novel than CIL founders had hoped. Many of the women who applied to the League had insufficient formal education, and the published details of those who were located in employment indicate the unvarying colonial demand for female domestic service, rather than for moral worth, gentility, and even qualified professionalism.

Could certain forms of domestic service be made suitable for 'educated' (genteel) emigrants? This was a question which haunted female emigrators for decades. Both reluctance and incompetence generally precluded gentlewomen from taking up paid domestic work, even in a distant colony where loss of caste might be less acutely felt. Strenuous efforts were made by all the female emigration societies to invest colonial housework with new job titles and new meanings which would make it more appealing to middle-class emigrants. Writing in *The Imperial Colonist* of November 1904, Miss Perkins of the BWEA claimed that the colonies offered opportunities for working women to discover their true feminine vocation as 'household helps'. Though household work was often hard in Australia and Canada, 'women emigrants should be of as superior and refined a type as possible', so that they could withstand difficulty and eventually prove 'better mothers . . . of the future citizens of the State'. Colonial housewives were increasingly recognizing the advantages of 'household helps, living with the family and treated as one of themselves':

> These things being granted, why should not gentlewomen go out in larger numbers? It would be an excellent thing if they more frequently joined their brothers . . . What can be more ennobling, more healthy, or more truly womanly than the doing of domestic work as our ancestors did it? [13]

Discussion of the merits of 'Home Helps' formed an important part of the private emigration conference at Princess Christian's London home in August 1904.[14] Lady Lyttelton (wife of Sir Neville Lyttelton) opened with a paper which depicted the favourable possibilities:

> I wish to accentuate the fact that the Society can put its hand upon women, who are really gentlewomen, but who are willing and able and trained to do the real, practical work of a

family. To make the beds, mend, sew, push the perambulator, cook, wash the children's clothes, and do the elementary teaching, and even at a push scrub the floors. When I say this, I do not mean that we can produce women, who can, or who should be expected to do, the whole work of a family every day, but who are as much willing to turn their hand to every job, when necessary, as an elder daughter of a family is usually willing to do.

Mrs Joyce next took up the theme, with an account of 'where she is to be found' (in the country homes of the clergy and of retired officers, and among high school graduates), and of how she might be further trained for colonial usefulness at the Leaton Colonial Training Home in Shropshire. This harmonious picture of mutual benefits bestowed was disrupted, however, by the forthright comments of visiting South Africans. Mrs Fuller, of the Cape Town Immigration Association, pointed out bluntly that 'practically the demand, as far as their Association was concerned, was limited to domestic servants'. Mrs Gardiner, of the Maritzburg Branch of SACS, 'objected to women doing manual labour out of doors, contending that it would bring them down to the level of Kaffirs'. Moreover, as Lady Lyttelton herself pointed out, 'these women require exceptionally careful selection. The families in which they can be placed require equally careful selection': a time-consuming process which inevitably held more appeal for British emigrators than for prospective employers.

The SACS Annual Report of 1903 had already admitted the problems of genteel domestic labour, blaming failures upon 'insufficient training'. Here was another area where enthusiastic female emigrators might assist. *The Imperial Colonist* published detailed information about schemes to equip departing emigrants with basic housewifery skills, and even a modicum of more specialized technical training. The Leaton Home (by 1909 'College') had been established as early as 1890 by two GFS Council members connected with Ellen Joyce's Canadian emigration work. Though it took in a few poorer girls at the outset, it was soon established that the Home's purpose would be to make it 'possible for well-born women to fit themselves for Colonial life, by the instruction it gives in the practice of all household duties, together with laundry work, poultry and bee-keeping'.[15] By 1904 the Home had acquired the patronage of Princess Christian, and offered courses of between three and six months for '15s weekly for a single bedroom, 10s for sharing a double room'. Instruction had extended to include dairy work and dressmaking, and advertisements boasted that 'The pupils do all the work of the house, taking it in turn to perform the various duties'.[16] Over a twenty-year period more than 400 newly competent female emigrants emerged from Leaton. 'Their success has been remarkable,' wrote Miss Vernon proudly in 1907. 'It may fairly be claimed that, in Canada at any rate, they have made such a name for their Training Home that over and over again applications come from mistresses who only wish for a girl trained at Leaton.' Among the 'successes' (carefully chronicled, in the usual 'personal' style of female imperialism) were to be found one student who 'gained the Royal Red Cross during the siege of Mafeking', another who had cleaned and planted a homestead in New Mexico 'by her own efforts', and 'the very large number who are most usefully filling posts in Canada and British Columbia which could never be adequately filled by a servant'.[17]

Leaton had its competitors. Some enterprising county councils, and other voluntary organizations such as the Yorkshire Ladies' Council of Education, took up similar training schemes with a residential component. In 1903 the Swanley Horticultural College was offering 'Practical training in Gardening, Dairying, Poultry, Cooking, Fruit Bottling and Jam Making, Laundry, Hygiene, Sanitation, South African Languages etc . . . Training in *separate Colonial House and Garden.*'[18] The Countess of Warwick's rural training school, linked through Halford Mackinder to the nascent Reading College, was a similar effort to link genteel education with colonial employment and home-making.[19] Even in the heart of London, by 1904 it was possible to receive 'Domestic Training for Gentlewomen for Colonial and Home Life, in a small private Ladies' Residential Club in Chelsea, at very moderate fees . . . Worked in connection with the British Women's Emigration Association.'[20]

These various schemes had in common a fundamental respect for the significance of the class distinctions which, superficially at least, their activities seemed designed to undermine. Emigrators believed that the Empire required the civilizing influence of gentlewomen almost as much as many gentlewomen required opportunities for paid employment and (potentially) marriage. Even the Colonial Intelligence League persisted in the view that inherent gentility could triumph over the rigours of apparently menial labour. The League's Princess Patricia Ranch, launched inauspiciously a year before the First World War, was the Leaton Training Home transplanted on to Canadian soil, this time under the royal patronage of the Duke and Duchess of Connaught. In the same year the League hit upon an ingenious scheme for enticing 'educated women' to take up domestic work in Melbourne. Members of the National Council of Women of Australia undertook to 'see that those ladies going out through the League shall in their leisure hours be received in their houses, and enjoy during these hours the social advantages they have always had at home'.[21] Though gentility was no substitute for efficiency, the female emigrators believed that the ideal emigrant should and could possess both qualities in equal measure. As Caroline Grosvenor put it in her conclusion to the first Annual Report of the Colonial Intelligence League:

> We should like to say that we believe this movement for the organisation of educated women's work in the Empire to be one of the most important of the day. If it succeeds it will employ a vast amount of splendid material which is now being either wrongly used or entirely wasted, it will bring hope and a future to many thousands for whom life at present looks infinitely dark and difficult, and last, and most important of all, it will help to keep the British Empire for the British race.[22]

The female emigration societies spent a good deal of time and effort trying to square the circle of genteel female employment although the settler colonies were crying out for straightforward domestic servants. The emigrators' own faith in social hierarchy, and its indissoluble links with imperial greatness, prevented them from accepting the obvious. They were also uncomfortably aware of the 'servant problem' nearer home as service became steadily less attractive to working-class women, but was still generally perceived as essential to comfortable life in middle- and upper-class British homes. From the 1880s onwards the BWEA fought off hostile accusations of 'servant-stealing', stemming partly from the Girls' Friendly Society's growing interest in emigration. In the philanthropic context of church congresses, Ellen Joyce was happy to publicize the 'preventive' value of emigration for working-class girls who might otherwise suffer from 'starvation wages' or be tempted by 'the allurements of earning money more easily in vicious ways'.[23] She also publicized the high wages and healthy living she had observed during her visits to Canada in 1884 and 1890. But she took care to disassociate herself from 'servant-stealing' by emphasizing matrimony rather than employment as the likely outcome of emigration by poorer girls; and by underlining the value of domestic service as matrimonial training for the great majority of working-class girls who would remain in Britain. By the early 1900s, as her emigration interests became steadily more aligned with Empire-building and her philanthropic work was subordinated to this higher cause, Mrs Joyce ceased even this modest encouragement towards servant emigration. The opening issue of *The Imperial Colonist* lauded middle-class employment opportunities in post-war South Africa. It also stated bluntly the female emigrators' view on domestic service: 'Servants will of course be wanted in all the Colonies, but their emigration does not require to be stimulated; it only needs to be guided and protected.'[24]

This basic attitude was maintained in following years. Paradoxically, however, the BWEA and SACS found themselves guiding and protecting departing servants in ever-increasing numbers. The realities of the colonial labour market asserted themselves not only through employer demand but also through government policy which eased the emigration of servants by providing free or subsidized passages for those female workers who were most evidently needed. As early as the 1860s, Maria Rye diverged from her FMES commitments to take advantage of opportunities to emigrate servants cheaply to New Zealand and Australia. By the 1890s the BWEA was doing likewise, in response to the provision of free passages for female servants by the governments of Queensland and Western Australia and cheap passages to Canada. The South African trade in servants had also begun, costs being divided between prospective employers and the emigrants themselves, a minority of whom were assisted by BWEA loans. Personified by Mrs Joyce as the 'Organizing Referee', the BWEA seems to have regarded its protective function as a service to be offered even-handedly to the emigrants, to their employers, and to British and colonial governments.

Points of conflict between these varied interest groups required careful negotiation. The BWEA depended upon the support of employers both in Britain and the colonies; emigrants might require 'protection' from self-interested demands for an uninterrupted flow of cheap labour; and governments both at home and overseas were often under-informed about the detailed needs of working-class emigrants. Reception committees in the colonies were vital to the success of protected emigration, but also extremely sensitive to implied criticism from Britain. A BWEA letter book of 1900 recorded interesting exchanges between Mrs Joyce and her equally forthright counterpart, Mrs Notcutt of the Cape Town committee. Mrs Joyce's detailed 'suggestions' to this committee on servants' terms of employment included the bold statement: 'It will be understood that nothing lower than the current wages given in the vicinity in which the Employer lives must be offered.'[25] Such a directive would undoubtedly have been resented by South African ladies who had already asserted their independence by criticizing the unsteady, ambitious behaviour of servants emigrated to Cape Town and suggested improvements to BWEA policies. Mrs Joyce's carefully drafted and redrafted replies to criticisms reveal her need to preserve a delicately balanced relationship.

Other correspondence in the same letter book shows Mrs Joyce prepared to take both employers and servants individually to task where necessary. A Burghersdorp doctor was told in no uncertain terms that his expectations of 'a good, sensible girl', to arrive without cost to himself and to stay for a minimum of three years at a wage of only £2 a month, were beyond what was reasonable or possible.[26] An unhappy new arrival called Hilda Waide, on the other hand, was firmly advised to 'stay on . . . and make yourself contented with any little difficulties there may be'.[27] Many servants were tempted to break their engagements by the higher wages on offer elsewhere. Writing from Rhodesia, Mrs Lyttelton Gell unequivocally defended the stance of colonial employers in such cases:

> No encouragement should be given to women who will merely trade on their sisters' emergencies . . . A great deal of cant is talked about not lowering 'the current rate of wages'. This may be sound economy in an old-established country, but in a new one, where 'the current rate' means what one plutocrat can afford to pay and leaves the majority unable to employ anyone at all in the same capacity, the 'current rate' theory is obviously fallacious.[28]

This letter was published approvingly in *The Imperial Colonist*, a journal directed towards a female imperialist readership of the employing classes rather than towards domestic servants. The launch of the journal coincided with a peak of government support for servant emigration, as Milner and Chamberlain briefly joined with South African financiers in an attempt at mass sponsorship for female British settlers who were intended to help outnumber the defeated Boers.[29] Free passages were offered in returning empty troop-ships, and the Transvaal Women's Immigration Department undertook to pay all expenses from London to Johannesburg for 'young women of British birth, good character, good health, and experience in domestic service', to be selected and chaperoned to their destination under the BWEA's auspices.[30] In some ways this was a moment of glory for the female emigrators. Lady Knightley and others who had had no involvement in earlier, smaller-scale emigration efforts were inspired to undertake the post-war work in a mood of fervent patriotism. However, both the BWEA and SACS retained their commitment, first and foremost, to the middle-class, 'educated' emigrant. Servant emigration was a duty rather than a choice, and even at the height of post-war government support efforts were made to leaven large-scale servant departures with smaller numbers of 'lady helps'. The Transvaal Department's own statistics, reproduced in the SACS Annual Report for 1905, show that this point of principle had little effect on the overall emigration outcome. By June 1905 a total of 995 wage-earning women had arrived in the Transvaal, comprising 866 domestic servants, twenty-five lady helps, twenty-three governesses and teachers, seventeen housekeepers, eighteen nurses, eight clerks and typists and thirty-eight 'other denominations' (laundry maids, ladies' maids, serving maids, dairy maids, dressmakers and waitresses). In the following year numbers began to fall off, and in 1907 the newly representative government of the Transvaal withdrew its financial support. British emigrators persevered with small-scale work in South Africa while redirecting most of their efforts towards Canada (see Appendix 1).

The South African servant emigration of the 1900s was an exceptional development, not only because of the scale of government support but also because the racial context gave new meanings to the emigrators' 'guidance and protection'. It is interesting to note, however, that in some respects the specific destination of servants made little difference to the general attitude of the emigrators. In July 1903 *The Imperial Colonist* reported on a week-long conference of the Canadian National Council of Women.[31] Many local councils had put forward resolutions urging 'the need for securing a better supply of duly qualified domestic servants, of which there is at present so great a lack; and of promoting for this end the immigration of suitable classes of domestic servants'. Mrs Joyce's published reply to the conference was a firm restatement of BWEA principles, from which there could be no deviation despite the urgency of colonial needs:

> We concern ourselves more with quality than quantity. We undertake the work as one of Imperial importance in effecting the distribution of women to a part of the Empire where women are scarce; but it is very important to remove one misapprehension – we have no superfluity of good hardworking servants, there is nearly as great a shortage here as with you.

A necessary compromise between imperial and British needs was reached by 'sending out those who apply to us, without ourselves stimulating their exodus'. The demands of South Africa – 'which many of your brave volunteers helped us to secure' – were adding to the pressures upon supply and wages. However, South Africa had agreed to accept a proportion of 'women above the servant class'. Mrs Joyce went on to propose a similar arrangement to the Canadians:

> The means which would attract us to help you more than any other in your call for domestics would be that it should be part of your scheme to endeavour to find out where openings exist for the employment of the class of women we can best spare.

Redolent with the metropolitan superiority which had already irritated South African committee ladies, this reply may not have been altogether well received in Toronto. Large numbers of servants certainly travelled to Canada over the next few years on their own initiative, or under arrangements initiated by the Dominion rather than by the BWEA. However, the British society successfully selected and protected several thousands, and also prided itself upon its 'lady help', 'mother's help' and 'help-companion' placements. Whether or not the Canadians fully accepted the female imperialist reasoning behind genteel emigration, they presumably could not afford to turn away scarce workers and wives, especially from the remoter areas of western Canada.

Meanwhile, the BWEA also sought out employment opportunities in Canada for working-class women who were not trained servants. The philanthropic urge behind much late-nineteenth-century emigration was far from eclipsed by Edwardian Empire-building. During the winter months of 1903 *The Imperial Colonist* began to offer 'an open door of escape' to women machinists and other underpaid and underemployed female workers in London's East End.[32] Appealing over the heads of these women to philanthropic emigrators, Mrs Joyce wrote of the factory opportunities in Montreal: 'We are asked for three hundred workers at once, *and are told that all that we can send for a year can be employed*.' Ladies were needed to spread this good news in factory clubs and evening classes, and funds required for fares and the expenses of a Matron, since 'we cannot expect much self-help from this class of toiler'. Several hundred women eventually departed under the scheme, though it soon became clear that the Canadian manufacturers' needs were not indefinite, that only skilled workers had good prospects, and that applicants must be prepared to fall back on domestic work if factory employment was not available. By August 1904 the BWEA was insisting that its emigrant factory workers should 'state in writing their readiness to take up domestic work': an unpopular demand intended to reassure Canadian immigrators and to guarantee repayment of BWEA loans, but likely to deter many of the women whom the scheme was intended to help.

If British factory workers drifted towards servanthood in Canada, this was still more inevitably the fate of the pauper child emigrants who remained another of Mrs Joyce's favoured causes in the early 1900s. Twenty years earlier she had begun to advocate emigration as a remedy for pauperism. Here she was following in the footsteps of Maria Rye, who had spent her later years 'rescuing' over 4000 poor girls and relocating them mainly in Canada. This was a tiny proportion of the estimated 100,000 children who were sent to Canada by more than twenty different organizations between 1870 and 1925, but Miss Rye's efforts attracted unusual hostility when the Doyle Report of 1876 publicized detailed criticisms of her lack of adequate supervision. Canadians, in their turn, criticized the moral and physical quality of the young migrants, and their depressing effects upon adult colonists' wages.[33] During the 1900s their numbers began to gradually rise again, for reasons which had as much to do with adult enthusiasm for Empire-building as with helping children and reducing local rates. Kingsley Fairbridge, brother of the South African loyalist Dorothea Fairbridge, meanwhile led the way in developing imperial farm schools in Western Australia. Ellen Joyce's renewed enthusiasm for such schemes was no doubt also linked to her own imperialism. She briefly used *The Imperial Colonist* to publicize a new scheme for child emigration in July 1904, but official BWEA support for child emigration was disclaimed soon afterwards.[34]

This was perhaps the nearest that Mrs Joyce ever came to a public climb-down. The incident indicates that even the most authoritarian of female emigrators could not necessarily bend her key associates to her own viewpoint, especially after the BWEA and SACS had attracted the support of women of higher social standing and greater influence than their foundress herself. The Edwardian female emigrators were unanimous in their devotion to Empire and in their support for middle-class emigrants seeking employment against the odds. Working-class and pauper employment were more contentious issues, and far less fundamental to the civilizing mission of British female emigration.

Even domestic servants who settled overseas were eventually likely to become imperial wives and mothers. This fact was welcomed by the emigrators although, as has been noted, they made sustained efforts to refute accusations of 'matrimonial colonization'. This attitude helped to dignify the efforts of the emigration associations in the eyes of their supporters and also (very importantly) in the eyes of respectable emigrants. Histories of the immorality endemic to earlier, indiscriminate female emigration took a good deal of living down. The emigrators' emphasis upon moral guardianship was closely linked to a cautious attitude to marriage. Thus, when the BWEA Secretary was questioned over emigrants' marital ambitions by a newspaper journalist in 1895, she replied diplomatically, 'Well, of course, we do not know what they have in their mind, but we certainly do not think it wise to encourage that idea . . . although we find, as I have said, that a fair proportion do marry, it is not, as a rule, until they have been in the colony for some time.'[35] From the pages of *The Imperial Colonist*, Mrs Ross advised the BWEA's 'country workers' on how to counter 'the accusation that we are a matrimonial society, which in a cowardly manner conceals its aims':

> Nothing can be less true – Work is inscribed on our banner, the security of immediate employment – and this does not commend itself to the woman whose primary object is to 'get settled'. That emigration leads to marriage is true, and which is the better, to marry here for fear the men should not go round . . . or to marry where the choice of affinity is possible, and when, having taken the first brave step towards independent action, the girl, in marrying, desires an honest self-dependence to the end of her days.[36]

There was nevertheless a certain disjuncture between the public and private views of emigrators on the marriage question. Writing in 1906 to Alicia Cecil, chair of the SACS Transvaal subcommittee, Maud Selborne proposed recruitment of 'a good class of untrained girls at £3 a month' to work in outlying rural areas. She followed up with the matter-of-fact comment:

> I think you may take it for certain that the majority of the girls will drift into Johannesburg after a year or two's service. From an imperial point of view I don't think this matters in the least. The majority of men are in Johannesburg, and as one real object is to provide English wives for them, there is no harm in the girls coming up there.[37]

Edith Lyttelton was equally direct in her Cape Town correspondence with her sister-in-law:

> There is a tremendous demand for servants – and though it doesn't do to say this too much, for wives. B. Powell is just enrolling 6000 policemen – if they don't have wives it means Kaffir women and more of that odious mixed race, which have never yet come to any good. I am amused by hearing that Rhodes says 'for goodness sake send us some decent looking ones'.[38]

The breeding potential of British women was discussed with even less inhibition by the male imperialists who were most closely associated with organized female emigration. Louisa Knightley found Sir John Ardagh (husband of Lady Malmesbury, a leading SACS supporter) 'simply crazy on the importance of sending out women in large – enormous numbers' in July 1902.[39] His man-to-man correspondence with Chamberlain spelled out unvarnished aims to expand the British population. Though female emigrants must be protected from 'evil influences',

> opportunities should be afforded to them for social intercourse with eligible young men, among whom they are likely to find husbands . . . The project thus baldly stated is open to the insinuation that it is in fact a matrimonial agency. This is to a large extent true, and it should be the aim and care of the administration to organise the details in such a way as to let this object appear subsidiary to that of providing suitable and remunerative occupation.[40]

It seems unlikely that the leading ladies of the emigration societies were equally duplicitous in their emphasis upon employment. For the majority, employment and marriage were not necessarily competing priorities. If marriage crowned an emigrant's success, then a double benefit would have been secured, both from an individual and an imperial viewpoint. Despite the delicacy of the issues involved, female emigrators sometimes allowed themselves to expand upon the joys and importance of colonial marriage. Mrs Shepstone urged South African emigrants to look towards marriage for 'a wider, brighter, fuller life . . . there should be no shame to any woman in anticipating and hoping for that supreme development of her own being which should make her part of the most important and powerful influences necessary for our Empire'.[41] An anonymous writer on 'Woman's Life in South Africa' dwelt upon the social class advantages of a colonial marriage, and upon the chivalrous behaviour extended towards women by 'the up-country colonist'.[42] Even the sternly moral Ellen Joyce hinted at pleasures to come in a farewell address to a party of teachers sailing for Alberta, Canada:

> I want you to bear in mind that women are on a higher pedestal, less approachable than here. They are so few, they are so precious, they must be reverently won; the women have the choice, not the men. Women have splendid opportunities of settling, but they must not give themselves away in a hurry; wait for the best man.[43]

Such visions of carefully chosen companionate marriage were at some distance from the race preservation measures planned by Rhodes, Milner, Ardagh and Chamberlain. A partial convergence of aims between female emigrators and their powerful male patrons need not be construed simply as successful manipulation. Later emigrators had a surprising amount in common with the early feminists of the Langham Place circle when they insisted that marital opportunity, and a welcome expansion of British overseas population, could be achieved upon women's own terms.

The annual reports of the South African Colonisation Society proudly record marriage statistics alongside those for new arrivals and for different categories of employment. Out of the 995 women who had emigrated under the Transvaal scheme by June 1905, 191 had already achieved matrimony, '88 of these having married between June 1904–5'. The previous year's report noted that those who married had done so 'extremely well and happily'. The society was proud to extend its guardianship of emigrants right up to their wedding day, and even beyond:

> One of the last weddings which took place on February 15th, was of a Typist who had gone out under this Society about two years ago. She had got on very well and was earning about £20 a month. The ceremony was at the house of one of the members of the Committee, several of them being present. She was much liked and respected by all who knew her, and her happiness is a great source of pleasure to all the girls.[44]

Reports of domestic bliss after marriage were also published from time to time in *The Imperial Colonist*. The intention was probably less to entice potential emigrants than to reassure the British supporters of emigration that the societies were succeeding in fulfilling 'matrimonial colonization' in ways which were uplifting rather than demeaning to women.

Marriage was about motherhood and the reproduction of the British race, but it was also very much about home-making and the transmission of cultural values. There was a role here for daughters and sisters as well as for mothers and wives. In its simpler forms, imperial culture could be transmitted by British women of any social class. However, in this sphere, as in others, the 'educated', middle-class woman had more to offer. According to Ellen Joyce, western Canada needed 'women of some culture . . .

who will keep up the tone of the men with whom they mix by music and book-love when the day's work is over.'[45] At the GFS Imperial Conference in 1913 she expanded upon this theme:

> Educated women have a very special part in laying the foundation, and in raising the arches in Empire-building. They are imbued with the traditions which are so all-important in forming character and moulding customs in a new country . . . I only wish that my acquaintance with English Literature had been half as good as that of the wife of a Major in the North West Mounted Police, or that I had kept up my music as she had kept up hers. One happy use she made of her music was, that she had an open door on Sunday evenings for the young Englishmen, who liked to drive in from their ranches or Stations. Part of the evening became a 'Service of Song', and the words these young pioneers had sung with their mothers in the fine Churches of old England, kept alive their religion, while their aesthetic tastes were preserved by a sonata of Beethoven or Mozart.[46]

While the Major's wife appropriated European composers to the British civilizing mission, working-class female emigrants might arrange vases of wild flowers or varnish their husbands' home-made furniture. Such beautifying touches were woman's special province. Their absence weakened the fabric of the Empire, as did any forgetfulness of religion and the power of prayer. Canada was 'waiting for the presence of women to make it possible for men to anchor themselves on the land'.[47] The actual number of British settlers was important, warding off the 'cosmopolitan' influx in Canada and the Boer threat in South Africa, but marriage and home-making had a higher symbolic value as the embodiment of virtues which underlay British rule. As we have seen, familial and domestic metaphors were continuously used to exalt the imperial enterprise.[48] Dora Gore Browne's poem, 'To England's Daughters', made a memorable contribution in this vein on the front page of *The Imperial Colonist* in December 1904:

> To you 'tis now entrusted, with a meaning larger, higher,
> You, my daughters, as you go to join your kinsfolk o'er the foam,
> 'Tis for you to keep the flaming torch of loyalty on fire,
> In the land of your adoption, for the honour of your home.
> Yes! for God and your country now 'tis yours to make the story
> You, the future nursing mothers of the English race to be.
> In your arms His love will lay them, and He looks for England's glory
> To her loyal sons and daughters in her homes beyond the sea.[49]

The language of female imperialism was pre-eminently a language of feminine duty and responsibility. Was there space among the multiple meanings of work, home and family for a woman emigrant to seek self-fulfilment, and even perhaps emancipation from the constraints of her British lifestyle? There can be little doubt that many emigrants departed with greater personal freedom in view. The emigration associations warned against dangerous delusions on this score, but did not entirely dispel such hopes. Necessity, duty and opportunity were interestingly juxtaposed within the female emigration movement. For Victorian emigrators, female self-support in the colonies was unambiguously a route out of poverty and humiliating dependence. While their Edwardian successors were inclined to place heavier emphasis upon the responsibilities of Britain's imperial mission, changes in British society made it inevitable that emigrants and emigrators alike would be influenced by current debates over women's education and employment, family life and the Vote. Some were active participants in this wider movement, while others merely absorbed a little of its rhetoric. Female Christian ethics militated against encouraging 'selfish' emigration aims. However, despite their emphasis upon female altruism and their widely differing attitudes towards organized feminism, many Edwardian emigrators believed that Empire-building contributed to a more rewarding future for individual women.

The rewards of a colonial lifestyle went beyond the purely material, important though liberation from poverty clearly was to most emigrants. In an 1896 article entitled 'A Woman's Life at the Cape, by one who has tried it', the author depicted a businesslike partnership with her husband in the running of their farm. She found hard work in plenty, and challenges to her ever-growing range of practical skills:

> But life is not all work, even on a farm. There are numberless things to enjoy. First of all, the beautiful climate; then the new and strange things to see . . . the long rides over the veldt in search of lost cattle, or to inspect and marvel over the wondrously rapid growth of crops and trees. It is a life to love, with all its drawbacks.[50]

The themes of natural beauty and healthy outdoor life were taken up by other commentators. Hard work was not only compensated by such enjoyments, but became its own reward when it involved the challenges of novelty and improvisation, and when it was undertaken in congenial company. In rural Canada or South Africa more equal marriages were a practical necessity rather than an abstract dream. Even single wage-earning women extolled the egalitarianism of work relationships in isolated surroundings. There was also widespread praise for a general lowering of class barriers which opened the way to abandonment of restrictive social rituals for middle-class women, as well as improved marriage prospects for poorer settlers. Such commentary reached Britain through emigrant letters published in *The Imperial Colonist* and quoted in female emigrators' speeches. The practice of publication and extensive quotation suggests that the emigration associations acknowledged the liberating consequences of their work, though these were usually carefully counterbalanced by more conservative messages.

Addressing the South African Expansion Committee in June 1902, Millicent Fawcett dwelt on South Africa's opportunities, and 'appealed to the love of adventure of young Englishwomen to induce them to go forth and take advantage of them'.[51] Adventurousness was not unexpected from this famous feminist, but it is perhaps more surprising from the Mothers' Union delegate Mrs Phillip, who toured South Africa in 1904 and returned to write in *The Imperial Colonist* of the 'large compensations' of female settlers' arduous lives:

> Such home-making as this appears to me the career of all others to attract the best type of girl, and to afford endless opportunity for the enormous number of girls here in England who are leading aimless, useless lives: unhappy, restless and discontented because they have not enough to occupy their time and exercise their talents, or chance to burgeon out all that is within them . . . To all such girls I would say go to South Africa, where women are not superfluous; or to one of our other colonies; and *live*, even if you have to work hard and long. It is a thousand times better than stagnating or drudging for inadequate pay at home.[52]

The 'chance to burgeon out all that is within them' frequently involved vigorous outdoor activity for women, in both their work and leisure hours. Many correspondents dwelt upon the joys of horse-riding. 'The pleasures of a country life appeal to me very much,' wrote a 'help' from Alberta in 1908.

> Words fail to express how much I enjoy the drives, and, above all, the rides, which are my crowning pleasure. I had never been mounted until I came here; but, to my surprise, it came quite easily, and although very nervous when driving, [I] am quite fearless on horseback.[53]

'Women Who Can Do Things' was the title of a 1914 article, again from the Canadian prairies, in which Eve Graham brought together the aspects of her new life most calculated to appeal to an adventurous streak in British readers:

> The girl who goes out in the right spirit is soon accepted as a chum. Indeed, she is very often the centre of interest, for the time, as girls are decidedly in the minority and everyone is anxious to give her a friendly 'shake'. Many girls find their keenest enjoyment in the saddle . . . She who is sufficiently brave to face the hard work will be more than compensated for any hardships she may undergo. The climate is ideal for young people. Whether in summer or winter there is always some form of outdoor enjoyment to be had. These pleasures are shared equally and are not, as in many countries, the monopoly of the wealthy.

Ultimately, there was 'almost a certainty of marriage' for those girls who chose to settle: though 'those who do not wish to marry certainly need not'. Again, an interesting slant upon conventional middle-class matrimony is implied by a female emigrant who had discovered that 'a Canadian man makes a most attentive and sympathetic husband . . . there is none of that utter lack of understanding between members of the opposite sex which is so often apparent in this country'.[54]

Self-fulfilment might take different, often interrelated forms. By the later Edwardian period an ageing Ellen Joyce must have appeared as an oppressive adviser to many young emigrants, but even she had begun to extol women's work as a source of fulfilment as well as subsistence. In a formal paper read at the Caxton Hall in 1906, she reviewed recent changes in the status of women, singling out the fact that 'nowadays, happily, it is expected that the majority of our girls should do something with their lives'. While economic circumstances forced many into paid employment, 'There is another and a nobler motive power at work – the independence of the young woman, her desire not to be a burden to her family, and her consciousness of her own power.'[55] Such pronouncements perhaps represented a sensible concession to current realities rather than her innermost convictions. In a contrasting speech she begged emigrating teachers to 'reconstruct the idea of the primitive purpose of woman in relation to man and the home-life' by helping each Canadian pupil to become 'a good housewife, a good help-mate for a practical working husband . . . a woman first, before she is a scholar'.[56] However, many of the BWEA's correspondents were indeed infused with consciousness of their own power. Moreover, they were anxious to share this assertive outlook with other British women.

In *The Imperial Colonist* of April 1914, Claire Malcolm described a visit with her sister to 'A Woman's Farm in Rhodesia'. Here, they discovered a total absence of fatherly or husbandly guidance. The owner was 'an enterprising lady who had recently taken up 15000 acres of land and was farming it on her own account', with only her mother and sister and African workers to help her. A thatched mud house had been 'erected by·natives under the supervision of Miss G. and her sister who camped out in grass huts the while'. It transpired that 'our energetic hostess' had gone on to make most of her own furniture, 'with no more technical training than is gained by a carpentry course at Oxford'; that she had fitted up a kitchen range and boiler, set up a forge, sunk a well, and made her own farm gates, apart from raising a first crop of mealies and establishing herds of cattle, sheep and pigs. Inspirational though this story was, it concluded with 'a word of warning' on the 'real difficulties and dangers' of native labour.[57] Here, at least, the author would have found herself on common ground with a majority of the leaders of the female emigration associations. The freedoms of colonial life were circumscribed, especially in Africa, by sexual and racial threats, as well as by feminine responsibilities and duties.

The protective aspect of emigration work was often taken more seriously than any other by the female emigrators, if not by the emigrants themselves. The BWEA established its high moral tone from the 1880s onwards, when its leadership was dominated by Church patrons and clerical wives. Despite the entry of a more secular aristocratic and imperialist element in the early 1900s, both the BWEA and SACS remained closely linked to the Anglican Church hierarchy. British and colonial bishops were popular platform speakers, and the overseas network of reception centres and protective guidance rested heavily upon the voluntary work of the clergy. Nor was it only the Church which encouraged the emigrators to see themselves primarily as moral guardians. A number of the leading emigrators were active within the British social purity movement which coincided with the advent of female imperialism, and almost all were in general sympathy with its aim of exposing the moral and sexual double standards which underpinned male exploitation of women through prostitution, pornography and abusive marital relationships.

Laura Ridding, for example, who took up emigration work after her visit to South Africa in 1908, was already active in 'rescue' work on behalf of prostitutes in London and Winchester. She had the White Slave Trade firmly on her investigative agenda during her time in South Africa. In Cape Town she visited a rescue home funded by Anglican women, argued with social reformers and politicians for further raising the age of consent, and was duly shocked by the 'awful morality' of Johannesburg. A ploy to engage Milner's former Kindergarten in 'vigilance work' apparently failed; but she remained convinced that 'a Men's Vigilance Society' was as necessary as the protective work of girls' hostels and the YWCA.[58] Louisa Knightley had similar 'eye-opening' discussions with South African ladies.[59] Like Laura Ridding and Ellen Joyce, her background in Girls' Friendly Society work had heightened her sensitivity to the moral and sexual dangers which threatened young women – never more so than when they were thousands of miles from home, and possibly revelling in a sense of new-found freedom.

The BWEA had always defined 'the right sort of woman' in terms of her moral qualities as well as her practical competence and employability. The first of its long-standing objectives was 'To emigrate only such women and girls as are of good character and capacity'. Thorough enquiries and multiple references were needed before any women received an emigration loan, and emigrants' virtue was preserved intact by chaperonage throughout the journey, followed by further guidance and protection at the place of arrival. The BWEA and SACS publicized these arrangements in minute detail, as much to reassure their own funders and colonial employers as for the benefit of emigrants. Approved departure arrangements included an overnight stay by each complete party of emigrants at the emigration association's hostels in London or Liverpool, where the women received full instructions for the journey and a departure speech from a lady emigrator dwelling on the imperial duties ahead of them. Approved shipboard arrangements required segregated sleeping and (where possible) exercise space for female emigrants, and a matron equipped to exercise any necessary moral discipline as well as to keep her charges usefully occupied with sewing, reading and prayers. Whether they docked in Cape Town or Quebec, emigrants could expect to be met by friendly escorts who would usher them to nearby hostels or on to reserved train accommodation for the last leg of their journey. The BWEA remained sternly critical of ports, mainly in Australasia, which failed to provide this level of reception, and put successful pressure upon the British and colonial authorities to improve matters. Meanwhile, inland hostel accommodation for single women continued to expand up to the First World War. Meriel Talbot believed this to be the female emigrant's most urgent requirement as she toured Canada in 1910, and Maud Selborne took a close personal interest in raising funds for and equipping new hostels in South Africa. Apart from providing cheap, safe lodgings, the hostels were seen by emigrators as the final link in the chain of guidance and support binding new settlers to the Mother Country.

Lady imperialists protected female emigrants with the most benevolent of imperial intentions. However, there was a fine line to be drawn between welcome protection and an unwelcome level of moral surveillance. Many of those emigrants who opted out of the emigrators' protective care were women who rejected the moral policing upon which the associations so prided themselves. As in other aspects of their work, the associations were highly sensitive to social class differences. Working-class women, and especially domestic servants, were regarded as careless, self-interested and morally vulnerable, even if they had led hitherto blameless lives. Unless firmly regulated, such emigrants risked bringing the whole movement into disrepute. Thus the BWEA and SACS reserved their most rigorous procedures for such groups even when under intense government pressure to accelerate emigration at the end of the South African War. The more independent-minded applicants were weeded out as unsuitable, and qualities of initiative and adaptability valued only insofar as they could be harnessed to employers' needs. Despite all precautions, a certain number of 'failures' and 'black sheep' slipped through. SACS annual statistics categorized these women as 'unsatisfactory' either 'morally', 'physically', through 'drink' or 'as employees'. Numbers were reassuringly low in all categories, but every individual 'moral failure' generated considerable anxiety.[60] Letters flew between London and South Africa on such shocking cases as those of Lewis (seduced by a ship's engineer), Richmond (who fell in love with a ship's steward and deserted her employer for a hasty marriage), Tulloch (found to be pregnant on arrival) and Riddock (not alone in opting for the lucrative perils of barmaiding in place of domestic service).[61] When Louisa Knightley visited South Africa she made efforts to follow up on fallen women, as well as having tea parties with 'successes'. This suggests a level of involvement which went beyond mere fear of bad publicity. Organized female emigration remained true to its roots in Victorian philanthropy, moral commitment and religious duty. No branch of activity provided a better outlet for the 'personal' and 'practical' talents of womanly imperialism.

The emigrators' published advice also dwelt heavily upon moral dangers. 'Letter to Young Women Leaving England' was in its seventh edition by 1913.[62] Composed by Ellen Joyce, it contained a lengthy preface by Louisa Knightley and rather grand portraits of both ladies demonstrated their seniority and high social standing. Lady Knightley exhorted emigrants

> to raise, and not to lower, the standard of womanhood in your new country . . . to uphold the standard of purity, to be gentle and refined, real ladies in the truest sense of the word. Above all, in South Africa, be more than careful in your intercourse with the natives with whom you may have to do.

Mrs Joyce reminded them that 'the New England is going to be what you women make it', before proceeding to give more specific advice on employment opportunities and the avoidance of moral danger. She had much to say on the perils of hotel dinners, evening entertainments, 'stray acquaintances' and 'making free with strangers'. Still more forceful warnings were included in another pamphlet of the same year, entitled 'Warning Signals for Young Women Travellers'.[63] The front cover depicted a railway signal set at 'Danger', and further sets of signals appeared within under the titles 'Before you take your Ticket', 'For the Voyage', 'For Landing' and 'For Colonial Railway Travelling'. A lurid tale unfolded, apparently intended to frighten off all but the most determined of emigrants. Women who neglected to obtain their tickets from the BWEA risked finding themselves locked into unsuitable employment, perhaps having 'entered into a dangerous contract with an unknown man'. Those unchaperoned by the BWEA might be 'berthed in the next cabins to young men'. Emigrants who disembarked at ports of call risked a still worse fate: 'YOU MIGHT NEVER BE HEARD OF AGAIN.' Upon landing, those who trusted strangers were likely to be '*robbed of every penny*'; while on the Canadian railways the prospect of mixed-sex sleeping accommodation once again reared its ugly head. The logic of consigning one's person and property to the emigration society's care was irresistible, however irksome its restrictions.

Like other writers before them, both Louisa Knightley and Ellen Joyce dwelt on the special dangers of South Africa. Not only were there exceptionally large numbers of male 'adventurers' heading out from Europe, but there was also the lurking threat of 'black peril' once a young woman had reached her destination. The origins of this fear were considered in Chapter 6. In the present context it is worth noting that black sexuality held particular meanings for white female servants, in addition to those generated by white communities at large. The enormous post-war demand for white domestic labour in the Transvaal was linked with the growth of Johannesburg from a city of 109,000 in 1902 to over 250,000 by 1914, with an ever-increasing proportion of white settlers establishing homes and families. At the height of the mines' labour shortage which led to the controversial arrival of indentured 'Chinese labour', more than 20,000 black male servants were working in white Witwatersrand households.[64] It was inevitable that newly arrived white female servants would find themselves working, and even living, in close proximity to these men. SACS took its usual close interest in sleeping arrangements, insisting that its emigrants should be housed under the same roof as the employing family rather than in any form of outhouse accommodation (the standard provision for black servants).

In addition, lady emigrators offered extensive warnings on how to 'handle' the natives. On the one hand, white servants had an inescapably managerial role. As Mrs Chapin told departing women in November 1902, 'the Kaffir "boys" were like children, who could only do a thing well if they were shown how to do it. If shown, for instance, how to peel a potato they would patiently and cheerfully peel a bucketful.'[65] The prospect of instructing others was an incentive to the more genteel prospective servant:

> Where the rough work of the house is done by natives, it is obvious that someone is needed who can both teach and direct, and that conscientiousness and common-sense are more necessary than 'scrubbing' or the wearing of 'caps', as Miss Johnson put it in an article on 'Domestic Helps in Natal'.[66]

Louisa Knightley took up the same theme in an extensive paper on 'Domestic Service in England and South Africa', composed during her 1905 visit. Native labour was 'a great attraction to English servants, accustomed to do all the rough work themselves', but it also posed a potential problem:

> the danger is that they may take advantage of this help and not do their fair share of the work . . . Too often they get their heads turned on the voyage, and the fact that the white woman must necessarily occupy a position of superiority with regard to the native servant does not tend to mend matters.[67]

Colonial mistresses writing in *The Imperial Colonist* echoed this view. A careful balance needed to be struck between whiteness and servanthood, between establishing instructive, civilizing contact and maintaining a necessary degree of distance. For an even greater danger threatened those servants who befriended black co-workers rather than despising and exploiting them. The problem was summarized in May 1903 by 'a lady long resident in Pretoria':

> I do not think that too much could be said to the new maids who come out upon their attitude towards natives. They should be civil and kind, not dictatorial or imperious; but they should never allow any familiarity. They should not touch their hands, or sit in a room where there are boys, or do anything whereby an insolent native may take liberties. A girl is often inclined to think of a native boy as a 'thing', a 'machine', an 'animal', not as a man, and if she never rouses any feeling he will usually do his work mechanically and never think of molesting her.[68]

However, one could never be sure. When the dread of sexual assault occasionally became a reality, the news raced round the white population of South Africa and further increased the vigilance of the female emigrators.

Racial duty was of paramount importance to Edwardian imperialists. Emigrants to any of the colonies were likely to be reminded, at the point of departure, that they were serving the British race. Though emigration held varied meanings for emigrants, emigrators and their male imperialist backers, there was a general coalescence of views on this point. Imperial rule was in itself beneficial, but the presence of growing numbers of British settlers was ultimately essential to its strengths and virtues. Female emigration societies were not alone in investing the woman emigrant's role with great significance.

Women were widely encouraged by male imperial propagandists to become 'the future nursing mothers of the English race to be'.[69] The particular contribution of the female emigration organizers was to underline the responsibility of motherhood for the highest attributes of British civilization, for women were key agents of cultural as well as biological reproduction. In this sense, the whole Empire required mothering in order to sustain the finest qualities of British rule.

Mrs Chapin, of Johannesburg and the BWEA, gave the grandest possible expression to the female imperial mission when she described 'the Ethics of Emigration' in terms of 'imperious maternity'.[70] Like other leading female emigrators, she believed that only women could both create and serve the Empire through their selfless fostering of loyal colonial settlements. By so doing, they placed themselves at the core of the Empire's racial future. In the long term no more important contribution could be made to the exercise of imperial power, so it was logical for the nurturing ideals of women's emigration to assume a particularly central and symbolic role within the spectrum of organized female imperialism. Gendered duty stood forth clearly for the emigrators, linking together racial mission, motherhood and moral education. If the lure of individual opportunity could unite intending emigrants with these ambitious idealists, then so much the better both for women and for the Empire. Varied and contrasting motives need not prevent a successful racial outcome which would reinforce British world power while enhancing women's status as standard-bearers of British civilization.

Notes

1. See J. Hammerton, *Emigrant Gentlewomen, Genteel Poverty and Female Emigration, 1830–1914* (London: Croom Helm, 1979) for a survey of the subject focused mainly on the earlier period. Hammerton's conclusions on the growing distance between female emigration and feminism during the Edwardian era are revised in this book, and in J. Bush, '"The Right Sort of Woman": Female Emigrators and Emigration to the British Empire, 1890–1910', *Women's History Review* (1994), 3, 3: 385–409. The South African context is examined in C. Swaisland, *Servants and Gentlewomen to the Golden Land* (Oxford: Berg Publishers, 1993). An organizational history is presented in U. Monk, *New Horizons: A Hundred Years of Women's Migration* (London: HMSO, 1963).
2. Monk, p. 20.
3. Bessie Parkes, 'A Year's Experience in Woman's Work' (paper read at the National Association for the Promotion of Social Science, August 1860, and reprinted in *The English Woman's Journal*, October 1860), quoted in C. Lacey (ed.), *Barbara Leigh Smith Bodichon and the Langham Place Group* (London: Routledge & Kegan Paul, 1986), pp. 187–8.
4. Maria Rye, 'On Assisted Emigration' (published in *The English Woman's Journal*, June 1860), quoted in Lacey, p. 344.
5. Frances Power Cobbe, 'What Shall We Do With Our Old Maids?' (published in *Frazer's Magazine*, November 1862), quoted in Lacey, p. 357.
6. William Greg's article is reprinted in J. Horowitz Murray (ed.), *Strong-minded Women and Other Lost Voices from Nineteenth Century England* (London: Penguin, 1984).
7. For a critical account of Maria Rye's later career, see M. Diamond, 'Maria Rye: The Primrose Path', in C. Campbell Orr, *Wollstonecraft's Daughters: Womanhood in England and France 1780–1920* (Manchester: Manchester University Press, 1996). Ellen Joyce's early interest in emigration work was inspired by personal contact with Maria Rye, who helped her to send orphan girls to Ontario from the Hampshire village where her husband was rector. I am

indebted to Joyce Goodman for this information, published in *The Hampshire Chronicle*, 3 January 1920.

8. Some of the female emigration societies' own statistical data for the Edwardian years are reproduced in Appendix 1. Unfortunately, full statistics on general female emigration to the British Empire are not available before the 1920s, and the societies' statistics for assisted emigration are also inconsistent and incomplete. For discussion of the general statistics, see W. Carrothers, *Emigration from the British Isles with Special Reference to the Overseas Dominions* (London: P.S. King, 1929), pp. 275 and 305–18; and Dominions Royal Commission: Final Report (1918) *Parliamentary Papers 1917–18*, Vol. X, Chapter VIII. Cd8462. For discussion of the societies' statistics, see Hammerton, pp. 176–7; Swaisland, pp. 167–9.

9. *The Imperial Colonist*, I/1, January 1902.

10. *Ibid.*, I/3, March 1902.

11. Mary Hervey, on behalf of 'The Education Sub-Committee of the South African Expansion B.W.E.A.', in *The Imperial Colonist*, I/2, February 1902.

12. Colonial Intelligence League First Annual Report 1910–11 (1911).

13. *The Imperial Colonist*, III/35, November 1904.

14. Reported fully in *The Imperial Colonist*, III/32, August 1904.

15. The early history of the Leaton Home is summarized in *The Imperial Colonist*, VII/94, and has also been researched by Donald Harris for his forthcoming PhD thesis on emigration from Shropshire to Canada (Department of American and Canadian Studies, University of Birmingham). I am indebted to Mr Harris for an 1891 census extract demonstrating that the original group of five adult students were self-supporting or provided for by their parents, but that in addition one younger 'pupil' was subsidized by the Bedford Union.

16. *The Imperial Colonist*, III/32, August 1904.

17. *Ibid.*, VI/61, January 1907.

18. *Ibid.*, II/5, May 1903.

19. See publicity material for the Lady Warwick Hotel, 1898–99, sent by the Countess of Warwick to Cecil Rhodes, including leaflets and the First Annual Report. Rhodes papers, C28/140–142. Rhodes House Library, Oxford.

20. *The Imperial Colonist*, III/32, August 1904.

21. Colonial Intelligence League Third Annual Report 1912–13 (1913).

22. Colonial Intelligence League First Annual Report 1910–11 (1911).

23. Ellen Joyce, published speeches made at the Portsmouth Church Congress, October 1885 and the Rhyl Church Congress, October 1891. GFS Archive.

24. *The Imperial Colonist*, I/1, January 1902.

25. Ellen Joyce to Helen Notcutt, 'Information and suggestions for the use of the proposed Cape Town Committee', endorsed with a letter dated 9 March 1900. BWEA South African committee correspondence 1899–1900. FL 4/4. Fawcett Library.

26. Ellen Joyce to H. Caiger Esq., 24 March 1900. BWEA South African committee correspondence 1899–1900. FL 4/4.

27. Ellen Joyce to Hilda Waide, 17 March 1900. BWEA South African committee correspondence 1899–1900. FL 4/4.

28. *The Imperial Colonist*, I/2, February 1902.

29. A detailed account of the post-war South African emigration, emphasizing the roles of governments and financiers rather than female emigrators and emigrants, is provided in J. Van-Helten and K. Williams, 'The Crying Need of South Africa: The Emigration of Single Women to the Transvaal 1901–10', *Journal of South African Studies* (1983), **19**, 1: 17–38.

30. *The Imperial Colonist*, I/10, October 1902.

31. *Ibid.*, II/7, July 1903.

32. *Ibid.*, II/12, December 1903.

33. See P. Bean and J. Melville, *Lost Children of the Empire* (London: Unwin Hyman, 1989), Chapters 4 and 5.
34. *The Imperial Colonist*, III/31 and III/32, July and August 1904.
35. 'Why Do Single Women Emigrate?', from *Cassell's Saturday Journal*, July 1895, preserved in BWEA Scrapbook 2, 1890–1901. FL 3/2.
36. *The Imperial Colonist*, VI/65, May 1907.
37. Maud Selborne to Alicia Cecil, 20 April 1906. SACS correspondence. FL 3/2.
38. Edith Lyttelton to Kathleen Lyttelton, 26 September 1900. Chandos II, 3/14. Chandos papers. Churchill College, Cambridge.
39. Louisa Knightley's journal, 2 July 1902. Northamptonshire Record Office.
40. John Ardagh to Joseph Chamberlain. Draft scheme for an 'Association for facilitating and promoting the emigration of selected young women under proper supervision to South Africa'. January 1901. JCII/3/4. Chamberlain papers. Birmingham University Library.
41. *The Imperial Colonist*, I/9, September 1902.
42. *Ibid.*, I/8, August 1902.
43. E. Joyce, (?1908) 'Words Addressed to the Teachers Sailing for Alberta, Canada'. GFS pamphlet in the GFS Archive.
44. SACS Annual Report 1904 (1905).
45. *The Imperial Colonist*, I/1, January 1902.
46. E. Joyce, 'The Imperial Aspect of GFS Emigration', published paper read at the GFS Imperial Conference at the Imperial Institute, 19 June 1913. GFS Archive.
47. *The Imperial Colonist*, I/1, January 1902.
48. See D. Alessio, 'Domesticating "the Heart of the Wild": Female Personification of the Colonies, 1886–1940', *Women's History Review* (1997), **6**, 2: 239–69.
49. *The Imperial Colonist*, III/36, December 1904.
50. 'A Woman's Life at the Cape, by One Who Has Tried It', from *The Queen*, 25 September 1896, preserved in BWEA Scrapbook 2, 1890–1901. FL 3/2.
51. *The Imperial Colonist*, I/6. June 1902.
52. *Ibid.*, IV/37, January 1905.
53. *Ibid.*, VI/80, August 1908.
54. *Ibid.*, XII/148, May 1914.
55. *Ibid.*, V/55, July 1906.
56. Joyce, 'Words Addressed'.
57. *The Imperial Colonist*, XII/147, April 1914.
58. Laura Ridding's notebook, January 1909, pp. 47–8. 9 M68/61. Hampshire Record Office.
59. Louisa Knightley's journal, 25 and 30 August 1905. In Pretoria Lady Knightley visited 'the Diocesan School of the Wantage sisters – to make some enquiries as to some of our girls who have drifted into their House of Mercy: I am thankful to say a very small proportion of those we have sent out'.
60. SACS Annual Report 1905 (1906) indicated that of 193 emigrants to the Transvaal 131 were 'very satisfactory' and only 27 in the categories of 'fair', 'unsatisfactory' or 'unknown'.
61. See letters from Alicia Cecil to the Johannesburg committee of the SACS dated 28 November 1902, 23 January 1903, 5 and 27 February 1903, 25 March 1903, and 3 and 17 July 1903. SACS correspondence. FL 3/1. See also letters from Helen Notcutt and Madeleine Goatly, of the Cape Town committee, to Ellen Joyce, dated 4 July 1899 and 16 August 1899. BWEA South Africa committee correspondence 1899–1900. FL 4/4.
62. E. Joyce, 'Letter to Young Women Leaving England' (Winchester: Warren and Son Ltd, 1913).
63. E. Joyce, 'Warning Signals for Young Women Travellers' (London: BWEA, 1913).
64. See C. Van Onselen, *Studies in the Social and Economic History of the Witwatersrand, 1886–1914*, Vol. Two, *New Nineveh* (London: Longman, 1982), pp. 13, 25. Walter Vivian

estimated that there were 'thirty thousand kaffirs engaged in domestic employment' in Johannesburg alone, in an article which summarized the economic connections between white female servants, the black male labour supply and the high cost of living. *The Imperial Colonist*, III/39. March 1905.

65. *The Imperial Colonist*, II/1, January 1903.
66. *Ibid.*, II/4, April 1903.
67. *Ibid.*, IV/48, December 1905.
68. *Ibid.*, II/5, May 1903.
69. *Ibid.*, III/36, December 1904.
70. *Ibid.*, II/8, August 1903.

10 Imperialism, the Women's Movement and the Vote

The female imperialist associations gathered momentum during the turn-of-the-century floodtide of new imperialism. However, the 1890s were also the decade of the new woman, an increasingly assertive and self-reliant individual who demanded the Vote as an essential adjunct to education, employment and a more independent lifestyle. The turbulent politics of the early twentieth century included the climax of the women's suffrage campaign, as well as challenges from the labour movement and, from 1906, the advent of a Liberal government committed to social and constitutional reform. Simultaneously, Britain's worldwide pre-eminence required shoring up against economic and military competition. Historians have pointed out the congruence between responses from the imperially thinking Establishment to these various problems.[1] From 1903 Joseph Chamberlain, the leading political prophet of imperialism, campaigned to impose tariff reform upon his reluctant party. Beneficiaries of protectionism were to include the British working man whose job was threatened by European or American imports, as well as British and colonial supporters of imperial unity. The alternative to 'making the foreigner pay' was to make the wealthier British taxpayer bear the expense of subsidizing cheap food, social reforms and rearmament. This was an alternative eventually preferred by a majority of the voting public and the pre-war governments of Asquith and Lloyd George. By 1910 the issues of tariffs, imperial defence and social reform were inextricably linked with the constitutional crises of House of Lords reform ('the peers versus the people'), suffrage reform and Home Rule for Ireland. Were Britain's traditional upper-class, male rulers equipped to find a way forward? This question often transcended the expediencies of short-term party politics. It infused the defence of Empire, and the debate over women's position in society, with a particular intensity.

The leading ladies of organized female imperialism were far from immune to the political excitements of their age. As members of ruling-class families, most were knowledgeable about parliamentary affairs and closely followed the day-to-day conflicts which shaped the changing face of British politics. With varying degrees of insight, they perceived their own interests to be at stake. As members of the upper class, as imperialists and as women, they were dissatisfied with the role of sidelined spectators. The existence of the female imperialist associations is evidence of this fact. The associations frequently declared themselves to be 'non-political' in order to emphasize their aspiration towards an inclusive, cross-party imperialism expressed through gendered women's work, but at both an organizational and an individual level, the business of government and the political debates surrounding it influenced many of their activities. The imperial politics of tariff reform, Chinese labour and Home Rule were part of the cut and thrust of party conflict at successive general elections. Social reform politics intersected with the multiple concerns of the wider British women's movement, to which many female imperialists had developed allegiance. Most divisively of all, suffrage politics were an inescapable part of the Edwardian context of female imperialism. This chapter examines the ways in which the imperialist associations handled political controversy, and especially the controversy over the Vote. Their successful containment of political divergence serves to underline those ideas and activities which the women themselves regarded as the essence of their cause.

At first glance it certainly appeared likely that organized female imperialism might founder on the rocks of suffragism. 'Votes for Women' had been demanded in Parliament and campaigned for in the country since the 1860s. In 1897 the moderate suffragists allied together into the National Union of Women's Suffrage Societies, headed by Mrs Fawcett, while from 1903 to 1914 the Pankhursts' Women's Social and Political Union added first stridence, then violence, to the demand. Indifference to the campaign was impossible, and the leading ladies did not attempt it. Analysis of the known views of prominent imperialists suggests that approximately equal numbers lined up for and against the Vote (see Appendix 2). Among the leaders, a small majority probably favoured women's suffrage. Among supporters in the country, these proportions may well have been reversed.[2] What is certain is that the official neutrality of the female imperialist associations on this and other 'political' matters did nothing to inhibit their most prominent leaders from making a strong public stand. Louisa Knightley, for example, was a consistent and outspoken supporter of moderate suffragism. As early as 1871 she had astonished herself with the extent of her subconscious ambitions:

> I dreamt that I had been elected to the House of Commons, though I tried in vain to recollect for what constituency I was about to take my seat. The floor of the House was covered with members through whom I threaded my way very shyly. There were other ladies in the House but as I was the only MP they had to leave when the debate began . . . I was deeply impressed with the responsibility of my new position. Suddenly I awoke and realised where I was, and began to ask myself if this were an omen of the future.[3]

The following year she succeeded in persuading her deeply traditionalist husband to vote for a Women's Franchise bill – 'much to my joy. The more I think about it, the more convinced I feel that it is only just women should have the vote, and that many injustices under which they labour will never be removed until they do have it.'[4] A few days later she raised the issue with Lord Salisbury, who 'can see no reason against it, although he does not consider it to be a pressingly needed reform at the present time'.[5]

Even at the height of her imperialist activity during the 1900s, Louisa Knightley found time for lobbying politicians and speaking at drawing-room meetings in support of the suffrage cause. In the same period the female members of the 'Hotel Cecil' perpetuated Salisbury's own suffragism from within the vanguard of female imperialism. Maud Selborne, Gwendolen Cecil and Alice, Betty and Frances Balfour were all keen suffrage supporters. Maud herself became the founding President of the Conservative and Unionist Women's Franchise Association in 1907, and later a vice-president of the National Union of Women's Suffrage Societies. In 1911 she accompanied Millicent

Fawcett and Christabel Pankhurst on a Downing Street deputation, and in the following years became increasingly active in suffrage journalism and meetings, despite her detestation of militancy. Meanwhile, Frances Balfour spoke from the plinth in Trafalgar Square in 1906, and between 1910 and 1912 was the leading guest at suffrage meetings up and down the country, as well as a somewhat reluctant participant in demonstrations. In her memoirs she recorded her pride in a 'common cause' which had numbered Josephine Butler, Ellice Hopkin, Florence Nightingale and Sophia Jex Blake among its adherents.[6] Despite claiming to be 'no good at organization', she chaired the largest London suffrage organization, and accepted historical credit for 'being a sort of liaison officer between suffrage and the Houses of Parliament'.[7] Like her sister-in-law, Betty Balfour, she greatly admired Mrs Fawcett. No doubt the association between these women was assisted by their shared enthusiasm for Empire. Unlike the Fawcett ladies, many female imperialists prioritized imperial activism or other forms of women's work above Votes for Women, but were nevertheless supportive of the cause. Such women included Conservatives and Unionists Meriel Talbot, Edith and Kathleen Lyttelton, Laura Ridding, Beatrice Cartwright, Lady Brassey and Lady Willoughby de Broke, as well as prominent Liberals such as Elizabeth Haldane and the Countess of Aberdeen, and the Fabian socialist Beatrice Webb. The evidence of committed suffragism among the female imperialists helps to undermine the still widely held view that Edwardian suffragism was overwhelmingly Liberal and middle class, linked to non-conformity and the labour movement but inimically hostile to Toryism, Anglicanism and Empire.[8]

Leading lady imperialists were almost equally to the fore within organized anti-suffragism. The novelist Mary Ward seized the initiative with her influential 'appeal against female suffrage', published in the *Nineteeth Century* in June 1889 and signed by many well-known ladies.[9] Twenty years later she joined Lady Jersey at the inaugural meeting of the Women's National Anti-Suffrage League. The eighteen ladies nominated to its executive committee included Beatrice Chamberlain (daughter of Joseph, and another Victoria League stalwart) and Gertrude Bell, the famous imperialist traveller and writer who was a close friend of Violet Markham.[10] Violet herself rapidly moved to prominence within the movement. Brian Harrison's history of the National League for Opposing Women's Suffrage emphasizes the control exerted from within by male leaders who included such renowned imperialists as Lord Cromer, Lord Curzon, Sir George Goldie and Sir Alfred Lyall, together with some of the most distinguished cultural exponents of Empire: Elgar, Newbolt and Kipling. Within the united Anti organization of 1911, Margaret Jersey became Deputy to Cromer as President. However, Mary Ward and Violet Markham, in particular, remained vital platform assets. In February 1909 Mary Ward was trounced by Millicent Fawcett at a public debate, but a month later made a triumphant reappearance at a large Anti-Suffrage Rally in the Queen's Hall.[11] Even this achievement was eclipsed by Violet Markham's spectacular success before a crowd of 10,000 at the Albert Hall on 28 February 1912. Georgina Frere was one of the many Victoria League members present who afterwards wrote to congratulate her on '*the* speech of the evening!'[12] Her other female imperialist admirers included Mary Harcourt, Ethel Colquhoun, Mary Jeune and Lady Lugard.

In retrospect, perhaps the most striking characteristic of Violet Markham's speech was its confident assertion of the value of women's participation in government, despite her rejection of the parliamentary vote as an appropriate means to that end. She stirred her audience, and perhaps particularly the organized female imperialists among it, with a resoundingly positive call to action:

> In the first place, we are here to affirm that a woman's citizenship is as great and as real as that of any man, that her service is as vitally necessary to the State . . . We believe that men and women are different – not similar – beings, with talents that are complementary, not identical, and that, therefore, they ought to have different shares in the management of the State, that they severally compose. We do not depreciate by one jot or tittle woman's work and mission. We are concerned to find proper channels of expression for that work. We seek a fruitful diversity of political function, not a stultifying uniformity.[13]

Such sentiments ultimately jarred a little with Cromer and Curzon, but brought a welcome rush of short-term publicity and support to the Antis' cause. There was corresponding displeasure in the pro-suffrage camp, especially among those who felt wounded by Violet Markham's criticism of women's failure to take up the appropriately gendered work of local government which already lay open to them.[14] However, it was also clear to many imperialist suffragists that only a fine line divided Violet's views from their own so far as gender difference and patriotic service were concerned. There was widespread agreement on the importance of connecting women's essentially different nature with suitable forms of participation in national and imperial affairs. This general viewpoint has been commented on by a number of recent historians of the women's movement, including Barbara Caine, who warns against false dichotomies between 'equality' and 'difference' feminism.[15] Victorian women inevitably conceptualized greater equality in terms defined by the prevailing domestic ideology, though some were more prepared to test its boundaries than others. For many female imperialists, regardless of their views on the Vote, feminine patriotism was merely distinctively feminine virtue and ability writ large. Thus when Violet Markham eventually came over to support for women's suffrage during the First World War, she did not need to jettison her fundamental belief in womanly talents any more than had earlier distinguished converts such as Beatrice Webb and Louise Creighton, friend of Mary Ward and founding President of the National Union of Women Workers.

Despite the common underlying beliefs held by many female imperialists, the divide on the suffrage issue remained a conspicuous one. There was a danger that it would be deepened by the leading ladies' disagreements on other key subjects which divided Edwardian politicians. Fortunately for the progress of organized female imperialism, its leaders were less inclined to take to the platform or the press on tariff reform, the House of Lords or Home Rule. Though some individuals held strong views, there was no concerted axis of support between the anti-suffragists and other campaign groups, despite the fact that a male imperialist axis of 'die-hard' opponents of reform has been identified by historians.[16] Basically, the lady imperialists were inclined to leave campaigning on most matters of high politics to their male relatives. Violet Markham made outspoken speeches from Liberal election platforms against tariff reform and in favour of constitutional reform, invoking her knowledge of Empire to support the case for Irish self-government.[17] However, there was certainly no unanimous female imperialist viewpoint on any of these subjects, even among those who shared a common party allegiance or a common view on suffrage. Chamberlain's efforts to convey tariff reform as an imperial touchstone successfully drew some lady imperialists into the auxiliary Women's Tariff Reform Association, including Edith Lyttelton and Violet Brooke-Hunt (who became its secretary).[18] But the privately hostile ladies included Margaret Jersey; Louisa Knightley found the whole subject confusing and a little boring; and Maud Selborne was uncomfortably positioned between a protectionist husband and anti-protectionist brothers. The Cecil brothers closed ranks with Selborne and Milner in defence of the House of Lords' prerogatives, while Maud anxiously debated compromise solutions with her husband. She strongly opposed Home Rule on both imperialist and traditionally Conservative grounds. However, even here she sought a pragmatic compromise, rather than following her sister-in-law Violet Cecil into bellicose support for the Unionism of Sir Edward Carson and Lord Milner.[19]

Most of the female imperialist associations had a long history of successfully containing political diversity. Only the Primrose League had a clear association with a single political party. Since the Conservative Party was itself divided and at odds for much of the Edwardian period, there was little difficulty in accommodating the differences of its female supporters. The imperialist propaganda of the Primrose League naturally dwelt on what united rather than on what divided. Interestingly, however, the League decided to permit open debate on the suffrage issue, presumably on the grounds that the issue was non-fundamental as well as irredeemably divisive. Louisa Knightley presided over a Towcester Habitation meeting in 1901 which resolved in favour of women's suffrage.[20] In contrast, Betty Balfour was driven into a conspicuous resignation from the Dame Presidency of her Woking Habitation when the local Conservative candidate mounted an anti-suffrage election campaign in 1910.[21] Martin Pugh concludes that, on balance, the Primrose League made a positive contribution towards the achievement of Votes for Women by undermining assumptions about women's political ability and interests and by providing them with a form of apprenticeship in party activism.[22] This was despite the fact that, on any count, it was the least feminist and indeed the least female of the organizations considered in this book.

In contrast to the Primrose League, the other female imperialist associations made conscious efforts to distance themselves from any formal connections with party politics. The Victoria League's attempts to construct a politically balanced executive have been described, and Violet Markham's aim to achieve a broad membership and even links to the labour movement must be construed as part of the same attempt. Like most other associations with a predominantly female membership, the Victoria League found itself unable to ignore totally the suffrage issue, despite an evident wish to do so at leadership level. The executive committee sternly avoided the subject, on the basis that it was divisively 'political'. When the South African suffragist Nina Boyle sent in her resignation from the Victoria League as a protest against Lady Jersey's anti-suffragism, it was left to the pro-suffrage Meriel Talbot to mend fences by 'calling the writer's attention to the support given to the League by those holding opposite opinions on controversial questions'.[23] Invitations to get involved in suffrage campaigns were also regularly recorded by the British Women's Emigration Association and its offshoots. Louisa Knightley's dual commitments to emigration and suffrage no doubt fostered the expectation that this all-female movement founded by first-wave feminists might be persuaded to take up the cause. However, all such overtures were politely declined on the grounds that the emigration associations' work lay elsewhere.

The same viewpoint was expressed by the Girls' Friendly Society. An occasional echo of the external battle for the Vote reached the pages of the GFS journals, only to be swiftly suppressed. For example, *Friendly Leaves* contained an educative 'GFS Dialogue' in 1903 on the subject of 'Our rights as women to stand firm, as a compact body':

> Ethel – What, to get into Parliament?
>
> Marian – No; to band ourselves together in a crusade against evil – in the GFS army – women as Associates, girls as Members, children as Candidates – standing shoulder to shoulder, foot to foot, in the effort to raise the standard of our men – brothers, husbands and sons – to a higher level by attaining to it ourselves.[24]

Five years later the same journal mused poetically:

> The Rights of woman, what are they?
> The Right to labour, love and pray;
> The Right to weep with those who weep,
> The Right to wake when others sleep.[25]

However, as Brian Harrison has pointed out, it would be very misleading to assess the GFS's contribution to 'women's emancipation' from such evidence alone.[26] A counterpoint to the anti-feminism of much GFS propaganda exists in the Society's frequent assertions of 'the great power of women in the world' and in its adulation for 'notable Women'.[27] Many suffragists, as well as anti-suffragists, felt comfortably at home within the GFS and enjoyed its invocations to female solidarity.

As the only female imperialist association with formal religious links, the GFS was more prone than other societies to self-conscious reflection on the spiritual powers of womanhood. However, each of the imperialist women's associations in its own way prompted its supporters to consider and discuss woman's nature and its relationship to female roles and responsibilities. The virtues of 'practical' altruism were as deeply embedded in womanly work for the Empire as they were in the many other forms of social action which attracted the support of Victorian and Edwardian ladies. Jane Lewis has described the extent to which shared attitudes towards social action could unite women who disagreed over the suffrage issue, and there is no doubt that her conclusions are of considerable relevance to organized female imperialism.[28] The female imperialist associations were shaped by imperial patriotism, linked to faith in the moral authority and superior abilities of a social hierarchy headed by royalty itself. However, they were also powerfully linked to a broader British women's movement, fed by the mingled currents of feminist equal rights activism and gender-conscious social reform. The organizational continuity of a suffrage-divided female imperialism seems less remarkable when the associations are viewed in this wider context. Women's work was seen as all-important, both as a fulfilment of female duties and abilities and as a contribution to the soundness and strength of Nation and Empire. Moreover, these convictions had materialized into a formidable network of interlinked organizations by the end of the nineteenth century. Though the female imperialist associations were potentially divided by the strength of their leaders' views on the Vote, they proved capable of drawing upon deeper well-springs of shared conviction and shared activism extending beyond their own immediate work.

The National Union of Women Workers was the largest Edwardian women's organization which promoted the importance of womanly work as a distinctive and valuable contribution to British society. In 1912 Lady Jersey welcomed representatives of no fewer than 170 loosely linked women's societies to the Union's Annual Conference at Oxford.[29] As a broad-based and largely philanthropic organization, the NUWW played a significant role in bringing together socially concerned middle-class women with the largely aristocratic leadership of female imperialism. During the Edwardian years it was also to supply another example of divisive suffrage debate within a forum where women were striving to maintain the continuity and unity of their long-term gendered work. Early twentieth-century presidents of the NUWW included female imperialists Kathleen Lyttelton (1899–1901), Constance Battersea (1901–03) and Laura Ridding (1910–11), to be followed in the post-war decade by Maud Selborne (1920–21) and Frances Balfour (1921–23).[30] Social rank no doubt played a part in these appointments, but the imperialist associations gained as much as they gave within the broad church of the British women's movement which the NUWW so impressively represented. The presidency of elite women signified recognition from within the powerful inner circles of Society and government. It was also a magnet which helped to attract less powerful women into the NUWW's orbit. On the other hand, the benefits to aristocratic participants were also important. For many upper-class women, NUWW conferences proved a key formative experience, opening avenues to collective organization and to female self-help on a larger scale than they had previously thought possible. A wider range of social contacts introduced a new range of knowledge and broader political horizons shaped by gender, as well as by existing class-based assumptions about female roles in society and government. The NUWW, like organized female imperialism itself, can scarcely be labelled as feminist since it happily tolerated the presence of extremely conservative women within its ranks. But it opened doors to feminism for some women. Above all, the NUWW convinced those whom it gathered together that they were indeed a 'movement'; that women (at least of the upper and middle classes) were united by important bonds of common interest, and that their shared convictions might influence the future.

Laura Ridding described this sense of collective female strength in her auto-biographical account of the Union's early history.[31] Founded in 1895, the NUWW aimed to link voluntary 'women workers' in the overlapping fields of philanthropy, social and educational reform and local government. Objectives included 'the encouragement of sympathy of thought and purpose among the women of Great Britain and Ireland; the promotion of their social, civil and religious welfare; the gathering and distribution of serviceable information'. Edith Lyttelton, Beatrice Webb and Laura Ridding were members of the first executive, while the founding vice-presidents included Millicent Fawcett, the Honourable Mrs Talbot, Lady Battersea and Lady Frederick Cavendish. The most distinguished imperialist foundress was the Countess of Aberdeen, who had presided two years earlier over the inauguration of the worldwide International Council of Women, to which the NUWW soon affiliated. Eventually, during the First World War, the NUWW fell into line with most overseas affiliates by changing its name to the National Council of Women (NCW). In 1899 the British organization hosted an international congress at which, true to its already inclusive traditions, delegates were offered 267 papers at sixty-seven separate meetings. Laura Ridding remembered, in her old age, the dominant presence of leading American and British suffragists, but also the overwhelming pleasure of her encounter with a widely varied mainstream of female activists eager both to learn and to teach:

> As our road surveyors transform lanes into highways, by extending their space on either side, so the path of life has been widened for us, unexplored country and broader horizons have been opened out before us, as we have travelled along the NCW road. We have also had the joy of meeting fellow pilgrims on that road, from among whom we have won some of our most cherished friendships.[32]

The issues debated at NUWW gatherings included virtually every established branch of upper- and middle-class social welfare work. Aside from educational work, the most frequently discussed subjects were poor relief, the employment of women, health issues and the rescue and preventive work of moral reform. From the 1870s onwards, these interconnected subjects had been at the heart of Victorian social action and mainstays of an increasingly organized and politicized women's movement. The Girls' Friendly Society and the British Women's Emigration Association sprang from the same fount of social concern. At the turn of the century all the female imperialist associations drew heavily upon the collective and individual commitment of women who wished to dedicate their existing convictions and experience to the service of Empire. As the networking chart in Appendix 2 demonstrates, very few of the leading lady imperialists turned to imperialist social action without a parallel, and usually preceding, experience of other voluntary 'women's work'. The direction of their interests and the extent of their commitments varied. But the NUWW, alongside more specialized organizations, had already set forth a shared programme of gendered duty and gendered achievement. Acceptance of this common agenda helped the female imperialists to overcome the suffrage divide, though not always without difficulty.

The desire to exclude suffrage debates from the imperialist associations' formal activities was no doubt increased by the simultaneous experience of suffrage-related problems within the NUWW. Leading executive members changed sides during the 1900s and by 1910 Mary Ward and other NUWW anti-suffragists found themselves in an embittered minority. Laura Ridding bravely decided to use her presidential authority to exclude both pro- and anti-suffrage literature from the hall during the 1910 NUWW Annual Conference, despite the vociferous criticism of 'ardent suffragists' with whom she privately sympathized.[33] Fellow-imperialist and suffragist Louisa Knightley was among the supporters of her decision, and helpfully to hand when a vote of confidence in the president required a seconder. Delegates who chose to debate the franchise issue were invited to do so after the main conference business was concluded. Lady Knightley once again stepped in, this time to take the chair at the pro-suffrage meeting. In her journal she recorded the interesting information that she had shared a railway carriage with Laura Ridding on the way to the conference; their chief topic of conversation had been Mary Ward's position on the Vote, which both women clearly wished to understand better.[34] The NUWW had by this date moved cautiously towards official support for moderate suffragism, but remained extremely reluctant to allow this particular battle to overshadow other issues and to undermine older alliances. In 1912 the National League for Opposing

Women's Suffrage formally conceded defeat within the NUWW by withdrawing its affiliation. Many suffragists regarded this as a matter of regret, and continued to emphasize the issues which united rather than divided women. This was the preferred, and largely successful, tactic pursued by the Victoria League, the British Women's Emigration Association and the Girls' Friendly Society.

It is clear that the Edwardian women's movement was broad enough to encompass, and indeed to link, middle-class social reformers, aristocratic female imperialists, and equal rights feminists whose priorities lay in the direction of legal and political reform. Votes for Women can no longer be regarded as the keystone of this arch,[35] though the issue remained an unavoidable one, even within organizations which had strong reasons for wishing to avoid it. The connections between female social action and female imperialism are evident enough, but the suffragist presence among the leading women imperialists is strong enough to prompt further enquiry into the influence of consciously expressed feminism within their associations. The existing substantial literature defining and redefining feminism provides an additional spur. Despite the fact that the term 'feminism' was little used in Britain before 1914, particularly extensive academic study has been devoted to its late-nineteenth- and early-twentieth-century characteristics.[36] In general, this work reinforces the view that feminism lacked a singular, distinct identity. It must therefore be explored through its many and varied manifestations in the campaigns of the women's movement and in women's lives in order to be well understood. Female imperialism provides a further site for such exploration, at both organizational and individual levels.

Certain characteristics which other historians have judged to be 'feminist' have already emerged in the course of this study, and a growing body of historical literature emphasizes the existence and significance of the feminist–imperialist link. Olive Banks identified the evangelizing face of Western feminism, and its connection to visions both of social progress and national greatness.[37] The Christian maternalism of the female emigrators undoubtedly united many female imperialists with this conservative strand of feminism. More sustained studies of the interconnections between feminism and Empire have been undertaken recently by Vron Ware, Barbara Ramusack, Antoinette Burton, Inderpal Grewal, Barbara Bush and Clare Midgley.[38] Working from varied evidence, they conclude that both direct and indirect connections were strong and endorse the view of post-colonial theorists that this subject is of critical importance to modern feminists who aspire to free themselves from the incubus of an imperial past. Not only was Empire-building a demonstrably gendered activity but women activists consciously made it so, emphasizing the importance of female roles and asserting women's ability and their duty to change the world and contribute to patriotic endeavour. Inderpal Grewal concludes, with others, that the Empire and its subject people offered a convenient footstool to Western women's political power.[39] Antoinette Burton's earlier work remains the most comprehensive account so far of the links between British feminism and British imperialism. The two categories were virtually inseparable for the suffrage-supporting 'imperial feminists' whose public discourse forms the main focus of her study: 'Claiming their place in the empire was – along with educational reform, suffrage campaigns, and battles against the sexual double standard – one of the priorities of liberal British feminists during the period under consideration' (1865 to 1915).[40]

Some of the leaders and supporters of the female imperialist associations certainly belong in Burton's category of 'imperial feminists', including Millicent Fawcett herself. However, the present study has shown that 'imperial feminists' and 'female imperialists' are by no means interchangeable categories. Even among those who supported the suffrage cause, there were some who rejected much else which 'liberal British feminists' regarded as the essence of their cause. A majority of the leading imperialist ladies were both Conservatives and, in some respects, conservative. Maud Selborne supported women's suffrage, but opposed women's entry into parliament; though a highly assertive person herself, she believed in feminine discretion. Louisa Knightley dreamed of entering parliament in the 1870s, but struggled to curb her ambitions and to conform to modest and altruistic expectations of Christian womanhood. A considerable number of female imperialists were hostile even to the suffrage demand, though this did not necessarily inhibit their participation in the social and educational campaigns of the wider women's movement. Both Mary Ward and Violet Markham believed womanly qualities would be compromised by female participation in national government, and that the loss would be detrimental to family life, Nation and Empire. Ellen Joyce urged emigrant Canadian teachers to strengthen the Empire by restoring women to their domestic roles.[41] All these women were engaged in the collective womanly work of organized female imperialism and a majority shared some sense of belonging to a British women's movement. However, a negation of most accepted historical meanings of the term 'feminism' is required in order to extend this category to include the members of the female imperialist associations. Though some female imperialists were influenced by aspects of contemporary feminism, only a small minority were 'imperial feminists'.

The problems of such political labelling have been widely acknowledged in recent historical writing. The emphasis of this study, like many others, is upon the permeability of political definitions and boundaries within women's history. Unexpected conjunctions between suffragists and anti-suffragists, feminists and anti-feminists were an outcome of the varied and variable commitments of those engaged in organizing female support for the Empire. Most female imperialists were not 'feminists' because they did not seriously contest existing gender relations and the inequalities of power which these embodied.[42] Inequality and oppression were simply not part of the female imperialist vocabulary, despite their currency in the interlinked suffrage movement. Even those imperialist ladies who supported suffrage generally positioned themselves at the most conservative end of the equal rights spectrum, rejecting both confrontational tactics and the development of any systematic critique of male power. As we have seen, their chosen imperialist activities sometimes implied male error by omission, but this was as far as the critique usually went. The female imperialists accepted the fundamentals of gender difference and sought opportunities to provide their own service to the Empire alongside the admired achievements of British men. Even the partially expressed consciousness of a need to 'feminize' imperial values was represented as a gently ameliorative task rather than a radical challenge to the gendered status quo. The non-confrontational gender politics of female imperialism were, of course, linked to social class. While feminists made angry claims on behalf of universal womanhood, the universe of the lady imperialists was circumscribed by their willing integration into a male-dominated social and political elite. For most upper-class women, equal rights issues were of abstract, or sometimes altruistic, interest. Gendered class status, on the other hand, carried with it the immediacy of social and economic authority and indirect forms of political power. All the strengths of an upper-class leadership were turned to good effect within the female imperialist associations.

Though female imperialists were usually resistant to feminist concepts of gender oppression, they did share in some of the positive and optimistic characteristics which historians have identified with Victorian and Edwardian feminist politics. Philippa Levine associated 'the feminist distinctiveness of the woman's movement' with pride in female identity, consciousness of the merits and strengths of autonomous female organization, and reliance by activists upon a network of emotional and intellectual female support.[43] Such characteristics were strongly evident within all the women's imperialist associations, and indeed provided a vital ingredient in linking them together. A degree of gender separateness was built into middle- and upper-class Edwardian social life, and must therefore not be too readily attributed to 'feminism'. Yet it is interesting to observe the extent to which the female imperialists derived conscious enjoyment (even empowerment?) from their women-only, or women-led, societies. 'We sat down eleven ladies to dinner!' exulted Louisa Knightley on the eve of a GFS conference at her country home.[44] Much of her extensive hospitality was afforded to women as individuals or in groups, and the commentary in her journal suggests this was very much a matter of choice and not merely a consequence of widowhood. It was Louisa Knightley who, in 1903, rejected the 'horrible idea' of a male secretary for the South African Colonisation Society.[45] It is clear that, while welcoming male co-operation and relying upon male patronage, the leading ladies were wary of the excessive incursion of male authority into their organizational affairs. External credibility was sustained through a masculine-style panoply of formal committees, but female friendships were of fundamental importance to the smooth working of the ladies' associations.

The interesting subject of friendship is connected with other conjunctions of personal and political behaviours within female imperialism. Recent historians have delved into the lives of politically active Victorian and Edwardian women in order to uncover more profound levels of motivation and to explain the potentially disruptive consequences of women's arrival upon a male-defined political stage.[46] The leaders of female imperialism form another group of women whose individual lives are, to some extent, open to investigation. While much of this study concerns collective organization and activity, due attempt has also been made to acknowledge the importance of individual personal experience. Philippa Levine's Victorian feminists 'made public their private lives'.[47] To an extent, the same is true of many female imperialists, though 'feminist' credentials were not necessarily established thereby. Leading feminists were also the subject of Barbara Caine's study of distinguished Victorian women, in which 'their personal experiences help us to understand the genesis of their feminist beliefs'.[48] However, a similar combined approach to 'private' and 'public' experience proved equally productive in Jane Lewis' exploration of the lives and ideas of five social activists whose relationship with feminism was, at best, problematic. Her subjects included Beatrice Webb, Mary Ward and Violet Markham. These women, like the majority of other female imperialists, grappled with political ideas concerning 'relationships between the individual, the family and the state', while at the same time attempting to reconcile their own public activism with their commitments to domestic duties and female propriety.[49] Violet Markham's correspondence with Lord Milner and Earl Grey contained anguished descriptions of the restraints imposed upon her by her mother's infirmities. Milner counselled that virtue would prove its own reward (as, on an earlier occasion, he had urged a reluctant Violet Cecil to reconcile herself to the rewards of motherhood).[50] Grey, on the other hand, advised Violet to look into the possibility of acquiring a paid replacement for her daughterly services.[51] Violet Markham's own ambivalent conclusions were reflected in her successfully sustained caring role as a daughter, but her postponement of marriage and avoidance of motherhood. On the political front, she chose to associate with the gendered imperialist activism of the Victoria League throughout the Edwardian years, despite her self-evident ability to make a serious contribution in other, mixed-sex company.

Both in public and in private, the female imperialists were intensely preoccupied with marriage and motherhood. These feminine functions were believed to represent the essential fulfilment of woman's nature, and also her most important contributions to Nation and Empire. An earlier chapter highlighted the advantages which upper-class married status bestowed upon a majority of the leading ladies of Edwardian imperialism.[52] More detailed biographical research shows that these advantages were variously enjoyed, with different political consequences for each individual. For example, the marriages of Maud Selborne and Edith Lyttelton present interesting points of contrast. Though Maud Selborne became a leading lady imperialist, and an important suffragist besides, she can scarcely be judged as 'woman-centred' or 'feminist' in her private attitudes. Her performance of conventionally feminine public duties as wife of the South African High Commissioner never restrained her appetite for involvement in the masculine world of government. Her political enthusiasms rested upon experience rather than purely a domineering personality, as is implied in Kenneth Rose's rather disapproving portrayal in *The Later Cecils*.[53] She was her father's politically astute daughter, reared in a household filled with governmental debates, and as Selborne's wife was fortunate enough to retain the role of a well-informed and respected adviser.[54] Maud was thus largely spared the stresses and strains which afflicted the marital relations of other politically ambitious women. She scorned the dullness of apolitical middle-class South African women, instead deriving immense satisfaction from operating through the politics of the men in her life. For Maud Selborne, the relationships of daughter, mother and wife were equally a source of political strength. She derived from them an assertive but non-confrontational attitude towards women's role in public life. Both the extent and the limitations of her general outlook on women, politics and the Empire were closely related to her own personal opportunities.

Edith Lyttelton's correspondence with her husband Alfred provides an equally impressive picture of married devotion. In their forties and fifties they celebrated the lasting qualities of their mutual physical passion. Ardent love letters were exchanged during the long periods of rest and recuperation which Edith's doctors urged her to take, with Alfred's anxious support, at German spas and Italian resorts. These absences were, in fact, further evidence of the nature of their partnership. As a youthful member of the Souls, Edith had succeeded in raising herself into the political and intellectual company of future prime ministers, viceroys and members of leading aristocratic families. Her keen intelligence and social conscience soon drew her into the somewhat contrasting orbits of the London literary world and the women's movement. Despite the happiness of her marriage, she frequently felt herself tugged in too many different directions. The Lytteltons were less securely cushioned by social status, wealth and political power than the Selborne and Cecil families. Alfred's personal uncertainties opened up a role for Edith as his confidante, but there was a price to be paid in terms of his extensive demands upon her time and energies. As early as 1898, before Edith Lyttelton had got into her stride as a female imperialist and would-be dramatist, her husband warned:

> I sometimes doubt whether I ought not to stop your doing so much . . . you must think what it would be to damage your health seriously and what a wretched exchange I should be for Oliver and Mary for your darling self: and also of what kind of life I should ever have here without you.[55]

The problem was insoluble, as Edith's public work flourished while she repeatedly promised her husband to avoid 'overdoing'.[56] Ironically enough, Alfred himself died suddenly in 1913 at the age of 56, while Edith continued to pursue an active public life until shortly before her death in 1948. Profound mutual affection could not reconcile this couple's ambivalent views on womanhood and women's work, and the depth and diversity of Edith Lyttelton's political commitments perhaps reflects this fact. It is not surprising to find that the suffrage issue presented Alfred Lyttelton with a dilemma. As Edith put it in her biography, 'his chivalry and reverence for women made him dislike their entry into the rough and tumble of political life. But, as he often said, his reason could find no reason for excluding women from their share in the government of the country.'[57]

A resolution of competing claims was necessary for many of the women who became active female imperialists, and the available evidence suggests that this may often have been rather difficult to achieve. The experience of each individual's family life undoubtedly permeated her politics, influencing her ideas on womanhood, the women's movement and the Empire, as well as either enlarging or restricting her opportunities to engage in public work. The progress of the female imperialist cause, like the growth of the other interlocked branches of the women's movement and feminism, was bound into private lives as well as into their more easily generalizable gendered and class-bound social context. It follows from this conclusion that most women found it very difficult to compartmentalize their politics. If they engaged in multiple forms of 'women's work', including suffrage or anti-suffrage campaigns alongside female imperialism and the social activism of the wider women's movement, it was because there were sensible connections between these different commitments. The connecting ideas were widely perceived and understood, if not always systematically theorized. It therefore remains to review in more detail the bedrock of shared beliefs which enabled organized female imperialism to flourish while its leadership stood divided over Votes for Women. Unity could not have been preserved merely by the formal silencing of suffrage debates within the Victoria League, the Girls' Friendly Society and the emigration associations. Instead, it rested upon joint convictions concerning gender difference, women's work and Empire.

Britain's imperial responsibilities were viewed as a key aspect of the suffrage debate both by the supporters and opponents of Votes for Women. When active female imperialists entered the arena they naturally brought with them their enthusiasm for the Empire, and for women's important role within it. Opposing conclusions on suffrage were in some cases based upon surprisingly similar premises. In other cases women who disagreed on the suffrage issue simply chose to deploy contrasting imperial evidence to support their different conclusions. Even within the separate camps of suffragists and anti-suffragists, there were differences of emphasis in relation to the Empire and the Vote. The twists and turns of the suffrage controversy provide a revealing index of opinions on many aspects of class, gender and citizenship, and illustrate the extent to which each of these categories had become imbued with imperial purpose during the Edwardian years. Antoinette Burton's study of 'imperial feminism' demonstrates the widespread currency of Empire in the discourse of leading suffragists.[58] Brian Harrison's older study of the anti-suffrage movement, on the other hand, makes much of the role of male imperialist leaders in setting the opposition's terms of debate.[59] The evidence of female imperialist contributions to suffrage discussion can be used to support the main conclusions of both of these studies. However, if attention is focused (as it was by the women imperialists themselves) upon the ideas which united rather than those which divided, then it becomes apparent that neither suffragists nor anti-suffragists deserve full credit for successfully appropriating the Empire's needs to their cause. However strongly the leading ladies felt about the Vote, they refused to elevate its importance to an extent which would jeopardize the work of organized, constructive female imperialism.

Violet Markham's Albert Hall speech achieved merited fame as the most persuasive piece of female oratory in the anti-suffrage cause. It was not immediately obvious to the grateful male leaders of the NLOWS that her chosen emphases diverged significantly from their own. While Violet endorsed the Antis' central belief in a natural and beneficial separation of spheres, she rejected the essentialization of women's weaknesses which had become a commonplace male anti-suffragist argument. Instead of dwelling on women's illogicality, emotionalism and fickle inability to sustain political loyalty, she emphasized the possibility of innately different but equally respected public roles for men and women. Both should share in 'the management of the State' in ways suited to their particular strengths and responsibilities. Violet extended women's primary maternal responsibility to include 'the aged, the sick, the destitute, the erring, the welfare of little children', and developed a strong plea for anti-suffrage women's deeper commitment to social action. Local government offered women 'splendid opportunities for civic betterment and the uplifting of the race', a conjunction with strong female imperialist overtones. For Violet, as for many other social reformers and imperialists within the women's movement, there was no inconsistency between promoting the vital moral and practical qualities of femininity in all appropriate governmental fields while accepting that 'work such as defence, commerce, finance, tropical administration is . . . work of a nature which lies outside woman's practical experience, and with which man is best fitted to deal'.[60]

Parliament's responsibility for defence was associated, in the minds of both male and female anti-suffragists, with the 'physical force' argument against Votes for Women. Ultimately, imperial rule depended upon military power which only men could exert. It seemed logical enough for many female imperialists to conclude that military decision-making should remain in the hands of men, however valuable women might be to other aspects of Empire-building. Some male imperialist Antis were eager to extend this negative argument by suggesting that a feminized British government would become a weakened object of derision, in particular in India. But the leading imperialist ladies in the Anti-Suffrage League joined with Violet Markham in emphasizing the positive face of opposition. Mary Ward gave particularly effective support to the concept of an alternative, but equally patriotic, citizenship for women. On the eve of the First World War she argued daringly that the 'local' caring and practical work of imperialist women should be extended beyond elected local government in Britain to include all the 'Minor Parliaments' of a federated British Empire. A consensual solution to the suffrage dispute might emerge from a scheme which (condescendingly) equated county councils with the parliaments of the Dominions and a future home-ruled Ireland:

> That women should ultimately have equal rights with men over the whole social and domestic sphere of delegated power covered by these local assemblies of the future, and that men only should possess the Imperial vote, and sit on the Imperial Parliament, is surely a distribution of responsibilities which corresponds broadly to the natural differences between the sexes . . . in social and domestic affairs a vast new field might open to women.[61]

During the previous year Mary Ward had written her novel *Delia Blanchflower*. While castigating the unwomanly dangers of militancy, the book also set forth extended and sympathetic portraits of a range of pro-suffrage and anti-suffrage women who shared a common devotion to useful 'women's work'.[62]

Meanwhile, Mary Ward and Violet Markham were joined by a number of other prominent anti-suffrage women in promoting a new Local Government advancement committee from 1912 onwards. Among its members were Margaret Jersey and Gladys Pott, secretary of the NLOWS and another ambitious, competent female imperialist who was later to lead the unified post-war female emigration society. Despite the importance of these women to the Antis' cause, Lord Cromer flatly refused to integrate the new committee into the NLOWS on terms which they found acceptable. A major row broke out when Mary and Violet offered their association's support to an excellent woman candidate, of discreetly pro-suffrage views, in preference to an outspokenly anti-suffragist man. A retreat was forced upon them as they planned 'an absolutely independent Committee for the support of women candidates' in the future.[63] In private exasperation, Mary's daughter wrote to Violet: 'If only the *men* on the League would realise that *mere* anti-ism is and above all *will* be, a simply fatal policy to back . . . They sometimes seem to me to see no further than the nose on their face.'[64] Violet Markham responded to this setback for her vision of patriotically 'useful' anti-suffragism with a characteristically frank warning to Cromer:

> All women who are interested in women's work will feel they have been rather badly treated in this matter of West Marylebone . . . We must show that we do take positive views of women's work and do not meet the whole feminist movement with a blunt *non possumus*.[65]

Her own independent thinking around the alternatives to women as voters and in parliament included schemes for a Women's Council (1910) and support for a joint parliamentary committee for women's questions, neutral on suffrage but committed to supporting legislation which would benefit women (1912).

When female imperialists spoke from anti-suffrage platforms they remained loyal to their ideals of Empire and of women's work. The same was equally true of imperialists upon pro-suffrage platforms. In many ways they had a stronger hand to play because as British and overseas suffrage organization strengthened it became increasingly possible to wheel forward supporters from the white settler colonies. The indirect importance of 'dependent' Indian women to the late Victorian suffrage cause has been thoroughly demonstrated.[66] However, the women of New Zealand and Australia, who had obtained the vote in 1893 and 1901 respectively, were to the forefront of the Edwardian suffrage debate. Several outstanding women returned from Australia to Britain to join the campaign, and Dominion contingents were prominent in suffrage processions. 'Trust the women, Mother, as I have done', advised a banner carried by a united Australian and New Zealand contingent at the suffragist Coronation March in 1911.[67] Though some of those involved had militant or socialist leanings and would have been unlikely to consort with the leading ladies of British imperialism, others included the wives of the Australian Prime Minister and the New Zealand Chief Justice. Among the most valuable New Zealand supporters of the suffrage cause was Maude Pember Reeves, well known as the author of a Fabian women's study of London poverty, but also an active Victoria League lecturer and committee member. Despite the daughterly banner of 1911, many suffragists from the Dominions took particular pride in their ability to offer British women a lead. In their literature, they bolstered claims of female-inspired legislative success and reproached the backwardness of the British parliament. A few sympathetic Australians were found to speak at anti-suffrage gatherings, but it is clear that the pro-suffrage movement had more to gain from this aspect of the imperial connection. Attitudes such as those of Mary Ward and Violet Markham towards 'minor parliaments' and 'local assemblies' inevitably strained the loyalty to the Antis' cause even of sympathetic colonial visitors.

The imperial scope of suffragism was strengthened by the South African and Canadian suffrage connections of Maud Selborne and the Countess of Aberdeen, as well as by the holding of international congresses and the activism of the successful Australasians. Despite the need for a 'non-political' stance while their husbands were in office, the suffrage views of both of these Governors' wives were well known and acted as a magnet for local supporters. After Maud Selborne returned to Britain she made a particular point of arguing the franchise cause on the basis of Dominion examples. The *Anti-Suffrage Review* sternly took her to task for misinterpreting the data she gathered from Australian correspondents on the much-contested issue of maternal and child health reforms.[68] Infant mortality was declining satisfactorily and, as we have seen, the work of the New Zealand reformer Dr Truby King was much admired by female imperialists. The issues of population growth and racial health were so central to imperialism that it is understandable that suffragists were eager to claim credit, while imperialist anti-suffragists were particularly anxious to undermine their arguments. Lady Selborne found herself incongruously accused of latent socialism by fellow-imperialists Gladys Pott and Margaret Jersey, as she admired Australasian achievements and as the British suffragists allied themselves to a suffrage-supporting British Labour Party.[69] Undeterred, she continued to praise the enfranchised Australian mothers and their government and to represent the suffrage case in terms of women's responsibility for the racial and imperial future.

In the summer of 1914 the *Daily Graphic* published a series of pro-suffrage letters, including one from an Ulster suffragist, headed 'Real Imperialists':

All these questions of women's wages, housing families, safeguarding of girls, are at the back of national defence; and it is we suffragists, who love our country and are willing to give our time and strength for its welfare, who are real Imperialists and claim our right to share political responsibilities with men. Looking over and beyond such questions as sex, we see that you cannot have a strong nation unless its women as well as its men realise their national responsibility and are allowed to work for the good of the Empire.[70]

This letter, like many others, claimed for women a political equality premised upon acceptance of gender difference. Equality of imperial responsibility was the argument of many anti-suffragist women too, despite their 'renunciation' of the unsuitable responsibility of voting. As Mary Ward put it in a leaflet for her Local Government Association:

no law affecting women and children is ever made nowadays without the cooperation and advice of women. But when the law is made comes the question – the all-important question – of carrying it out and making it work. Here it is that we appeal to women. Let us leave men to their own task of Imperial Government. But every day, under existing laws, there is work at home and at our doors, that clamours to *us* – us women – to be done. Shall we not bestir ourselves and do it?[71]

The gap between these political positions was far from unbridgeable. It was bridged within the female imperialist associations, but also in many other areas of the women's movement. 'By the expression, the Women's Movement, we indicate not only the agitation for the granting of the vote, but the general movement among women desirous of taking a more active part in the efforts to improve the conditions of life', noted Maud Selborne in her own contribution to the *Daily Graphic* suffrage correspondence.[72] This conciliatory, inclusive view was aligned to her own membership of multiple organizations, and to her confidence in imperial social and political progress which was already drawing upon the special talents of women – whether or not they were current supporters of Votes for Women. Complementarity and unity between the sexes, rather than equality and competition, were her points of emphasis. Like other upper-class imperialist suffragists, her belief in political equality was circumscribed to support for a limited suffrage which would exclude poorer working-class men and women alike. Adult suffrage, so contentious elsewhere in the suffrage movement, never became a serious issue among the female imperialists. It was rarely even mentioned, and still more rarely supported. Suffragists had no more intention than anti-suffragists of disturbing the social hierarchy which underpinned the female imperialist associations. Class allegiance maintained its importance within the associations as a defining characteristic which held together women whose political outlook varied, and largely determined their organizational style and choice of imperialist work.

Some of the most interesting evidence of the ideological common ground linking female imperialism and the women's movement, and imperialist suffragists and anti-suffragists, is to be found in the private correspondence between women who publicly disagreed over the Vote and other matters of national politics. An active search for this common ground was sometimes a priority for the female imperialists themselves. Edith Lyttelton and Violet Markham were antagonists in party political as well as in suffrage matters. Yet they corresponded amiably about their common work for the future after the Liberals' landslide election victory in 1906, and the ejection of Alfred Lyttelton from the Colonial Office. 'There is very much the Liberals will try to do which I shall deeply sympathise with,' wrote Edith to Violet in January 1906; 'on most of the home social questions I am with them. But it is the Empire and the colonies which claim my allegiance first, and I am frankly terrified as to what may be done in South Africa . . . To hand back the country to the Boers will be – well I know what you think on this.'[73] Another issue which concerned both ladies equally was the impact of the Labour vote:

> They are going to determine all elections in the future – not only by returning the Labour members but by their solid vote . . . This means that in future we must try and get at them more than at any other class. Never mind which party they put into power, we must see that they care for the Empire. The Victoria League must work harder than ever. I want to see you about all this.[74]

Eighteen months later Edith and Violet were co-operating within the Personal Service Association as well as the Victoria League. This new organization aimed to bring together working-class needs for guidance and support with upper- and middle-class women's need for self-fulfilment through womanly social action. Moreover, it linked individual service to the work of local and national government by organizing visits to the unemployed in connection with the distress committees set up by the Unemployed Workmen's Act of 1905. The headquarters of the Personal Service Association was at Mary Ward's Passmore Edwards settlement in Bloomsbury. Its supporters included Millicent Fawcett and Margot Asquith, two other important women who were in outspoken opposition to each other on the question of the Vote.

For Maud Selborne, a lasting divide over Votes for Women was unthinkable. She wrote a series of seven long letters to Violet Markham during 1913 urging unity over essentials, while at the same time freely discussing their points of disagreement. Her opening letter accepted Violet's criticism of the 'wildly absurd' hopes of suffragists for a transformed world under the Vote. A further commentary upon the links between the women's franchise and social reform in Australia and New Zealand followed. Maud emphasized that 'sex antagonism' had been safely avoided there:

> The fact is that men and women work together very well and do each other good, and this is just as true in politics as it is in home life, or city life . . . No theory would make me in favour of giving votes to women if it did not work well. No theoretical objections are going to frighten me, seeing it does work well.

This pragmatic endorsement would not necessarily mean the end of separate forms of gendered women's work: 'the sooner they have it, the sooner a confusing and possibly dangerous question will be removed from politics, and we shall all get back to our ordinary work again.'[75] Maud also agreed with Violet that 'A sound public opinion does more than voting power to improve things.' However, she argued that 'the process of voting might itself educate public opinion. Is women's opinion worth having or not? As you say, they are perhaps more ignorant than men, but their moral standard on a good many points is higher.'[76]

In a final exchange of letters, the two women agreed to co-operate in a project to investigate the social outcomes of female suffrage in America. Maud Selborne stated plainly:

> I never can see that difference of opinion should prevent friendship. I feel myself much more in accord with some anti-suffragists than with some suffragists. It is really the end we have in view that is the important thing. Some suffragists appear to think the vote is the end, whereas the right view seems to me that it is only a means – one of many – to obtain what we want.[77]

She went on to explain 'what we want' in terms of the classic demands of the British women's movement. There was a need for 'an adequate amount of parliamentary time and thought devoted to the women's side of life'; a need for opportunities for women as well as protection, for women's employment and the removal of unfair legal barriers as well as for social care. Violet Markham and the vast majority of female imperialist anti-suffragists would have applauded this litany. Maud Selborne acknowledged as much by commenting, 'I expect you are just as keen for these things as we are, only you think you can get them all by "influence" only, and we think that influence and the vote would be more effective.'[78] The vote was needed as an adjunct to the women's movement and to organized female imperialism. It was not an alternative, and in the final analysis it was not important enough to obstruct those other more enduring causes.

Maud Selborne's disdain for 'theoretical' approaches to political and social issues was shared by many female imperialists.[79] It may have reflected some lack of confidence in their own under-trained intellectual powers, coupled with the knowledge that most 'theories' were man-made. However, the rejection of theorizing in favour of 'personal' and 'practical' women's work for the Empire was more frequently a very positive choice. It enabled the upper-class leaders of the imperialist associations to carry forward into an extended (even worldwide) public arena their existing traditions of hospitality, philanthropy, education and indirect political influence. Social leadership in these spheres was an assumed duty and a practised art. The imperialist dimension added patriotic glamour and drew upon the increasingly common family experience of service overseas, as well as upon the fount of imperial propaganda from which Edwardians of all social classes derived part of their world view. Female imperialism served to consolidate social hierarchy and acceptable gender roles, but it also opened up new avenues for collective action. Whether suffragist or not, these women chose to self-organize around agreed common work. As they debated the principles and practice of their work, they strengthened existing links with a wider British women's movement as well as infiltrating their priorities into the male circles of imperial rule. An engagement with contemporary discussions of the nature of womanhood, and the nature of female citizenship, was the inevitable result. The outcomes of this encounter have been considered not only in this chapter but throughout the book. A unified and clearly conceived doctrine of female imperialism was not one of them. Instead, individual women and groups of women developed their ideas slowly and expressed them inconsistently and incompletely.

The organized female imperialism of the Edwardian years was an overt exercise of upper-class female and imperial power, despite its many inconsistencies. Its historical interest lies partly in the fresh perspectives which it offers upon larger and better-known political movements, such as suffragism, feminism and popular imperialism. However, the female imperialists also deserve to be studied on their own account. They left a revealing record of aristocratic lifestyles as well as imperialist commitment; of lives lived in a turbulent and ultimately transformative period of British and colonial gender politics; and of women's social and political action organized on women's terms, though within the parameters of a male-dominated British establishment.

Notes

1. See, e.g., J. Charmley, *A History of Conservative Politics 1900–1996* (London: Macmillan, 1996); B. Harrison, *Separate Spheres: The Opposition to Women's Suffrage in Britain* (New York: Holmes & Meier, 1978); P. Marsh, *Joseph Chamberlain: Entrepreneur in Politics* (Yale: Yale University Press, 1994); G. Phillips, *The Diehards: Aristocratic Society and Politics in Edwardian England* (Cambridge, MA: Harvard University Press, 1979).
2. The organized anti-suffragists produced effective propaganda concerning the views of the 'silent majority' in the country, including several local referendums which endorsed anti-suffragism. *The Anti-Suffrage Review* had some basis for its confidence that most women did not want the vote, and it is likely that less active members of the female imperialist associations would have shared in the widespread inertia and even hostility.
3. Louisa Knightley's journal, 21 May 1871. Northamptonshire Record Office.
4. *Ibid.*, 1 May 1872.
5. *Ibid.*, 3 May 1872.
6. Each of these women represented a different aspect of the broader women's movement which also encompassed suffragism. Josephine Butler led the campaign against the Contagious Diseases Acts; Ellice Hopkin was a leading figure in the social purity campaign; Florence Nightingale founded the modern nursing profession; Sophia Jex Blake was a pioneer in the struggle for women's medical training.
7. F. Balfour, *Ne Obliviscaris: Dinna Forget* (London: Hodder & Stoughton, 1930), p. 140.
8. This view was prevalent in older suffrage histories, such as R. Evans, *The Feminists* (Beckenham: Croom Helm, 1977). Its legacy is evident in many more recent works, including J. Rendall (ed.), *Equal or Different: Women's Politics 1800–1914* (Oxford: Basil Blackwell, 1987). However, B. Campbell, *The Iron Ladies* (London: Virago, 1987) began to put Conservatism and upper-class women more securely back into the frame of suffrage and feminist history.
9. Signatories included, from among the ladies associated with turn-of-the-century organized imperialism, Jennie Churchill, Louise Creighton, Beatrice Webb, Mary Ward, Margot Asquith and Victoria Buxton.
10. See Harrison, p. 119.
11. See J. Sutherland, *Mrs Humphrey Ward: Eminent Victorian, Pre-eminent Edwardian* (Oxford: Oxford University Press, 1991), p. 303.
12. Georgina Frere to Violet Markham, 6 March 1912. VMar26/30. BLPES.
13. Violet Markham's speech was published as a pamphlet by the National League for Opposing Women's Suffrage, under the title 'Miss Violet Markham's Great Speech at the Albert Hall'. VMar28/92i.
14. Pro-suffrage officials of the Women's Local Government Society wrote a letter bitterly criticizing Violet Markham's Albert Hall speech to the *Manchester Guardian*, 22 March 1912. VMar 26/30.
15. See B. Caine, *Victorian Feminists* (Oxford: Oxford University Press, 1992), pp. 16–17.
16. See Phillips. He concludes that the opponents of House of Lords reforms represented 'the traditional conservative goals of aristocratic dominance and British imperial power', and

offered integrated support to 'tariff reform, compulsory military service, a vastly strengthened army and navy, the introduction of a referendum system, and armed resistance to Home Rule for Ireland' (p. 158).

17. See, e.g., Violet Markham's published speech during the December 1910 election campaign in Chesterfield, headed 'The Great Struggle. PEERS v. PEOPLE. Defence of the People's Rights'. VMar 28/91ii.

18. See D. Porter, 'The Unionist Tariff Reformers 1903–14' (Manchester University PhD thesis, 1976), pp. 243–4.

19. Maud Selborne to William Selborne, 6 and 10 June 1914. Ms Selborne adds. 3, pp. 156, 157.

20. Louisa Knightley's journal, 21 April 1901.

21. *Primrose League Gazette*, 1 September 1910.

22. M. Pugh, *The Tories and the People 1880–1935* (Oxford: Basil Blackwell, 1985), p. 66.

23. Victoria League Executive Committee Minutes, 26 October 1911.

24. *Friendly Leaves*, April 1903.

25. *Ibid.*, February 1908. The poem was by Mrs Isabel Reaney, author of *Our Daughters: Their Lives Here and Hereafter* (1881). See F. Prochaska, *Women and Philanthropy in Nineteenth Century England* (Oxford: Clarendon Press, 1980), p. 15.

26. B. Harrison, 'For Church, Queen and Family: The Girls' Friendly Society 1874–1920', *Past and Present* (1973), **61**: 120–1.

27. E.g. in *Friendly Leaves*, August 1908.

28. See J. Lewis, *Women and Social Action in Victorian and Edwardian England* (Aldershot: Edward Elgar, 1991).

29. NUWW, *Papers Read at the Conference Held in Oxford, 1–4 October 1912* (London: NUWW, 1912). Fawcett Library.

30. See D. Glick, *The National Council of Women of Great Britain: The First One Hundred Years* (London: NUWW, 1995), Appendix 2.

31. Laura Ridding, MS account of 'The Early Days of the National Union of Women Workers', 9M68,73/35. No date, but she refers to herself as 'one of the few surviving matriarchs of the National Council of Women of Great Britain' (p. 1) Hampshire Record Office.

32. *Ibid.*, p. 12.

33. Laura Ridding's diary, 12 October 1910. 9M68/30.

34. Louisa Knightley's journal, 11 and 14 October 1910.

35. This view is implied by many suffrage histories, including the classic account by R. Strachey, *The Cause: A Short History of the Women's Movement in Great Britain* (London: Virago, 1978; first published 1928).

36. See, e.g., discussions of definition in O. Banks (ed.), *Faces of Feminism* (Oxford: Basil Blackwell, 1986), Introduction; B. Caine, *Victorian Feminists* (Oxford: Oxford University Press, 1992), Introduction; F. Dubois *et al.*, 'Politics and Culture in Women's History: A Symposium', *Feminist Studies* (1980), **6**, 1: 29–53; P. Levine, *Victorian Feminism 1850–1900* (London: Hutchinson Education, 1987), Introduction; P. Levine, *Feminist Lives in Victorian England: Private Roles and Public Commitments* (Oxford: Basil Blackwell, 1990), Chapter 1; M. Maynard, 'Privilege and Patriarchy. Feminist Thought in the Nineteenth Century', in S. Mendus and J. Rendall (eds), *Sexuality and Subordination* (London: Routledge, 1989); J. Rendall (ed.), *Equal or Different. Women's Politics 1800–1914* (Oxford: Basil Blackwell, 1987), Introduction.

37. See Banks, Chapter 2.

38. See esp. chapters by B. Ramusack and A. Burton, in N. Chaudhuri and M. Strobel (eds), *Western Women and Imperialism* (Bloomington: Indiana University Press, 1992); V. Ware, *Beyond the Pale: White Women, Racism and History* (London: Verso, 1992); A. Burton, *Burdens of History: British Feminists, Indian Women and Imperial Culture, 1865–1915* (Chapel Hill:

University of North Carolina Press, 1994); I. Grewal, *Home and Harem: Nation, Gender, Empire and the Cultures of Travel* (London: Leicester University Press, 1996); C. Midgley (ed.), *Gender and Imperialism* (Manchester: Manchester University Press, 1998).

39. Grewal, Chapter 2.
40. Burton, p. 7.
41. E. Joyce (?1908) 'Words Addressed to the Teachers Sailing for Alberta, Canada'. GFS pamphlets, undated. GFS archive.
42. These defining characteristics of emergent feminist activism and thought are emphasized in M. Maynard, 'Privilege and Patriarchy: Feminist Thought in the Nineteenth Century', Chapter 7 in S. Mendus and J. Rendall (eds), *Sexuality and Subordination* (London: Routledge, 1989).
43. Levine, p. 18.
44. Louisa Knightley's journal, 20 May 1901.
45. *Ibid.*, 1 July 1903.
46. E.g. P. Levine, *Feminist Lives in Victorian England: Private Roles and Public Commitment* (Oxford: Basil Blackwell, 1990); B. Caine, *Victorian Feminists* (Oxford: Oxford University Press, 1992).
47. Levine, *Feminist Lives*, p. 179.
48. Caine, p. 9.
49. J. Lewis, *Women and Social Action in Victorian and Edwardian England* (Aldershot, Hants: Edward Elgar, 1991), p. 5.
50. Alfred Milner to Violet Markham, 21 February and 29 June 1908. VMar25/56; Alfred Milner to Violet Cecil, 26 June 1895. VM85: 'I do not at all despair of convincing you of my belief that Motherhood is the highest of all things.' See also Violet Markham to Alfred Milner, 29 December 1907. Milner papers VM33/257: 'I am wanted about a hundred trifles a hundred times a day, and outside interests and even friendships have had to go entirely to the wall . . . You don't know how much at times I mourn the goodly days when I was fighting under your banner.' Bodleian Library.
51. Lord Grey to Violet Markham, 30 June 1906. VMar 25/33.
52. See Chapter 2.
53. K. Rose, *The Later Cecils* (London: Weidenfeld & Nicolson, 1975).
54. Her respected status within the marriage partnership is evidenced throughout the couple's correspondence during Selborne's South African Governorship, but remains virtually unnoticed by the latest historian of this subject. See D. Torrance, *The Strange Death of the Liberal Empire* (Liverpool: Liverpool University Press, 1996). Lord Selborne suppressed any qualms about speaking from suffrage platforms after their return to England and even defended his wife's position on this subject to King George V. William Selborne to Maud Selborne, 14 June 1914. Selborne Papers 102. Bodleian.
55. Alfred Lyttelton to Edith Lyttelton, 26 July 1898. Chandos II, 3/10. Churchill College, Cambridge.
56. Edith Lyttelton to Alfred Lyttelton, 2 and 3 October 1910. Chandos II, 3/11.
57. E. Lyttelton, *Alfred Lyttelton: An Account of His Life* (London: Longmans, Green & Co, 1917), p. 374.
58. Burton.
59. B. Harrison, *Separate Spheres: The Opposition to Women's Suffrage in Britain* (New York: Holmes & Meier, 1978).
60. V. Markham, 'Miss Violet Markham's Great Speech' (1912). VMar, 28/92i.
61. Article by Mary Ward in *The Times*, 15 May 1914. The heading was 'A Way Out?', which rather accurately summarized her wish for an end to the dilemma and division by this date. Cutting in NLOWS scrapbook, 2474d.66. Bodleian Library.
62. M. Ward, *Delia Blanchflower* (London: Ward Lock, 1915).

63. Mary Ward to Violet Markham, 11 February 1912. VMar26/30.

64. Dorothy Ward to Violet Markham, 9 February 1912. VMar 26/30.

65. Violet Markham to Lord Cromer, 10 February 1912. VMar 26/30. In response to the crisis, Violet spelled out to Mary Ward her own terms for a workable Local Government Association with close NLOWS links but also an adequate degree of independence: 'I could not join any Society which promoted the candidature of an inferior Anti in opposition to that of a capable Suffragist. Finally, I could not join a Society which involved the smallest obligation upon me as *an individual* to refrain from supporting the candidature of suffragist friends for any given public office.' March 1912. VMar 26/30.

66. Burton.

67. See A. Oldfield, *Woman Suffrage in Australia: A Gift or a Struggle?* (Cambridge: Cambridge University Press, 1992).

68. See Editorial in *The Anti-Suffrage Review*, May 1914, and article by Gladys Pott attacking Maud Selborne in July 1915. The issue of Australian social reforms was also addressed by the *Review* in November 1912 and November 1913. 'No vote helped us; it was all private work,' claimed an Australian anti-suffragist in the edition of August 1914.

69. *Anti-Suffrage Review*, December 1913 and January 1914. Cuttings in NLOWS scrapbook, 2474d.66.

70. Article by Cecil Donne in the *Daily Graphic*, 20 July 1914. NLOWS scrapbook, 2474d.71.

71. Draft leaflet by Mary Ward sent to Violet Markham on 11 August 1912. In an accompanying draft letter to newspaper editors she wrote: 'We want more good and qualified women to help their own sex, to help children, to help the nation.' VMar 26/30.

72. Article by Maud Selborne in the *Daily Graphic*, 29 June 1914. NLOWS scrapbook, 2474d.70.

73. Edith Lyttelton to Violet Markham, 22 January 1906. VMar 25/51.

74. *Ibid.*

75. Maud Selborne to Violet Markham, 27 February 1913. VMar 26/30.

76. Maud Selborne to Violet Markham, 1 March 1913. VMar 26/30.

77. Maud Selborne to Violet Markham, 11 July 1913. VMar 26/30.

78. *Ibid.*

79. This was firmly restated in Maud Selborne's short chapter on 'The Imperial Issue', published in *The Men's League Handbook on Women's Suffrage* (London: Men's League for Women's Suffrage, 1912). In the same publication she wrote 'the effect of giving women a vote will be good for a sane Imperialism'. It would be 'the natural sequence of the political activity to which they have been accustomed for the last thirty years' (the Victoria League and the Primrose League being her leading examples of organizations 'largely run by women', and 'associating women with the political life of the nation') (p. 69). I am indebted to Angela John for this reference.

11 Postscript: World War and After

The First World War provides a convenient ending point for this book, as for so many others. In recent years there have been important historical challenges to the view that the war was a watershed in British social and political affairs. It is therefore appropriate to conclude by briefly reviewing the war's impact on organized female imperialism. Were the activities and outlook of the ladies' associations transformed by the war? In what ways do their reactions to the war mirror the pre-war characteristics analysed in this study? The answers to these questions are bound up with longer-term issues concerning the changing nature of British society, the evolution of the women's movement and women's politics, and the future prospects for national strength based upon imperial unity.

The first conclusion which must be drawn is the obvious one that any wartime gains for the imperialist associations were achieved at the cost of devastating personal tragedies. As we have seen, these organizations drew their impetus from an upper-class leadership. Analysis of war casualties reveals the extent to which the British aristocracy suffered disproportionate losses, especially in the early months of the war when a traditional 'warrior class' strove to prove its patriotism and leadership qualities. By the end of 1914 the casualties included a total of six peers, sixteen baronets, ninety-five sons of peers and eighty-two sons of baronets. More than one in seven junior officers died in the first year, compared with one in seventeen from all ranks, and it was to this group of precipitate enthusiasts that most of the sons belonged.[1] Among them was Violet Cecil's only son, an 18-year-old fresh from Winchester whose notions of war were tied into childhood memories of lighting a celebratory bonfire at Hatfield on the night when Mafeking was relieved. George Cecil's father had been among Mafeking's defenders, and in the spring of 1914 he followed in his footsteps as a second lieutenant in the Grenadier Guards. In June he delighted his mother by looking handsome in his uniform, 'dancing with very nice girls', and making a good job of carrying a regimental banner at a rehearsal for the Trooping of the Colours.[2] On 12 August she saw him off to war from the station at Nine Elms, pursuing him down the platform with a parcel of fruit for the journey:

> my last vision of him was his flushed, excited face thrust out of the window behind John
> Manners and I waved until the train was out of sight . . . somehow my pen falls from my
> hand when I think of the boat, the fatigue, the plains of Belgium, where I understand our
> troops are going.[3]

Her worst fears were realized sooner than anyone had imagined possible. On 20 August she received his first letter from active service, written the day after his departure. Twelve days later he was reported missing. No amount of agitation at the British War Office and in the French government (where Violet Cecil had friends and influence) could alter the torment of uncertainty, then eventual certainty of the deaths of both young men during their first attack. John Manners' mother wrote to Violet in a language of grief which bore the legacy of their shared Victoria League politics:

> No pioneers of our Empire ever led a more forlorn hope than our two boys were called on to do, they who had never even been in manoeuvres! . . . Yes, they both lived flawless lives and died *heroic* deaths and they *loved* each other, and added immeasurably to each other's happiness and these are priceless possessions for us to live by.[4]

Many other imperialist ladies were forced to dig deeply into their reserves of patriotic stoicism and family pride over the following years as nearly one in five of the serving British peers and their sons eventually succumbed. Maud Selborne secretly rejoiced when her two younger sons were despatched to India rather than to the Western Front – 'though there is danger everywhere in wartime, I feel this will be less risky' – but by February 1916 Robert was also missing.[5] Maud received the news while sailing out to search for him; she elected to sail on, and to tell no one on board her ship. 'I wanted to be alone to get used to it,' she explained to her husband: 'We ought to think ourselves lucky in having had such a perfect son for 27 years, and not repine that now he is called elsewhere. Be brave, and help me to be brave.'[6] Laura Ridding set to work on her nephew's biography, just as she had commemorated her husband thirteen years earlier. The shock waves from each death spread out across the closely woven networks of aristocratic kinship, and overshadowed every form of war work. By the end of the war five of Lord Salisbury's ten grandsons were dead. However, among the survivors from the leading imperialist families was Oliver Lyttelton, Edith Lyttelton's only son, who believed in 1914 that 'winning in war is at all times a beautiful and exhilarating experience' and emerged unscathed in 1918 after four years at the battle front.[7] John Kipling, hurried to the front by his patriotic father at the earliest possible moment, was to be less fortunate.[8]

Personal reactions to bereavement are fully recorded in the letters and diaries of those enduring it. There can be no doubt that for women of all social classes war work of various kinds was an important means of coming to terms with anxiety and loss. Here, too, the British aristocracy proved more than ready to do their bit. 'All England is preparing hospitals', marvelled Violet Cecil in August 1914.[9] Aristocratic ladies were as prominent in these early efforts as were their male relatives among the first military contingents. In May 1915 the Countess of Warwick, whose eldest son was at the front, boasted in general terms to the *Daily Chronicle* that 'the hostess of yester-year is the head of some centre of philanthropic endeavour today'.[10] She could point to the hospital work of her two sisters, the Duchess of Sutherland and Lady Algernon Gordon Lennox, to the hospitals opened in stately homes (including Londonderry House and Grosvenor House), and to the nursing and VAD work of younger women from titled families. Such individual efforts were outshone by the collective contribution from many pre-war women's organizations, including the female imperialist associations themselves. Suffragists and anti-suffragists combined, and sometimes competed, to demonstrate female patriotism and women's capabilities in a crisis. The political message of a joint suffragist/suffragette demonstration to demand greater war work opportunities, in July 1915, was shunned by organized anti-suffragists. But it was impossible to resist the urge to co-operate over such issues as female unemployment, the needs of women munitions workers, support for war refugees and later for colonial troops stationed in Britain, care for servicemen's families, and the special demands for moral education and protection created by the war emergency.

Though the scale of wartime needs was unprecedented, organized caring by the women's movement plainly was not. In many respects the First World War provided a finest hour for voluntary social action, while at the same time laying foundations for a more socially interventionist post-war state. Female imperialists had multiple personal and political motives for bringing their existing organizations to the fore within this broader effort. The Victoria League made a direct transition from its pre-war organized hospitality into mass entertainment for the wives of overseas officers, then into the organization of overseas servicemen's clubs which provided meals and sleeping accommodation for thousands of colonial troops.[11] Another element of continuity lay in continued royal support. King George and Queen Mary, the League's joint patrons, requested that its first London club should bear their name and paid a personal inspection visit in April 1916. The League's educational work also continued. Wartime pamphlets included 'A Free Empire in Wartime' and 'The Meaning of the War: For Labour-Freedom-Country', and lecturing activities were extended, with financial help from the Daughters of the Empire, to include hospitals and Canadian camps in Britain.

The Girls' Friendly Society could equally claim to be relatively well prepared for the sudden expansion of its responsibilities. As its 1926 history proudly recorded:

> For nearly forty years it had been training itself in habits of practical organisation, understanding, sympathy, and generous helpfulness. Every year it had been studying the special needs and capacities, the temptations and the opportunities of womanhood, and had been training itself to deal with these efficiently. Now in the August of 1914 it was faced by a new and unprecedented situation . . . Fresh demands were made upon the country by the changing circumstances of its womanhood, and the GFS was one of the first to come forward and meet them.[12]

In the first weeks of the war the Society's Lodges housed refugees and displaced members from abroad, while its Central Employment Office struggled to find jobs for the unemployed. Later, the flood of war work opportunities in shops, offices and factories created its own problems, and the GFS turned its attention to supplying rest and recreation facilities, and the all-important spiritual guidance and moral protection which were more than ever needed at a time of crisis and increased population mobility for both sexes. GFS branches in the Dominions made a major contribution to the funds which sustained this work. Money was spent as fast as it could be raised, but the GFS made the most of its ambitious War Emergency Fund target of £20,000. In October 1918 Princess Mary received donations from more than 500 purse-bearers representing British and colonial branches at a great delegates' meeting in the Central Hall, Westminster.

For the Primrose League and the emigration societies, the route into war work was less clearly mapped out but proved equally beneficial. As its chief chronicler has pointed out, the Primrose League suffered badly during the years leading up to the war from the Conservative Party's internal divisions over protectionism, social and constitutional reform, and the question of Ulster.[13] The war provided a respite from internal conflict, and from the erosion of the League's support by the development of other forms of Conservative constituency organization, including women's groups. Ultimately the war hastened the processes of social and political change which rendered the Primrose League obsolete, but in the short term it found a new lease of life through patriotic activities which were both charitable and educational. Dames came to the fore, since so many male leaders of the League were on active service or otherwise preoccupied by war work. A needlework committee supplied garments to the Red Cross, the Belgian refugees and the British troops; large sums of money were raised for war charities; Habitations made it their business to entertain and care for soldiers' wives, while juvenile branches 'adopted' prisoners of war. The League's lecture programme continued to convey its patriotic and imperialist message, and strenuous efforts were made through local canvassing to sustain the flow of recruits to war work and the armed forces.

The emigration societies similarly endeavoured to link their work as closely as possible with the national cause. Emigration was at a standstill during the war years, but the BWEA's office remained staffed and the *Imperial Colonist* continued to appear, since former emigrants still required support and the concept of emigration to the Dominions soon seemed more than ever an appropriate contribution to a reconstructed post-war world. This was the eventual conclusion of the British government which, after the final publication of the findings of its Dominions' Royal Commission in 1917 to 1918, established an Oversea Settlement Department under the Colonial Office. The three main women's emigration societies had already formed a consultative Joint Council in anticipation of official recognition. This formed a useful base from which negotiations took place with government officials and representatives of other women's interests over the creation of a new, semi-official body to co-ordinate female emigration. The Society for the Oversea Settlement of British Women was finally in business by early 1920, handling the cases of thousands of ex-servicewomen somewhat in the old style, but buoyed up by a government grant towards administrative costs and by new-style recognition of the Society's worth as an advisory body able to influence government emigration policy.[14]

One of the most interesting aspects of the newly united Society was its leading personnel. Continuity with the past was indicated by the active involvement of Princess Christian and the honorary presidency of an aged Mrs Joyce until her death in 1924. But alongside various ladies from the BWEA's pre-war past were to be found recruits to female emigration who had proved their value in other spheres of women's war work. For many patriotic ladies, especially those who had obtained previous administrative experience in the imperialist societies or in other women's organizations, the war created undreamt-of opportunities to move closer to the exercise of government power. The first chair of the SOSBW executive committee was Gladys Pott, encountered in Chapter 10 as the formidable Secretary of the Anti-Suffrage League, but respected in government circles as a wartime Travelling Inspector of the Women's Branch of the Board of Agriculture. By 1919 she had acquired extensive firsthand knowledge of the Dominions, and soon found herself in partnership with former Victoria League Secretary (and suffragist) Meriel Talbot, whose wartime career had been equally successful. In 1915

Meriel was invited to join the government's advisory committee for the repatriation of enemy aliens. During the following year she resigned her Victoria League post in order to join Gladys Pott at the Board of Agriculture as Chief Woman Inspector with special responsibility for the Land Army. By the end of the war she was directing the Women's Branch of the Food Production Department, and also representing women's interests on the new overseas development committee. Her subsequent post at SOSBW was that of Publicity Officer; it extended to include editorship of the *Imperial Colonist* (adopted by the new society until 1926) and acting chairmanship of the executive during Miss Pott's frequent absences abroad.

The list of wartime achievements can be extended to include other prominent lady imperialists. Violet Markham was invited on to the executive of the National Relief Fund in 1914; she moved on to chair the Central Committee on Women's Employment, and to become the Deputy Director of the Women's Section of the National Service Department in 1917. Among her colleagues on the employment committee were fellow-Victoria Leaguers May Tennant, Lady Midleton and Edith Lyttelton. Edith's war work also included a spell at the Ministry of Agriculture, and membership of the war refugees committee from 1914 to 1918. The networks of female imperialism, as well as of upper-class society and the wider women's movement, were clearly at work here, influencing government choices which were also swayed by these women's proven patriotism and administrative skills. There is some evidence of a two-way flow of talent. For example, Margot Glyn, who acted as an aide to Victoria League member Lady Londonderry as she built up her Women's Legion, became drawn into issues concerning post-war female emigration. She joined the joint committee of emigration societies in 1918, and was later to chair SOSBW into the demanding years of the Second World War. The overwhelming impression remains that the First World War provided new and important work for female imperialists which reached beyond the scope of amateurish Edwardian voluntary work. Though the war ended with determined attempts to turn back the clock for the majority of women workers at all levels of society, there could be no retreat from the realization that different and more influential avenues to social change and to imperial activism were opening up for a select minority of leading ladies.

This realization was, of course, strongly reinforced by the enfranchisement of women over the age of 30 and by their admission to parliament in 1918. The passage of the Representation of the People Act was a complex process with multiple causes. It had much to do with calculations of party advantage and caution over advancing democracy, as well as constituting a 'reward' for women's war work and for the cessation of suffragette militancy. However, the experience of war undoubtedly accelerated some significant changes in attitudes towards women, and equally important changes in self-perception. Lord Curzon, while still presiding over the Anti-Suffrage League, decided to abstain in the final House of Lords division on the suffrage proposals because he now feared the destabilizing effects of another Lords veto more than he feared women's suffrage itself. More positively, Violet Markham had the courage to declare a public change of heart. Before doing so she explained herself to Lord Cromer, the imperialist and anti-suffragist mentor whom she continued to admire:

> I cannot pretend that the experience of the war has left me unmoved as to the principle of woman's suffrage . . . As a matter of practical politics I put it to you, can we say with

one breath that women have helped to save the state and with the next deny them any share in its management? That is my difficulty at the present time. I do not think my opinions have changed very fundamentally. The man as worker, the woman as home-maker remains my ideal of society. But in this difficult world one has to take facts as they are.[15]

In the same letter she described her growing concern for the disadvantaged position of women in the labour market, and her sense of an inescapable burden of public duties for women like herself. The Vote would not transform women's lot, any more than it would alter her own convictions on gender difference. But it was becoming necessary, and probably inevitable. Even Mary Ward admitted as much in a very private letter of her own to Cromer, written seven months earlier: 'I sometimes wonder in my secret thoughts whether we are not already beaten! . . . the war has changed so many things.'[16] Unlike Violet, she allowed herself to be persuaded that the anti-suffrage campaign must continue to the bitter end, but, like Violet and so many other leading imperialists, she found herself inevitably drawn to the wheel of government service. At their country home Dorothy and Mary Ward organized a force of land girls, while in London their voluntary work at the Passmore Edwards settlement became part of a Treasury-funded national scheme of play centres for the offspring of working mothers. Mary's most important patriotic contribution was probably her war journalism, which has been credited with influencing American public opinion towards entry into the war.

Mary Ward was certainly not alone as an effective female propagandist. In her 1916 work *England's Effort* she paid full tribute to women's contribution to the war effort. It is interesting to compare the stance of this famous anti-suffragist with the patriotic propaganda of the suffragists. As in the pre-war period, there are important similarities of emphasis upon feminine strengths. Women's ability to serve their country rested in the longer term upon their *womanly* qualities, and not upon their ability to 'copy' the achievements of men. In June 1915 Christabel Pankhurst voiced her appeal for fuller national service opportunities in remarkably similar terms. Women's economic contribution was of course needed, but

> More important still is it that women's thinking power, women's intelligence, women's moral and spiritual force shall now be put directly at the service of the nation. History shows that men can gain an Empire, but cannot keep it. That is because they do not possess the creative and the conservative force especially and by Nature appertaining to women. Therefore in the history of nations the feminine element plays a part analogous to that played in human reproduction. Indeed, the woman's movement of the past forty years, and especially of the last ten years, has been an evolutionary process – the feminine principle in our national life trying to find expression and to work national regeneration.[17]

This appeal was deliberately couched in universalist terms in order to appeal across the barriers of party politics and suffrage controversy. Nowhere would it have received a warmer reception than among those female imperialists who succeeded in overcoming their scepticism towards its author. Less problematically, similar sentiments were expressed by moderate pro-suffrage members of the pre-war ladies' associations, including Frances Balfour, Maud Selborne and Millicent Fawcett. In an October 1915 article titled 'Woman after the War. Her new position', Lady Selborne wrote: '"National service" for men means, to most people, the duty that is incumbent on men to fight for their country. National Service for women should mean the preservation of life. What wisdom can there be in denying them the opportunities to do so on its public side?'[18] Her question encompassed the gendered contributions which women were prepared to make as both paid and voluntary workers, as voters and as mothers.

The female imperialists made demonstrable gains from wartime's heightened patriotism and heightened consciousness of women's vital role in building the national and imperial future. Yet from a longer-term perspective it is equally clear that by 1918 the writing was on the wall for organized female imperialism in its Edwardian mould. The war years did not amount to an absolute and definitive watershed in British social and political life, but they did represent a period of accelerated transition. In the first place, aristocratic predominance in economic, social and political life was on its way out. This was arguably the case by 1914, when landed wealth had already suffered damage and competition, Society was increasingly open to the moneyed and educated upper-middle class, the Court was losing its mystique, and the House of Lords had suffered defeat in its challenge to advancing democracy. The war further advanced all these trends, most notably by setting firmly in power a Lloyd George-led coalition government which enriched and rewarded efficiency, with scant respect for titles and tradition. Government by family connection and behind-the-scenes influence was drawing to a close, and with it one of the most important sources of authority for the female imperialist associations.

The changing social composition of government was linked to a broader process of democratization which received a war-related impetus from the 1918 enfranchisement measures. Socially, government and the electorate remained a long way distant from each other at the end of the war. However, the existence of mass politics, already uneasily sensed by Edwardian lady imperialists, was becoming an inescapably dominant reality which would sweep away amateur propagandists and organizers and focus politicians' attention firmly on the electorate and the media. The power of social deference, manifested so prominently in both the larger and smaller female imperialist societies, could no longer be relied upon. Changing political priorities indirectly reflected the changed social composition of British politics. As the war drew to a close, the government expressed its appreciation of the female associations' war work, heaped honours upon their leaders, and invited some to participate in aspects of post-war reconstruction. But appreciation of voluntary work was yoked to an evident determination to redirect it selectively towards government ends. The enormous increase in state power and in its fields of application was to remain one of the war's most lasting legacies. Voluntary social action, whether for domestic or imperial purposes, would never again exert the same influence, except insofar as its priorities became swallowed up in party politics and policy-making.

Like other processes of social and political change, the enfranchisement of women was linked with the war but not entirely caused by it. How far did Votes for Women (and entry into parliament) pull the rug from under the feet of long-established women's organizations? Such an outcome was certainly not anticipated by the thousands of organized women, including many leading imperialists, who had campaigned for this recognition of their citizenship. Obviously a multi-faceted women's movement survived and developed into the interwar years and beyond. However, its form and content evolved to accommodate new political and social realities. According to Brian Harrison, 'inter-war Britain gradually unravelled much of the feminist commitment that women's organisations had acquired since 1880s'.[19] The cohering influence of the suffrage campaign was missed, and party political divisions inevitably assumed greater importance as women voted, organized mass electorates and stood as parliamentary candidates. Even the organizations of female imperialism stood to suffer, insofar as their mainly non-feminist and non-party activities had been assisted by the interconnectedness, breadth and catholicity of the Victorian and Edwardian women's movement.

For the female imperialists, as for other women activists, the route to survival lay in successful adaptation and acceptance of the fact that women's increasingly diverse interests required differentiated, separate organizations. The female emigration societies retreated from a generalized imperialist commitment into the specialized work of a government-funded agency. The Victoria League abandoned its attempts at mass propaganda as lecture audiences declined, and instead focused on what it already did best: hospitality for overseas visitors, the work of settlers' welcome in the Dominions, long-distance exchange of books, magazines and letters, and support for Empire troops in wartime. The two larger imperialist associations were markedly less successful in their attempts to change with the times. The Primrose League resisted incorporation into the Conservative Party machine, and found itself marginalized and declining as a result. Politically active women moved across to the more up-to-date ideals and forms of activism of the burgeoning Conservative Party women's associations. The Girls' Friendly Society also entered into a period of accelerating decline as its imperialist work lost appeal and its associates failed to heed the warnings of a far-sighted leadership against outdated social attitudes.

During the interwar years the associations all survived in one form or another, and adapted to a changing Britain with a greater or lesser degree of success; but there was one insurmountable obstacle to their future as female imperialist organizations. The Empire itself failed to take shape in the form dreamed of by Rhodes, Chamberlain and Milner, and imperial idealism in both Britain and the Dominions became steadily submerged by the preoccupations of domestic politics. Though the British Empire reached its greatest extent in the interwar years, recreational aspects of popular imperialism flourished, and the political heirs to Milnerite imperialism strove to bring imperial federalism to life, fewer and fewer members of the ruling-class elite chose to 'Think Imperially'. A sentimental pride in the trappings of Empire remained, and patriots continued to take comfort in a vague consciousness of vast territories held and lesser peoples ruled; but this was far from determined, unitary imperialist politics. As the Dominions obstinately asserted their separateness and Indian nationalism grew too powerful to be ignored, it was increasingly implausible to assert that the hopes of British men or women should be invested in Empire. Patriotism and imperialism gradually parted company. The pre-war patriotic societies remained active into the late twentieth century, yet their continuities with Edwardian female imperialism rapidly became more apparent than real. Both women and Empire were acquiring new voices. The older style of socially hierarchical gender politics had become an anachronism, and the Empire itself was beginning to erode beneath the imperialists' feet.

Notes

1. D. Cannadine, *The Decline and Fall of the British Aristocracy* (London: Macmillan, 1992 edn), p. 74; F.M.L. Thompson, *English Landed Society in the Nineteenth Century* (London: Routledge & Kegan Paul, 1963), p. 327.
2. Violet Cecil to Edward Cecil, 28 May and 23 June 1914. VM62.
3. Violet Cecil to Edward Cecil, 13 August 1914. VM62.
4. Lady Manners to Violet Cecil, 8 October 1914. VM56.
5. Maud Selborne to William Selborne, 27 September 1914. MS Selborne adds. 3.
6. Maud Selborne to William Selborne, 3 February 1916. MS Selborne adds. 3.
7. See O. Lyttelton, *The Memoirs of Lord Chandos* (London: The Bodley Head, 1962), pp. 31–6.
8. John Kipling's enlistment and subsequent fate are fully recorded in Caroline Kipling's letters to Violet Cecil. VM 44.
9. Violet Cecil to Edward Cecil, 19 August 1914. She added, with naive optimism, 'I must say that this general teaching of the British to anticipate the going to bed of all their defenders seems to me morbid.' VM 62.
10. Countess of Warwick in the *Daily Chronicle*, 18 May 1915. NLOWS scrapbook, 2474.d.70.
11. The wartime activities of the Victoria League are recorded in its minute books, reports and journal.
12. M. Heath-Stubbs, *Friendship's Highway* (London: GFS, 1926), p. 91.
13. M. Pugh, *The Tories and the People* (Oxford: Basil Blackwell, 1985). Pugh identifies the outbreak of war with 'a final reassertion of the chivalric spirit so recently aroused during the South African war'. The casualty rate in the Primrose League Imperial Chapter reached 36 per cent (p. 175).
14. The wartime history of the emigration associations is summarized in U. Monk, *New Horizons* (London: HMSO, 1963), pp. 18–19.
15. Violet Markham to Lord Cromer, 2 November 1916. VMar 26/30.
16. Quoted in B. Harrison, *Separate Spheres* (New York: Holmes & Meier, 1978), p. 205.
17. Christabel Pankhurst in *The Observer*, 27 June 1915. NLOWS scrapbook, 2474.d.71.
18. Maud Selborne in the *Daily Graphic*, 6 October 1915. NLOWS scrapbook, 2474.d.71.
19. B. Harrison, *Prudent Revolutionaries: Portraits of British Feminists Between the Wars* (Oxford: Clarendon, 1987), p. 7.

Appendix 1: The Growth of Female Imperialism

Table 1   Victoria League income 1901 to 1914

Year	Receipts			Subscriptions			Branch income			Donations		
	£	s.	d.	£	s.	d.	£	s.	d.	£	s.	d.
1901	403	8	10	343	8	10		–		60	0	0
(from May)												
1902	748	17	10	367	9	6		–		224	3	9
1903	617	9	8	353	9	6		–		39	15	6
1904	614	17	6	468	5	6	10	13	11	29	10	0
1905	808	10	6	461	4	0	17	18	8	8	8	6
1906	881	2	10	472	6	6	20	4	1	104	7	3
1907	1900	8	2*	1237	12	8	34	10	2	359	2	11
1908	2063	2	1	1223	14	0	39	17	5	98	6	3
1909	2209	6	4	1308	17	3	48	5	3	493	12	0
1910	2165	6	8	1386	1	0	52	7	10	358	16	4
1911	2682	19	5	1484	3	6	47	0	9	818	11	10
1912	2701	0	11	1397	16	3	45	19	7	358	18	1
1913	2903	15	2	1422	6	8	48	14	10	668	15	9
1914	4105	10	2**	1433	2	0	40	2	8	1841	13	6

* From 1907 to 1914, includes £500 p.a. from Rhodes Trust (within Subscriptions).
** Includes £1052 Special Endowment Fund and £625 19s. 1d. War Fund (within Donations).

Note
The table is based upon the Victoria League's annual balance sheets. The League's accounting procedures were not entirely consistent through the period 1901 to 1914. However, these extracted figures demonstrate the growth of the League's activities; its heavy dependence upon donations (including Rhodes Trust funding, listed as 'subscription'); and the modest role of branch income. Many donations were earmarked for special purposes, for example, the lectureship scheme (1902), book prizes (1903), Miss Talbot's Tour (1909 and 1910), the North of England extension scheme (1911), the Endowment Fund and War Fund (1914). Other receipts not listed included affiliation fees and sales of tickets, badges, flags and publications. It should be noted that the League's subcommittees kept separate accounts which included their own subscriptions and donations, sometimes for amounts as large as those entering the central funds.

Table 2   Victoria League subscriptions 1909 to 1914

Year	Council (£1.1.0 plus)			Members (10s plus)			Members and Associates (under 10s)		
	£	s.	d.	£	s.	d.	£	s.	d.
1909	602	6	0	629	17	0*	76	14	3
1910	677	15	6	110	7	0	77	18	6
1911	738	15	0	136	1	0	89	7	6
				Members (5s plus)			Associates (under 5s)		
1912	667	16	9	196	7	6	21	13	6
1913	664	8	8	223	15	6	25	1	6
1914	656	6	0	230	19	6	24	0	0

* Error: £129 17s. 0d. is more likely.

Note

Additional subscriptions were received from 'Local Centres' and 'Affiliations', as well as from the Rhodes Trust. The democratizing efforts of 1911 to 1914 were reflected to only a minor extent in the Victoria League's bank balance. Upper-class ladies remained predominant, and it seems probable that the regular collection of small subscriptions was not high on their list of priorities. The Victoria League had other, more lucrative, sources of income and never truly aspired to a mass membership in Britain.

Table 3   Victoria League British branch memberships in 1913

Branch (founding year)	Council members	Members	Associates	Junior associates	Affiliated schools
Bath (1904)	–	110	60	1	–
Blackheath (1908)	2	69	54	130	–
Bournemouth (1907)	–	55	42	27	4
Cheltenham* (1902)	1	37	53	–	6
Cirencester (1906)	5	19	40	–	7
Crowborough (1907)	2	50	122	28	–
Denbighshire (1909)	–	12	29	–	–
Eastbourne (1908)	2	36	79	6	–
E. Suffolk (1907)	2	58	69	–	15
Edinburgh* (1907)	–	102	7	3	–
Elstree (1904)	4	32	88	–	7
Essex (1903)	11	53	163	151	8
Gloucester (1903)	2	34	36	9	2

Table 3   (continued)

Branch (founding year)	Council members	Members	Associates	Junior associates	Affiliated schools
Harrow (1905)	2	51	118	720	6
Leatherhead (1908)	2	38	15	–	–
Leeds (1906)	No figures given				
Liverpool (1913)	£14.1.0 total subs				
Nairnshire (1902)	£8.11.0 total subs				
Newcastle (1912)	15	74	92	2	–
Newlands Corner (1903)	2	57	122	16	11
N.Somerset (1905)	1	27	21	1	12
Oxford (1910)	–	29	25	4	–
Severn and Wye Valley (1907)	3	38	81	3	–
Sheffield (1913)	11	24	89	–	–
Weybridge (1910)	–	46	8	–	–
Woking (1904)	–	23	51	111	–

*1914 figures are given, as no 1913 details were provided.

Note
These figures are extracted from branch reports published in the Victoria League's Annual Report. Not all branches sent in reports, and some did not include membership totals in their reports.

Table 4   Victoria League overseas branch memberships in 1913

The following branches were recorded in the Twelfth Annual Report (1913). Not all reports gave membership figures. The overseas branches seem to have been reluctant to reproduce the British Victoria League's hierarchical classification of members in relation to the size of their subscriptions. The bracketed date is the branch's year of formation.

Australia	
Victoria League of Tasmania (1903)	£48.17.6 subscription receipts
Victoria League of Victoria (1908)	442 members of Council, 800 'ordinary' members
Victoria League of Western Australia (1909)	250 members
Victoria League of Broken Hill, NSW (1909)	39 senior, 3 junior members
Victoria League of South Australia (1911)	290 members

New Zealand	
Victoria League of Otago (1905)	370 members
Victoria League of Wellington (1907)	'Marked progress', but report 'accidentally destroyed in New Zealand just when it was ready to be sent off'
Victoria League of Hawkes Bay (n.d.)	No report received
Victoria League of Canterbury (1910)	672 members
Victoria League of Auckland (1910)	Report, no figures: 'owing to the magnitude of the work now it is almost impossible to detail it.'
Victoria League of Hamilton (1912)	107 members, 38 junior associates

Jamaica	
Victoria League of Jamaica (1910)	110 members

South Africa	
Transvaal (1911)	
Johannesburg Central	58 members
Northern Suburbs	55 members
North East Suburbs	41 members
Pretoria	31 members
Lichtenberg	No figure
Vereeniging	No figure
Provincial councillors not included in branches	64
'Scattered members'	29
Junior associates	28
Orange Free State (1911)	
Bloemfontein	166 members
Heilbron	30 members
Kaffir River	35 members
Ladybrand	18 members
Parys	13 members
Bulfontein	10 members
Unattached members	40
Cape of Good Hope (1913)	
Wynberg	72 members
Cape Town and Sea Point	42 members
Rondebosch	35 members
Claremont	60 members
Maitland ('just formed')	6 members
Natal (1913)	
Maritzburg	84 members
Ladysmith	45 members

Table 5   British Women's Emigration Association: Emigrant numbers for ten years (1913 Annual Report)

Year	Canada	NZ	Australia	Tasmania	USA	India
1904	474	17	17	1	19	–
1905	575	7	9	–	12	–
1906	677	50	5	2	10	–
1907	825	53	11	–	23	–
1908	417	71	6	–	11	–
1909	464	86	21	–	29	–
1910	927	92	15	–	23	–
1911	1086	72	31	1	6	–
1912	1203	152	19	1	4	2
1913	1062	94	37	–	8	–

Note

Of the 1913 emigrants assisted by the BWEA, 1007 were women, 170 children, 17 men and 7 'families'; 1122 travellers were received at the Wortley hostel during the year: 1104 of the emigrants were English, 32 'Scotch', 43 Irish, 17 Welsh and 5 'other'. Of 1062 travelling to Canada in 1913, 372 travelled second class and 690 third class. Among these emigrants were 91 'educated women', 41 teachers, 27 nurses, 6 stenographers and 8 'middle-class and business' women; 216 women were servants. These figures reflect the predominant attraction of Canada for Edwardian emigrants once the post-war glamour of South Africa had faded. They also illustrate the BWEA's continuing determination to assist the ladylike emigrant, despite the much greater demand for servants.

Table 6   South African Colonisation Society: Emigrant numbers and destinations from 1903 to 1914

Year	Total	Transvaal	Orange River	Cape	Natal	Rhodesia
January 1903 to March 1904	1218	734	24	274	82	39
1904–1905	339	206	32	82	12	7
1905–1906	346	161	36	85	48	16
1906–1907	341	192	47	69	7	25
1907–1908	299	135	53	74	13	23
1908–1909	266	129	15	55	22	45
1909–1910	308	157	30	67	20	32
1910–1911	365	193	20	99	14	35
1911–1912	401	164	36	94	47	53
1912–1913	482	180	33	128	55	80
1913–1914	469	140	28	139	59	92

Note

These figures are from SACS Annual Reports 1903–1914. The totals include a handful of SACS emigrants to Basutoland and to British East Africa.

Table 7   South African Colonisation Society receipts and payments

Year	Subscriptions			Donations			Capitation grants			Passage money			Passage refunds		
	£	s.	d.	£	s.	d.	£	s.	d.	£	s.	d.	£	s.	d.
1903	136	13	0	352	1	6	618	10	0	3560	3	4	–		
1904	196	6	6	672	13	0	163	15	0	2547	1	9	–		
1905	203	18	6	1731	17	7	135	2	6	1843	5	0	–		
1906	231	13	0	1061	15	1	162	10	0	1911	14	0	–		
1907	178	9	0	1929	5	0	130	0	0	2409	0	8	20	0	5
1908	198	3	3	1404	9	10	75	6	3	2613	18	5	633	4	10
1909	173	18	2	1562	10	9	11	18	9	2088	9	5	1754	8	11
1910	158	6	9	634	10	10	17	8	0	2874	4	9	2061	9	11
1911	151	1	9	354	3	5	13	4	6	3293	13	9	2200	12	4
				(1695	10	0)									
1912	143	15	0	285	6	3	16	6	3	4214	5	11	2435	19	3
				(1070	10	0)									
1913	320	5	0	200	9	6	22	12	6	4775	14	6	2365	14	5
				(875	10	0)									
1914	285	3	6	207	10	0	–			3525	8	1	1185	6	9
				(545	10	0)									

Note

The figures are from SACS annual reports and represent the main income categories of the Society's central organization. Subcommittees had their own separate funds. In theory at least, subscribers paid one guinea per year and working members five shillings. However, SACS made only limited efforts to increase subscription income, preferring to rely upon donations. The amounts in brackets for 1911 to 1914 show the income from the Princess Christian Appeal which attracted large donations from South African financiers and mining companies. In earlier years the Rhodes Trust made regular donations. The source of capitation grants and passage refunds is not entirely clear; together, these categories demonstrate the substantial amount of financial assistance provided to South African emigrants both by governments and by employers. Loan repayments from emigrants were listed separately.

Table 8   Girls' Friendly Society membership, 1895 to 1912

Year	Branches	Associates	Members	Candidates
1895	1270	31 783	147 770	44 938
1896	1287	32 193	150 055	47 210
1897	1315	32 486	153 092	49 685
1898	1330	32 390	154 170	53 126
1899	1345	32 436	155 708	55 575
1900	1361	32 103	152 398	55 521
1901	1359	32 189	152 174	58 077
1902	1371	32 502	152 431	62 335
1903	1382	32 891	156 885	65 125
1904	1404	33 448	160 673	65 941
1905	1442	34 009	164 174	68 639
1906	1485	35 014	170 614	71 397
1907	1534	35 187	175 354	73 026
1908	1554	37 004	180 396	78 408
1909	1606	38 006	186 499	80 234
1910	1653	38 401	191 269	82 526
1911	1707	38 580	194 617	80 905
1912	1742	39 433	196 321	83 684

Note

The Girls' Friendly Society grew steadily in all departments. There was concern at headquarters that the number of members, and especially of juvenile candidates, was growing at a faster rate than the number of guiding associates. Ultimately, the success of the organization depended upon the associates. Like many mass organizations, the Society was more diligent in adding new recruits than in removing the names of lapsed supporters. There is some inflation in these figures, but the GFS attached considerable practical and symbolic importance to the payment of subscriptions, and its large and growing financial income in this period supports the view that membership expansion was genuinely occurring. The figures are taken from Agnes Money, *The Story of the Girls' Friendly Society* (1913 edition).

Table 9   Primrose League membership

Evidence on official enrolment figures is from the Special Issues of the *Primrose League Gazette* produced to coincide with the annual Grand Habitation meeting in late April or early May (1905–14).

Date	Total enrolments	Date	Total enrolments
1884	957	1896	1 315 128
1885	11 366	1897	1 376 428
1886	237 283	1898	1 430 019
1887	565 861	1899	1 475 352
1888	672 606	1900	1 518 561
1889	810 228	1901	1 558 750
1890	910 852	1902	1 603 939
1891	1 001 292	1903	1 636 601
1892	1 075 243	1904	1 670 118
1893	1 131 821	1905	1 703 708
1894	1 198 431	1906	1 752 632
1895	1 259 808		

Note

These figures are deeply misleading, since they were reached by a constant process of addition with no provision for subtracting those who left or transferred. From 1907 to 1913 the Grand Habitation received, instead, a total number of new members:

1906/07	68 960
1907/08	75 573
1908/09	74 806
1909/10	81 052
1910/11	96 241
1911/12	70 853
1912/13	60 439

In 1914 the Special Issue reported: 'the result of a careful examination into the strength of the Habitations indicates that the present Roll of the League comprises over 800,000 Knights, Dames and Associates.' This impressive figure was a mere 35 per cent of the 'total enrolments' since 1884.

Unfortunately, the gender division of members was not fully recorded. Martin Pugh produces evidence relating to Knights and Dames only which suggests that in 1901 there were 75,260 Knights and 64,906 Dames (total enrolments). By 1910 the equivalent totals were 87,235 and 80,038 (*The Tories and the People*, 1985, p. 27).

The geographical spread of membership has been extensively researched and recorded by Martin Pugh. By 1912, the 'live' membership was divided between England and Wales (495,463), Scotland (22,500), Ireland (1500) and Juvenile branches (65,000) (*The Tories and the People*, p. 168).

Table 10 Primrose League Habitation reports: gender roles

A striking characteristic of the *Primrose League Gazette* was the amount of space devoted to local Habitation reports. An analysis of the editions of January 1905 and May 1907 provides indicative evidence of gender roles within the Primrose League at local level. The following figures relate to English and Welsh Habitations only.

Roles reported	1905	1907
Dame President with male Ruling Councillor	6	5
Dame President without male Ruling Councillor	6	5
Female Ruling Councillor	8	6
Male Ruling Councillor	23	15
Female Secretary	29	15
Male Secretary	17	15
Female Speaker	5	5
Male Speaker	44	28

Appendix 2: Female Imperialist Networks

Name	FI affiliations	Other 'women's work'	Suffrage views	Party politics
Countess of Aberdeen	Aberdeen Association/VL	International Council of Women, Settlements, nursing organizations in Canada and Britain, NUWW	Suffragist	Liberal
Margot Asquith	BWEA, VL*	East End visiting, political hostess	Anti-suffragist	Liberal
Alice Balfour	VL,* PL,* SACS*	Supporter of Octavia Hill, founded East London Nursing Association	Suffragist	Conservative
Betty Balfour	VL,* PL*	Support for improvements in maternal and child welfare	Suffragist	Conservative
Frances Balfour	VL,* PL	Travellers' Aid Society, Working Ladies' Guild, NUWW	Suffragist	Liberal
Constance Battersea	VL	Philanthropy, social purity, temperance and education work, prison visiting, NUWW		Liberal
Violet Brooke-Hunt	VL, SACS	Tariff Reform League Women's Association, South African War work		
Adelina Brassey	BWEA, SACS		Suffragist	Conservative
Beatrice Cartwright	PL,* GFS, BWEA	Poor Law guardian, NUWW	Suffragist	Conservative
Alicia Cecil	BWEA,* VL, SACS, PL		Suffragist	Conservative
Gwendolen Cecil	PL,* VL,* SACS	Philanthropy, hospital-building, church work	Suffragist	Conservative
Violet Cecil	VL*	Support for South African War refugees and Ulster women and children	?Anti-suffragist	Conservative
Beatrice Chamberlain	VL		Anti-suffragist	Conservative
Mary Chamberlain	BWEA, VL		Anti-suffragist	Conservative
Jennie Churchill	PL*	Organized women's hospital ship in South African War, political hostess before 1900		Conservative

Note: * indicates committee member.

Name	FI affiliations	Other 'women's work'	Suffrage views	Party politics
Mary Curzon	VL	Support for development of nursing in India	Anti-suffragist	Conservative
Millicent Fawcett	VL, BWEA	Support for campaigns for women's education, property rights, social purity, NUWW	Suffragist	Liberal Unionist
Philippa Fawcett	BWEA*	Work in education in Britain and South Africa	Suffragist	Liberal
Georgina Frere	PL, VL,* BWEA		Anti-suffragist	Conservative
Lily Frere	PL, VL		Anti-suffragist	Conservative
Caroline Grosvenor	CIL,* BWEA	Philanthropy		Conservative
Susan Grosvenor	CIL,* SACS, VL	Settlement work, Personal Service Association, Charity Organization Society worker		Conservative
Victoria Grosvenor	GFS,* BWEA,* SACS, CIL			Conservative
Elizabeth Haldane	CIL, VL*	Poor Law work, nursing and hospital reforms, settlement work, child welfare	Suffragist	Liberal
Annie Hanbury Williams	BWEA,* VL	Government House hostess in Cape Town		
Mary Harcourt	VL*		Anti-suffragist	Liberal
Mary Hervey	SACS,* CIL,* VL*		Anti-suffragist	Conservative
Margaret Jersey	PL,* VL*	Philanthropy, NUWW, political hostess	Anti-suffragist	Conservative
Mary Jeune	VL	Philanthropy, women's education, social purity, political hostess	Suffragist	Conservative
Ellen Joyce	GFS,* BWEA*	Church work, philanthropy	?Anti-suffragist	Conservative
Louisa Knightley	GFS,* PL,* BWEA,* SACS,* VL,* CIL	Philanthropy, education, church work, NUWW, local government	Suffragist	Conservative
Lady Londonderry	PL, GFS, VL	Political hostess	Anti-suffragist	Conservative
Edith Lyttelton	VL,* GFS, CIL	Anti-sweating campaign, Personal Service Association, NUWW	Suffragist	Conservative (Liberal Unionist)

Name	Memberships	Activities	Suffrage stance	Party
Katherine Lyttelton	SACS*	Philanthropy, church work, NUWW	Suffragist	
Kathleen Lyttelton	VL		Anti-suffragist	Conservative
Susan Malmesbury	SACS,* PL, VL*	Settlement work, Personal Service Association, local government	Anti-suffragist	Liberal
Violet Markham	VL,* CIL			Liberal
Helen Munro-Ferguson	BWEA, SACS,* VL*			
Meresia Nevill	PL, VL	Daughter of Dorothy Nevill, political hostess		Conservative
Maud Pember Reeves	VL	Poverty research	Suffragist	Fabian/Liberal
Eleanor Percy Taylor	VL,* CIL*			
Gladys Pott	SOSBW*		Anti-suffragist	Conservative
Laura Ridding	GFS, BWEA, SACS	Church work, social purity campaigns, NUWW	Suffragist	Conservative
Adelaide Ross	BWEA*	Church work, philanthropy		
Maud Selborne	SACS, VL*	Support for reforms in nursing, housing, female education and employment, NUWW	Suffragist	Conservative
Lady Talbot	VL, BWEA*		Suffragist	Conservative
Meriel Talbot	VL,* SOSBW*	Secretary to Lambeth Charity Organization Society		
May Tennant	VL,* CIL	First woman factory inspector, supporter of women's employment reforms, Women's Trade Union League, divorce reform	Suffragist	Liberal
Mary Ward	BWEA,* CIL, VL*	Settlement work, local government, women's education, child welfare, NUWW	Anti-suffragist	Conservative
Countess of Warwick	BWEA, VL	Women's employment and education reforms, many social(ist) causes, Poor Law work, political hostess	Suffragist	Socialist

Note: * indicates committee member.

Appendix 3:
Biographical Summaries of Leading Ladies

Alice BALFOUR (1850–1936)

Devoted unmarried sister of Arthur Balfour, Prime Minister 1903–1906 and Conservative Party leader until 1911. Mistress of Whittinghame, the Balfours' Scottish home, from her mother's death in 1876, and Downing Street hostess. Travelled in South Africa in the 1890s and published an account of her journey. London philanthropist (supporter of Octavia Hill) and founder of the East London Nursing Association in 1898. Very active in the front ranks of the Primrose League, the Victoria League and the South African Colonisation Society.

Frances BALFOUR, née Campbell (1858–1931)

Daughter of the Duke of Argyll, sister-in-law to one of Queen Victoria's daughters (Princess Louise) and sister-in-law on her husband's side to Prime Minister Arthur Balfour. Her husband, Eustace Balfour, was an architect and an alcoholic. Her family conflicts became notorious, but personal energy also fed into the women's movement. President of the London Women's Suffrage Association, and involved in imperialist activities through her social connections and her social work as founder of the Travellers' Aid Society. Primrose League membership conflicted with allegiance to the Women's Liberal Unionist Association (she followed in her father's rather than her husband's political footsteps), but became Secretary of the Victoria League's hospitality committee. Published five memoirs, as well as her own two-volume autobiography, and received two honorary degrees. Five children.

Gwendolen CECIL (1860–1945)

Unmarried daughter and eventually private secretary and biographer to her father, Lord Salisbury. Extensive political knowledge and social work interests in philanthropy and housing and hospital design. Prominent role in both the Primrose League and the Victoria League. After her father's death in 1903, retired from Hatfield House to a smaller residence on the estate where she wrote four volumes of her Salisbury biography alongside other activities. Devoutly religious and famed for her compassion and unworldliness.

Violet CECIL, née Maxse, later Milner (1870–1958)

Daughter of unconventional parents, an atheistic Admiral and an artistic, literary mother, who separated when Violet was five. Brought up largely by her mother, who encouraged her artistic talents. Married Lord Edward Cecil (son of Lord Salisbury) in 1894, but became estranged from him after her return from South Africa in 1900. Devoted admirer of Alfred Milner, whom she married in 1921 after her husband's death. Founder of the Victoria League, inspired by experiences of the South African War. Active in various imperialist and nationalist causes, including the National Service League and Ulster Women's Defence Association. Took over editorship of the *National Review* from her brother, and edited it successfully from 1932 to 1948. Close friend of the Kiplings, who were her neighbours. Two children.

Millicent FAWCETT, née Garrett (1847–1929)

Daughter of a middle-class JP and wife of Henry Fawcett, blind Liberal politician, academic and feminist sympathizer. Introduced to feminist politics through the Langham Place circle and her female relatives (sister Elizabeth Garrett Anderson and aunt Emily Davies). Lifelong suffrage campaigner and organizer of the National Union of Women's Suffrage Societies (1897), but also active in other women's causes including social purity, temperance and education work as well as female imperialism. Widowed in 1884, she opposed Home Rule and supported the South African War, leading an investigation into the Boer concentration camps in 1901. Supported female emigration and returned to South Africa as a Victoria League lecturer in 1903. Fully occupied with the suffrage campaign in the pre-war years, but remained committed to imperialism. Continued to be active in post-war feminism, living to celebrate the attainment of suffrage in 1928. DBE in 1925. One child (Philippa Fawcett).

Susan GROSVENOR, later Buchan, then Tweedsmuir (1882–1977)

Daughter and niece of female imperialists, Caroline and Victoria Grosvenor. Member of a 'liberal' branch of a great Conservative family, she developed both a social conscience and a patriotic commitment to Empire. Charity Organization Society work led to involvement in Mary Ward's London settlement and the Personal Service Association. Followed her mother into female emigration work. Involved in the Victoria League through her friendship with Violet Markham. Married imperialist writer and Milner supporter John Buchan, who became Governor-General of Canada (1935). Published several novels, plays, histories and autobiographical works. Four children.

Elizabeth HALDANE (1862–1937)

Strict religious upbringing in Edinburgh, where prospects of a wealthy future were damaged by her father's early death. Resisted limitations on her education and became a supporter of Liberalism and women's rights. Very active public life, which included supporting her brother, Cabinet Minister and Liberal imperialist Richard Haldane. Campaigned for Poor Law reform, became a manager of the Edinburgh Royal Infirmary from 1892, and supported demands for improved training and pay for nurses. Author of twelve historical and literary works. Awarded an honorary doctorate by St Andrews University in 1906. Active within the Victoria League and Colonial Intelligence League, though female imperialism was a limited part of her busy agenda. Gave evidence to the 1909 Royal Commission on the Poor Laws, served on a National Insurance Act committee from 1911 and contributed to the 1912 Royal Commission on the Civil Service. First female JP in Scotland.

Margaret Villiers, Countess of JERSEY, née Leigh (1849–1945)

Daughter of Baron Leigh and sister of the Duke of Westminster, she married the Earl of Jersey in 1872 and established an influential salon. Literary and political interests combined in her extensive travels. Lived in New South Wales from 1891 to 1893 (as wife of the Governor-General) and visited New Zealand, Samoa and the Far East. Queen Victoria admired her writings. Lady Jersey acted as Victoria League President for twenty-six years. During the Edwardian period also well known as an active opponent of women's suffrage. Writings included plays and stories for children and an autobiography. Positions held included Presidency of the Ladies' Grand Council of the Primrose League and Vice-Presidency of the National League for Opposing Women's Suffrage. DBE in 1927. Five children.

Ellen JOYCE (1832–1924)

Limited biographical information is available on this key figure in the history of late Victorian and Edwardian female emigration. Married to a country clergyman who later served at Winchester Cathedral, she had one clergyman son who actively supported her emigration work and accompanied her to the Canadian West in 1884. Emigration work for the Girls' Friendly Society led to establishment of the United Women's Emigration Association in 1884, reformed into the British Women's Emigration Association four years later. As Organizing Referee, Mrs Joyce had direct personal control of correspondence and key decisions concerning individual emigrants and became an influential organizer and propagandist. Gave evidence to the Royal Commission on the Dominions in 1912 and appointed President of the united post-war Society for Oversea Settlement of British Women. Member of an important group of patriotic Winchester ladies, united by devout Anglicanism as well as imperialism; close friend of Lady Louisa Knightley.

Louisa KNIGHTLEY, née Bowater (1842–1913)

Daughter of Sir Edward Bowater, equerry to Prince Albert, and became friendly with the Queen and royal princesses. Married a Conservative Northamptonshire landowner and MP in 1869 and developed philanthropic, social and religious interests alongside her wifely role. Joined the GFS in 1876 and the Primrose League in 1885 and her talents soon placed her among the leaders of both. Persuaded by Ellen Joyce to take up emigration work, and became first President of the South African Colonisation Society in 1901 and founding editor of *The Imperial Colonist*. Author of sixty volumes of journals (from 1856 to 1913), she wrote press articles and was regarded as an effective speaker. Toured South Africa in 1905 and worked for emigration alongside other female causes which included education, genteel employment, moral reform and the suffrage campaign. Held office as Vice-President of the National Union of Women Workers and President of the Conservative and Unionist Women's Suffrage Society.

Edith LYTTELTON, née Balfour (1860–1948)

Daughter of a London businessman, she shone in the social and intellectual company of the Souls during the 1880s. Married Alfred Lyttelton in 1892 and supported his political career as MP then Colonial Secretary from 1903 to 1905. Her enthusiasms included theatre, writing and social reform. She was active in the anti-sweating campaign, the Personal Service Association and the National Union of Women Workers and a convinced suffragist. Founding member of the Victoria League and active on a wide range of committees, despite her husband's pleas to reduce her public work. After his sudden death in 1913, developed interests in psychic research, took up war work at the Ministry of Agriculture and on the War Refugees Committee, and later became an active worker for the League of Nations. Published several plays, a fine biography of her husband and books on psychic research. Campaigned for the establishment of a National Theatre. DBE in 1917. Three children (one died in infancy).

Violet MARKHAM, later Carruthers (1872–1959)

Daughter of a Chesterfield industrialist, she rapidly developed an appetite for research and public work. Investigated social and political conditions in South Africa in 1899 and became a leading defender of Alfred Milner's policies. Played an important role in the Victoria League, influencing it towards more social and democratic forms of imperialism through an industrial committee and branches committee. Strong supporter of Liberal politics and opponent of female suffrage. During the First World War, worked for a number of government bodies, including the central committee on women's employment. Stood unsuccessfully for parliament in 1918, then continued a busy career of public service culminating in membership of the Unemployment Assistance Board from 1934 to 1946. During the Second World War, chaired a government committee on welfare in the Women's Services. Other posts included membership of various trades boards and of the Industrial Court, from 1920 to 1946. Councillor, then Mayor of Chesterfield and founder of the Chesterfield Settlement after an inheritance in 1901. Married in 1917, but continued her independent work. Publications included three books on South Africa and social and political journalism.

Laura RIDDING, née Selborne (1855–1939)

Daughter of the Earl of Selborne, and sister-in-law of Maud Selborne. Married the headmaster of Winchester School in 1876, later the first Bishop of Southwell until his death in 1904. Active as a clerical wife and social reformer, concerned primarily with the social purity movement, the Girls' Friendly Society and the Mothers' Union. A visit to South Africa in 1908 helped to convert her to the causes of imperialism and female emigration. Established a local society to emigrate white female servants to Natal, as well as intervening in the British Women's Emigration Association. Leading figure in the National Union of Women Workers, of which she was President between 1910 and 1911, and a strong suffragist. Authored pamphlets and articles, and biographies of her husband and nephew, as well as keeping copious diaries from 1884 to 1939.

Maud SELBORNE, née Cecil (1858–1950)

Daughter of Prime Minister Lord Salisbury. Grew up in an intensely political household, then formed another by marrying Liberal Unionist William Palmer, Earl of Selborne from 1895 and holder of a range of senior government posts: Under-Secretary for the Colonies 1895–1900, First Lord of the Admiralty 1900–05, High Commissioner in South Africa 1905–10. Followed government affairs closely all her life. South African experience led her into imperialist emigration work and the Victoria League. Acted as a useful go-between for her husband during visits to Britain, and received his support for her suffrage campaigning. President of the Conservative Women's Suffrage Society from 1907. Converted her home into a military hospital during the First World War. After the war, continued her efforts to influence political affairs and to preserve world peace. Four children.

Meriel TALBOT (1868–1956)

Member of the extensive Talbot and Lyttelton families, also related to the Gladstone family. Showed no inclination towards marriage and made a successful career as an administrator and in government service. Began work in the Lambeth Charity Organization Society before becoming the indispensable Secretary of the Victoria League from 1901 to 1916. Extended her knowledge and tested her diplomatic skills during a World Tour of Australia, New Zealand, Canada and South Africa from 1909 to 1911. During the First World War joined the advisory committee for the repatriation of enemy aliens, before moving on to the Board of Agriculture where she directed the Women's Branch of the Food Production Department. Served on government committees after the war and became publicity officer of the Society for the Oversea Settlement of British Women, a post which included editorship of *The Imperial Colonist*. Made many broadcasts and became Chairman of the BBC central appeals advisory committee and of the London Council for the Welfare of Women and Girls. DBE in 1920.

Mary WARD, née Arnold (1851–1920)

Born in Hobart, Tasmania, she was the granddaughter of Arnold of Rugby and niece of Matthew Arnold. Married Oxford Fellow and future journalist Humphrey Ward in 1872. Began to study and write, and in 1879 became Secretary to Somerville College, Oxford. In 1881 moved to London and began the first of twenty-five novels, many of which enjoyed major commercial success. Founded the Passmore Edwards settlement in Bloomsbury in 1890, and devoted herself to social work alongside her writing. Actively opposed women's suffrage from 1889, when she organized a published protest letter with multiple signatures. From 1908 headed the Anti-Suffrage League, absorbed two years later into the male-dominated National League for Opposing Women's Suffrage. Founded the Local Government Advancement Committee in 1911, and was one of the first women magistrates appointed in 1920. Active within the female emigration movement and the Victoria League. Influential patriotic journalist during the First World War. Three children.

Frances Greville, Countess of WARWICK, née Maynard (1861–1938)

An heiress at the age of five, she enjoyed unusual independence from an early age. After a youth of immense social success, became the Prince of Wales' mistress during the 1890s. Dedicated her later life to social causes including education, relief of poverty and the advancement of women. Poor Law Guardian and founder of a women's agricultural training school and a home for crippled children in Warwickshire, and technical schools alongside her Essex estates. An active imperialist, working through her own schemes and political friendships rather than the imperialist organizations. Converted to socialism, under the influence of Robert Blatchford and Henry Hyndman, and gave away much of her fortune. Unsuccessful Labour Party candidate in 1923. Authored several books, mainly autobiographical. Five children.

Bibliography

Personal papers

1. Leading female imperialists

Violet Cecil
Milner papers, Bodleian Library, Oxford

Louisa Knightley
Knightley papers, Northamptonshire Record Office, Northampton

Edith Lyttelton
Chandos papers, Churchill College, Cambridge

Violet Markham
Markham papers, British Library of Political and Economic Science,
London School of Economics

Laura Ridding
Selborne papers, Hampshire Record Office, Winchester

Maud Selborne
Selborne papers, Bodleian Library, Oxford
Selborne papers, Hampshire Record Office, Winchester

Meriel Talbot
Talbot papers, Centre for Kentish Studies, Maidstone

2. Other personal papers

Joseph Chamberlain
Chamberlain papers, Birmingham University Library

Alfred Lyttelton
Chandos papers, Churchill College, Cambridge

Alfred Milner
Milner papers, Bodleian Library, Oxford

Cecil Rhodes
Rhodes papers, Rhodes House Library, Oxford

William Selborne
Selborne papers, Bodleian Library, Oxford
Selborne papers, Hampshire Record Office, Winchester

3. Autobiographies

Aberdeen, Lord and Lady (1925) *'We Twa': Reminiscences of Lord and Lady Aberdeen*. London: Collins.

Aberdeen, Lady (1960 edn) *The Canadian Journal of Lady Aberdeen, 1893–98*, ed. J. Saywell. Toronto: Champlain Society.

Asquith, Margot (1936 edn) *The Autobiography of Margot Asquith* (2 vols). London: Penguin.

Asquith, Margot (1995 edn) *The Autobiography of Margot Asquith*, ed. M. Bonham Carter. London: Weidenfeld & Nicolson.

Balfour, Frances (1930) *Ne Obliviscaris: Dinna Forget*. London: Hodder & Stoughton.

Battersea, Constance (1922) *Reminiscences*. London: Macmillan.

Churchill, Jennie (1908) *The Reminiscences of Lady Randolph Churchill*. London: Edward Arnold.

Fawcett, Millicent (1924) *What I Remember*. London: Fisher Unwin.

Greville, Frances, Countess of Warwick (1929) *Life's Ebb and Flow*. Plymouth: Mayflower Press.

Greville, Frances, Countess of Warwick (1931) *Afterthoughts*. Plymouth: Mayflower Press.

Haldane, Elizabeth (1937) *From One Century to Another*. London: Alexander Maclehose.

Jeune, Mary, Lady St Helier (1909) *Memories of Fifty Years*. London: Edward Arnold.

Knightley, Louisa (1915) *The Journals of Lady Knightley of Fawsley*, ed. J. Cartwright. London: John Murray.

Lyttelton, Edith (1917) *Alfred Lyttelton*. London: Longmans, Green & Co.

Markham, Violet (1953) *Return Passage*. London: Oxford University Press.

Milner, Violet (1951) *My Picture Gallery*. London: John Murray.

Nevill, Dorothy (1906) *My Own Times*. London: Methuen.

Stewart, Edith, Marchioness of Londonderry (1938) *Retrospect*. London: Frederick Muller.

Tweedsmuir, Susan (1952) *The Lilac and the Rose*. London: Gerald Duckworth.

Villiers, Margaret, Countess of Jersey (1922) *Fifty-one Years of Victorian Life*. London: John Murray.

Ward, Mary (1918) *A Writer's Recollections*. London: Collins.

Organizational records

1. Female imperialist organizations

Female emigration societies

Archives in the Fawcett Library, London Guildhall University

Female Middle Class Emigration Society 1862–1886
Colonial Emigration Society 1884–1892
United Englishwomen's Emigration Association 1884–1886
British Women's Emigration Association 1884–1919
South African Colonisation Society 1902–1919
Colonial Intelligence League 1911–1919
Society for the Oversea Settlement of British Women 1920–1962

Girls' Friendly Society

Archives in the Girls' Friendly Society Central Office,
Townsend House, London

Primrose League

Archives in the Bodleian Library, Oxford

Victoria League

Archives in the Victoria League for Commonwealth Friendship Central Office, Leinster Square,
London

2. *Other organizations*

East End Emigration Society: Papers in the British Library
League of the Empire: Archive in the League for the Exchange of Commonwealth Teachers
    Central Office, Clapham, London
Mothers' Union: Archive in the Mothers' Union Central Office, Mary Sumner House, London.
National League for Opposing Women's Suffrage: Archive of newspaper cuttings in the Bodleian
    Library, Oxford
National Union of Women Workers: Records in the Fawcett Library, London Guildhall
    University, and in the British Library for Political and Economic Science, London School
    of Economics
Navy League: Papers in the British Library
Royal Colonial Institute: Archives in the Royal Commonwealth Society Collection in Cambridge
    University Library

Contemporary journals

1. *Female imperialist journals*

Associates' Journal and Advertiser (GFS)
Friendly Leaves (GFS)
Friendly Work for Friendly Workers (GFS)
The GFS Reporter (GFS)
The Girls' Quarterly (GFS)
Our Letter (GFS)
The Imperial Colonist
Primrose League Gazette
Victoria League Notes of the Month

2. *Other contemporary journals*

The Anti-Suffrage Review
The Boy's Own Paper
Britannia
The Empire

The English Woman's Journal
The Federal Magazine
The Girl's Empire
The Girl's Own Paper
Girls' Special Missionary Union Magazine
League of the Empire Monthly Record
Mothers in Council
The Mothers' Union Journal
Navy League Quarterly
The Nineteenth Century
United Empire

Parliamentary papers

Royal Commission on the Dominions:
    First Interim Report. PP1912–13. Cd.6515
    Evidence and Appendices. Part 1. Migration. PP1912–13. Cd.6516
    Final Report. PP1917–18. Cd.8462

Unpublished theses

Pickles, C. (1996) 'Twentieth Century Colonial Identity: The Imperial Order Daughters of the Empire (IODE)'. McGill University PhD thesis.
Porter, D. (1976) 'The Unionist Tariff Reformers 1903–14'. Manchester University PhD thesis.
Reynolds, K. (1995) 'Aristocratic Women and Political Society in Early and Mid-Victorian Britain'. Oxford University DPhil thesis.

Books and articles

Afshar, H. and Maynard, M. (eds) (1994) *The Dynamics of 'Race' and Gender: Some Feminist Interventions.* London: Taylor & Francis.
Alberti, J. (1989) *Beyond Suffrage. Feminists in War and Peace, 1914–29.* London: Macmillan.
Alessio, D. (1997) 'Domesticating "the Heart of the Wild": female personification of the colonies, 1886–1940', *Women's History Review* 6(2): 239–69.
Banks, O. (1968 edn) *Faces of Feminism.* Oxford: Blackwell.
Bean, P. and Melville, J. (1989) *Lost Children of the Empire.* London: Unwin Hyman.
Beckett, J. (1989) *The Aristocracy in England 1660–1914.* Oxford: Blackwell.
Benstock, S. (ed.) (1988) *The Private Self: Theory and Practice of Women's Autobiographical Writings.* London: Routledge.
Biddiss, M. (1972) 'Racial ideas and the politics of prejudice, 1850–1914', *Historical Journal* 15(3): 570–82.
Birkett, D. (1989) *Spinsters Abroad: Victorian Lady Explorers.* Oxford: Blackwell.
Bland, L. (1995) *Banishing the Beast: English Feminism and Sexual Morality, 1885–1914.* London: Penguin.
Bolt, C. (1971) *Victorian Attitudes to Race.* London: Routledge & Kegan Paul.
Bowie, F. *et al.* (eds) (1993) *Women and Missions: Past and Present Anthropological and Historical Perspectives.* Oxford: Berg.
Bristow, J. (1991) *Empire Boys: Adventures in a Man's World.* London: HarperCollins.
Brookes, B. (1997) 'Nostalgia for "innocent homely pleasures"', *Gender and History* 9(2): 242–61.

Burton, A. (1994) *Burdens of History: British Feminists, Indian Women and Imperial Culture, 1865–1915*. Chapel Hill: University of North Carolina Press.

Bush, J. (1994) '"The Right Sort of Woman": female emigrators and emigration to the British Empire, 1890–1910', *Women's History Review* 3(3): 385–409.

Bush, M. (1984) *The English Aristocracy: A Comparative Synthesis*. Manchester: Manchester University Press.

Caine, B. (1986) *Destined to Be Wives: The Sisters of Beatrice Webb*. Oxford: Clarendon Press.

Caine, B. (1992) *Victorian Feminists*. Oxford: Oxford University Press.

Callaway, H. (1987) *Gender, Culture and Empire: European Women in Colonial Nigeria*. London: Macmillan.

Campbell, B. (1987) *The Iron Ladies*. London: Virago.

Campbell Orr, C. (1996) *Wollstonecraft's Daughters: Womanhood in England and France, 1780–1920*. Manchester: Manchester University Press.

Cannadine, D. (1992) *The Decline and Fall of the British Aristocracy*. London: Macmillan.

Cannadine, D. (1995 edn) *Aspects of Aristocracy*. London: Penguin.

Carrothers, W. (1929) *Emigration from the British Isles with Special Reference to the Overseas Dominions*. London: P.S. King.

Castle, K. (1996) *Britannia's Children: Reading Colonialism Through Children's Books and Magazines*. Manchester: Manchester University Press.

Chamberlain, J. (1987) *Foreign and Colonial Speeches*. London: Routledge.

Chancellor, V. (1970) *History for Their Masters*. Bath: Adams and Dart.

Chandos, O. (1962) *The Memoirs of Lord Chandos*. London: The Bodley Head.

Chandos, O. (1968) *From Peace to War: A Study in Contrasts, 1857–1918*. London: The Bodley Head.

Charmley, J. (1996) *A History of Conservative Politics 1900–1996*. London: Macmillan.

Chaudhuri, N. *et al.* (eds) (1992) *Western Women and Imperialism*. Bloomington: Indiana University Press.

Clark, P. (1985) *The Governesses: Letters from the Colonies, 1862–82*. London: Hutchinson.

Collini, S. (1991) *Public Moralists: Political Thought and Intellectual Life in Britain, 1850–1930*. Oxford: Clarendon Press.

Corbett, M.J. (1992) *Representing Femininity: Middle Class Subjectivity in Victorian and Edwardian Women's Autobiographies*. Oxford: Oxford University Press.

Curthoys, A. (1993) 'Identity crisis: colonialism, nation and gender in Australian history', *Gender and History* 5(2): 165–76.

Davidoff, L. (1973) *The Best Circles: Society Etiquette and the Season*. London: Croom Helm.

Davidoff, L. (1995) *Worlds Between: Historical Perspectives on Gender and Class*. Cambridge: Polity Press.

Davidoff, L. and Hall, C. (1987) *Family Fortunes: Men and Women of the English Middle Class, 1780–1850*. London: Hutchinson.

Davin, A. (1978) 'Imperialism and motherhood', *History Workshop* 5: 9–65.

Dawe, C.S. (1902) *King Edward's Realm: Story of the Making of the Empire*. London: Educational Supply Association.

Dawson, G. (1994) *Soldier Heroes: British Adventure, Empire and the Imagining of Masculinities*. London: Routledge.

Dubois, E. *et al.* (1980) 'Politics and culture in women's history: a symposium', *Feminist Studies* 6(1): 29–53.

Dunae, P. (1980) 'Boys' literature and the idea of Empire, 1870–1914', *Victorian Studies* 24: 105–21.

Dyhouse, C. (1989) *Feminism and the Family in England 1880–1939*. Oxford: Blackwell.

Egremont, M. (1980) *Balfour: A Life of Arthur James Balfour*. London: Collins.

Eldridge, C. (ed.) (1984) *British Imperialism in the Nineteenth Century*. London: Macmillan.

Ellenberger, N. (1990) 'The transformation of London "Society" at the end of Victoria's reign: evidence from the court presentation records', *Albion* 22(4): 633–53.

Else, A. (ed.) (1993) *Women Together: A History of Women's Organisations in New Zealand.* Wellington: Daphne Bresell Associates Press.

Evans, R. (1979) *The Feminists.* Beckenham: Croom Helm.

Fletcher, S. (1997) *Victorian Girls: Lord Lyttelton's Daughters.* London: The Hambledon Press.

Fry, R. (1992) *Maud and Amber: A New Zealand Mother and Daughter and the Women's Cause 1865–1981.* Canterbury, NZ: Canterbury University Press.

Fryer, P. (1984) *Staying Power: The History of Black People in Britain.* London: Pluto Press.

Gerard, J. (1987) 'Lady Bountiful: women of the landed classes and rural philanthropy', *Victorian Studies* 30(2): 183–209.

Glick, D. (1995) *The National Council of Women of Great Britain: The First One Hundred Years.* London: National Council of Women.

Gollin, A. (1964) *Proconsul in Politics: A Study of Lord Milner in Opposition and in Power.* London: Anthony Blond.

Gordon, P. (1982) 'Lady Knightley and the South Northamptonshire election of 1885'. *Northamptonshire Past and Present* 6 (5): 265–73.

Grant, J. (ed.) (1996) *Women, Migration and Empire.* Stoke-on-Trent: Trentham.

Green, M. (1980) *Dreams of Adventure, Deeds of Empire.* London: Routledge & Kegan Paul.

Grewal, I. (1996) *Home and Harem: Nation, Gender, Empire and Cultures of Travel.* London: Leicester University Press.

Grieve, N. and Burns, A. (1986) *Australian Women: New Feminist Perspectives.* Australia: Oxford University Press.

Grimshaw, P. (1987) *Women's Suffrage in New Zealand.* Auckland: Auckland University Press.

Grimshaw, P. *et al.* (eds) (1994) *Creating a Nation 1788–1990.* Victoria: McPhee Gribble.

Hall, C. (1992) *White, Male and Middle Class: Explorations in Feminism and History.* Cambridge: Polity Press.

Halperin, V. (1952) *Lord Milner and the Empire.* London: Odhams.

Hammerton, E. and Cannadine, D. (1981) 'Conflict and consensus on a ceremonial occasion: the Diamond Jubilee in Cambridge in 1897', *Historical Journal* 24: 111–46.

Hammerton, J. (1979) *Emigrant Gentlewomen: Genteel Poverty and Female Emigration, 1830–1914.* London: Croom Helm.

Harrison, B. (1973) 'For Church, Queen and Family: the Girls' Friendly Society 1874–1920', *Past and Present* 61: 107–138.

Harrison, B. (1978) *Separate Spheres: The Opposition to Women's Suffrage in Britain.* New York: Holmes & Meier.

Harrison, B. (1987) *Prudent Revolutionaries: Portraits of British Feminists Between the Wars.* Oxford: Clarendon Press.

Headlam, C. (1933) *The Milner Papers, South Africa.* London: Cassell.

Heath-Stubbs, M. (1926) *Friendship's Highway.* London: GFS.

Heilbrun, C. (1988) *Writing a Woman's Life.* New York: Ballantine Books.

Hollis, P. (1987) *Ladies Elect: Women in English Local Government, 1865–1914.* Oxford: Oxford University Press.

Holton, S. (1986) *Feminism and Democracy: Women's Suffrage and Reform Politics in Britain, 1897–1918.* Cambridge: Cambridge University Press.

Holton, S. (1996) *Suffrage Days: Stories from the Women's Suffrage Movement.* London: Routledge.

Horn, P. (1991) *Ladies of the Manor: Wives and Daughters in Country House Society, 1830–1918.* Stroud: Alan Sutton.

Horowitz-Murray, J. (ed.) (1984) *Strong-minded Women and Other Lost Voices from Nineteenth Century England.* London: Penguin.

Imperial Order Daughters of the Empire (1950) *Golden Jubilee 1900–1950.* Toronto: IODE.

Jalland, P. (1988) *Women, Marriage and Politics 1860–1914*. Oxford: Oxford University Press.

James, L. (1994) *The Rise and Fall of the British Empire*. London: Abacus.

Jones, J. (ed.) (1994) *Duty and Citizenship: The Correspondence and Political Papers of Violet Markham, 1896–1953*. London: The Historians' Press.

Lacey, C. (ed.) (1986) *Barbara Leigh Smith Bodichon and the Langham Place Group*. London: Routledge & Kegan Paul.

Lake, M. (1993) 'Colonial and colonising: the white Australian feminist subject', *Women's History Review* 2(3): 377–86.

Lake, M. (1996) 'The inviolable woman: feminist conceptions of citizenship in Australia, 1900–1945', *Gender and History* 8(2): 197–211.

Levine, P. (1987) *Victorian Feminism 1850–1900*. London: Hutchinson.

Levine, P. (1990) *Feminist Lives in Victorian England: Private Roles and Public Commitments*. Oxford: Blackwell.

Lewis, J. (ed.) (1987) *Before the Vote Was Won: Arguments for and against Women's Suffrage, 1864–1896*. London and New York: Routledge & Kegan Paul.

Lewis, J. (1991) *Women and Social Action in Victorian and Edwardian England*. Aldershot: Edward Elgar.

Lorimer, D. (1978) *Colour, Class and the Victorians*. New York: Holmes & Meier.

Lyttelton, K. (1901) *Women and Their Work*. London: Methuen.

Lyttelton, N. (1927) *Eighty Years: Soldiering: Politics, Games*. London: Hodder & Stoughton.

McCann, P. (ed.) (1977) *Popular Education and Socialisation in the Nineteenth Century*. London: Methuen.

McClintock, A. (1995) *Imperial Leather: Race, Gender and Sexuality in the Colonial Contest*. London and New York: Routledge.

MacKenzie, J. (1984) *Propaganda and Empire*. Manchester: Manchester University Press.

MacKenzie, J. (ed.) (1986) *Imperialism and Popular Culture*. Manchester: Manchester University Press.

Mackenzie, J. (1988) *The Empire of Nature: Hunting, Conservation and British Imperialism*. Manchester: Manchester University Press.

Malmgreen, G. (1986) *Religion in the Lives of English Women, 1760–1930*. Beckenham: Croom Helm.

Mangan, J. (1988) *Benefits Bestowed: Education and British Imperialism*. Manchester: Manchester University Press.

Mangan, J. (1989) *The Games Ethic and Imperialism*. Manchester: Manchester University Press.

Marchant, B. (1909) *Daughter of the Dominion*. Glasgow: Blackie.

Marchant, B. (1910) *Molly of One Tree Bend: A Story of a Girl's Heroism on the Veldt*. Glasgow: Blackie.

Markham, V. (1900) *South Africa, Past and Present*. London: Smith, Elder & Co.

Markham, V. (1904) *The New Era in South Africa*. London: Smith, Elder & Co.

Markham, V. (1913) *The South African Scene*. London: Smith, Elder & Co.

Marlowe, J. (1976) *Milner: Apostle of Empire*. London: Hamish Hamilton.

Marsh, P. (1994) *Joseph Chamberlain: Entrepreneur in Politics*. London: Yale University Press.

Maynard, M. and Purvis, J. (eds) (1996) *New Frontiers in Women's Studies: Knowledge, Identity and Nationalism*. London: Taylor & Francis.

Meath, Earl (1928) *Brabazon Potpourri*. London: Hutchinson.

Mendus, S. and Rendall, J. (eds) (1989) *Sexuality and Subordination*. London: Routledge.

Midgley, C. (1992) *Women Against Slavery: The British Campaigns, 1780–1870*. London: Routledge.

Midgley, C. (ed.) (1998) *Gender and Imperialism*. Manchester: Manchester University Press.

Miller, C. (1993) *Painting the Map Red: Canada and the South African War 1899–1902*. Quebec: Canadian War Museum.

Mills, S. (1991) *Discourses of Difference: An Analysis of Women's Travel Writing and Colonialism.* London: Routledge.

Milner, A. (1904 edn) *England in Egypt.* London: Edward Arnold.

Milner, A. (1913) *The Nation and the Empire.* London: Constable.

Money, A. (1897 and 1913 edn) *History of the Girls' Friendly Society.* London: GFS.

Monk, U. (1963) *New Horizons: A Hundred Years of Women's Migration.* London: HMSO.

Nicolson, N. (1977) *Mary Curzon, 1870–1906.* London: Weidenfeld & Nicolson.

Oldfield, A. (1992) *Woman Suffrage in Australia: A Gift or a Struggle?* Cambridge: Cambridge University Press.

Pederson, S. and Mandler, P. (eds) (1994) *After the Victorians: Private Conscience and Public Duty in Modern Britain.* London: Routledge.

Pelling, H. (1979 edn) *Popular Politics and Society in Late Victorian Britain.* London: Macmillan.

Penny, B. (1967) 'Australia's reactions to the Boer War – a study in colonial imperialism', *Journal of British Studies* 7(1–2): 97–103.

Peterson, M.J. (1989) *Family, Love and Work in the Lives of Victorian Gentlewomen.* Bloomington: Indiana University Press.

Phillips, G. (1979) *The Diehards: Aristocratic Society and Politics in Edwardian England.* Cambridge, MA: Harvard University Press.

Porter, B. (1984 edn) *The Lion's Share.* London: Longman.

Prentice, A. *et al.* (eds) (1988) *Canadian Women: A History.* Toronto: Harcourt Brace.

Prochaska, F. (1980) *Women and Philanthropy in Nineteenth Century England.* Oxford: Clarendon Press.

Pugh, M. (1985) *The Tories and the People: 1880–1935.* Oxford: Blackwell.

Pugh, M. (1933 edn) *The Making of Modern British Politics 1867–1939.* Oxford: Blackwell.

Purvis, J. (ed.) (1995) *Women's History: Britain 1850–1945.* London: VCL Press.

Reese, T. (1968) *History of the Royal Commonwealth Society 1868–1968.* Oxford: Oxford University Press.

Rendall, J. (ed.) (1987) *Equal or Different: Women's Politics 1800–1914.* Oxford: Blackwell.

Rich, P. (1986) *Race and Empire in British Politics.* Cambridge: Cambridge University Press.

Robb, J. (1942) *The Primrose League, 1883–1906.* New York: Columbia University Press.

Rose, K. (1969) *Superior Person: A Portrait of Curzon and His Circle in Late Victorian England.* London: Weidenfeld & Nicolson.

Rose, K. (1975) *The Later Cecils.* London: Weidenfeld & Nicolson.

Rowbotham, J. (1989) *Good Girls Make Good Wives.* Oxford: Blackwell.

Rubinstein, W.D. (1987) *Elites and the Wealthy in Modern British History.* Sussex: Harvester.

Samuel, R. (ed.) (1989) *Patriotism: The Making and Unmaking of British National Identity.* London: Routledge.

Sanders, V. (1989) *The Private Lives of Victorian Women.* Hemel Hempstead: Harvester.

Scott, J. (ed.) (1996) *Feminism and History.* Oxford: Oxford University Press.

Shkolnik, E. (1987) *Leading Ladies: A Study of Eight Late Victorian and Edwardian Political Wives.* New York: Garland.

Smart, C. (ed.) (1992) *Regenerating Womanhood: Historical Essays on Marriage, Motherhood and Sexuality.* London: Routledge.

Smith, I. (1996) *The Origins of the South African War.* London: Longman.

Springhall, J. (1970) 'Lord Meath, youth and empire', *Journal of Contemporary History* 5: 97–111.

Springhall, J. (1977) *Youth, Empire and Society.* London: Croom Helm.

Stasiulis, D. and Yuval-Davis, N. (eds) (1995) *Unsettling Settler Societies.* London: Sage.

Strauss, W. (1952) *Joseph Chamberlain and the Theory of Imperialism.* Washington, DC: American Council on Public Affairs.

Strobel, M. (1991) *European Women and the Second British Empire.* Bloomington: Indiana University Press.

Summers, A. (1975) *Damned Whores and God's Police*. Victoria: Penguin.

Swaisland, C. (1993) *Servants and Gentlewomen to the Golden Land*. Oxford: Berg.

Swindells, J. (ed.) (1995) *The Uses of Autobiography*. London: Taylor & Francis.

Thompson, D. (1990) *Queen Victoria. Gender and Power*. London: Virago.

Thompson, F.M.L. (1963) *English Landed Society in the Nineteenth Century*. London: Routledge & Kegan Paul.

Torrance, D. (1996) *The Strange Death of the Liberal Empire*. Liverpool: Liverpool University Press.

Tweedsmuir, S. (1966) *The Edwardian Lady*. London: Duckworth.

Van Helten, J. and Williams, K. (1983) 'The crying need of South Africa: the emigration of single women to the Transvaal, 1901–10', *Journal of South African Studies* 19(1): 17–38.

Van Onselen, C. (1982) *Studies in the Social and Economic History of the Witwatersrand, 1886–1914*. London: Longman.

Vicinus, M. (1985) *Independent Women: Work and Community for Single Women, 1850–1920*. London: Virago.

Vickery, A. (1993) 'Golden Age to separate spheres? A review of the categories and chronology of women's history', *Historical Journal* 36(2): 383–414.

Walker, C. (1990) *Women and Gender in South Africa to 1945*. Claremont: David Philip.

Ward, M. (1915) *Delia Blanchflower*. London: Ward Lock & Co.

Ware, V. (1992) *Beyond the Pale: White Women, Racism and History*. London: Verso.

Yuval-David, N. and Anthias, F. (eds) (1989) *Woman-Nation-State*. London: Macmillan Press.

Index

b